Anglicanism and Orthodoxy
300 Years after the
'Greek College' in Oxford

Edited by
Peter M. Doll

Anglicanism and Orthodoxy 300 Years after the 'Greek College' in Oxford

PETER LANG

Oxford · Bern · Berlin · Bruxelles · Frankfurt am Main · New York · Wien

Bibliographic information published by Die Deutsche Bibliothek
Die Deutsche Bibliothek lists this publication in the Deutsche National-
bibliografie; detailed bibliographic data is available on the Internet at
‹http://dnb.ddb.de›.

British Library and Library of Congress Cataloguing-in-Publication Data:
A catalogue record for this book is available from *The British Library*,
Great Britain, and from *The Library of Congress*, USA.

Cover illustration: Icon of the Mother of God Hodegitira, Worcester College
Chapel. Written by Patricia Fostiropoulos.
Commissioned as a memorial of the Greek College. Photograph ©Ander J McCol.

Cover design: Adrian Baggett, Peter Lang AG

ISBN 3-03910-580-9
US-ISBN 0-8204-7957-8

© Peter Lang AG, International Academic Publishers, Oxford 2006
Hochfeldstrasse 32, Postfach 746, CH-3000 Bern 9, Switzerland
info@peterlang.com, www.peterlang.com, www.peterlang.net

Printed in Germany

Contents

Part 2: Anglican Reflections on Orthodox Relations

Appendices: Documents

List of Plates

Cover: Icon of the Mother of God Hodegitria, Worcester College Chapel. Written by Patricia Fostiropoulos. Commissioned as a memorial of the Greek College. Photograph © Alexander J. McIntyre.

Preface

The beginning of September 2001 marked the 300th anniversary of a central event in the life of the Greek College: the visit of Archbishop Neophytos of Philippopolis to Oxford to receive an honorary D.D. This seemed an appropriate time for Worcester College to remember and celebrate an important episode in its earlier history as Gloucester Hall, since, as the senior history fellow and Vice–Provost, James Campbell, observed, the Greek College represented the only time when Worcester had ever attempted to play a part on the international stage. As college chaplain at the time, I felt that this brave experiment deserved to be remembered as more than the failed dream of an eccentric, Principal Benjamin Woodroffe, and as something other than an ecumenical aberration in the midst of eighteenth–century Anglican Oxford. The following papers, originally presented at the commemorative conference, demonstrate that the Greek College was a vital and audacious sign of the ongoing engagement between Anglicanism and Orthodoxy, very much representative of the concerns of its time and place.

I would like to thank all those who made the conference and this publication possible. Above all, I am grateful to the conference patrons: His Royal Highness the Prince of Wales; His Eminence Archbishop Gregorios of Thyateira and Great Britain; and the Lord Bishop of London, Richard Chartres. Their gracious encouragement and support draws fresh attention to the wider significance of the living ecumenical hope that the Greek College represents. Many individuals and organisations have made generous financial contributions to defray the cost of the conference, the publication of this book, and the writing of the two icons commissioned for the College chapel as a memorial of the Greek College. I would like particularly to acknowledge the support of The Hellenic Foundation, the A. G. Leventis Foundation, the C. H. Wilkinson Trust, the Fellowship of St Alban and St Sergius, the Anglican and Eastern Churches Association, and the Provost and Fellows of Worcester College.

Many members of the Worcester College community ensured the smooth running of the conference. I am especially grateful to Helen Russell, Nighat Malik, Helenann Hartley, and Gregory Platten. I am grateful also to the contributors to this volume, who all submitted their papers in timely fashion (especially to Colin Davey for his work in translating Aptal and Prossalentis), and to Graham Speake and his staff at Peter Lang who bore with patience the delays to the editing after my return to parochial ministry.

I would like to add my personal thanks to those who from the first believed in the conference and enabled it to become a reality, particularly Edward Wilson and Richard Sharp of Worcester College. Finally, without the loving support and generosity of my wife Helen, and our children Emily, Andrew, Nicholas and Eleanor, I could not have had the opportunity to bring this strange but not quite mythical creature, the Greek College, back to life.

Photographic Acknowledgements

Conference Greetings

ST. JAMES'S PALACE

I am delighted, as Patron of this important Conference, to salute the enduring significance of the initiative which led to the foundation of the Greek College. Short-lived as it was, the College stood for a noble vision, remarkable for its time, which sought to build bridges between Christian traditions, East and West.

In our own day, in the midst of a debate about the " soul of Europe", our understanding will be incomplete if we do not appreciate the contribution of both hemispheres of the Christian mind, East and West, to our common heritage. At a time when old tensions have not been resolved, the legacy of Benjamin Woodroffe and the generous spirit which lay behind the foundation of the College, deserve to be remembered, celebrated and translated into terms appropriate to the challenge of our own day.

I hope that your Conference will play a part in strengthening the ties of respect and love between Christians of East and West and that the Tercentenary Celebrations themselves will be enjoyable and memorable.

ΙΕΡΑ ΑΡΧΙΕΠΙΣΚΟΠΗ ΘΥΑΤΕΙΡΩΝ ΚΑΙ ΜΕΓΑΛΗΣ ΒΡΕΤΑΝΙΑΣ
ARCHDIOCESE OF THYATEIRA AND GREAT BRITAIN
5 Craven Hill, London W2 3EN. Tel: 020 - 7723 4787. FAX: 020 - 7224 9301

30th August 2001

Dear Members of the Organising Committee of the Conference
"Anglicanism and Orthodoxy: 300 Years after the 'Greek College' in Oxford",

I am delighted that it has been decided to commemorate the albeit short-lived 'Greek College' in Oxford by way of a scientific conference which will have as its focal point that particularly interesting and perennial subject: the efforts to cultivate and achieve (as far as is possible) closer links between the Orthodox Church and the Anglican Communion; and that, in particular, the Conference has elected to examine the 17th and 18th centuries, a time when religious differences still divided Christians in Europe − even to the extent of their warring about them.

I am confident that the eminent speakers who have been invited to address you will deal with the various subjects on which they have consented to speak both in depth and in detail. For my part, I should like to make a brief mention of one or two of those who, as pioneers, worked so hard to achieve some form of *rapprochement* and in so-doing to express my gratitude to them.

In the first place, I ought to mention Christophoros Angelos, the first Hellene who is known to have taught Greek at the University of Oxford (that being at the beginning of the 17th century). Next, there was Metrophanes Critopoulos, who was probably the most eminent student of this University during the first quarter of the 17th century (and we should not overlook the fact that the then Anglican archbishop of Canterbury, George Abbot, undertook to cover the expenses of his studies). At the same time, we should not forget Cyril Loukaris, the great Patriarch of Constantinople, who had sent Metrophanes to London.

The next significant personality was the former Archbishop of Samos, Joseph Georgerenes, who arrived in England in the middle of the 1670s, and with whom two major events are associated − namely, the building in the area of London's Soho of the first known Greek Church, which was dedicated to the Mother of God but which, sadly, was soon to be confiscated on the orders of the Anglican bishop of London, Henry Compton, so that it might be handed over to the French Huguenots; and, secondly, the idea for the establishment in Oxford of the so-called 'Greek College'.

This idea, however, was not to be realised until after Georgerenes' death; and, then, it was by an Anglican clergyman, Dr. Benjamin Woodroffe. However, this College did receive a visit from another Orthodox hierarch, Metropolitan Neophytos of Filippoupolis, together with his entourage − that being in 1701. Indeed, he not only received an Honorary Degree of Doctor of Divinity from the University, but also met with Dr. Woodroffe and the College's handful of students. Unfortunately, this praiseworthy attempt had to face insurmountable obstacles − in particular, the negative reaction of the Oecumenical Patriarchate on account of the very real danger of the College's students being seduced from the Orthodox Faith. Indeed, the College was to dissolve itself less than ten years after its official opening.

However, the question of religious contacts was reopened by Metropolitan Arsenios of Thebaïs of the Patriarchate of Alexandria, who was in direct and prolonged contact in London with the Non-Jurors during the first two decades of the 18th century. However, his efforts at *rapprochement* were also unsuccessful – not so much due to Arsenios' short-comings as to the fact that the Non-Jurors' movement was in itself condemned to fail from the outset.

It would probably not be out of place to stress that, three centuries later, the efforts of these pioneers have borne fruit. I say this because, in our own days, we see how Christians of East and West are showing a heartfelt desire for deeper and closer relationships, and this is also felt in this country. Consequently, it is not an exaggeration to say that the efforts of those Christians of the 17th and 18th centuries have not simply borne fruit but have surpassed any expectations that they might have had.

Thus, we as Orthodox Christians, owe a deep debt of gratitude to the University of Oxford for the facilities that were granted to Greek students, in particular during the period of Ottoman rule, to enable them to pursue their studies at this outstanding educational establishment. A similar debt is due to the various archbishops of Canterbury and bishops of London for their encouragement and support (apart, that is, from the unhappy incident in the late 17th century). I am therefore delighted to have this opportunity to express my sincere thanks and gratitude to them all.

Needless-to-say, I also thank and congratulate Worcester College on its initiative in agreeing to host this Gathering and, more particularly, its Chaplain, the Reverend Dr. Peter Doll, who (together with others) has worked so hard to bring it to fruition. As one of the Patrons of this Conference, I should also like to thank those eminent speakers who have so kindly consented to deliver papers and, at the same time, to welcome all those who will share in its sessions.

Confident of the success of your deliberations and discussions and praying that Almighty God will bless you all,

    I remain,

       With best wishes and love in Christ

        Gregorios
       Archbishop of Thyateira
        and Great Britain

The Organising Committee of the Conference
 "*Anglicanism and Orthodoxy: 300 Years after the 'Greek College' in Oxford*",
Worcester College,
OXFORD OX1 2HB.

The Revd Dr Peter Doll
Chaplain
Worcester College
Oxford
OX1 2HB

21 June 2001

Dear Peter

I am delighted to greet you as you assemble for your conference on Anglicanism and
Orthodoxy.

Anglicans, although separated by geography, language and culture from the Church of the
East, have looked to the Orthodox as a living link with the Church of the first centuries.
We have sought to build on the traditions we share through Patristic scholarship, in
maintaining 'the godly and decent order of the ancient Fathers' of our liturgy and through
ecumenical dialogues. We are committed to strengthening the visible unity of the Body of
Christ.

May your experience over the next few days inspire us to build upon Benjamin
Woodroffe's vision and seek ever more diligently and prayerfully that unity which is both
our calling and our Lord's gift. I pray that through your worship together, discussions and
fellowship our two traditions would be better ready for this task that lies ahead.

Yours in Christ

+ George Cantuar

Introduction

Peter M. Doll

The Greek College at Oxford emerged out of an 'ecumenical moment'. The fissures in the body of the Church opened by the Reformation in the West prompted the churches of the Reform to seek a common identity and purpose with one another, a process abetted not only by the normal processes of scholarly and commercial exchange but also (for Anglicans) by the Marian and Commonwealth exiles which enabled much ecumenical contact.[1] Out of a desire both for Christian unity and for political, commercial, and theological advantage, churches on both sides of the Reformation also sought out those Christians from whom they had been divided by an even older schism, that between East and West in 1054. Western Christians regarded the Orthodox as faithful witnesses to ancient tradition and therefore sought their judgement on

---

1   For an overview of the subject, see Ruth Rouse and Stephen Charles Neill (eds), *A History of the Ecumenical Movement 1517–1948*, 2nd edn (London: S.P.C.K., 1967). Among more focussed studies are *Anglican Initiatives in Christian Unity. Lectures Delivered in Lambeth Palace Library 1966.* (London: S.P.C.K., 1967); W. B. Patterson, *King James VI and I and the Reunion of Christendom* (Cambridge: Cambridge University Press, 1997); Lars Österlin, *Churches of Northern Europe in Profile. A Thousand Years of Anglo–Nordic Relations* (Norwich: Canterbury Press, 1995); Norman Sykes, *William Wake, Archbishop of Canterbury* (Cambridge: Cambridge University Press, 1957); Eamon Duffy, '*Correspondance Fraternelle*; The SPCK, the SPG, and the Churches of Switzerland in the War of the Spanish Succession'. *Studies in Church History* Subsidia 2 (1979) 251–280.

matters of debate between Rome and the Reformers. Had Rome been faithful to ancient tradition or had it made unwarranted additions to it? Was the Reformation truly a return to the doctrine and practice of the early Church, or had it also deviated from the original?

The Church of England for its part particularly prided itself on its adherence to the standards of the 'primitive church' of the first centuries. Its theologians were students and admirers of the Greek Fathers and the Greek Liturgy. Like the Orthodox, Anglicans refused to acknowledge the supremacy of Rome and maintained the equality of all bishops and the apostolic succession. For international support of its position against Roman Catholicism, the Church of England therefore looked to the Eastern Orthodox churches (most of them under the rule of the Ottoman Empire). Anglicans saw the Orthodox both as the legitimate heirs of the early Church and as potential allies against the papal pretensions of Rome and the political and commercial ambitions of Catholic France and Spain.[2]

For the Orthodox, all this attention from the West was a decidedly mixed blessing. While it opened to some access to higher education not otherwise available to them under Turkish rule, it also meant that their would–be benefactors

---

2   Vasilios N. Makrides (ed.), *Alexander Helladius the Larissaean* (Larissa: Ethnographical Historical Museum of Larissa, 2003); Judith Pinnington, *Anglicans and Orthodox: Unity and Subversion 1559–1725* (Leominster: Gracewing, 2003); V. T. Istavridis, *Orthodoxy & Anglicanism*, trans. Colin Davey (London: S.P.C.K., 1966); A. M. Allchin, ed., *We Belong to One Another: Methodist, Anglican & Orthodox Essays* (London: Epworth, 1965); Methodios Fouyas, *Orthodoxy, Roman Catholicism and Anglicanism* (London: Oxford University Press, 1972); Nicholas Lossky, *Lancelot Andrewes the Preacher: The Origins of the Mystical Theology of the Church of England* (Oxford: Clarendon Press, 1991); Christopher Knight, '"People so beset with saints": Anglican Attitudes to Orthodoxy 1555–1725', *Sobornost* 10 (1988) 2, 25–36.

put Orthodox traditions and identity under severe pressure. The *Collegio San Atanasio* in Rome (founded 1577) insisted on acknowledgement of papal supremacy; even when they allowed the Greeks their liturgical tradition, the Romans demanded they accept the Western doctrine of transubstantiation, imposing a scholastic idiom foreign to the Greek tradition. Both the Greek College in Oxford and the *Collegium Orientale Theologicum* run by the German Pietists in Halle would likewise expose the Greeks to modes of thought that challenged Eastern church life. In all cases, the danger was that the Orthodox students might become estranged from the living tradition to which they belonged, adopting (in what George Florovsky called a *pseudomorphosis*) theological categories, terminology, and forms of argument alien to the Orthodox tradition.[3] Some of the students who came to the West, most notably Metrophanes Kritopoulos, were able not only to familiarise themselves with currents in Western thought but also to be articulate defenders of the Orthodox tradition (see chapter 2). Others, such as Frangiskos Prossalentis and Alexander Helladius, would retreat behind a defensive position of Orthodox superiority (see chapter 11).

While at first glance a college for Greeks might seem an anomaly in an eighteenth-century Oxford not noted for its international links, the college was in fact the culmination of contacts between Anglicans and Orthodox over nearly a century. The conference 'Anglicanism & Orthodoxy 300 Years after the "Greek College" in Oxford', held at Worcester College, Oxford, from 30 August to 2 September 2001 (and from which the papers in this volume are drawn), sought to place the existence of the college within both its immediate historical context and a broader perspective on Anglican–

---

3   See Florovsky in Rouse and Neill, *History of the Ecumenical Movement*, 183.

2|2140689

Orthodox relations at the beginning of the twenty–first century. The late twentieth century has itself been another 'ecumenical moment', a time that has awoken in many Christians a deep longing for unity and has inspired painful yet abundantly fruitful ecumenical dialogue among many churches. Nevertheless, the ecumenical movement seems to have left most denominations agonisingly far from unity in word and sacrament. Is it possible that the experience of the Greek College and of Anglican and Orthodox relations in the seventeenth and early eighteenth centuries can offer any guidance or inspiration to the relations between these two communions in the present?

In chapter 1, Brown Patterson outlines the initiative that marks the genesis of the Greek College – the invitation from King James VI and I and Archbishop George Abbot to Patriarch of Constantinople Cyril Lukaris to send Orthodox scholars to study at the English universities. In the process, official relations between the Church of England and the Greek Orthodox Church were established. Lukaris represented just the sort of churchman the Anglicans wanted to work with – deeply anti-Roman Catholic, well acquainted with and sympathetic to Calvinist theology, determined to bring the Orthodox Church out of its isolation and to help it come to terms with new theological ways of thought. The scheme brought to Oxford two scholars who made the most of the opportunity provided, Metrophanes Kritopoulos and Nathaniel Konopios. In the words of another contemporary Greek scholar, Christophoros Angelos, England proved to be a place where the Orthodox might find wise men among whom they might keep their religion and yet not lose their learning.

Colin Davey explores further the experience of Kritopoulos in England in chapter 2. At Balliol College he engaged in the study especially of the church Fathers and of the

ancient Greek language and literature. Among contemporary Orthodox theologians, he was seen as having the finest education and the widest ecclesiastical horizons. Although he engaged fully in the life of the college, he seems not to have received communion there (though this was unlikely to have been the case with Konopios, who was appointed a Canon of Christ Church by William Laud). Kritopoulos put his knowledge of Western theology to the best possible use, working continuously for a rapprochement between the Orthodox and the Reformed churches, encouraging them to accept the Orthodox respect for Tradition, including his church's full sacramental and devotional life and the Fathers as authoritative interpreters of Scripture.

John Barron in chapter 3 gives an illuminating account of the complicated saga of Joseph Georgirenes, one-time Archbishop of Samos and builder of a Greek Orthodox church in London. All opponents of the papacy in this period were sure of a warm welcome in London, whose bishop, Henry Compton, was heartily – 'even fanatically' – anti-papal. While he warmly supported plans for the Greek church, he was determined (in a period seething with rumours of the popish plot) that its worship should bear no taint of anything remotely popish, hence his forbidding the use of icons and of prayers for the dead. Georgirenes had the further misfortunes of making politically inappropriate friendships and of falling foul of sharp building practice and a devious landlord so that in the end the Greeks lost their church. The archbishop tried to recoup his position by proposing in 1677 a college for Greeks in Oxford, but this too proved an idea in advance of its time. Although contemporary Anglicans proved sadly incapable of seeing Orthodox worship except through spectacles tinted by fear of popery, it is notable that although Compton forbade the use of icons and prayers for the dead,

no further alteration of the Orthodox Liturgy seems to have
been contemplated.

One of Georgirenes' closest Anglican contacts was Dr
Thomas Smith of Magdalen College, Oxford, whose career
Charles Miller surveys in chapter 4. Because of his zeal for
oriental languages, Smith was known by his contemporaries at
Oxford as 'the Rabbi', and he put this linguistic facility to
good use when from 1668–1670 he was chaplain to the British
ambassador to the Sublime Porte. As a result of his time
there, he published an *Account of the Greek Church* as an
introduction to Orthodoxy for western Christians. It was also
an apologia for Compton's strictures on the Greek church in
London. Smith sums up in his own person many of the
tensions that constrained a fuller Anglican understanding of
the Orthodox position – a genuine sympathy and respect for
the Greeks living under persecution; a recognition of the
primitive emphases that bound Orthodox and Anglicans
together; and an inability to see much of the Eastern tradition
except as corrupted by some of the same faults as Romanism.

John Covel succeeded Smith as chaplain in Constantinople, and he too would eventually publish a careful account
of what he saw and did there. In chapter 5, Ephrem Lash
explores his role in the debate over that most controverted
of doctrines, transubstantiation. Covel was familiar with the
key players, both Greek and French, in the drama that led
to the declaration of the Synod of Jerusalem (1672, sometimes known as the 'Synod of Bethlehem') which marked the
closest approximation of Eastern Orthodoxy to Tridentine
Catholicism. While Covel's *The Greek Church with Reflections
on their Present Doctrine and Discipline* (1722) is written in an
aggressive polemical style often unfriendly to the Orthodox,
his journals reveal another side to him – full of painstaking
detail and sympathetic interest in the people and religious
practices he met.

Although E. D. Tappe's article on the Greek College is more than fifty years old, it remains the most complete account of the story of the college's existence (chapter 6). The Levant Company, the government, the churches and the university did cooperate in Woodroffe's project, but they had no common vision for the purpose of the institution, from which each hoped for something different. It was seemingly more imperative to the Roman Catholics that the Greek College should fail than to the British and Greeks that it should succeed. Cyril Lukaris had been prepared to send men of the highest quality to England; those who came to the Greek College were not of the same calibre. When the activities of the Roman agents and the profligacy of Seraphim of Mitylene threw the life of the College into confusion, the Orthodox needed no encouragement to withdraw their support from what had proved more of a headache than a blessing to them.

The failure of the Greek College marked the end of official cooperation between the Greek and English churches. With the accession of the House of Hanover to the British throne, high church concerns no longer had priority, and the internal disputes within the church that led to the suspension of Convocation in 1717 meant that the opportunity for ecumenical initiatives was more circumscribed than ever. But the Non-Jurors kept alive Anglican contact with the Orthodox in the hope of receiving a lifeline from the wider church. Ann Shukman (chapter 7) recounts how they sought unity with not only the Greek but also the Russian Orthodox. Although the Non-Jurors' correspondence with the Orthodox Patriarchs was cordial and constructive in many ways, the Orthodox insisted the Anglicans must submit on all points of disagreement; the invocation of saints, the worship of images, and transubstantiation remained intractable barriers to unity. Shukman also chillingly reveals how the friendship of Bishop

Gilbert Burnet with Peter the Great contributed to the Erastian captivity of the Russian Church under the 'Holy Governing Synod' established by Peter's *Ecclesiastical Regulation* of 1721.

Chapter 8 turns to matters of liturgy and architecture. Peter Doll explores how both Orthodox and Anglicans came to share much common ground (not fully recognised at the time) in their understanding of the Eucharist and in the use of their church buildings. This arose not out of any Anglican dependence on Orthodox theology or practice, but from a shared devotion to Scripture and the Fathers and a shared conviction that the origins of Christian worship were to be found in the worship of the Temple in Jerusalem. Both traditions were united in a profound sense of the joining together of earth and heaven in the Church's Eucharist. The vast difference between the visual cultures of the two churches testifies to the distinctive ways in which communities reliant on the same beliefs and sources can express that common tradition in different cultural circumstances.

The remaining three chapters in the first part of the book survey Anglican–Orthodox relations from an Orthodox point of view. The theme of worship continues in chapter 9 as Gregory Woolfenden considers Orthodox influences on Anglican liturgy, focusing particularly on the 'history of the Anglican epiklesis'. Although seventeenth- and eighteenth-century Anglicans had a keen sense of the necessity of the invocation of the Holy Spirit to the consecration of the eucharistic elements, by the time liturgical revision became possible in the Church of England in the early twentieth century, the western tradition of the 'words of consecration' had reasserted itself. Woolfenden is clear that even though there is an ecumenical consensus that the whole of the eucharistic anaphora is consecratory, it may be some time yet before the practice of Orthodox, Roman Catholics and Anglicans clearly witness to this agreement.

Vasilios Makrides in chapter 10 is concerned with the varieties of Orthodox response to approaches from the West. The legacy of the collapse of Byzantium coloured the Greek view of western developments in technology, trade, and learning. Those who rejected pro–western currents in the East developed compensatory strategies to show the emptiness of western progress and the real superiority of the Orthodox East. Central to these strategies were the insistence that modern Greeks were the only true heirs and guardians of the classical Greek tradition and that the Orthodox faith was the one true expression of Christianity.

Many Englishmen in the seventeenth and eighteenth centuries were drawn to Greek culture in both its classical and Orthodox Christian forms. Very few were in a position or were sufficiently committed to embrace it fully. The most notable exception was Frederic North, fifth Earl of Guilford, whose conversion to Orthodoxy is the subject of Kallistos Ware's moving contribution in chapter 11. While there is no indication that anything in his Anglican upbringing predisposed Guilford toward Orthodoxy, he took the opportunity of a sojourn in Greece as a young man to be baptized into the Orthodox Church. Never happy to acknowledge publicly a new allegiance that might damage his family's reputation and limit his ability to serve his country, he nevertheless made sure that he died in the communion of the Orthodox Church.

Whereas the first section of this collection has put the Greek College within a broad historical context, the second part brings together contemporary Anglican reflections on its relationship with Orthodoxy. In one of the keynote addresses from the conference, Donald Allchin (chapter 12) offers a salutary reminder that given the depth of mutual ignorance that accompanied the beginning of official ecumenical dialogue in 1973, we can hardly be surprised at the abundance of misunderstandings in the seventeenth and eighteenth centuries. He points out what a deep impact Orthodox music, iconography, and ways of prayer are having on contemporary western worship and spirituality. He reflects also on the way in which the patristic mind so deeply inspired Thomas Rattray, Daniel Brevint, and Charles Wesley that their liturgical theology is marked by a mutual 'resonance' with Orthodox thought. A fuller appreciation of what each has to contribute of what Derwas Chitty called the 'miraculous glue' of the traditions we share would help Orthodox and Anglicans grow into both greater self-awareness and greater mutual trust and understanding.

Derwas Chitty was an Anglican priest who devoted his ministry to a witness to the common life of the undivided Church. Edward Every in chapter 13 explains how, although Chitty at one time felt called to become Orthodox, he remained an Anglican called to serve both churches spiritually in the cause of unity. As a parish priest (and with the tacit acquiescence of his bishops) he always omitted the *filioque* in public worship – an act of nonconformity in the strictest sense, yet a prophetic symbol of the unity for which he worked and prayed.

As the historical papers in this volume constantly reveal, ecumenism is a highly personal business. In the modern church, those Anglicans who have been personal points of contact between the churches have been the apokrisarioi, the personal ambassadors of the Archbishop of Canterbury to the various Patriarchs of the Orthodox churches. In chapter 14, Chad Coussmaker offers his lively and personal reminiscences of his appointments as apokrisarios not only to the Ecumenical Patriarch but also to the Patriarch of Moscow, the Patriarch of Georgia, and the Catholicos-Patriarch of Armenia in the heady days of the restitution of the churches after the fall of communism. The apokrisarios retains a crucial role at a time when advances in communication, far from clarifying relationships, seem sometimes to exacerbate the potential for misinformation and misunderstanding.

If the apokrisarios may expect a life with more than its share of incident and high drama, then representatives to ecumenical dialogue must be prepared for the hard slog of detailed theological argument engaged in sporadically over periods of years and for the frustration of being at the mercy of church politics and decisions beyond their control. While William Green has known all this during his long service to the Anglican–Orthodox dialogue (chapter 15), he has also seen mutual suspicion and a dogmatic defensiveness on each side give way to a mutual recognition of 'the hidden life of the Trinity at the heart of our communities'. His account of the progress of the dialogue is a valuable testimony to the crucial importance of this largely unseen and little acknowledged work.

The best hope that the scholarships of King James and the Greek College represented, of providing a place in England where Anglicans and Orthodox could meet and pray together and learn from one another has only recently been realised in the Institute for Orthodox Christian Studies in Cambridge. In fact, as its first Principal John Jillions explained to the conference, the original model has been improved; it is as if the competing colleges – the *Collegio San Atanasio,* the *Collegium Orientale Theologicum*, and the Greek College – have all joined together with the Orthodox as equals. The Institute is an integral part of the Cambridge Theological Federation, representing a range of Christian traditions (Roman Catholic, Anglican, Reformed, Methodist, and now Orthodox). The Institute is pan–Orthodox and is thus ideally placed to share Orthodox insights on the common Christian inheritance.[4]

In the final address to the conference, Richard Chartres (chapter 16) brought together the many strands shared by the speakers in their papers – that common anamnetic sense of identification with the undivided Church; the patristic mind of Anglicanism that liberated the Church of England from scholasticism and drew it back towards Orthodoxy; the crucial importance of mutual hospitality and fellowship of the heart to complement the fellowship of the mind; the scope for misunderstanding (comical only in hindsight); the extent to which the Orthodox tradition today is enriching Christianity in the West. Anglicans and Orthodox have a responsibility not only to seek that unity which is Christ's will for his Church but also (as the Prince of Wales remarked in his greetings to the conference) to engage in the common task of ministering to the 'soul of Europe' at a time when churches and nations are caught up in struggles to redefine communal identity in a post-colonial and post-communist world.

The third section of the volume comprises a selection of primary documents related to the existence of the Greek College. Appendix A is Woodroffe's *A Draught or Model of a Colledge or Hall to be Settled in the University for the Education of some Youths of the Greek Church*, Appendix B some of Woodroffe's correspondence on the establishment of the College. Appendices C and D are the most significant parts of the collection, as Colin Davey has translated two documents (previously available only in Greek) that give valuable insight into the working of the Greek College. The first is Ἡ τῶν Ἁγίων Γραφῶν αὐτάρκεια (*The Sufficiency of the Holy Scriptures*), a publication by Woodroffe of the public disputations

---

4   Full information on the Institute is available on its website, www.iocs.cam.ac.uk.

presented by two students of the Greek College, Georgios Aptal and Georgios Maroules. Here is evidence of Anglican and Orthodox veneration of the Scriptures and the church Fathers, but here is evidence also of the tensions that the Anglican need to attack Roman Catholicism placed on this joint venture. When Aptal rejected the Roman Catholics' 'unwritten traditions additional to Scripture', he did not acknowledge that such an argument could be used against the Orthodox view of the 'unwritten Word of God'. The rejection of unwritten tradition so enraged Frangiskos Prossalentis that he penned an attack on Woodroffe, Ὁ αἱρετικὸς διδάσκαλος ὑπὸ τοῦ ὀρθοδόξου μαθητοῦ ἐλεγχόμενος (*The Heretical Teacher Cross-Examined by his Orthodox Pupil*), from which Colin Davey has translated the introductory material together with the author's own summaries of each chapter in Appendix D. While Woodroffe had shown himself insufficiently sensitive to the Orthodox tradition, Prossalentis responded with a blanket condemnation of his effort to educate the Greeks.

Appendix E gathers documents relating to one of the high points of the existence of the Greek College, the visit of Archbishop Neophytos of Philippopolis to Oxford, where he and several members of his retinue received honorary degrees. Whether or not the fuss made over him in Oxford, Cambridge, and London (where the noted engraver Robert White published his portrait) can be directly linked to the existence of the Greek College, certainly no other visiting Orthodox prelate in the seventeenth or eighteenth centuries was honoured as he was.

Edward Stephens was foremost among Anglican admirers of the Greek Church, and he did his utmost to continue the work of the College after it folded. He believed (Appendix F) that all that was necessary to encourage the 'restitution of Catholick Communion' between the Greek and English churches was the establishment of a house of studies for

Greek clerics and scholars, including an oratory for their use. This, he thought, would repair the damage done by the scandals accompanying the failure of the Greek College.

The final document (Appendix G) lies at the heart of the conference itself. It is Bishop Thomas Rattray's edition of the liturgy of St James, *An Office for the Sacrifice of the Holy Eucharist being the Ancient Liturgy of the Church of Jerusalem.*

The conference took place at Worcester College, the successor to Gloucester Hall and the very institution Woodroffe hoped the Greek College would help bring into being. The delegates to the conference, representing many countries and Christian traditions, heard and discussed these papers in the midst of three days of talking, thinking, eating, praying, and relaxing together. The visits to the conference of Archbishop Gregorios of Thyateira and Great Britain and of Bishop Richard Chartres of London intensified our awareness of meeting three hundred years to the day after Archbishop Neophytos' triumphant visit to Oxford. The daily worship according to both traditions that took place in the college chapel, in the presence of the two new icons commissioned as a memorial to the Greek College, heightened the sense of 'resonance' between the traditions that emerged from the conference papers. The celebration of the Eucharist according to Rattray's *Office*, at once deeply Orthodox and yet also clearly Anglican, linked our offerings of mind and heart to the offering of the Church in worship, joining us ultimately to Christ's self-offering to the Father in the heavenly Temple.

* * *

From the perspective of the 'ecumenical moments' of the seventeenth century and of the late twentieth century, what assessment can be made of the Greek College in Oxford? For Steven Runciman, the scheme was ill-thought-out, and an Oxford education was inappropriate for Greek priests destined to live under Turkish rule.[5] Tappe believes it was useful to some of the students who came, but Judith Pinnington, the most recent historian of Anglicanism and Orthodoxy, has dismissed it as an 'ill-judged and exceedingly ill-timed project for Greek education in England',[6] an aspect of the 'subversion' of Orthodoxy referred to in her title. This judgement arises in part out of her conviction that the Church of England was crippled by the twin traps of establishment and western epistemology, so that even the Caroline divines found it impossible to achieve a theological rapprochement with Orthodoxy or 'to break through to a spirit of liberty in the Divine Presence'.[7] Pinnington's conviction that by the eighteenth century any Anglican 'hidden givenness of sacramental life' had been 'largely buried under massive historical detritus' has convinced her that by the time of the Greek College Anglicans and Orthodox were a universe apart.[8] But it is possible to concur with this assessment only by steadfastly ignoring the abundant recent scholarship testifying to the continuing vitality of the high church sacramental tradition in the eighteenth century.[9]

---

5   *Anglican Initiatives in Christian Unity*, 12.
6   Pinnington, *Anglicans and Orthodox*, 96.
7   Ibid., 40, 220.
8   Ibid., 223.
9   Pinnington acknowledges the existence of J. C. D. Clark's 'theories' concerning the eighteenth-century Church of England (referring primarily to his landmark study *English Society 1688–1832* (Cambridge: Cambridge University Press, 1985) and she admires the work of Peter Nockles (*The Oxford Movement in Context: Anglican High Churchmanship 1760–1857* (Cambridge: Cambridge University Press, 1994), but she could profitably also have consulted John Walsh, Colin Haydon, and Stephen Taylor (eds), *The Church of England c.1689–c.1833* (Cambridge: Cambridge University Press, 1993); F. C. Mather, *High Church Prophet: Bishop Samuel Horsely (1733–1806) and the Caroline*

In the seventeenth and eighteenth centuries progress towards unity for both Anglicans and Orthodox depended on the other church submitting in all points of disagreement. The Anglicans expected the Orthodox to worship without icons and prayers for the dead and to deny transubstantiation. The Orthodox Patriarchs expected the Non-Jurors to accept all these unequivocally. If submission is the only standard of success we can apply in our ecumenical endeavours, then both the Greek College and more recent ecumenical dialogue will indeed be disappointing. As Donald Allchin has noted, relations between Orthodox and Anglicans have never been comfortable or easy. But they have been enduring because there has been an underlying sense of spiritual and theological 'resonance' – a common apprehension of the sources of our Christian identity – which continues to draw the two to one another. This resonance of theological ideas and practice is a recurring theme in a recent study of Orthodox and Wesleyan sprituality; it promises to be 'of great service to ecumenism and contemporary Christian and human understanding'.[10] The hymns and other writings of the Wesleys are paradigmatic of the patristic mind in eighteenth-century high church Anglican spirituality, and Orthodox scholars are full of admiration for the living Spirit of the Divine Presence these works evince.

For all those who search for mutual understanding between Orthodox and Anglican, organic unity must remain a

---

Tradition in the Later Georgian Church (Oxford: Clarendon Press, 1992); Jeremy Gregory, *Restoration, Reformation, and Reform, 1660–1828: Archbishops of Canterbury and Their Diocese* (Oxford: Clarendon Press, 2000); W. M. Jacob, *Lay People and Religion in the Early Eighteenth Century* (Cambridge: Cambridge University Press, 1996). These and other studies confirm and deepen Clark's insights.

10   S. T. Kimbrough (ed.), *Orthodox and Wesleyan Spirituality* (Crestwood, N. Y.: St Vladimir's Seminary Press, 2002), 17.

gospel imperative and ultimate goal. For some Anglicans (like the Earl of Guilford) and other western Christians, that unity is most appropriately achieved by conversion to Orthodoxy – either to the Greek or the Russian church, or by seeking an authentically British expression of Orthodoxy, perhaps by harking back to the life of the British church prior to the Great Schism.[11] But others (like Edward Stephens and Derwas Chitty) will wish to continue to work for that goal from within the body of Anglican churches as they are for all their limitations. Such Anglicans perceive in themselves, as they do in the Orthodox churches, bodies of faithful Christians seeking to live out the Gospel in communities shaped by the contingency of history; they also recognise resonances of faith and practice drawing them toward the Orthodox despite those barriers of history and culture. In the Anglican–Orthodox Dialogue, a mutual recognition of the hidden life of the Trinity at the heart of both communities is asserting itself. As Anglican and Orthodox alike recognise (in the words of Richard Meux Benson, S.S.J.E.) that 'we have not to maintain the truth, but to live in the truth so that it may maintain us', so then the Spirit of truth will lead them into all truth.

Speakers at the conference often had reason to refer with gratitude to the example and inspiration of Michael Ramsey, so it is appropriate to turn to him for a final reflection (entirely if unintentionally appropriate) on the contribution of the Greek College to Anglican–Orthodox relations. In *The Gospel and the Catholic Church* he wrote:

> While the Anglican church is vindicated by its place in history, with a strikingly balanced witness to Gospel and Church and sound learning, its greater vindication lies in its pointing through its own

---

11   See, for example, the website of the British Orthodox Church, www.britishorthodox.org.

history to something of which it is a fragment. Its credentials are its incompleteness, with the tension and the travail in its soul. It is clumsy and untidy, it baffles neatness and logic. For it is sent not to commend itself as 'the best type of Christianity', but by its very brokenness to point to the universal Church wherein all have died.[12]

The Greek College shared in full measure that clumsiness and untidiness. But Anglicans at that time had a strong sense of their obligation to abide by the witness of the universal church, and they sought to make concrete expressions of unity with the whole Church. For all its faults the College was such a sign of Anglicans recognising their incompleteness, of reaching out to Orthodoxy to receive its primitive continuity and apostolic witness and in turn to offer such of their own gifts as they hoped might serve the needs of the Greeks. If Woodroffe's College appeared a failure in its own day, the fruits of the conference to commemorate its existence give good reason to hope that his vision was not in vain, but still strikes resonant chords despite all that divides us. May both Anglicans and Orthodox grow into a fuller understanding and appreciation of the tradition that unites them, so that that 'miraculous glue' may yet more powerfully draw Christians today toward rediscovering that unity which is the Lord's gift to his Church.

---

12   Arthur Michael Ramsey, *The Gospel and the Catholic Church*, 2nd edn (London: Longman, Green and Co, 1956), 220.

PART I

The Greek College in its Context

1. Cyril Lukaris, George Abbot, James VI and I, and the Beginning of Orthodox–Anglican Relations

W. B. Patterson

In about 1615, Cyril Lukaris, the Orthodox patriarch of Alexandria, wrote a letter in Greek to George Abbot, the archbishop of Canterbury, which expressed his gratitude to both Abbot and to 'James, the most righteous and gracious king'.[1] As the letter makes clear, Lukaris had been invited to send men of his choosing to England for further education, so that the Greek Church would have able spokesmen for its theology and polity. The need for such spokesmen, he explained, was acute, since 'the evil-natured Jesuits' were trying to separate the Greeks from their traditional faith, and Greek Christians in the Turkish dominions were being kept in ignorance.[2] Lukaris's letter was a reply to one from Abbot, which had been a response to an initial letter from Lukaris. Though the first two letters in the correspondence have not survived, the first may be presumed to have been a plea

---

1   Oxford, Bodleian MS. Smith 36, pp. 39, 41. The letter, which was printed with a brief commentary by Timotheos Themelis, Ἐπιστολὴ τοῦ Λουκαρεως πρὸς τὸν ABBOT', Νέα Σιών viii (1909), 30–33, is dated July 16, with no year given.

     It is a pleasure to acknowledge the generous assistance of Kallistos Ware, Andreas Tillyrides, and Colin Davey in my research on Orthodox–Anglican relations.

2   Bodl. MS. Smith 36, p. 39.

40 W. B. Patterson

for assistance and the second an offer by Abbot and King James VI and I (of Scotland and England) to maintain Greek scholars at the English universities.[3] Together, the letters inaugurated a promising scholarship programme and, more importantly, established official relations between the Greek Orthodox Church and the Church of England. What was it that brought these three leaders together despite a vast expanse of sea and land and the differences of language, culture, and religious traditions that separated the Orthodox Church in the East and the reformed Church of England in the West?

Let us begin with the patriarch. One thing that is striking about Cyril Lukaris is that he was thoroughly familiar with many aspects of the intellectual culture of western Europe. He was a native of Crete, which had been under Venetian control since the infamous Fourth Crusade in 1204. At the age of twelve he visited Venice, where he studied Greek, Latin, and philosophy under Maximos Margunios, a poet and scholar who was bishop of the Greek island of Cythera, also under Venetian control. A few years later, he studied philosophy and graduated with honours at the University of Padua, on the Venetian mainland.[4] In this way, Lukaris took advantage

3   See the discussions in George A. Hadjiantoniou, *Protestant Patriarch: The Life of Cyril Lucaris (1572–1638), Patriarch of Constantinople* (Richmond: John Knox Press, 1961), 45; and Colin Davey, *Pioneer for Unity: Metrophanes Kritopoulos (1589–1639) and Relations between the Orthodox, Roman Catholic and Reformed Churches* (London: British Council of Churches, 1987), 71–72.

4   For Lukaris's life and career, see Hadjiantoniou, *Protestant Patriarch, passim;* Steven Runciman, *The Great Church in Captivity: A Study of the Patriarchate of Constantinople from the Eve of the Turkish Conquest to the Greek War of Independence* (Cambridge: Cambridge University Press, 1968), 259–288; Cyrille Lucar, *Sermons, 1598–1602,* ed. Keetze Rozemond (Leiden: E. J. Brill, 1974), 1–17; Gunnar Hering, *Ökumenisches Patriarchat und Europäische Politik, 1620–1638* (Wiesbaden:

of the links between several of the Greek islands and Venice, receiving his secondary and higher education in one of the leading centres of learning in Europe. Venice was home to a community of Greeks and it had a tradition of hospitality to Greek scholars. Though the Venetian Republic was officially Roman Catholic, its citizens enjoyed a large measure of religious and intellectual freedom and the state maintained a considerable degree of autonomy in its relations with the papacy in Rome.[5] Another striking thing about Lukaris is that he had extensive experience with the problems of the Orthodox Church in eastern Europe. He knew at first hand of its struggle against well-trained Roman Catholic priests, especially Jesuits, who sought to bring the Orthodox under the jurisdiction of the papacy. After being ordained, probably by his kinsman, the patriarch of Alexandria, Lukaris journeyed with a fellow Greek cleric to Poland, where Roman Catholicism was being vigorously advanced by King Sigismund III at the expense of both Protestantism and Orthodoxy. Lukaris attended the Council of Brest in 1596 where an agreement of the previous year was confirmed, that the Orthodox Church in the kingdom would submit to the authority of the pope, while retaining its liturgy, calendar, and tradition of married priests. Lukaris, who resolutely opposed the agreement,

---

Franz Steiner, 1968); and Germanos [Strenopoulos], Metropolitan of Thyateira, *Kyrillos Loukaris, 1572–1638: A Stuggle for Preponderance between Catholic and Protestant Powers in the Orthodox East* (London: S.P.C.K., 1951).

5   Deno J. Geanakopolos, *Greek Scholars in Venice: Studies in the Dissemination of Greek Learning from Byzantium to Western Europe* (Cambridge, Mass.: Harvard University Press, 1962), 41–70; William J. Bouwsma, *Venice and the Defense of Republican Liberty: Renaissance Values in the Age of the Counter Reformation* (Berkeley: University of California Press, 1968); David Wotton, *Paolo Sarpi: Between Renaissance and Enlightenment* (Cambridge: Cambridge University Press, 1983), 45–77.

worked to support those Orthodox who sought to remain free of the union. His experience taught him that poorly educated Orthodox clergy were at an immense disadvantage when confronted by Jesuits urging the union. He spent several years in eastern Europe, directing an Orthodox school, founding another, and helping to establish a printing house.[6]

Finally, it is striking that Lukaris was well acquainted with Protestant, especially Calvinist, theology and was attracted to it. Soon after his arrival in Alexandria from eastern Europe in 1601, Lukaris was elected patriarch of Alexandria in succession to his recently deceased cousin. On a visit to Constantinople in the following year, he became acquainted with Cornelius van Haga, a Dutch traveller who was to become the ambassador of the United Provinces of the Netherlands at the Ottoman capital. From van Haga he received a set of books of Protestant theology. In subsequent correspondence with the Dutch theologian Jan Uytenbogaert, Lukaris showed that he was receptive to at least some of the tenets of western Reformed theology.[7] Thus, Cyril Lukaris was familiar with western religious ideas and practices of a variety of kinds, he was exceptionally well educated himself, and he was an advocate of the further education of the Orthodox clergy. Moreover, he was determined to oppose the proselytizing activities of Roman Catholic clergy in the East. As he commented in his letter to Abbot cited above, Jesuits were active among the Orthodox in the city of Constantinople itself, with the result that 'children give no heed to their parents, two religions exist in one house together

---

6   Hadjiantoniou, *Protestant Patriarch*, 32–33; Lucar, *Sermons, 1598–1602*, ed. Rozemond, 7; Runciman, *The Great Church in Captivity*, 262–264.

7   Hadjiantoniou, *Protestant Patriarch*, 40–42. For Lukaris's letters to Uytenbogaert in 1612–1613, see Christiaan Hartsoeker (ed.), *Praestantium ac eruditorum virorum epistolae ecclesiasticae et theologicae* (Amsterdam: Franciscus Halma) 1704, third ed., 314–315, 357–365.

with conflict and argument,' and there is 'no one to rescue them.'[8] With opportunities for advanced education for Greek Christians virtually non-existent in the Ottoman Empire,[9] it is understandable that Lukaris would seek an opportunity to send promising young clergymen abroad to become skilled in the intellectual techniques employed in the West and to immerse themselves more deeply in the classical sources of their own faith.

George Abbot was an Oxford-educated Calvinist theologian who had been master of University College, Oxford, and Dean of Winchester before being named bishop of Lichfield in 1609, and then, in rapid succession, bishop of London in 1610 and archbishop of Canterbury in 1611.[10] Although his election as primate was a surprise to some of his contemporaries, Abbot had earned the respect and gratitude of King James in ways that made him seem well qualified for the position.[11] As the king's representative, he had visited

---

8   Bodl. MS. Smith 36, p. 39.
9   See Apostolos E. Vacalopoulos, *The Greek Nation, 1453–1669: The Cultural and Economic Background of Modern Greek Society,* trans. Ian and Phania Moles (New Brunswick, N.J.: Rutgers University Press, 1976), 151–186; Runciman, *The Great Church in Captivity,* 208–225; and Timothy Ware, *Eustratios Argenti: A Study of the Greek Church under Turkish Rule* (Oxford: Clarendon Press, 1964), 5–11.
10   Paul A. Welsby, *George Abbot: The Unwanted Archbishop, 1562–1633* (London: S.P.C.K., 1962), 5–27.
11   Welsby, *George Abbot,* 28–39. Welsby's interpretation, that 'in the end the appointment pleased nobody' (p. 13) has been effectively countered by S. M. Holland, 'George Abbot: "The Wanted Archbishop"', *Church History,* 56, 2 (June 1987), 172–187, and Kenneth Fincham, 'Prelacy and Politics: Archbishop Abbot's Defence of Protestant Orthodoxy', *Historical Research,* 61, 144 (February 1988), 36–64, esp. 40–47. For Abbot's career as bishop and archbishop, see also Fincham, *Prelate as Pastor: The Episcopate of James I* (Oxford: Clarendon Press, 1990), 24–53, 248–304.

Scotland in 1608 to help restore bishops in the Scottish Kirk, and as bishop of London in 1610 he presided over the consecration of three bishops in the historic or apostolic succession to serve in Scottish sees. Abbot was, like the king, both an episcopalian in polity and a Calvinist on fundamental theological issues. Like James, he sought to reconcile Puritans to the established Church rather than persecute and thus alienate them.

Abbot was, much more than the king, anti-Roman Catholic, regarding the Habsburg powers abroad as threats to the very existence of Protestantism in Europe, and Catholics at home as dangerous subversives. In an era in which King James was being attacked by Roman Catholic writers across Europe for the Oath of Allegiance, Abbot's support was probably much appreciated by the king.[12] If Abbot and James had much in common, Abbot had special reasons to be interested in the Greek East. He showed a keen interest in Venice, which he saw as a bulwark against papal influence on the domestic and foreign policies of Roman Catholic states, and he was well acquainted with the growth of English trade in the eastern Mediterranean. Abbot's brother Maurice was an active member of both the East India Company and the Levant Company, the trading company whose representative to the Sublime Porte – the Turkish government – served also as the English ambassador there. Abbot corresponded with Dudley Carleton, the English ambassador in Venice. Carleton was, in turn, in touch with Paul Pindar, a merchant who was to become English ambassador in Constantinople in 1614, and was in residence in Constantinople when Lukaris first made contact with Abbot. Pindar wrote to Carleton from Pera, in

---

12   Peter Milward, *Religious Controversies of the Jacobean Age: A Survey of Printed Sources* (London: Scholar Press, 1978), 86–119; Johann Peter Sommerville, 'Jacobean Political Thought and the Controversy over the Oath of Allegiance', Ph.D. thesis, Cambridge University, 1981.

Constantinople, in 1612, that the patriarch of Alexandria 'seemeth much to affect our profession (whereof he is well informed by reading) and to detest the Jesuits in vehement manner.'[13] Abbot probably saw the Greeks as trading partners and, potentially, as ideological allies in the struggle of his king against supporters of the pope. Abbot and James had almost certainly heard of Lukaris's anti-Roman Catholic views and his receptivity to Protestantism before they received a letter from him, and they may well have viewed him as someone close to being a co–religionist.

King James VI and I, who had been brought up by the Calvinist party in Scotland after the deposition of his mother, Mary Queen of Scots, had a broader view of the Church than most Protestants or Roman Catholics. For political as well as religious reasons he had worked hard to reconcile Roman Catholics to the Kirk and to exert his own authority over the sessions of its general assemblies. After his accession in England, he sought to reconcile moderate Catholics and moderate Puritans to the Church of England. He saw religious pacification as one of the keys to domestic and international peace.[14] He asserted in an address to the first Parliament of his reign, in 1604, that he wished 'that it would please God to make me one of the members of such a generall Christian

---

13   Welsby, *George Abbot*, 4; Fincham, 'Prelacy and Politics', 50–51; Alfred C. Wood, *A History of the Levant Company* (Oxford: Oxford University Press, 1935), 42; Bodl. MS. Smith 36, pp. 30–31 (Paul Pindar to Dudley Carleton, April 25, 1612).

14   Kenneth Fincham and Peter Lake, 'The Ecclesiastical Policy of King James I', *Journal of British Studies*, 24, 2 (April 1985), 169–207; Gordon Donaldson, *Scotland: James V to James VII* (Edinburgh: Oliver & Boyd, 1965), 171–196. For James's efforts to bring the major Christian churches together see W. B. Patterson, *King James VI and I and the Reunion of Christendom* (Cambridge: Cambridge University Press, 1997), *passim*.

vnion in Religion, as laying wilfulnesse aside on both hands, wee might meete in the middest, which is the Center and perfection of all things'.[15] Edward Bruce, Lord Kinloss, a Scot who served as a privy councillor, explained in 1603 to the Venetian secretary in England how this might be achieved:

> True it is that if the Pope wished to summon a General Council, which, according to the ancient usage, should be superior to all Churches, all doctrine, all Princes, secular and ecclesiastic, none excepted, my master [. . .] would be extremely willing to take the lead and to prove himself the warm supporter of so great a benefit to Christendom.[16]

Neither James nor Kinloss specifically mentioned the Greek Church in this context, though there can be no doubt that 'according to the ancient usage' meant that the ancient eastern sees would be included in such a council.

In 1612, when the distinguished Huguenot scholar, Isaac Casaubon, sought to answer the charge made by Cardinal Jacques Davy du Perron, that King James was not entitled to be called 'Catholic', Casaubon quoted James as saying:

> The Church of Rome, the Greek Church, the Church of Antioch, and of Aegypt, the Abyssine, the Moschouite and many others, are members much excelling each other in sinceritie of doctrine, and faith; yet all members of the Catholike Church, whose ioynture, in regard of the outward forme, was long since broken.[17]

---

15   Johann P. Sommerville, ed., *King James VI and I: Political Writings* (Cambridge: Cambridge University Press, 1994), 140.

16   *Calendar of State Papers and Manuscripts Relating to English Affairs Existing in the Archives and Collections of Venice and in Other Libraries of Northern Italy*, 40 vols. (London: Public Record Office, 1864–1947), vol. X, 22.

17   Isaac Casaubon, *The Answere of Master Isaac Casaubon to the Epistle of the Most Illustrious and Most Reverend Cardinall Peron* (London: William Aspley, 1612), 11.

The Church of England, James asserted, was likewise a member of this Church. Casaubon claimed that no cause was more important to the king than that of procuring peace 'amongst the dissenting members of the Church'.[18] Not even in the midst of the battle of the books that ensued after the Gunpowder Plot in 1605 and the imposition of the Oath of Allegiance in the following year did James's resolution weaken.[19] He was committed to furthering peace among his European neighbours and to achieving a religious reconciliation among the major Christian traditions as a means of avoiding an international war.[20] James saw the Greek Orthodox not just as potential allies in his ongoing controversy with Roman Catholic spokesmen over the supposed right of the papacy to depose princes, he also saw the Orthodox as potential partners in the reunion of the Church.

The scholarship scheme got under way with the arrival in 1617 of Metrophanes Kritopoulos, a Macedonian who had been educated as a member of the monastic community on

---

18   Casaubon, *The Answere*, 2.
19   See James VI and I, *An Apologie for the Oath of Allegiance . . . Together with a Premonition of His Maiesties to All Most Mightie Monarches, Kings, Free Princes and States of Christendome* (London: Robert Barker, 1609), 45–46, 110–111.
20   For James's peace diplomacy, see Maurice Lee, Jr., *James I and Henri IV: An Essay in English Foreign Policy, 1603–1610* (Urbana: University of Illinois Press, 1970), 12–13, 17–18, 61–70, 118–142, 175–176; Charles H. Carter, *The Secret Diplomacy of the Habsburgs, 1598–1625* (New York: Columbia University Press, 1964), 109–133; Arthur Wilson White, Jr., 'Suspension of Arms: Anglo-Spanish Mediation in the Thirty Years War, 1621–1625', Ph.D. thesis, Tulane University, 1978; and Maurice Lee, Jr., *Great Britain's Solomon: James VI and I in His Three Kingdoms* (Urbana: University of Illinois Press, 1990), 262–298. For the contemporary reputation of King James as peacemaker, see James Doelman, *King James I and the Religious Culture of England* (Cambridge: D. S. Brewer, 2000), 83–101.

Mount Athos, where Lukaris had met him on a visit.[21] Kritopoulos entered Balliol College, Oxford, where Archbishop Abbot had been an undergraduate and where he had been a fellow for seventeen years. The archbishop's brother Robert Abbot, bishop of Salisbury, had been master of Balliol until 1615.[22] Another possible reason for the selection of Balliol was that another Greek scholar, Christophoros Angelos, a native of the Peloponnese, was already a member there, providing instruction in the Greek language.[23] Kritopoulos studied in Oxford for five years, and then stayed almost two years in London, partly spent in collecting books, before setting out for home on an overland journey across Europe in 1624.[24]

Was there any attempt to effect a union between the Church of England and the Greek Orthodox Church during the period of Kritopoulos's residence? There was, though it was unofficial. In 1619 Marco Antonio De Dominis, archbishop of Spalato, the modern city of Split, wrote from

21   Davey, *Pioneer for Unity*, 23, 69–73.
22   Welsby, *George Abbot*, 5; James Bass Mullinger, life of Robert Abbot, *Dictionary of National Biography*, 22 vols. (Oxford: Oxford University Press, 1959–60), vol. I, 24–25.
23   Johannes Kempke, *Patricius Junius (Patrick Young), Bibliothekar der Könige Jacob I. und Carl I. von England* (Leipzig: M. Spirgatis, 1898), 122–124; Anthony à Wood, *Athenae Oxonienses: An Exact History of All the Writers and Bishops Who Have Had Their Education in the University of Oxford*, ed. Philip Bliss, 4 vols. (London: F. C. and J. Rivington, 1813–20), vol. II, cols. 633–634.
24   Davey, *Pioneer for Unity*, 88–111; Kempke, *Patricius Junius*, 124–130; H. R. Trevor-Roper, 'The Church of England and the Greek Church in the Time of Charles I', in Derek Baker (ed.), *Religious Motivation: Biographical and Sociological Problems for the Church Historian* (Oxford: Blackwell, 1978), Studies in Church History, XV, 222–224, 240; F. H. Marshall, 'An Eastern Patriarch's Education in England', *Journal of Hellenic Studies*, 40 (1926), 185–202.

London to a Greek ecclesiastic, presumably Lukaris, to propose a close association between the two churches.[25] De
Dominis had left his see for London in 1616 as a result of
disputes with the papacy and his desire to see his massive
study of ecclesiastical polity published where he would be free
from papal interference.[26] Like King James he was ambitious
to further the coming together of the churches across
national and denominational lines. His letter proposed a
meeting in England that would include four patriarchs, two
bishops, and a learned presbyter from the Greek Church to
meet with leaders of the Church of England and King James
about plans to link the two churches more closely together.[27]

De Dominis's proposal for what might be the terms of
union revolved about the mutual recognition of the juris-
dictions of the patriarchs, metropolitans, and archbishops of
the two churches, and the affirmation of their common adherence to the ancient creeds, the Apostles', Nicene, and
Athanasian, and the ecumenical councils. He proposed that
the first five ecumenical councils be recognised jointly, along
with certain provisions of the sixth and seventh. The issue of
the *filioque* clause of the Nicene Creed, which had long
divided East and West, would, he proposed, be seriously
discussed, but not be allowed to stand in the way of a com-
pact. The liturgical and other traditions of both churches, as

---

25   Marco Antonio De Dominis to Cyril Lukaris (?), London, 1619, in
      J. H. Hessels (ed.), *Ecclesiae Londino-Bataviae archivum*, 3 vols. in 4
      (Cambridge: Cambridge University Press, 1887–1897), vol. II, 946–
      954.
26   Noel Malcolm, *De Dominis (1560–1624): Venetian, Anglican, Ecumenist
      and Relapsed Heretic* (London: Strickland and Scott, 1984), 42–44;
      Patterson, *King James VI and I*, 222–232. De Dominis's scholarly study
      was published as *De republica ecclesiastica*, vols. I–II (London: John
      Bill, 1617–20), vol. III (Hanau: L. Hulsius, 1622).
27   Hessels (ed.), *Ecclesiae Londino-Bataviae archivum*, vol. II, 953.

well as their teachings about the nature and number of the sacraments, would continue. The centrality of baptism and the Eucharist in the life of the Church, however, would be mutually affirmed.[28] The letter did not have specific backing from English officials, though the fact that De Dominis offered to pay the travel expenses of the Greek visitors suggests that he may have consulted those with deeper pockets than his own.[29] In any case, there seems to have been no response from Lukaris. De Dominis subsequently returned to the Roman obedience, but he seems never to have repudiated his vision of a reunited Church. After being welcomed to Rome by Pope Gregory XV, he was, after Gregory's death, confined to prison by the Inquisition on suspicion of heresy. He died there in 1624 and was posthumously declared a relapsed heretic.[30] King James VI and I himself died in the spring of 1625. There was no immediate follow-up to the plans De Dominis had sketched, perhaps because Lukaris as well as James and his successor Charles I were preoccupied with more pressing concerns. For the British monarchs, these concerns revolved particularly around the outbreak of the Thirty Years' War on the continent. Archbishop Abbot lost influence with James towards the end of the king's reign because his accidental shooting of a gamekeeper in a hunting accident in 1621 resulted temporarily in his duties being exercised by others. He was also at cross-purposes with James

---

28   *Ecclesiae Londino-Bataviae archivum*, vol. II, 950–953.

29   Ibid., vol. II, 953.

30   Patterson, *King James VI and I*, 251–257. The anonymous *A Relation Sent from Rome, of the Processe, Sentence, and Execution, Done upon the Body, Picture, and Bookes of Marcus Antonius De Dominis, Archbishop of Spalato, after His Death* (London: John Bill, 1624), lists sixteen heresies, five of which concern his views on church unity, including one that affirmed the catholicity and orthodoxy of the Church of England (Sig. B2–B2 verso).

over foreign policy, the archbishop favouring a vigorous intervention on the continent, while the king favoured negotiations to end the war.[31]

The only other officially sponsored Greek scholar was Nathaniel Konopios, a native of Crete, who was chosen by Lukaris in the late 1630s, when Lukaris was patriarch of Constantinople. He was sponsored by Archbishop William Laud and King Charles I.[32] In 1639 Konopios entered Balliol College, where he received his Bachelor of Divinity degree in January 1643, in the midst of the English Civil War. In 1645, with the war going badly for the king, he left Oxford for the University of Leyden in the Netherlands, where he sought and apparently received financial support from the States-General. He subsequently served for a time as chaplain at Christ Church, Oxford, until he was ejected by the parliamentary commissioners in November 1648, after which he returned to the East. Like Kritopoulos, he collected books of theology to take back home, since books, including the works of the ancient Greek theologians, were in extremely short supply among the Orthodox. Both Kritopoulos and Konopios wound up in conspicuous ecclesiastical positions, Kritopoulos as patriarch of Alexandria, Konopios as metropolitan of Smyrna. Anthony à Wood, the late seventeenth-century historian of Oxford, credited Konopios with another achievement. 'It was observed', wrote Wood, 'that while he continued

---

31   Welsby, *George Abbot,* 91–104; Fincham, 'Prelacy and Politics', 52–64; Patterson, *King James VI and I,* 345–348. After Charles I's accession in 1625, Abbot lost influence at court to the party of William Laud, who succeeded Abbot as archbishop of Canterbury after Abbot's death in 1633.

32   Kempke, *Patricius Junius,* 136–138; Wood, *Athenae Oxonienses,* vol. IV, col. 808. For Laud and the Greek Church, see Trevor-Roper, 'The Church of England and the Greek Church in the Time of Charles I', 213–214, 228–230, 235, 239.

in Bal. coll. he made the drink for his own use called coffee, and usually drank it every morning, being the first, as the antients of that house have informed me, that was ever drank in Oxon.'[33]

Why was the scholarship not continued after Konopios's residence? The most obvious answer is that the civil wars in England, Scotland, and Ireland in the 1640s brought about the downfall of both the episcopate and the monarchy. Laud and Charles I were, after all, executed. During the inter-regnum of the 1650s, there was no archbishop of Canterbury and no king to sponsor visiting Greek scholars. When the Restoration came in 1660, the scholarship had no advocate. But an important aspect of the story concerns Cyril Lukaris and the Greek Orthodox Church. Lukaris became patriarch of Constantinople in 1620, when Kritopoulos was at Oxford. But he found the patriarchate difficult to hold on to. He was deposed in 1623 by a rival party that favoured a pro-Roman policy and accused him before the Turkish authorities of being in contact with the Orthodox in Russia, the Ottoman Empire's potential enemy on its northern frontier. Lukaris was restored later in 1623, only to be deposed again in 1633, 1634, and 1635.[34] Lukaris's leadership was also weakened by the publication in Geneva in 1631 of the Greek version of his *Confession*, previously published in Sedan in French and Spanish in 1629.[35] The *Confession*'s synthesis of Orthodox and Reformed ideas gave the patriarch's enemies the evidence they needed to condemn him as a heretic. Lukaris met a

---

33 Wood, *Athenae Oxonienses,* vol. IV, col. 808.
34 Hadjiantoniou, *Protestant Patriarch,* 57–61, 113–121; Runciman, *The Great Church in Captivity,* 269–271, 282–284.
35 Runciman, *The Great Church in Captivity,* 275–276; Hadjiantoniou, *Protestant Patriarch,* 141–145. Lukaris acknowledged his authorship in conversation with the French ambassador in Constantinople. See Bodl. MS. Tanner 461, p. 81 (Cornelius van Haga, 7 January 1632).

violent end. Accused of encouraging the Russian cossacks to attack Ottoman territory on the Sea of Azov, he was executed by the Turkish authorities in June 1638. His *Confession* was condemned by synods in Constantinople in 1638 and 1642.[36] The outstanding patriarch of Constantinople in the seventeenth century, Lukaris was, nevertheless, unable to institutionalize the scholarship, any more than he was able to win acceptance in the East for his theological views.

What was the significance of this scholarship programme, and what might still be its relevance? Briefly, let us note the following. First, the Greek scholars who came to England were only a small part of the movement of Greeks in the seventeenth century.[37] Some Greeks in England were merchants, some were officials or landowners who had suffered at the hands of the Turks and sought financial assistance, some were students not on the official scholarships described here. Many of the Greeks returned home, but some of them stayed. In any case they enriched the culture of England. A recent article shows that in the period when coffee houses first came into vogue in the late seventeenth century it was in the Grecian Coffee House, one of several such establishments run by Greeks, that advanced political discussions took place. The patrons found it an appropriate setting in which to discuss Greek philosophy and literature, as well as the history of the ancient Greek city-states and the modern history of the Greeks, and apply the lessons to the

---

36   Runciman, *The Great Church in Captivity*, 285–286; Hadjiantoniou, *Protestant Patriarch*, 127–133; Timothy Ware, *The Orthodox Church*, revised edition (London: Penguin, 1997), 96.

37   Kempke, *Patricius Junius*, 118–122, 133–136, 138–139. See also Andreas Tillyrides, Ἀνέκδοτος Ἀλληλογραφία ἐκ τῶν ἐν Ἀγγλίᾳ Ἐπιδημησάντων Ἑλλήνων τινων τοῦ 17ου Αἰῶνος (reprinted from Θεολογία) (Athens, 1974), 5–55.

politics of their own day.[38] Second, it was the discovery of western religious ideas and practices by Lukaris, Kritopoulos, and others that helped to bring the Orthodox world out of its relative isolation in the seventeenth century. The Reformation had made little impact on the Greek East, though the Counter-Reformation did – many of the Orthodox experienced the latter as an assault on the independence of their Church. The Greek Orthodox Church found it urgently necessary to come to terms with new theological ways of thought. Lukaris's formulation proved to be unacceptable, though Kritopoulos's *Confession* of 1625, published in 1661, which was less influenced by Reformed thought, was generally welcomed. A theological revival took place in the East, partly in an effort to counter Lukaris's *Confession*. The stimulus that Lukaris provided helped theologians to define Orthodoxy, even as its struggle to survive within the regime of the Ottomans continued.[39] Third, the relationship that was established between Orthodoxy and the Church of England endured, despite the short-lived career of the scholarships. There was a great deal of interest in the Greek Church on the part of English scholars and officials in the late seventeenth century, and the establishment in 1699 of the Greek College at Gloucester Hall, Oxford (later Worcester College), was one of the results.[40] What began in the early seventeenth century was a relationship of mutual trust. In 1608, when Christophoros Angelos fled from the Turks in Athens, he asked

---

38 Jonathan Harris, 'The Grecian Coffee House and Political Debate in London, 1688–1714', *London Journal*, 25, 1 (2000), 1–13.

39 Ware, *The Orthodox Church*, 96–99; Ware, *Eustratios Argenti*, 8–16; John Meyendorff, *The Orthodox Church: Its Past and Its Role in the World Today* (Crestwood, N.Y.: St. Vladimir's Seminary Press, 1996), 83–89.

40 E. D. Tappe, 'The Greek College at Oxford, 1699–1705', *Oxoniensia*, 19 (1954), 92–111.

many merchants, 'where I might find wise men, with whom I might keepe my religion and not loose my learning. They told me: In England you may have both [...].'[41] England provided an atmosphere of acceptance. The Orthodox could remain Orthodox, while learning about the West and deepening their understanding of their own faith. This is surely a model for continuing relations.

41   Kempke, *Patricius Junius*, 123.

2. Metrophanes Kritopoulos and his Studies at Balliol College from 1617 to 1622

COLIN DAVEY

In a letter to one of his friends in Germany written in April 1627, Metrophanes Kritopoulos has left us his own account of his early life and travels, from Beroea, where he was born in 1589 and grew up, to England and elsewhere. This is what he writes:

Since you wish to know about my travels from Greece onwards, here is a brief summary of them. I left Beroea and went to Thessaloniki with my uncle, my mother's brother. From there we went to Mount Athos (which today is called the Holy Mountain) where at the age of seventeen I entered the monastic life, and there I remained with my uncle for seven years. One day the Patriarch of Alexandria, who is now Patriarch of Constantinople, came on a visit to see the Holy Mountain. And when he departed, I left my uncle and went with him, desiring to further my studies and education (for His Holiness Kyrillos is said to be the wisest of men). Together we travelled to Moldavia [...] and then to Wallachia. After that we made our way to Constantinople, but only remained there for a few days before journeying to Cairo by way of Rhodes and Alexandria. There His Holiness received letters from the Anglo-British inviting him to send a Greek to study there, and he sent me.

I wanted to say goodbye to my parents and my brothers before leaving for Britain [...]. So [...] after visiting my family in Beroea, I went to Constantinople [...] and from there I took a Dutch ship to the island of Zakynthos. There I boarded an English ship on which I went all the way to England without stopping at any other island, though we did go past several. On arriving in England I was sent by the Archbishop there to the University of Oxford, where I spent five years before returning to London.[1]

Kritopoulos's own primary motivation for coming to Oxford was his continued desire, as he put it, 'to further my studies and education'. The letter of commendation which he took with him from the Patriarch Kyrillos Loukaris to Archbishop George Abbot emphasises that he is 'a Greek, by rank a Presbyter, possessing a good knowledge of Greek literature, a child of our Alexandrian Church, of noble birth, and talents prepared to receive deeper learning'.[2] And the Patriarch continues: 'We trust that the advances he will make will be such as need not be repented of, if Divine Grace will breathe on him from Heaven, and Your Blessedness will lend him an assisting hand.' It is probable that his seven years on Mount Athos were spent at the monastery of Iviron, where there were well-educated monks and a fine library, which would have provided him with opportunities for study as well as for training in prayer and spirituality.[3]

Metrophanes Kritopoulos was the beneficiary of the initiative taken by the Patriarch Kyrillos Loukaris to explore the possibility of educating Greek clergy in England among Anglicans rather than accept the ambiguous assistance offered by the Roman Catholic Greek College of St Athanasios in Rome or the Jesuit school in Constantinople itself. For the Patriarch

---

1   Letter 16 to Johannes Braun, Minister of the Church of God in Sulzbach dated 3rd April 1627 in I. N. Karmiris, Μητροφάνης ο Κριτόπουλος καί η ανέκδοτος αλληλογραφία αυτού (Athens, 1937), 197; Colin Davey, *Pioneer for Unity: Metrophanes Kritopoulos (1589–1639) and relations between the Orthodox, Roman Catholic and Reformed Churches* (London, 1987), 23, 33, 73.

2   J. M. Neale, *A History of the Holy Eastern Church, Alexandria* vol. II, (London, 1847), 385–386. The letter is dated March 1st 1616 (i.e. 1617).

3   See Colin Davey, op. cit., 25–6 referring also to Deno J. Geanakoplos, *Byzantine East and Latin West* (Oxford, 1966), 180–182.

was fully aware of Rome's ulterior motive: to persuade Orthodox students to submit individually to papal jurisdiction, in
order eventually to bring about corporate reunion of the
Orthodox with Rome while retaining Orthodox liturgical
rites and other customs and practices, including married
parish clergy. As the English Ambassador in Constantinople
Sir Thomas Roe wrote in 1623 to the Archbishop of Canterbury George Abbot:

> This we know [...] that the Pope nourisheth a Greek church in
> Rome, who are his emissaries into these parts [...] and the whole plot
> is that [...] the metropolitan seats shall be, in a few years, filled with
> those of the Romish faction, and by degrees, that doctrine sowed in
> the church, and final obedience in the end.[4]

And Kyrillos Loukaris had written in 1613 to one of his Dutch
correspondents in these terms, deploring the limited educational opportunities for Greeks under Turkish rule:

> It is a great dissatisfaction to me that our Pastors and Bishops should
> be sunk in the darkness of ignorance. With this I reproach my coun-
> trymen, but without avail. And the Jesuits, taking the opportunity,
> have laid the foundation of a plan for educating boys at Constantin-
> ople, and have as undisputed success as foxes among poultry; and at
> length the Roman doctrine will overspread the world, if the satellites
> of the Court of Rome employ equal diligence in the business, unless
> God is merciful to us.[5]

This was the reason why Kyrillos Loukaris opened a correspondence, through the English Ambassador Sir Paul Pindar

---

4   *The Negotiations of Sir Thomas Roe in his Embassy to the Ottoman Porte*
     (London, 1740), 146. Sir Thomas Roe was Ambassador from 1621 to
     1628.

5   J. M. Neale, op. cit., 381–382. Letter to J. Uytenbogaert dated 20
     October 1613.

and his Chaplain the Revd William Foord,[6] with the Archbishop of Canterbury, as he explains in his reply on 16 July 1615 to the latter's favourable response to his request:

> You will understand the difficult times we live in, and what a comfort it was to me to read and re-read your gracious letter, the proof of your eagerness to help us [...]. The Jesuits would deprive us of Christ himself, making another to be the head and foundation of the Church, thus contradicting the words of Paul [...]. I judged therefore that this evil could best be allayed with your help, which I am sure will be most useful to our Church, especially since your gracious and compassionate King has given approval of it. Now, with God's help, I am on my way to Alexandria, and from there I shall choose and send to you those whom I consider to be well-pleasing to Christ and able ministers of the Gospel, who will both gratify our benefactors and fulfil our highest expectations.[7]

In addition to pursuing his further education and studies, Metrophanes Kritopoulos undertook two other tasks while he was in England and later in Germany and Switzerland: first to inform those he met about the present state and teachings of the Greek Orthodox Church under Turkish rule, for, as he wrote later, 'some seem to question and, when reassured, are amazed at the survival of Christianity in the East, where Antichrist reigns and persecutes it relentlessly.'[8]

---

6   J. B. Pearson, *A biographical sketch of the Chaplains to the Levant Company* (Cambridge, 1883), 41. Sir Paul Pindar was Ambassador in Constantinople from 1611 to 1619; William Foord was his Chaplain from 1611 to 1615, when he was succeeded by Thomas King.

7   T. P. Themelis, Νέα Σιών 8 (1909), 30–33. The first two letters in this correspondence are lost.

8   Metrophanes Kritopoulos, *Confession of the Catholic and Apostolic Eastern Church*, Preface. Greek text in I. N. Karmiris, Τα Δογματικά καί Συμβολικά Μνημεία τῆς Ορθοδόξου Καθολικῆς Εκκλησίας, Τόμος Β (Athens, 1953), 496 ff.

Second, as the Company of Pastors and Professors of Geneva were later to hear from him, he had been sent by the Patriarch Kyrillos Loukaris (as the Minutes of their meeting with him recorded)

> to visit the Churches and Universities of Western Europe so that by staying a long time in our company, conversing with our scholars and reading our books, he might report to the said Patriarch the doctrine preached and taught in our Churches, so that there might thus be an opening for negotiating some sort of unity and conformity of the Greek Churches with our own.

However, his hosts in Geneva felt correctly that his instructions were 'only to see and learn what doctrine is taught in our Churches' and to report back to the Patriarch, not to engage in any negotiations as such, although, they concluded, 'on his return to his country he should assure the said Patriarch and others who are of the same mind, that if they will show the way in which reunion can be achieved, we shall most gladly open our arms to welcome such a great and holy work.'[9]

Metrophanes Kritopoulos arrived in London in the summer of 1617. He was welcomed by Archbishop George Abbot and his chaplains to Lambeth Palace and was sent for a short time to Gresham College in the City, possibly to help him begin to learn English and Latin.[10] He was accompanied by his brother Demetrios, for whom the archbishop found accommodation and the promise of an apprenticeship, rather than employing him as one of his servants, as Kritopoulos had

---

9   Minutes of an extraordinary session of the Company of Pastors and Professors of Geneva on 6 October 1627, in E. Legrand, *Bibliographie Hellénique au Dix-Septième Siècle* (Paris, 1894–1903), vol. v, 203–206.

10   Colin Davey, op. cit., 75.

62   Colin Davey

perhaps suggested.[11] Then in early September he went up to
Balliol College, Oxford, where his name first appears on
the Bursar's Book of Battels on 6 September 1617.[12] He was
twenty-eight years old.

Archbishop Abbot had chosen Balliol College for Kritopoulos because of his own links with it. He had been a scholar
and then a fellow there, and was one of its more influential
patrons and benefactors.[13] Thanks to him, his elder brother
Robert Abbot had been appointed Master of Balliol in 1610
and he was then succeeded by the Archbishop's former
chaplain John Parkhurst in 1617.[14] Also among the College's
senior members was Christopher Angelos, a refugee from
Greece where he nearly died a martyr's death for his faith. He
had been in Oxford since 1610 'doing very good service among
the young scholars who were raw in the Greek tongue';[15] and
also Edward Sylvester, who 'ran a small but very successful
private grammar school in All Saints' parish [... and] was well

11   A. Tillyrides, Ἀνέκδοτος Ἀλληλογραφία εκ τών εν Ἀγγλία
      επιδημησάντων Ἑλλήνων τινων ιν Θεολογία (Athens, 1974), 34–35,
      Letters 20 and 21.
12   A.Tillyrides, Συμβολαί καί Διορθώσεις εις τήν Ἀλληλογραφίαν τού
      Μητροφάνους Κριτοπούλου τινων ιν Θεολογία (Athens, 1974), 9.
13   Paul A. Welsby, George Abbot, The Unwanted Archbishop 1562–1633
      (London, 1962), 5. In 1616 he had given £100 to the College and in
      1619 spent money on repairing old books in the College library and
      purchasing new ones 'after it had laid in a careless manner from the
      time of the Reformation of religion, or rather before that time.'
      Anthony à Wood, The History and Antiquities of the Colleges and Halls
      in the University of Oxford, ed. John Gutch (Oxford, 1786), 89; Paul A.
      Welsby, op. cit., 117.
14   John Jones, Balliol College, A History, 2nd ed. (Oxford, 1997), 92;
      A. Clark, Balliol College, Oxford, Yearly Lists, vol. II, 1591–1620, states
      that Parkhurst was elected Master 6 February 1616/7; Henry Savage,
      Balliofergus or a Commentary upon the Foundation, Founders and Affairs
      of Balliol College (Oxford, 1668) 126.
15   Anthony à Wood, Athenae Oxonienses (London, 1691), 618.

known [...] for his command of the Greek language and literature',[16] and who, according to Henry Savage, acted as 'interpreter to Metrophanes Critopylus'.[17] In fact, although, as Archbishop Abbot reported to Sir Thomas Roe five years later, 'he hath attained unto some reasonable knowledge of the English tongue, not neglecting his studies otherwise',[18] Kritopoulos himself was not so confident of his ability in the language and wrote to one of his English friends (in Greek) that, during a crucial interview in 1623, the archbishop 'did not completely understand me (with my bad English)' and therefore 'told his Chaplains to hear me out, write it down point by point, and take it to him'.[19] Certainly Kritopoulos conversed and corresponded in Greek whenever he could, and there were quite a number of people in Oxford, Cambridge and London with whom he could do so directly, as well as through his interpreter.

In November 1617 Archbishop Abbot wrote to the Patriarch Kyrillos Loukaris to say that

> the King has commanded me to receive your Metrophanes in a kind and friendly manner. I have already planted this generous young shoot of a Grecian school in a pleasant garden, where he may flourish amongst us, and in good time bring forth fruit; it is in the University of Oxford, where there is a most excellent library, and seventeen colleges, and where a numerous race of learned men are supported at the public expense, as in a Prytanaeum. Your Metrophanes is already entered on the books; and when he has come to maturity, and brought forth fruit, then, as shall seem best to your prudence, and be most for the advantage of your Church, he shall either take deep root

---

16   John Jones, op. cit., 95.
17   Henry Savage, op. cit., 119.
18   J. M. Neale, op. cit., 413, letter dated 22 November 1622.
19   A.Tillyrides, Συμβολαί καί Διορθώσεις, 40, letter 18.

amongst us, or be sent back to his native soil and there again planted.[20]

However, in his reply the Patriarch made it clear that the whole point of sending Kritopoulos abroad to study was that he should return home to serve the Greek Orthodox Church, not that he should remain indefinitely in England, nor indeed that he should become an Anglican:

> May the Lord grant him to make good progress and then return here and be of use in preaching the word and in all other parts of the ministry in the Church. For grievous wolves and evil workers lie in wait to attack us. They go about the cities and seek for opportunities to oppress our simple people.[21]

Balliol College in the year 1617 was larger than we might have expected in terms of overall numbers of people in residence.[22] First there were the Master, twelve Fellows and twelve Scholars and Exhibitioners; then twenty described as 'Doctors and Masters', that is to say those with or studying for higher degrees. This group included two of the three Praelectors (for Rhetoric, Greek Language and Logic) who were largely responsible for the official college teaching.[23] In Clark's Balliol College Lists Metrophanes Kritopoulos is put in this category, with a note adding that he 'was put on the list

---

20 J. M. Neale, op. cit., 388–389.

21 C. A. Papadopoulos, Νέα Σιών 3 (1906), 3–10.

22 These figures are taken from A. Clark, *Balliol College, Oxford, Yearly Lists,* vol. II, 1591-1620, 114 ff. These were compiled from the Buttery Books for each year, supplemented where necessary from the Bursar's Book of Battels, using the list for the last week in the fourth quarter in the college year and supplying additional information about people's ages, status, date of taking degrees etc. They exclude non-residents.

23 John Jones, op. cit., 95.

14th October 1617. He was given standing as an M.A., and as the first M.A. of that Academic Year.'[24]

In 1610 a new Statute had been made providing for the admission of Fellow-Commoners. There was an increased demand for such places from the upper strata of society and their presence was financially advantageous to the House.[25] In 1617 there were twenty-three of these Fellow-Commoners, and also seventy-one Commoners, who also paid their way but did not necessarily read for a degree.[26] If we add to these some twenty-nine servants in residence, that gives a total of one hundred and sixty-eight people in all.

Most of Balliol College's buildings, including the Hall and Library, dated from the fifteenth century. But the 'comely and decent Chapel, which', as Anthony à Wood wrote later in the seventeenth century, 'now stands on the north side of the quadrangle' was begun in 1521 and finished in 1529.[27] Here, we assume, Kritopoulos attended Anglican services, though he appears not to have received communion.[28] It is probable, however, that he kept up his monastic round of prayers and offices – he gives us a brief glimpse of his constancy in prayer during his many travels when he writes later:

---

24   A. Clark, op. cit., 123, College Lists for 1618. Kritopoulos then appears on these lists for 1619, 1620, 1621 and 1622. A. Clark, op. cit., II, 129, 136; III, 1621–1644, 11, 17.

25   John Jones, op. cit., 92.

26   M. H. Curtis, *Oxford and Cambridge in Transition 1558–1642* (Oxford, 1959), 130.

27   A. Wood, *History and Antiquities*, 87–89, 99.

28   As indicated in a letter to him in 1637 from the Propaganda in Rome which states that 'we know [...] what you did in England, refusing the execrable table of the heretics'. G. Hofmann, *Griechische Patriarchen und Römische Päpste* in *Orientalia Christiana*, vol. XXXVI, no. 97 (Oct. 1934).

If on a dark and moonless night I arrive at an inn, and it is difficult to tell where the East lies, I shall not leave out my prayers because of this. Nor shall I have to find out from the landlord exactly where the East lies before I can pray [...] but shall pray facing in whatever direction I like.[29]

Yet it is not known whether, as a priest, he celebrated or even attended the Orthodox liturgy between 1617, when he left for England, and 1627 when he arrived in Venice, where there was a Greek Orthodox Church and community.[30]

Metrophanes Kritopoulos was like other students who came to Oxford to study but not for a degree. He spent five profitable years reading and being tutored in the subjects of his choice. The Testimonial from King James I, which he received in 1623, records that

he has been assiduous in his reading of the Holy Fathers and Doctors of the Church and in all parts of Sacred Study, not neglecting meanwhile to converse with learned men of all kinds (as is clear from their own testimonials) and he has left behind him a great sense of loss on his departure from here on his travels. In him has been seen throughout his stay here holiness of life combined with modesty of character and outstanding erudition.[31]

And one of the Archbishop's chaplains, Dr Thomas Goad, wrote that same year:

He seems to be a living reincarnation of St Gregory and St Basil, if indeed, from our daily acquaintance, I have judged rightly the nature

---

29   Metrophanes Kritopoulos, *Confession,* in I. N. Karmiris, op. cit., 556–557.
30   Colin Davey, op. cit., 263 ff.
31   Latin original in the Library of Hamburg first published in A. K. Demetrakopoulos, Δοκίμιον περί τού βίου καί τών συγγραμμάτων Μητροφάνους τού Κριτοπούλου (Leipzig, 1870), 9–10.

of his great intellect and the great learning he displays, especially in the Fathers, for which he is famous, and in other writers.[32]

He also made a thorough study of ancient Greek language and literature. This is reflected in his own letters and writings, with their quite extraordinary beauty of style and vocabulary. These were described by Thomas Rhoedus, King James I's secretary, as 'most worthy of ancient Greece',[33] while Kritopoulos himself was praised for 'the elegance of his pure Attic language'.[34] The content of his classical studies was perhaps much the same as that recommended to him by Andrew Downes, the Regius Professor of Greek at Cambridge for another priest from Greece who had come to England for further studies. This was Nikodemos Metaxas, a monk from Kephalonia who had been educated there and in Athens, and on whose behalf Kritopoulos wrote to Professor Downes, whose attitude to Greece and the Greeks may also have been shared by many at Oxford. Downes replied to him:

> It would, I feel, be absurd if I, who spend my days teaching and training rather untalented barbarians, should refuse to welcome those who come from Greece itself, and who possess both ability and also a natural aptitude towards what is, after all, their native tongue. So if you send the young man here [...] in a short time we shall have him speaking like my Demosthenes [...]. I hope that my pupil will

---

32 *Philotheke* (Kritopoulos' autograph album, which has never been published in its entirety but on which I was able to work in 1964–5 in the Library of the Theological Faculty of Athens University where it is held) 46. Extensive use has been made of it by M. Renieris, Μητροφάνης Κριτόπουλος καί οι εν Αγγλία καί Γερμανία φίλοι αυτού (1617–1628) (Athens, 1893), and F. H. Marshall, *An Eastern Patriarch in England and Germany* (MS in the Gennadeion Library in Athens; the first half published in the *Journal of Hellenic Studies* 46 (1926), 185–202.

33 *Philotheke*, 64.

34 By Laurence Whitaker, a Cambridge graduate resident in London where he met Kritopoulos on 26 June 1623, *Philotheke*, 285.

learn to speak elegantly and clearly. For I have been a philhellene since I was a boy, and I am an admirer of Athens as you know [...]. But as for the scholar's arts which you wish the young man to attain, I feel that he should make a sufficient and adequate study of logic, pay special attention to rhetoric [by which he meant Greek grammar, language and literature], and add as much philosophy as is useful.[35]

(In fact Nikodemos Metaxas never went up to Cambridge, possibly because of the problem of paying for his tuition, board and lodging, but spent four years in London studying the art of printing and acquiring and using a Greek printing press which he took to Constantinople in 1627.)[36]

The Professor of Greek at Oxford, John Harris, referred in Kritopoulos' autograph album to their 'long friendship and acquaintance';[37] and Edward Sylvester, his interpreter, referring to Acts chapter 17, testified to his friendship with 'the most holy, devout and Orthodox of monks, one of the noblest of Berroeans'.[38]

Kritopoulos also answered the request of one of his Balliol friends, Matthias Turner, for extra instruction in Attic Greek,[39] and that of Meric Casaubon from Christ Church, for tuition in Modern Greek. However, he speaks disparagingly of Modern Greek, saying that his friend's aim must be 'to converse with Greeks who travel here, [rather than] in order to search, like a busy bee, for better things, for there are hardly any books written in it.' And he compares it very

---

35   Colin Davey, op. cit., 92–93.
36   Ibid., 117–118.
37   *Philotheke*, 164.
38   Ibid., 293; Acts 17.10–11.
39   Colin Davey, op. cit., 100–101. Matthias Turner was a Commoner, the son of a clergyman in London, who entered Balliol aged 15 in 1616 and gained his B.A. in April 1619 and his M.A. in 1622. A. Clark, *Balliol College, Oxford, Yearly Lists* II, 112, 131; III, 24.

unfavourably with Ancient Greek, calling his nine rules of grammar 'the nine errors of the Modern Greek language'.[40]

At Oxford Kritopoulos may have continued some study of Latin, but he did not get as far as might have been expected, though he seems to have made up for this later. In fact he wrote to Matthias Turner in early 1623 when he was back at Lambeth Palace to say

> about the grammar, this is what I would prefer. I do not want to make such a study of Latin that I could write in it, but only so as to be able to understand what is written by others. So I think that the grammar of Lilius would be sufficient.[41]

Kritopoulos was a frequent visitor to the Bodleian Library. Its librarian, John Rous, in 1622 'bade farewell to his learned, upright and modest Critopulus and urged him to remember the most venerable Bodleian, to which he often came'.[42] The Bodleian Library Catalogue of 1620 is among the two hundred and sixty-five books belonging to Kritopoulos which are still to be found in the Patriarchal Library of Alexandria.[43] These indicate not only that he was a fanatical collector of books but also the breadth of his interests and the generosity of those he met during his travels in Western Europe. They include Greek and Latin Classical authors, Philosophy, Grammars, Lexicons, Biblical Texts and

---

40 A.Tillyrides, Συμβολαί καί Διορθώσεις, Letter 20, 41–45. Kritopoulos later developed this into a 'Grammar of Modern Greek' for Matthias Bernegger, Professor of Grammar and Rhetoric at Strasbourg, in August 1627. See Colin Davey, op. cit., 244–247.

41 Colin Davey, op. cit., 114.

42 *Philotheke*, 80.

43 *Catalogus Universalis Librorum in Bybliotheca Bodleiana* (Oxoniae, 1620). T. D. Moschonas lists the 265 volumes collected by and given to Kritopoulos during his studies and travels which are still in the Patriarchal Library in Κριτοπούλεια in *Analecta* II (Alexandria, 1962).

Commentaries, Patristic authors, Councils and Canons, as well as works of Roman Catholic and Reformed Theology.[44]

There is one further observation to make about Kritopoulos during his five years at Oxford. He was often ill, as his correspondence with Patrick Young, the King's Librarian shows. In 1618 Kritopoulos wrote that he had 'suffered a truly terrible attack of kidney trouble. And it is only now that with God's help I have recovered a little [...] and I still have some difficulty in writing at all.'[45] In May 1620 he wrote to say that he had been ill again, this time for four months.[46] And his correspondence with Meric Casaubon in July that year again mentions his illness, while in August he says he has discovered what must have caused it. The letter is addressed 'To the sick Meric Casaubon from the very sick Metrophanes Kritopoulos'. And he writes of his illness:

> I think it happened because of my drinking nasty stinking beer (may its inventor perish!). I was not used to this drink (you would sooner find bird's milk in Greece than a drop of beer!). But as soon as I began to drink it, and not in small quantities either (and what else could I drink with the water being unsafe and wine not doing me any good) I suffered what I suffered.[47]

Metrophanes Kritopoulos greatly appreciated the welcome he had been given at Balliol, and expressed this in letters

---

44 Colin Davey, op. cit., 287–288. The numbers in each category are as follows: Classical Authors: Greek 49; Latin 12; Philosophy etc 36; Grammars and Lexicons 15; Biblical Works: Texts 7; Dictionaries etc. 3; O. T. Commentaries 14; N. T. Commentaries 11; Councils and Canons 10; Patristics 30; Roman Catholic Theology 17; Reformed Theology 58; Miscellaneous 3.

45 Ibid., 95–96.

46 Ibid., 96.

47 Ibid., 97.

he wrote in the summer of 1623 to its Master, John Parkhurst, and to 'the Balliolites'. To the former he said:

> Reverend Master, on many other occasions you have most cour-
> teously and generously shown to me your goodness and kindness;
> indeed you treasured me, a foreigner unknown to you, so graciously,
> and took such care of me, that I feel terribly ashamed, for I cannot
> thank you enough.[48]

And to his friends at Balliol he added:

> Every tribe and nation welcomes friends and treats them kindly
> while they stay with them. But it is rare, and found only among
> people of education and liberal character that friends are remem-
> bered after they have gone away, and people do all they can to help
> them then [...]. I am absent in body – but in body only, for in my soul
> I have never been parted from you, nor shall I be 'though many dark
> mountains and the echoing seas divide us'.[49]

In fact, as these letters indicate, Kritopoulos had already left Balliol some months before writing them. His name appears for the last time on the Balliol Butler's Book on 6 September 1622.[50] He then paid a short visit to Cambridge,[51] where he opened his autograph album, which he called his *Philotheke* (or 'Friendship Book'),[52] spent two weeks back in Oxford collec-ting signatures and comments from his friends and his teachers, and then travelled to London. He stayed at Lambeth Palace until mid-July 1623 and then moved into rooms in London until he left for Germany a year later.

However, the reason for his leaving Lambeth Palace was an unfortunate one, to put it mildly. His problem was that he

---

48   Ibid., 126.
49   Ibid., 127.
50   A. Tillyrides, Συμβολαί καί Διορθώσεις 9.
51   Colin Davey, op. cit., 102.
52   See footnote 32 above and M. Renieris, op. cit., 6.

was sure that the Patriarch Kyrillos Loukaris wanted him, if possible, to travel back home via Germany and Switzerland in order to visit and learn about and report to him on the other Reformed churches there. But the Patriarch's correspondence with Archbishop Abbot had given the impression that Kritopoulos should come straight back home by sea. And there was little hope in mid-1623 of Kritopoulos receiving the necessary authorisation for the alternative route, since the Patriarch had been deposed and exiled to Rhodes in April that year and was not restored again until October.[53]

Kritopoulos severely damaged his own reputation with Archbishop Abbot by refusing point blank to return home by ship direct to Constantinople on 15 July 1623. The Archbishop was infuriated by what he saw as an act of ingratitude and disobedience and poured out to Sir Thomas Roe his feelings about Greeks in general and Kritopoulos in particular:

> In brief, writing a kind of epistle unto me, that he would rather lose his books, suffer imprisonment and loss of life, than go home in any ship; but that he would see the parts of Christendom and better his experience that way, I found that he meant to turn rogue and beggar and more I cannot tell what; and thereupon I gave him ten pounds in his purse, and leaving him to Sir Paul Pindar's care, at my removing to Croydon a fortnight's since, I dismissed him. I had heard before of the baseness and slavishness of that nation; but I could never have believed that any creature in human shape, having learning, and such education as he hath had here, could, after so many years have been so far from ingenuity, or any grateful respect. But he must take his fortune, and I will learn by him to entreat so well no more of his fashion. Only I have thus at large acquainted you with the unworthy carriage of this fellow, which, though it be indecent in him, yet for the Patriarch's sake, I grudge it not unto him.[54]

---

53   On all this see Colin Davey, op cit., 119–120, 124–126.
54   Letter of 12 August 1623 in T. Roe, op. cit., 171, quoted in J. M. Neale, op. cit., 414–415.

This was a heavy blow, first for Kritopoulos himself, though he retained the goodwill of both King James I, who later in the year wrote him the warmly supportive letter of commendation and safe conduct already referred to,[55] and also of the Patriarch Kyrillos Loukaris, who eventually sent the authorisation required for his journey through continental Europe.[56] But it was a blow also to the possibility of any immediate continuation of the scheme for sending Greeks to be educated in England as far as Archbishop Abbot was concerned. 'I will learn by him to entreat so well no more of his fashion' he had declared. This episode has also damaged Kritopoulos' reputation with subsequent English historians, who have repeated J. M. Neale's quotation of the Arch-bishop's letter without understanding fully the dilemma in which Kritopoulos found himself.

So what were the results and significance of Kritopoulos' five-year stay at Balliol College Oxford? First, he has been described by the late Professor Karmiris as 'a theologian with the finest education of any of his contemporaries, a man approved for his steadfast devotion to Orthodoxy, possessing the widest of ecclesiastical horizons'.[57] He did indeed serve the Greek Orthodox Church with distinction, first as priest and schoolmaster for the Greek Community in Venice, then as Great Archimandrite of Alexandria, Bishop of Memphis

---

55   See footnote 31 above.
56   See footnote 9 above. The Minutes of the Extraordinary Session of the Company of Pastors and Professors of Geneva include the report 'that when he was ready to leave [England] to return to Greece, he received letters from the Patriarch which instructed him to see also the Churches and Academies of Germany. This he had done, and had remained there for three years. He had been to Basel [...] and from there had come to Berne, where he had made it known that he desired also to see Geneva'.
57   I. N. Karmiris, Μητροφάνης ο Κριτόπουλος, 169.

and Egypt, and, from 1636 until his death three years later, as Patriarch of Alexandria.

Second, as a result of his studies at Oxford and his travels elsewhere, he not only did as much as any one person could to make known to those he met the teachings and traditions of the Orthodox Church, but he did so in a way which showed his grasp and understanding of both Roman Catholic and Reformed theology and practice and of where the Orthodox agreed or disagreed with them. He wrote two accounts of the life and doctrines of the Orthodox Church, a short series of *Answers* to questions put to him by Dr Thomas Goad, the Archbishop's chaplain, in July 1623[58] and a much longer *Confession of the Catholic and Apostolic Eastern Church* which he wrote at the request of the Professors of the University of Helmstadt in May 1625.[59] In these, for instance, he defended the Orthodox practice of infant communion against those who said that babies had no awareness of it by replying 'that they have none of Baptism either. [...] Quite simply, we use about the Lord's Supper the same arguments that everyone else, except the Anabaptists, uses about Baptism'.[60]

He also suggests, in his *Confession*, a 'middle way' between those who argue that there are seven sacraments and those who say there are only two, by dividing them into three which are necessary for all for their salvation: Baptism, Communion and Penance; and others which are only for some, which he describes as 'sacramental rites which are similarly called sacraments by the Church, because of their mystical and

58   Text of the first set of *Answers to Goad* in K. I. Dyovouniotis, Μητροφάνης Κριτόπουλος (Athens, 1925) 51–60. The second set, entitled *Other Answers to the same Dr Goad from the same Metrophanes*, is found in I. N. Karmiris, Η Ομολογία μετά τών πρός Γώδον Αποκρίσεων τού Μητροφάνους Κριτοπούλου (Athens, 1948), 26–38.
59   See footnote 8 above.
60   K. I. Dyovouniotyis, op. cit., 54–55.

spiritual content: such as the Holy Chrism, which we receive immediately after Baptism, the Order of Priests, the first Marriage, and Unction'.[61] To these he adds, in his *Answers to Goad*, the Monastic Order and the Burial of the Dead.[62] And on the much disputed matter of 'where can the true Church be found?' he suggests four 'marks' which point clearly in fact only to the Orthodox Church. These are: unanimity between the Church's leaders; respect for tradition; being the victim, not the agent of persecution; and loyalty to the Word of God, both the written Scriptures and the Church's unwritten traditions.[63]

Third, he worked continuously for a rapprochement between the Orthodox and the Reformed Churches. Towards the end of his stay in Germany he was quite optimistic. He wrote that the German people's deep love for the Greek language

> made them true friends of the Greek nation. It also made them friendly towards our Christian Orthodoxy (and even if we differ in some matters, yet the differences can be easily healed and overcome, and I am convinced that complete unity will not be long in coming – so the Holy Spirit tells me).[64]

I think he would have felt the same about those he met in England and about the Anglican Church's view of the Orthodox Church. But later on, the publication of the Patriarch Kyrillos Loukaris's Calvinistic *Confession of Faith*[65] and the activities of Antoine Léger, the Calvinistic Chaplain to

61 *Confession,* chap. 5 in I. N. Karmiris, op. cit., 525.
62 *Other Answers,* in I. N. Karmiris, op. cit., 33.
63 *Confession,* chap. 7 in I. N. Karmiris, op. cit., 528.
64 Preface to Grammar of Modern Greek in K. I. Dyovouniotis, Μητοφάνους Κριτοπούλου Ανέκδοτος Γραμματική τῆς Ἁπλῆς Ελληνικῆς (Athens, 1924), 107.
65 See Colin Davey, op. cit., 282–286.

the Dutch Ambassador in Constantinople,[66] made Krito-poulos even more clear that the way to any rapprochement between the Orthodox and the Reformed Churches – any grand alliance against Rome, which had already proved possible politically but which was harder to achieve ecclesiastically – should be through the Reformers coming to accept his own Church's respect for tradition, including its full sacramental and devotional life and the Fathers as the authoritative interpreters of Scripture, not by the 'conformity of the Greek Churches with our own', as the Company of Pastors and Professors in Geneva had put it.[67] With this in mind he wrote to Antoine Léger on 8 January 1636 with less optimism 'about the future welfare of our churches, supposing that there is some hope of our coming together one day, by leaving aside all unseasonable objections and holding fast to the Church's rule of faith alone'.[68] And a month later he wrote again to Léger, first to say that

> the sad sight of the almost complete separation between the different parts of the Christian Church arouses in you a manifest zeal to work out, as far as you can, how they may come together in unity of faith. We cannot but praise your purpose, [he continues] which should be commended by both sides, and indeed it has been exactly our purpose also.

But he concludes by re-stating his own understanding of 'unity of faith', which is that all should accept

> that sound and saving doctrine, the foundations of which were laid down by the Prophets, which Christ our Lord revealed, the Apostles preached throughout the world, the Doctors and Pastors of the Church proclaimed and handed on to their successors, and which all

---

66   Ibid., 297–298.
67   See footnote 9 above.
68   E. Legrand, op. cit., IV, 418–419.

Orthodox Christians gladly accept and hold untainted up till now, and will maintain to the end of the world. This doctrine, I repeat, this doctrine revealed by God, I shall defend to my dying day.[69]

And he did.

---

69   Ibid., 430–432.

3. Archbishop Joseph Georgirenes and the Prehistory of the Greek College

John P. Barron

On 10 April 1677 the recusant Catholic dilettante Thomas Blount wrote from Shoreditch to his friend Anthony Wood, the antiquary of Merton College, 'I suppose you have heard, that the Archbp of Samos has got leave to build a Greek Church here, our Bps promoting it, because he disacknowledging the Pope's supremacy.'[1] Two months later, as Wood noted in his recollections,

> In the beginning of this month [...] the archbishop of Samos in Greece came to Oxon, aet. 40 or thereabouts [...] Quere whether he did not come in relation of having a college erected for them in Oxon, at Gloucester Hall. He came to get money towards the finishing of the Greek church at London. At that time there was a great talk of converting Gloucester Hall into a College for the educating of 20 or 30 Greeks in Academical learning and to send them home, but these only wanted pelf.[2]

1   Bodleian Library, MS Wood F.40, f. 225. This paper has been much improved by suggestions made at the conference, and subsequently by Miss Melanie Barber, Dr Sebastian Brock and Mrs Helen Hughes-Brock, Dr Jonathan Harris, Mr Peregrine Horden, Professor John Miller, Miss Sally Speirs, Mr John Steele, Dr Dimitris Theodossopoulos, Bishop Kallistos Ware, and the Prefects and Directors of archives at the Vatican and at Volterra.

2   *The Life and Times of Anthony Wood, Antiquary, of Oxford, 1632–1695, described by Himself*, ed. A. Clark, 5 vols (Oxford Historical Society, 1891–1900), ii, 379. For the Gloucester Hall project of 1677, see C. H.

Elsewhere Wood notes that the archbishop was in Oxford 'for some weeks'.[3] That his solicitation for the Greek church bore fruit we learn from the vice-chancellor's accounts for 1676–1677: 'given to the archbishop of Samos by consent of the delegates, 10 *li*'.[4]

In the long drawn-out but ultimately vain attempt of Anglican divines of the seventeenth and eighteenth century to achieve what they called 'the Restitution of Catholick Communion between the Greek Churches and the Church of England',[5] Joseph Georgirenes, sometime archbishop of Samos, for six short years seemed to hold the key to success.

Daniel and W. R. Barker, *Worcester College* (London, 1900), 134 f. It appears not to be mentioned in the *History of the University of Oxford,* iv, ed. N. Tyacke (Oxford, 1997), or v, ed. L. S. Sutherland and L. G. Mitchell (Oxford, 1986).

3   A. Wood, *Fasti Oxonienses*, ed. P. Bliss, 4 vols. (London, 1813–1830), ii, col. 219.

4   *Life and Times*, iv, p. 76. Interestingly, the next payment listed in the accounts is 'to Mr Rhodocanaces, the Grecian, by the same consent, 5 *li*'. A member of the London Greek community, Constantine Rhodocanaces was Charles II's personal physician. A 'Grecian of the Isle Chios', as he described himself on the title-page of his *Alexicacus, spirit of salt of the world* (London, 1664; repr. St Peter Port, 1977), he even wrote a poem in his native Greek to celebrate the Restoration: E. Legrand, ed., *Le retour de Charles II, Roi d'Angleterre: poëme grec du prince Constantin Rodocanakis, publié d'après l'edition de 1660* (Paris, 1873).

5   Cf. the broadsheet, *A Good and Necessary Proposal for the Restitution of Catholic Communion between the Greek Churches and the Church of England*, probably written by Edward Stephens, London, 1705, after the collapse of the second (Woodroffe's) attempted Greek college. Lambeth Palace Library has a manuscript draft significantly different from the printed version, among the Gibson collection: MS 935/30, cf. 938/13 (See Appendix F). I am deeply indebted to the former deputy librarian, Miss Melanie Barber, for this and other information.

As is well known, seventeenth-century England was a ready seed-bed for ecumenical ventures of the sort which Georgirenes and his English contacts had in mind. In the fashionable Greek coffee-houses which sprang up in London (and even earlier in Oxford), the conversation was of ancient Greece and its literature, certainly; but the suffering of contemporary Greeks at the hands of the Turks kindled new and powerful waves of sympathy for a civilisation brought so low.[6] Against this background, for the young Church of England the Ortho-dox Church seemed a most desirable partner – a church which spoke still the authentic language of the fathers, episcopal and apostolic, above all non-papist. The Church of England, of course, sat on the western side of the Great Schism over the procession of the Holy Spirit; but it joined the Orthodox in its rejection of Purgatory and prayers for the dead, and in more practical matters such as the administration of com-munion in both kinds, using ordinary (i.e. not unleavened) bread; and it could live with the eastern church's lack of precision or even equivocation over the issue of transub-stantiation.[7]

At the time of Georgirenes' visit to England no one was more heartily, even fanatically, anti-papist than the new bishop of London, Henry Compton – who had been lately but

---

6   J. Harris, 'The Grecian Coffee House and Political Debate in London 1688–1714', *London Journal* xxv (2000), 1–13. A Greek coffee-house appeared in Oxford as early as 1639, introduced by Nathaniel Konopios, a Greek sent to Balliol (below, n. 10). See, for instance, T. E. Dowling and E. W. Fletcher, *Hellenism in England* (London, 1915), 46, 67.

7   See S. Runciman, *The Greek Church in Captivity* (Cambridge, 1968), 235, 276 ff, and esp. ch. vii. See also H. R. Trevor-Roper, 'The church of England and the Greek church in the time of Charles I', in D. Baker, ed., *Religious Motivation: Biographical and Sociological Problems for the Church Historian, Studies in Church History* xv (1978), 213-240.

briefly bishop of Oxford, from December 1674 to November 1675. Compton's hostility to Rome and all her works brought him the implacable hostility of the Romish duke of York, and was to frustrate his otherwise well-grounded aspiration to the see of Canterbury.[8] But he never wavered. The bishops of London had long held particular responsibility for alien churches.[9] For Compton, this became sharply focused in two directions, support of anti-papist churches abroad and provision for immigrant and refugee protestant congregations in England – provided that their doctrines and practices were compatible with the tenets of the Church of England as by law established. On all these grounds and in this context, the archbishop of Samos and his English friends could expect a favourable hearing, whether for plans to provide a Greek church for the expatriates in London or for the more daring Oxford design of training a Greek élite to lead and serve their countrymen at home.[10]

So far as it is possible to separate Georgirenes' interlinked endeavours – the attempt to establish a Greek church

---

8   See the excellent biography by Edward Carpenter, *The Protestant Bishop* (London, 1956).

9   Andrew Pettegree, *Foreign Protestant Communities in Sixteenth-Century London* (Oxford, 1986), 137, the bishop of London appointed superintendent in 1559.

10   For the latter, they could point to two precedents dating from before the civil war, of Greeks sent to Balliol at the instance of Patriarch Loukaris and with the interest of archbishops Abbot and Laud. Metrophanes Kritopoulos, having studied Latin and Greek and the doctrines of the Church of England, returned home and at length became metropolitan of Memphis and then patriarch of Alexandria. Nathaniel Konopios studied theology and introduced coffee, was ordained and became chaplain of Christ Church. Ejected by the parliamentary forces in 1648, he also returned home, and in 1651 became bishop of Smyrna. See above, Colin Davey, 'Metrophanes Kritopoulos and his Studies at Balliol College from 1617 to 1622'.

in London, his contribution to theological dialogue, and his part in the design for a Greek college at Gloucester Hall – we shall examine them in that order. As well as the notices of his contemporaries, such as those already quoted, and official records of the time, we are fortunate to have from his years in England a small clutch of writings made by or for him: *A Description of the Present State of Samos, Nicaria, Patmos, and Mount Athos* [...] *Translated by one that knew the Author in Constantinople*, licensed for publication on 14 July 1677 while the author was in Oxford fund-raising for the Greek church, and published the following year;[11] an inscription formerly above the west door of the Greek church, and now preserved in the Greek Cathedral in Bayswater, recording his construction of the church in 1677;[12] two manuscript letters to Thomas Smith at Magdalen College attempting to resolve points of doctrine and church practice which were identified as stumbling-blocks in the way of intercommunion, from one of which Smith quotes *verbatim* in the preface to the 1678 edition of his *De Graecae Ecclesiae hodierno statu Epistola*;[13] a manuscript petition to Archbishop Sancroft to seek his support for the founding of a Greek college, undated but no doubt of 1678;[14] a manuscript petition to the King and his

---

11   Thomas Smith, *An Account of the Greek Church as to Its Doctrine and Rites of Worship* (London, 1680), 97 f, speaks of a version in French also, earlier than the English edition. This was never published however. There followed a German edition, 1689, reprinted in 1799. See below and nn. 52-56.

12   P. A. Bezodis in *Survey of London*, vol. xxxiii, *The Parish of St Anne Soho,* ed. F. H. W. Sheppard (London, 1966), 280 and pl. 16 *b*.

13   Bodleian Library, MS Smith 98, pp. 31–34 and 47–50, published in full by M. E. Martin, 'Some western images of Athos in early modern times, c. 1554–1678', *Byz. and Mod. Greek Studies* xxii (1998), 51–74; Appendix II, 72 ff. I owe this reference to the kindness of Dr Jonathan Harris.

14   Bodleian Library, MS Tanner 33, p. 57 (p. 58 is *verso*, blank).

Privy Council in November 1678, and a notice in the *London Gazette* in February 1680, when fund-raising for the church had suffered fraud;[15] a further petition for royal aid;[16] and – sad coda to a flawed endeavour – a broadsheet dated 1682 'From the Arch-Bishop of the Isle of Samos in Greece, An Account of his building the Greek Church in So-hoe Feilds, and the disposal thereof by the Masters of the Parish of St Martin's in the Feilds'.[17]

---

15 Bodleian Library, MS Tanner 33, p. 59: dated by *Calendar of State Papers, Domestic Series, 1678*, ed. F. H. Blackburne Daniell (London, 1913), p. 548; cf. Historical Manuscript Commission, *4th Report*, Pt. i (London, 1874), Appendix, p. 234, Coventry MS at Longleat. *London Gazette*, no. 1485v, 9–12 February 1679/80 ('1679', wrongly).

16 *Cal. State Papers, Dom. Ser., 1680–81*, ed. Daniell (London, 1921), 691 f.

17 London, printed for A. F. There are two copies in the Bodleian Library: MS Wood 417, no. 103, in a volume mainly of broadsheets and folios containing popular anti-papist songs; and MS Ashmole F.1 (74), in a collection of tracts favourable to the French protestant cause and hostile alike to papists and Quakers. In addition to all the above, the printed British Library catalogue (1975) and others attribute to Georgirenes *A True and Exact Relation of the Strange Finding Out of Moses his Tombe* [...] *communicated by a person of quality residing at Constantinople, to a person of Honour here in England* [...]: London, Printed by J. G. for Richard Lowndes, [...] 1657; repr. Luttrell Society No. 18 (Oxford, 1958). In his introduction to the latter reprint, C. H. Wilkinson notes that Aubrey and Wood exposed the *True and Exact Relation* as a hoax, the work of Thomas Chaloner the regicide and notorious drunkard, 1595–1661. The attribution to Georgirenes (of which Wilkinson says nothing) was made by the late seventeenth-century owner of a bound-up volume of pamphlets now in the library of Christ Church (Oxford), a.3.194, who wrote on the title-page of this, the first item, 'by Joseph Georgirenes ABP. of Samos', and made the same assertion in his list of contents on the facing fly-leaf. This owner, who presumably did not recognise the hoax, gives no reason for his attribution. Consciously or subconsciously, it may have been triggered by the initials of the printer, J. G., and apparently confirmed by the statement on the title-page that the story was told in

Joseph Georgirenes was a native of the island of Melos, born – if Wood judged his age correctly – in the mid 1630s. Of his early career we know only that he spent six years as a monk on Mt Athos.[18] On 7 October 1666, under Patriarch Parthenios IV, he was consecrated archbishop of Samos, the seventh since Samos broke away from the jurisdiction of the metropolitan of Rhodes to become directly subordinate to the patriarch. 'He sat here five years, till after the taking of *Candie*, the *Turks* grew more populous, and consequently more abusive: So that wearied with their injuries, he retired to the Holy *Grotto* of the *Apocalypse*, in the isle of *Patmos*.' And the new Patriarch Dionysios IV appointed one Philaretos as his successor.[19] So it was that when in 1676 Georgirenes came to London, he came not as archbishop of Samos in exile but as *ex*-archbishop. It was not a distinction he troubled to make clear. 'An indifferent tall man, and slender, with long black hair, having a wart on the right side of his nose just against his eye, a Cut under his right eye, and black whiskers with very little Beard', he was not, perhaps, in appearance a particularly commanding figure.[20] And he spoke no English.[21] But he had a

---

Constantinople, where Georgirenes certainly had English contacts (below and n. 52) – but later, in the 1660s. There is nothing to be said for the attribution, which remains a bibliographical curiosity. (See also Martin, op. cit., 70.)

18   Smith, loc. cit. (n. 11); A. Galland, quoted in E. Legrand, *Bibliographie Hellénique ou description raisonnée des ouvrages publiés par des Grecs au dix-septième siècle* (Paris, 1894–1903), vol. ii, 346. I owe this reference to Dr Jonathan Harris.

19   Georgirenes, *Description*, 37. The much disturbed sequence of the patriarchs of Constantinople in this period is clarified by G. Podskalsky, *Griechische Theologie in der Zeit der Türkenherrschaft (1453–1821)* (Munich, 1988), 399.

20   *London Gazette*, loc. cit. (n. 15).

21   Bodleian Library, MS Tanner 33, p. 59.

certain charisma, a gift for making friends and influencing people.

What is quite unclear is how much his English friends knew of Georgirenes' adventures and activities between his departure from Samos and his arrival in England. In his *Description* [...] *of Samos*, as we have seen, he speaks of having 'retired' to Patmos following his five-year tenure in Samos, which began in October 1666; so he no doubt withdrew to Patmos during the winter of 1671-2. Then, in his broadsheet *Account of* [...] *the Greek Church in So-hoe Feilds* he says that he arrived in England in 1676. The English reader is allowed to presume a quiet interval of monkish contemplation between the two dates. But there are in fact four or five years to be accounted for; and, in the light of his subsequent role as a figurehead of Anglican–Orthodox rapprochement in the face of Rome, the account is certainly surprising. After two years in Patmos he persuaded the abbot to let him travel to Italy to seek Catholic funding for the monastery; while in Italy he allowed himself to be recruited to attempt a reconciliation between Catholic and Orthodox elements in the Greek refugee community at Bibbona in Tuscany.[22]

He next appears early in 1676 in Paris, in the outer fringes of Louis XIV's court. A little must be said of Georgirenes' time in Paris, for it was there that he first made contact with Oxford. In the first place, he renewed his acquaintance with Antoine Galland, afterwards the translator of the *Thousand and One Nights*, whom he had met in Patmos two years previously, when Galland had served as secretary to the French

---

22   E. I. Stamatiades, Ἐπιστολιμαῖα διατριβὴ περὶ Ἰωσὴφ Γεωργειρήνου, ἀρχιεπισκόπου Σάμου *1666-1671* (Samos, 1892), 13–18. This is a translation of a document formerly in the Cathedral Archive at Volterra, *filza* 22, no. 203, which has, however, been missing since before 1935. I am grateful to Dott. Umberto Bavoni and Mgr Mario Bocci for their help in seeking the original document.

ambassador and collector, the marquis de Nointel. Passion-
ately interested in travel through the Turkish dominions, and
the Aegean in particular, it was Galland who persuaded Georgirenes to write down what he knew at first hand of the
manners and customs of the parts of Greece where he had
himself resided – Samos with Ikaria as archbishop, Patmos as
refugee from the hostile patriarch, Athos as a monk at the
start of his career. Galland has left a vivid impression of the
urgency with which the task was pursued, the archbishop
writing in vernacular Greek and Galland himself seizing and
translating it into French as each sheaf of pages was
complete.[23]

It was no doubt through Galland, whose rapid mastery of
'grec vulgaire' had been won through long discussions with
Orthodox prelates in Constantinople, leaving him with a lasting interest in the eastern churches, that Georgirenes first
came into contact with the Revd Dr Thomas Smith, Fellow of
Magdalen and Oxford's most devoted student of the Greek
church. Both of them energetic explorers of the Ottoman
dominions, Smith and Galland had coincided briefly in
Constantinople in 1670-71, in the service of their respective
ambassadors, and will have first met then. Now, in 1675–76,
Galland was briefly in Paris before setting out on a second
journey to the east, when Smith came there intent on improv-
ing his understanding of the Orthodox church and its beliefs.
On this subject he had already completed a book entitled *De
Graecae Ecclesiae Hodierno Statu Epistola*, at Magdalen on 20
August 1675 to be published in the following year. Already he

---

23 See Galland's introduction to his second, later, translation of Geor-
    girenes' book (Brussels, Bibliothèque Albert I, MS II – 5359, ff. 138–
    183), quoted by Legrand, op. cit. (n. 18), 345–347. I am most grateful
    to Mr John Steele for examining this manuscript on my behalf. I
    intend to publish elsewhere a full account of Georgirenes' activities
    in Italy and in Paris.

was amassing material for a second, London, edition to appear in 1678. A recurrent obsession, it was the practice of infant communion in one kind – wine only – that seemed to Smith a particularly objectionable item of Orthodox belief, in the context of Romish practice and the hated doctrine of tran-substantiation. In the preface to the 1678 edition he recalls a discussion of this matter in Paris with a learned bishop of the Greek church, who confirmed that communion in one kind was indeed the Orthodox practice with infants, and offered the 'ludicrous' explanation that this was done because their digestive systems were not yet equal to the digestion of flesh. Some years later, Smith revealed that this *egregius cavillator* was none other than Georgirenes, who was then intending to make his home in France, 'by favour of the Most Christian King'.[24]

That favour was easily bought, for Georgirenes knew well how to commend himself to the rich and powerful. He had evidently taken the precaution of including in his baggage a number of gifts from Patmos. In the Ancien Fonds Grec of the Bibliothèque Nationale are two thirteenth-century gospel manuscripts, each bearing in Greek an identical note:[25]

> This book of the four gospels was brought from the library at Patmos by me, Joseph Georgirenes, humble archbishop of Samos, and was given to the Most Christian and Mighty King Louis the Great, in the year 1676, 25 March.

The date cannot be many months before the archbishop left Paris for England, and the question arises, what favour he hoped to receive from Louis XIV in return for his gift. It may have been some privilege for the Greek community in Paris.

---

24   T. Smith, *Miscellanea, in quibus continentur Praemonitio ad Lectorem de infantum Communione apud Graecos*, etc. (London, 1686), prelims f. 4r.
25   Legrand, op. cit. (n. 18), vol. v, 301: no. 86, f. 12 v; no. 118, f. 238 v.

Or it may have been a letter of introduction for himself to Charles II, or to the overtly Catholic duke of York.

With or without an introduction, Georgirenes set out for England in 1676. He perhaps departed from Paris in some haste, and certainly to the confusion of Galland, for the latter was at that moment making arrangements for the publication of his French translation of Georgirenes' book. Instead, the archbishop took the French version with him, leaving the original Greek in Paris, and exacting from Galland a promise that the book would not appear in French until it had been first published in English.[26] The obvious but conjectural explanation of his hasty departure is that he had received an invitation to the two projects in London and Oxford to which we now return.

The establishment of a Greek church in London had been first pressed in a petition to the Privy Council in 1674 by three Greeks, 'Daniell Bulgaris, Lewis Orbinaty and Demetry of Constantinople'. Henry Compton had only recently become bishop of Oxford when permission was granted on 8 January 1675, and on 16 February Bulgaris was granted a warrant 'to be made a free denizen of England'.[27] For the moment, that was all. When Georgirenes arrived from Paris in 1676 seeking (as he said later) a publisher for his *Anthologion*, a liturgical book 'for the use of the Eastern Greek Church',[28] he added considerable weight to the initiative of

---

26   See Legrand, op. cit. (n. 18 above), vol. iii, 346.
27   Public Record Office, PC 2/64, p. 341, cf. Georgirenes, *Account of* [...] *the Grecian Church* (above, and n. 17); *Cal. State Papers, Dom. Ser., 1673–1675*, ed. Daniell (London, 1904), 591.
28   *Account of* [...] *the Grecian Church*. This is, *prima facie*, a curious motive for a visit to London: though Greek presses were severely discouraged in Constantinople, there was a great outpouring of such volumes from the printers of Venice. There is no evidence that the *Anthologion* was ever published.

Bulgaris and his friends. By then Bishop Compton had been translated to London. In his search for the means, methods and interest which had so far been wanting, Georgirenes approached the new bishop and secured Compton's support as well as his advocacy of the Greek initiative with his fellow bishops and other prospective donors. Before 19 March 1677 the archbishop (with Bulgaris) had obtained from the king through Compton's intercession a patent for the Greek community to exercise their religion freely.[29] Thus armed, he had approached Dr Nicholas Barbone, member of Parliament for Bramber (Sussex) and son of Praise-God Barbone. Barbone was then a speculator active in the developing suburb of Soho; he promised to give a site for the church and even to pay for its foundations.[30] On 19 March the king, noting that Georgirenes had already raised subscriptions from the archbishops and bishops of the Church of England 'towards the building of a little Church', agreed to contribute the substantial sum of £100.[31] There was further delay when the bishop of London offered an alternative location. In August 1677 he brokered a complicated property deal whereby the Greeks acquired a different and presumably better site in Soho, and he put them in touch with another of the local entrepreneurs of develop-

---

29   PRO, SP44/46, p. 164; *Cal. State Papers, Dom. Ser., 1677–78*, ed. Daniell (London, 1911), 38. For Compton's intervention, see Historical Manuscripts Commission, *Report on the Manuscripts of the Late Allan George Finch Esq., of Burley-on-the-Hill, Rutland*, [ed. Mrs S. C. Lomas], ii (London, 1922), 148.

30   Georgirenes, *Account of [...] the Grecian Church*. The history of the Greek church in Soho is comprehensively reconstructed in the *Survey of London* (n.12 above), 278–284 and pll. 16–19.

31   PRO, SP44/46, p. 164; *Cal. State Papers, Dom. Ser., 1677–78*, 38.

ment, Richard Frith, whom Georgirenes was to remember as 'Mr Thrift'.[32]

So, in that year, work started on the Church of the *Koimesis*, the Dormition of the Mother of God. It was a building of poor-quality brick from Mr Thrift – 'sammell and crasey and too short'[33] – with a bare minimum of stone dressing, the windows in two storeys, and over the eccentrically placed west door this inscription, the date of which evidently commemorates the beginning rather than the completion of the work:[34]

Ἔτει σωτηρίῳ AXOZ ἀνηργέρθη ὁ ναὸς οὗτος ὑπὲρ γένους Ἑλλήνων,
Βασιλεύοντος τοῦ γαληνοτάτου Καρόλου τοῦ Β, καὶ ἡγεμονεύοντος τοῦ Πορφυρογεν-
νήτου ἄρχοντος Κυρίου Ἰακώβου, ἀρχιερατεύοντος τοῦ αἰδεσιμωτάτου Κυρίου Ἐνρίκου τοῦ
Κομπτώνού, διὰ δαπάνης τῶν ἄνωθεν καὶ τῶν λοιπῶν ἀρχιερέων, συν-
δρομῆς δὲ τῆς ἡμῶν ταπεινότητος Σαμοῦ Ἰωσὴφ Γεωργειρήνου τοῦ ἐκ τῆς Νήσου
Μήλου.

In the year of Salvation 1677, this Church was built for the Greek nation, in the reign of the Most Serene Charles II, the royal prince Lord James being commander-in-chief, in the episcopacy of the Right Reverend Lord Henry Compton, at the expense of the above and other bishops and nobles, and with the concurrence of our Humility of Samos, Joseph Georgirenes, from the island of Melos.

Meanwhile the archbishop threw himself into the formidable task of fund-raising. We have seen that, no doubt

---

32   Georgirenes, *Account of* [...] *the Grecian Church*. PRO, KB27/2040, no. 1186, of 26 December 1684, rehearses the complex history of fifty-year building leases in the area; see especially ff. 4v–6r. See *Survey of London*, 278 f. The remark preserved in the Verney MSS at Claydon, 15 Nov. 1677, that 'A Greek Church has been long a building in St Giles' Fields; it goes on slowly' (HMC, *7th Report*, 1879, 494ʒ), is hard to understand, unless the author was thinking back to the petition granted in 1674.

33   London, Guildhall Library, MS 3047/2, quoted in *Survey of London*, loc. cit.

34   *Survey of London*, pl. 16 *b*. See illustrations 1 and 2.

through Compton's influence as a Privy Councillor, the king on 19 March 1677 had agreed to give Georgirenes and Bulgaris £100 towards the building. His brother the duke of York made a generous donation also; and it was, in consequence, to him that the archbishop dedicated his *Description of* [...] *Samos* in fulsome terms the following year – 'not as a thing of any merit, but as a manifestation of my *devoir* and gratitude, for those great Obligations, which I, and in me all the *Greek Nation* has received'.[35] We have seen also that the University of Oxford was an early donor, of £10 in the summer of 1677. The appeal for funds was complemented by a degree of self-help: on 14 December 1677 'Laurence Georgerini, late of Milo, an island in the Archipelago, now belonging to the Grecian Church planted in this kingdom', was granted a warrant entitling him to a patent for fourteen years of his 'art to pickle mackerel so as they shall continue for two years without decaying or perishing [...] towards the better support and maintenance of the said Grecian church'. Laurence's surname and origin would seem to identify him as a family member whom the archbishop had brought with him.[36]

As 1678 began, it must have seemed to Georgirenes that the project was assured of success. What remained to be settled was the nature of the worship which the bishop of London was willing to permit. In general, as is clear from his better-documented relations with the French protestants, his concern was for compatibility with the Church of England, if possible leading to intercommunion.[37] How was this requirement to be interpreted in relation to an eastern Orthodox

35 Dedication in Greek and English, the former presumably in Georgirenes' own words; for the duke of York's support, see the inscription above; cf. below, and n. 69.
36 PRO, SP44/40A, f.223; *Cal. State Papers, Dom. Ser., 1677–78*, 508: presence of family, ibid., *1680–81*, 691 f.
37 Carpenter, op. cit., 70ff., 322ff.

church? The answer is contained in a declaration of conformity to the doctrines of the Church of England, a copy of which, dated 2 April 1678, was received by Thomas Smith and is preserved in the Bodleian Library.[38] It is endorsed by Smith, 'The Archbishop of Samos his renouncing the superstition of the Romish and Greek Church, and his promise to give no scandal in the publick exercise of his Religion':

> We renounce transubstantiation of the Holy Mystery as a superstition recently established by the Romans; we renounce also the Synod of Bethlehem with all its false teaching which the Romans have introduced into the Eastern Church.[39] We promise not to place icons in our church in London, nor to worship, revere or serve anyone but God alone; nor to pray for the dead, as the Romans pray, nor to hold any service which would be contrary to that of the Anglican Church or would give scandal to it. Thus we renounce, thus we promise in the name of God, Amen.

This declaration appears to reflect a far harsher attitude than that expressed in the king's grant to Bulgaris and his colleagues in 1674 of 'liberty to build a Church [...] where they may freely exercise their Religion according to the Greek church'.[40]

---

38   Bodleian Library, MS Smith 98, pp. 47–50; two leaves or one folded (the binding conceals the edge), then folded again (apparently as a letter), text on p. 47 only, in a different (but similarly literary) hand from 31–34 (cf. n. 54), 48–49 blank, endorsed by Smith on 50. For the text see Martin, op. cit., 74. See also Georgirenes, *Description*, epistle to the reader, where it is said that 'they', the Greek Church, 'accord with us' (the Church of England) – itself a curious perspective – on a number of details of eucharistic practice.

39   On this synod, held in 1672, see Martin, op. cit., 74, n. 4, referring to M. Foucqueret, *Synodus Bethleemetica adversus Calvinistas Haereticos* (Paris, 1676).

40   PRO, PC 2/64, p. 341.

No doubt it reflects the almost paranoid preoccupation with the peril of popery which increasingly gripped England throughout the year 1678. In that year, Bishop Compton must have felt he had no choice but to require Georgirenes' declaration of conformity as a condition of the new church's operation.

The speed of the builders was limited by the pace of the archbishop's fund-raising, in which he suffered a number of setbacks, at least one of which could have proved fatal to his plans and perhaps even to himself. In 1678 he was forced to prosecute his own servant Dominico Gratiano, who had absconded in Bristol with a considerable part of the funds raised. In self-defence, Gratiano attempted to implicate Georgirenes in an alleged Popish Plot, claiming in a letter written from Bristol's Newgate Prison to have heard his master say that he hoped to hear Mass in Bristol cathedral, and that 'the Duke of York would soon be King, and that he should have a Bishoprick'. By his name clearly an Italian, Gratiano may have been with Georgirenes ever since his adventure in that country. If so, he knew all too much of Georgirenes' dalliance with the Catholic church, enough to make him a considerable embarrassment in the present circumstances. In the anti-popish hysteria of the moment, when everyone but the king himself was ready to believe in the greater Plot disclosed by Titus Oates, the accusation appears to have been taken seriously, and Georgirenes had to petition the king and the Privy Council for Gratiano to be brought to London, thereby affording the archbishop an opportunity to confront his accuser and to clear his name.[41]

---

41   PRO, SP44/51, p. 94, cf. *Cal. State Papers, Dom. Ser., 1678,* p. 548, 30 Nov. 1678, Secretary Coventry to the Attorney-General; HMC, *4th Report*, Pt. I, App., 234, 9 Dec. 1678, deposition of Gratiano. The whole episode is worked out with admirable clarity from a wealth of contemporary evidence in the *Survey of London*, 280.

On 30 November 1678 the House of Lords, having heard the accusation, issued a warrant for Gratiano to be brought under escort by the sheriff of Bristol; and on 21 December, having reached London, he was ordered to be detained in the Marshalsea to await interrogation. On both occasions both the king and the duke of York were present in the House, together with the archbishop of Canterbury and the bishop of London: Compton at least must have been startled by the accusation against his protégé. It will not have helped Georgirenes that when, a week later, in the presence of king, duke and archbishop of Canterbury (though the bishop of London was absent), the duke of Monmouth reported to the House on his investigations into the Popish Plot, he read the deposition of one Miles Prance, a silversmith, obtained in return for a pardon: in this it appeared that as the Plot unfolded, the body of the murdered magistrate Sir Edmundbury Godfrey, who had taken Titus Oates' deposition and could therefore he thought a plausible victim of Catholic revenge, had been carried from Somerset House in a sedan 'as far as the new Grecian Church in The Soho'.[42] Shortly after this, Parliament was prorogued and, then dissolved, the duke of York withdrew overseas, and the new 'healing' Parliament did not meet until 6 March 1679. Meanwhile, inquiries continued to be pursued by a committee of the Privy Council.[43] Georgirenes kept his nerve and emerged unscathed, except perhaps in the eyes of Bishop Compton; and he had lost his patron the duke of York. Later he was to write

---

42   *Journals of the House of Lords, Beginning Anno Vicesimo-septimo Caroli Secundi, 1675*, vol. xiii, 395, 412, 430, 438.

43   Bodleian Library, MS Rawlinson A 136, ff. 5, 31, 91. I owe this reference to the kindness of Professor John Miller, whose book *Popery and Politics in England 1660–1688* (Cambridge, 1973) is invaluable for the complexities of this period. See also John Kenyon, *The Popish Plot* (London, 1972; 2nd ed. 1983); A Marshall, *The Strange Death of Edmund Godfrey* (London, 1999).

ruefully that his own prosecution of Gratiano failed because of his ignorance of the English language and of legal procedure, to say nothing of the difficulty of assembling his witnesses in far-away Bristol.[44]

In 1679, his credibility evidently restored, Georgirenes resumed fund-raising on a broad front: how broad, we can see from records of two donations. On 28 May 1679 the earl of Rutland at Belvoir gave £5, and the next day the corporation of Lincoln agreed to give the archbishop a similar amount.[45] But solicitation beyond the circle of his acquaintance in London and Oxford still gave rise to fraud. In the *London Gazette* for 9–12 February 1680 Georgirenes complained that

> A Grecian Minister of a high stature, with black bushy hair and a long black beard, whose name is Joachim Cicileano, of the Isle of Ceffalonia, has gone up and down the country under the name of the Bishop of Samos in Greece, and hath been assisted with Christian contributions towards building the Grecian Church, which he hath lewdly spent, to the prejudice of the said Church and the scandal of the said Bishop.[46]

We must hope that the contributions of the earl of Rutland and the corporation of Lincoln were not the subject of this embezzlement!

Completion of the church did not of course remove the need for fund-raising. It is no doubt to this phase that we should ascribe an undated petition of 'Joseph Gogorino

---

44 Bodleian Library, MS Tanner 33, p. 59.
45 HMC, *Rutland* iv (1905), 553; HMC, *Fourteenth Report*, App. pt. viii (1895), 107.
46 *London Gazette*, loc. cit. (n. 10 above). *The Survey of London*, p. 281, notes that this may be the same Ciciliano 'of Caffalonia' whose departure for Greece in 1685 is recorded in *Cal. State Papers, Dom. Ser., 1685*, ed. F. Bickley (London, 1960), 434.

Archbishop of Samos, to the King', to be found among the State Papers:

> Petition for a brief throughout England for the benevolence of people whereby he may be enabled to maintain the Greek church and himself, and to relieve his countrymen who came to England in distress. The money given him was laid out in building the church, in supporting himself and family in assisting his countrymen that have been slaves and fled hither, so that now he has nothing left.[47]

Writing in 1682 when, as we shall see, the experiment of the Greek church had failed, Georgirenes gives the total raised for it as £1500, of which only £800 went to pay for the actual building work: 'the remainder of the money was expended in Charges, Servants wages, and Horse lines in going about the Country, and in my maintenance for these six years last past'.[48]

By the end of 1681 it seemed clear, says Georgirenes, that the church was in the wrong place, 'being too remote from the abodes of most of the Grecians, (dwelling cheifly in the furthermost part of the City)'. It cannot, of course, be the case that the Greek community had suddenly decamped to another part of town; the explanation of the failure of the church must have been more complicated, and we shall see that it was so. At any rate, the decision was taken to sell, and build elsewhere.[49] At first Bishop Compton is said to have promised renewed support, though he later grew cool when it seemed the church might become a meeting-house, perhaps for the hated Quakers. Georgirenes attempted to recoup his outlay by selling his building to St Martin-in-the-Fields. What

---

47 *Cal. State Papers, Dom. Ser., 1680–81*, pp. 691 f.
48 Georgirenes' broadsheet *Account of* [...] *the Grecian Church*.
49 Georgirenes' broadsheet *Account of* [...] *the Grecian Church*, though detailed, gives an inevitably partisan account of the events of 1681–1682. It is clarified and amplified in the Survey of London, 281 f.

he had not realised, however, in his innocence of English language and law, was that Compton's property deal of 1677 had left St Martin's with the head lease. An advantageous sale was impossible. St Martin's first made an insulting offer of £168, which the archbishop managed to 'gazump' with an offer of £230 from an alternative buyer. St Martin's finally offered £200. Bishop Compton thought he should accept, but Georgirenes rejected that advice. In the end he did not receive even £200, for when he declined their offer as being too far below the valuation of £626 – itself a disappointing enough figure – the men of St Martin's simply broke the door down and took possession. A desultory attempt was made to invoke the protection of the law, and when that failed Georgirenes gave up. St Martin's sold the church to Compton's favoured Huguenots, very numerous in the parish.[50] They held it until 1822, locally nicknamed 'les Grecs'. And that is the end of the story of the first Greek church, though we shall see that it is not by any means the whole story. There is no hint that Georgirenes made any second attempt. He died, it is said, four years later;[51] and all that survives of the project is the memory fossilised in street names: Greek Street and Frith Street – and Old Compton crossing the line of both, obliquely.

When Georgirenes came to Oxford in July 1677 and stayed 'some weeks', it will not have been simply to raise funds for the London church. Moved as his Oxford contacts were by the plight of Greece downtrodden by the Ottomans, and full of sympathy though they were for the refugee community

---

50 For Compton and the Huguenots, see Carpenter, op. cit., esp. 322–343.

51 Cf. M. Constantinides, *The Greek Orthodox Church in London*, 6f; no authority is cited for the date of Georgirenes' death. That no alternative church was built is not simply an argument from silence. In 1705 Edward Stephens (n. 5 above) remembered that 'this is almost the only considerable Nation, where the *Greeks* have no Church at all'.

in London, they had greater things in mind, not only a Greek church in London but a Greek college in Oxford. The arrival of a Greek archbishop entirely dependent on English charity for his project seemed a heaven-sent opportunity for practical progress in theirs, the promotion of intercommunion between the Anglican and Orthodox churches, to the exclusion of Rome.

Georgirenes had met the Oxford scholar Thomas Smith in Paris, and it may indeed have been Smith who urged him to come to London to lead the projected Greek church. He must in fact have made contact with at least one other Oxford acquaintance some time before the July visit, perhaps even already when he first reached England the previous year. For it was while he was in Oxford that summer that a licence was granted in London on 14 July for the publication of his *Description of the Present State of Samos, Nicaria, Patmos, and Mount Athos,* 'translated by one that knew the author in Constantinople'. If the book was ready for press by 14 July, Georgirenes must have handed over his text to the translator some time before that. Encouraged by the sight of a four-page dedication to the duke of York in Greek, a casual reader might suppose that the whole work was a translation from Greek, though the title page does not claim this. In fact we saw earlier that, according to Antoine Galland, the Greek original remained in Paris, and it was his French translation that the archbishop took with him to England. From local knowledge, Anthony Wood was able to identify the English translator as a Fellow of Queen's, Henry Denton, who had been chaplain to the English ambassador in Constantinople, Sir Heneage Finch (Lord Winchilsea), from 1664 to 1668.[52]

---

52   *Life and Times* (n. 2), ii, 379; cf. id., *Ath. Oxon.* ii, col. 219, where he
     says that Denton 'did translate "from Greek" into English'. That it
     was in fact done from French no doubt explains Wood's curious

Back at Queen's and rector of Bletchingdon, Denton must
have renewed the acquaintance when the text was handed
over, whether in London or in Oxford; and he may be judged
likely to have been one of the promoters of Georgirenes'
prolonged stay in Oxford in 1677. Though little is otherwise
known of Denton, the Queen's College network will have
been a fruitful source of contacts. Matriculating back in June
1653, Denton had already been a member of the College for
eighteen months when Henry Compton, the later bishop of
London, came up to Queen's in December 1654.[53] Though
they are not likely to have been on close terms as undergraduates, the one a 'nobleman', the other a 'servitor' working
his way through College, and Compton did not stay long
enough to graduate, Denton's election to a Fellowship in 1660
may have brought him to Compton's notice, and the acquaintance will certainly have been resumed in the year when
Compton was briefly bishop of Oxford, in 1675. It is possible
that Denton not only welcomed the archbishop to England,
and took over his manuscript, in 1676: he may also have been
in a position to help him with an introduction to Compton,
now newly in London. By 1676 the Queen's College network
had been further strengthened by the appointment of
Thomas Barlow, provost since February 1658, to the see of
Lincoln. Though bishop from June 1675 till his death in
October 1691, it is said that he never once visited his cathedral

---

punctuation. On Denton, see J. B. Pearson, *A Biographical Sketch of
the Chaplains to the Levant Company, maintained at Constantinople,
Aleppo and Smyrna, 1611–1706* (Cambridge, 1883), 12, 15, 51f., noting the
view of his successor in the rectory, preserved in the parochial
records, 'that he was sadly unfit to be entrusted at any rate with the
temporalities of a rectory.'

53   Carpenter, *The Protestant Bishop*, 10. Compton's academic career
progressed by fits and starts, however: ibid., p. 14, cavalry and
Cambridge, M.A. 1661; 16, Christ Church, M.A. 1666.

city. Significantly for Georgirenes, Barlow was still provost in 1677. In 1678, though no longer provost, he was given, and read, a copy of Georgirenes' book.[54]

The *Description of the Present State of Samos, Nicaria, Patmos and Mount Athos*, published in London by Moses Pitt, the University of Oxford's leading bookseller, seems to have enjoyed some success, for it exists in no fewer than three issues.[55] At first sight it may seem strange that a short work on four Aegean sites should have sold so well. Its significance, however, was that it was, in its Samian section, a primary source for the nature of contemporary Orthodox episcopacy and worship, and in the final part devoted to Mt Athos, an account of Orthodox monasticism and of the ritual of initiation undergone by the monks. It evidently caught the interest of the moment: the same year saw the composition of Paul Ricaut's *The Present State of the Greek and Armenian Churches Anno Christi 1678*, published in the following year 'with the Command of his Majesty'; 1678 is the date, too, of the first

---

54   On Barlow, see J. R. Magrath, *The Queen's College*, 2 vols. (Oxford, 1921), ii, 33 ff. The book, with *marginalia* in Barlow's hand, is Bodleian Library 8° C Linc. (2).

55   The first, to which Bishop Barlow's copy belongs, contains obvious misprints in the Greek dedication (which was separately printed on a pair of leaves designed to be bound in as A2–3 as well as 'comtemplations' at the foot of A4, the English version of the dedication. Barlow marked these errors in both the Greek and the English, but it was probably not from his copy that the second issue was made, the Greek corrected but 'comtemplations' left; John Locke's copy (Bod. Lib., Locke 8,136) belongs to this issue. Finally the English misprint was corrected; the copy which Dr Martin Lister, the distinguished conchologist, gave to the Ashmolean Museum (Bod. Lib., Lister I 3) has both the corrected Greek and 'contemplations'. For Moses Pitt, see for instance HMC, *Le Fleming* (London, 1890), 165.

London edition of Thomas Smith's *De Graecae Ecclesiae Hodierno Statu Epistola*, also published by Moses Pitt.

Whether or not the archbishop's arrival in England had been at the instigation of Thomas Smith, there was much for this most prominent of Oxford's scholars of the eastern church, a keen advocate of intercommunion, to discuss with him. Himself a former undergraduate at Queen's in Barlow's time, who received his BA degree the year after Denton was elected to the fellowship, Smith had directly followed Denton into the chaplaincy at Constantinople, where, by then a Fellow of Magdalen, he served the ambassador Sir Daniel Harvey from 1668 to 1671.[56] It was while he was there, he tells us, in 1669, that he conceived the idea of writing a general work on the current state of the Eastern Church, and did indeed compose a short draft.[57] But on his return to Magdalen other tasks seemed more pressing. He first wrote a Latin account of the customs and institutions of the Turks, and of the Seven Churches in Asia (preface dated 8 April 1672, published 1672) followed by *Brevis Constantinopoleos Notitia* (preface, 5 July 1673, published 1674).[58] By 1675 he had completed his resumed account of the Eastern Church in the form of an open letter, *De Graecae Ecclesiae hodierno statu Epistola*. A mixture of history, geography and theology, it is not a great work of organisation. Lists of major feasts and fasts are followed by an account of the ecclesiastical organi-

---

56   See Pearson, *Chaplains to the Levant Company*, pp. 12, 15 f. 52; see below, Charles Miller, 'Educating the English: Dr Thomas Smith and the Study of Orthodoxy in the Seventeenth Century' (chapter 4).

57   T. Smith, *An Account of the Greek Church as to its Doctrines and Rites of Worship, with Severall Historicall Remarks interspersed relating thereunto* (London, 1680), 'To the Reader'.

58   Cf. *Epistolae quattuor, quarum duae de moribus ac institutis Turcarum agunt, duae Septem Asiae Ecclesiarum et Constantinopoleos notitiam continent* (London, 1674).

sation of the patriarchate, with lists of provinces, *metropoleis* and bishops' sees, a description of monasticism and the priesthood, culminating in a discussion of the sacraments – Baptism and the Eucharist were basic, the others largely Romish accretions, he says – and a very full analysis of the Greek attitude to μετουσίωσις, transubstantiation, at the time a subject of much scholarly inquiry, and little enlightenment. The *Epistola* was completed on 20 August 1675, and published in Oxford at the Sheldonian Theatre in 1676, with the support of the new bishop of Oxford, Dr Fell.[59] That year also, Georgirenes arrived in England. By this time Smith was dean of Magdalen College, where luminaries of the Greek hierarchy were no strangers to his lodgings. That same year he entertained the archbishop of Thracian Tiberias; and his papers, bequeathed to Thomas Hearne and now preserved in the Bodleian Library, include 'A Paper in Greek about the Greek church's communicating, given to Dr Smith at Oxford by the Archbishop of Tiberias'.[60]

When the archbishop of Samos came to Oxford in 1677, he evidently spent some time with Smith, who amid his concern for Greek doctrine of the Eucharist in general had developed a particular obsession with the issue of infant communion. In the Greek church, if the parents wished it, communion was administered to newly baptised infants, communion apparently in one kind only, namely a drop of

59   See, for the sacraments, 73 ff; for the Eucharist, 83 ff; and for transubstantiation, 94 ff. For the publication of the Oxford edition of 1676, 140 pp. and prelims, see Smith, *An Account of the Greek Church*, loc. cit. Much of the raw material, in Greek, is preserved in the Bodleian Library, MS Smith 98. The *Epistola* had a second edition of 183 pp. (London, 1678), and a third (1698), which, though said to be *auctior et emendatior*, is almost entirely a reprint of the second.

60   *Epistola*, 1678 ed., introductory epistle to the reader, at A6 r-v; Bodleian Library, MS Smith 98, pp. 39 ff.

wine; in fact the wine contained tiny crumbs of bread, as blood contains flesh – a striking reversal of the Roman doctrine of the sufficiency of communion in one kind, bread, sufficient on the ground that flesh contains blood. To an enemy of transubstantiation this Greek practice of infant communion was an inevitable stumbling-block. If the Lord's Supper was purely commemorative – if, in the words of the Prayer Book of 1662, He 'made there (by his one oblation of himself once offered) a full, perfect, and sufficient sacrifice, oblation, and satisfaction, for the sins of the whole world' – then to appreciate its significance demanded that the recipient be of an age to understand: it could not possibly be of benefit to an infant. To administer communion to an infant, on the contrary, presupposed that it was a good in itself, independent of the awareness of the recipient. And that, together with talk of blood containing fragments of body, was too much for Dr Thomas Smith. He had already discussed the issue with Georgirenes when they met in Paris,[61] and again in Oxford with the archbishop of Tiberias, and was in correspondence about it with Henry Dodwell. In the preface to the second edition of the *Epistola*, published in London in 1678 (he dated the preface from Magdalen on 6 July that year) and dedicated to The Queen's College's most distinguished old member and greatest benefactor, Secretary Williamson, he speaks of his frequent discussions of the subject with Georgirenes, who had even written to him about it in a letter from which he quotes.[62] The whole letter is in

---

61   Cf. n.24.

62   *Epistola*, 1678 ed., loc. cit. An incidental mark of Smith's talks with Georgirenes is to be found ibid., p. 79, where in the list of metro-politans, "Η 'Ρόδος, *Rhodus*', of the first edition now carries the additional information 'Huic olim subjecti *Samius & Parius Antistites*': cf. Georgirenes, *Description*, 32 f. See also Smith's *Account,* of 1680, 89, where he distinguished the title of archbishop as given to bishops

fact preserved among Smith's papers. The archbishop makes a long and elaborate promise of 'a straight answer to a straight question', describing Greek practice, and being careful to note that the particles of flesh imbibed with the drop of wine placed in the mouth of infants are *spiritual* fragments: there is no admission of μετουσίωσις. The letter, received before July 1678, is undated and appears to have been delivered by hand. Smith has endorsed it 'Archb. of Samos's letter to mee'.[63]

We come finally to the Greek College, the project pursued concurrently with these publications and discussions. As we saw, Anthony Wood wondered whether Georgirenes' lengthy visit to Oxford was connected with the proposal then current for 'converting Gloucester Hall into a college for the educating 20 or 30 Greeks in Academical learning and to send them home'. As with the church in London, evidently, the scheme was not new: 'these only wanted pelf'.[64] In Georgirenes the Oxford enthusiasts had not only a suitable figurehead but one with a proven record of fund-raising, able to gain the ear of the king himself as well as the duke of York and the bishop of London – the last two an apparently impossible pair to yoke in a single team. To succeed, the college would need the support of the archbishop of Canterbury also, and it was decided that Georgirenes should make the approach, one archbishop to another. 1677 was a difficult

---

freed from the former jurisdiction of metropolitans, and now therefore autocephalous, 'as he of *Samos,* for instance, who before was under Rhodes'; cf. Georgirenes, *Description,* epistle to the reader, at end, and 32 f. (The text of the original source of Smith's list, Bodleian Library, MS Smith 98, pp. 1–6, is as the first edition.)

63   Bodleian Library, MS Smith 98, pp. 31–34: two leaves (or one folded double), folded originally as a letter, text on pp. 31–32, 33–34 blank except for Smith's endorsement. The text is printed by Martin, op. cit., 72 f.

64   See above, and n. 2.

year. London was preoccupied with the marriage of the duke
of York's daughter Mary to the Prince of Orange, Princess
Anne developed smallpox, and the aged Archbishop Sheldon
died in November. It was universally assumed – and widely
hoped – that the bishop of London would succeed him. However, on 30 December William Sancroft, dean of St Paul's, and
a friend of the duke of York, a keen student of the Greek
church's eucharistic doctrine, was appointed to Canterbury,
and the way was clear.[65] Among those of Sancroft's papers
which reached the Tanner Collection in the Bodleian Library,
is a petition in the name of Georgirenes, written for him with
some elegance, presumably by one of his Oxford friends.[66]
After a moving reminder of

> the Miseries and Misfortunes which the Grecians at this day groan
> under, being prohibited the use of publick Schooles, and reduced to
> Poverty by the Tyranny of the Turks; and also grown into so great
> Ignorance by the Corruption of theire Church, which dayly groweth
> more and more corrupt and that that famous Nation is in great
> danger of being utterly lost, which is to be avoided by all good
> Christians and Lovers of Learning,

we reach the appeal itself. It is far more startling, more
ambitious and less realistic than Wood's summary suggested.

> Your petitioner holds it very necessary that about 12 Schollers out of
> Greece be constantly here to be instructed and grounded in the true
> Doctrines of the Church of England, whereby (with the Blessing of
> God) they may be able Dispensers thereof, and so returne into
> Greece aforesaid to preach the same, by which means your peti-
> tioners conceive the said people may be Edified.

---

65   For the preoccupations of 1677, see for instance Carpenter, *The
     Protestant Bishop*, 35–41.
66   Bodleian Library, MS Tanner 33 f. 57; dated 1682 by Carpenter, op.
     cit., 362.

The petition concludes with a request that Sancroft intervene with the king and Bishop Compton, 'to the intent some Yearly Revenue may be allowed to carry on so pious and good a Work'. It is an astonishing proposal to come from an archbishop of the Orthodox Church, even an ex-archbishop and one dependent on others to clothe his thoughts in English.

Of Sancroft's response, we have no evidence at all, except the certainty that nothing came of the appeal. Nor do we know the date of the petition, except that it cannot be earlier than Sancroft's accession to the see of Canterbury in the last days of 1677, nor later, presumably than Georgirenes' falling out with the bishop of London over the disposal of the Greek church in 1681 or 1682. Within these limits we may perhaps be safe in supposing that the approach was made early in Sancroft's term, half a year or so after the discussions which coincided with Georgirenes' visit to Oxford. There may even be a clue in Smith's papers, the statement from Georgirenes dated 2 April 1678, 'renouncing the superstition of the Romish and Greek Church, and his promise to give no scandal in the publick exercise of his Religion'.[67] That text is a revelation as dramatic as that contained in the appeal to Sancroft, and entirely consistent with it in its equation of the Anglican and Orthodox churches: petition and declaration may be contemporary. By this time Georgirenes had evidently accepted that there was no tight-rope to walk between Orthodoxy and the Church of England, and leaped towards the latter as the only hope of support either for his congregation in London or for his poor oppressed countrymen in Greece.

His virtual conversion no doubt delighted Smith, who that year received also a copy of the archbishop's newly

---

67   See above, and n.38.

published *Description* of Samos and other parts of the Greece he had known so well but left behind. Two years later, when he published an English edition of his own *Epistola*, now under the title *An Account of the Greek Church as to Its Doctrines and Rites of Worship*, Smith made a point of citing Georgirenes' book for its first-hand account of the monasteries of Mt Athos, a part of Greece which he himself regretted he had never seen.[68]

Smith's English version is dedicated to Bishop Compton, with a fulsome tribute to that prelate's defence of 'the Church of England in this day of trial, against the furious assaults of her restless enemies the *Papists* on the one hand, and the Giddy *Sectaries* on the other', and to his concern for Greeks

> whom either curiosity and love of learning shall draw into these parts, or *Turkish* cruelty and persecution shall drive and force out of their own Country; and at the same time (he adds) to reduce them from those errours and corruptions, which have of late crept in among them, by bringing them into a nearer and more familiar acquaintance with the Doctrine, and rites of Worship establisht in the Church of *England*.

On the surface, the usual degree of flattery, perhaps with an element of self-congratulation on the process of reconciliation and indeed homogenisation for which the author had laboured and which the project for a Greek college was intended to complete. Between the lines, however, there is more than a hint of trouble approaching. 'If the Governors of their Church have not such a gratefull resentment of the favour,

---

68   Smith, *Account,* 97 f. This edition contains all of Smith's familiar preoccupations: the Romish influence on the Greek view of the sacraments, 107; transubstantiation not a Greek doctrine originally, but adopted lately from the Romans, perhaps introduced by Archbishop Gabriel of Philadelphia, in Venice in the late sixteenth century, but not generally accepted until the mid-seventeenth, 146 f.

[...] or if they, who enjoy the happiness and benefit, should render themselves less worthy of it', Compton can still look forward to 'reward with God', and the good opinion of good men. But here is the real menace:

> How highly your Lordship has merited of the *Greek* Church by taking it into your care, and by opening a Sanctuary for the poor distressed Bishops and Priests of that Communion to fly unto, is not unknown at Constantinople.

Would the patriarch welcome this benevolence? There follows an address 'To the Reader', dated 23 February 1680, so that is presumably the approximate date of the dedication to Compton.

It was then almost exactly a year since, on 17 February 1679, Patriarch Dionysios had sent to Sir John Finch, younger brother of Sir Heneage and now himself ambassador in Constantinople, a commission of five archbishops led by the archbishop of Herakleia with, as interpreter, an Italian-speaking priest of a Constantinopolitan parish who had seen the Greek church in London.[69] The patriarch was concerned, they said, to hear more of the circumstances of the foundation of that church. Finch replied that it had been established with support from the king and the duke of York, and that the bishop of London had set the conditions under which it operated, in conformity with the laws of church and state. He listed four conditions, the very four set out in Georgirenes' declaration sent to Smith on 2 April 1678: no icons in the church, no adherence to the doctrine of transubstantiation, no practice or advocacy of prayer to saints, no

---

69 HMC, *Report on the Manuscripts of the Late Allan George Finch, Esq., of Burley-on-the-Hill, Rutland,* ii, 148–150. The priest, who served in Galata, was regarded by Finch as the only educated priest in the city; he preached before the patriarch on alternate Sundays: ibid., 160.

conformity to the Council of Bethlehem (otherwise known as
the Council of Jerusalem, at which Patriarch Dionysios himself had been present in 1672 and which – in Thomas Smith's
view – had been corrupted by Roman flattery and cash). The
prelates' response was unanimous and unambiguous. To the
first condition they objected that

> they could not without pictures in their church officiate, and that
> they could upon no conditions be stript of them. To the second they
> gave an answer with much heat and exclamation, saying that they
> differ'd not from the Church of Rome as to the point of transub-
> stantiation, and then with one voice thundred out that the very Body
> of Christ that was crucify'd on Mount Calvery, was after conse-
> cration there present and that they would never alter this doctrine.

To the third condition they retorted that 'all their Liturgys
were composed of prayers to saints and to the Blessed
Virgin'. As to the Council of Bethlehem, they claimed rather
implausibly to know nothing of its import and so had nothing
to say of it.

Finch now warmed to the theme: in England Popery was
against the law, 'and t'wer the same thing to the government
of his Majesty, and scandal to the Church and people of
England, that these "tenents" should be published and practised in Greek as in Latin'. Icons and prayers to saints were
unknown to the early church; and the doctrine of transubstantiation was as much at odds with the chronology of the
Last Supper as it was with common sense. 'But I added that I
should acquaint my Lord of London with their resolution.'
The Greek archbishops did not yield an inch on those three
topics and now invoked the authority of the patriarch and the
Holy Synod to add three further demands: that leavened
bread might be allowed to be used for the sacrament, that in
the Creed the Holy Ghost be said to proceed from the Father
only, and – most provocatively – that the Greek church in

London be removed from the jurisdiction of the bishop of London and, like that in Venice, be placed instead under the jurisdiction of the patriarch himself. Finch replied that the use of leavened bread raised no difficulty: it was indeed the practice of the Church of England, against that of Rome. But the eastern view of the procession of the Holy Ghost was 'directly repugnant to the articles of our Church', and therefore quite inadmissible. As for their 'extravagant and unreasonable demand' for the London Church to be removed from the authority of the diocesan and transferred to that of the patriarch, Finch allowed that the patriarch might be given the right to appoint ministers of the church but left the commission in no doubt that, as to jurisdiction, 'my Lord Bishop of London would never be deprived of his right in his own diocese, of governing ecclesiastical affayrs under his Majesty, and that I could not give them the least hopes of such an ill-grounded demand'. At this the meeting broke up, Finch undertaking to acquaint the bishop of London with what had been said, and to bring the patriarch 'his Lordship's sense of the whole conference' in due course. Compton's reaction is not recorded, but is not hard to guess.

Discussions were evidently drawn out for one year more. Finally, on 27 January 1680 Finch sent a further letter from Pera to the bishop of London, 'being a fundamentall account of what relates to the Greeke church designed to be settled in England'.[70] Of course the patriarch could not trim and compromise as Georgirenes had been prepared to do. But his refusal to give way at any point was the death-knell of the Greek church in London, as it was for the proposal to establish a college in Oxford training Greek missionaries to propagate the Anglican gospel in their homeland. It was not in the end the removal of his congregation to another part of

---

70   HMC, *Finch* ii, 65.

London that precipitated the closure of the Greek church, as Georgirenes himself was to claim two years later, but the implacable refusal of his own patriarch to countenance the only terms on which it could continue.

Significantly, there is no evidence of further fund-raising after 1679. The archbishop of Samos remained in London to close the church and attempt to sell the building, bravely insisting that it would reopen at a more appropriate location. But by 1682 Georgirenes had not only lost his building to St Martin-in-the-Fields. More seriously, he had forfeited the confidence of the bishop of London: he had, after all, been far too close to the hated duke of York, had taken the latter's bounty for his church, had mentioned him alongside the king (and the bishop) in the stone inscription over its door, had dedicated his *Description* of Samos to the duke, and had even been reported (however falsely) as having looked forward to the duke's accession to the throne. Without Compton's support, and against the hostility of the patriarch, there was no hope of recovery, and no new church was built. Georgirenes found himself forced to issue an account of the sad affair, if only to defend himself against rumours of peculation: 'This relation *I* have thought fit to make, that thereby all persons may see, *I* never sold the said Church, nor received any sum for the building thereof '.[71] With that, he leaves the stage, saying nothing of the patriarch's judgement, which effectively declared him a heretic. And all the patriarch's arguments would be equally fatal to the project for a college in Oxford to train Greeks as Anglican missionaries for Greece.

---

71   Georgirenes, *An Account of* [...] *the Grecian Church*, end. It is interesting that the last clause, 'nor received any sum for the building thereof', is inked out in both Wood's and Ashmole's copies (n. 17): perhaps not everyone accepted the archbishop's denial.

4. Educating the English: Dr Thomas Smith and the Study of Orthodoxy in the Seventeenth Century

CHARLES MILLER

Dr. Thomas Smith (1633–1710) of Magdalen College, Oxford, was a contemporary of Benjamin Woodroffe.[1] Although Smith was not directly engaged with Woodroffe's efforts to establish a Greek College at Worcester at the turn of the eighteenth century, Smith's knowledge of and writing about the Greek Orthodox tradition provided an important contextual element in the wider field of ecclesiastical interest which gave impetus to the plan. For Thomas Smith was one of the most learned members of a loose circle of ecclesiastically conservative clerics who in many ways were the pride of the Restoration Church. Their scholarly and theological interest in ancient Christian tradition, together with a strong anti-papalism, provoked a critical interest in, and practical support for, the Greek Orthodox Church.

Thomas Smith was a thoroughly bookish man. By the end of his life he was envied for his library, and was reputed to possess the most thorough knowledge of books in England.[2] While not a practical ecumenist, Smith nevertheless aided the inter-confessional contacts of the late Restoration period

---

1   This is no biographical material on Smith apart from the entry in the *Dictionary of National Biography* XVIII, 539–541.

2   Ibid., 541.

with his learning and his writing on the subject of Orthodoxy. His contribution is exemplified in his most important work on the subject, namely, his *Account of the Greek Church* (to use its short title) published in Oxford in 1680.[3]

The long history of Anglican and Orthodox relations is one that began in the sixteenth century with mercantile concerns as the English sought to extend their emerging commercial empire. It was, after all, the age of commercially-inspired exploration. But as a result of such enterprises there soon emerged a literature which not only documented successful and unsuccessful contacts with hitherto unknown trading partners, but also opened to the literate English public, not least clergy, descriptions of Orthodox church life both in Slavic and Mediterranean territories. That connivance between commercial and 'ecumenical' interests, and the literature that resulted from it, was aided, of course, by the presence of chaplains and clerical scholars. In both cases linguistic and scholarly support for England's commercial and political aspirations went hand in hand with theological investigation, ecclesiastical observation, and even personal contact with the Orthodox. Dr. Thomas Smith's contribution to this growing literature, and to the ecumenical awareness that it could foster, resulted from precisely such a confluence.

---

3   The full title of the work is *An Account of the Greek Church as to its doctrine and rites of worship: with several historical remarks interspersed, relating thereunto. To which is added an account of the state of the Greek church under Cyrillus Lucaris, patriarch of Constantinople, with a relation of his sufferings and death* (London, 1680).

Thomas Smith

Smith was the son of a London merchant. He was born in 1633 and was only ten years old when the 'Root and Branch' bill for the abolition of episcopacy, signaling the point of no return for the Church of England, was passed by Parliament. We know nothing of the religion with which Smith grew up, but from later accounts, his time at the Queen's College, Oxford, did nothing to engender or strengthen any presbyterian sympathies he might have had. In fact, from later literary evidence where he extols Lancelot Andrewes, the prodigious James Ussher, and the learned and combative John Cosin,[4] and then from his Non-Juring commitments in old age, Smith seems to have been a man whose style of religion and theology was solidly episcopal and reformed according to 'the constant norm of religion', as Cosin himself once put it: 'one Canon, two Testaments' chiefly, followed by 'three Symbols, the first four Councils, the continuity and consensus of the catholic fathers of the church's five centuries'.[5]

---

4   Smith's *Vitae Quorundam Erudissimiorum et Illustrium Vivorum* (London, 1717) was published posthumously, and included 'Lives' of seven eminent scholars and clergy. The clergy included, viz. James Ussher and John Cosin, may well indicate something of Smith's theological pedigree: a moderately 'high' Anglicanism, philologically sophisticated, anti-Roman, deeply committed to the study and witness of Christian antiquity, to episcopacy and the Book of Common Prayer. A further indicator of Smith's sympathies is that his life of Cosin includes a reprint of the latter's apologetic tract *Regni Angliae Religio Catholica* first published at Edward Hyde's direction in Paris in 1652. Cosin's tract presents the credentials of the reformed Church of England, and spells out the authorities for its doctrine, worship and order.

5   From his *Religio Catholica*, ch. 1, from the *Library of Anglo-Catholic Theology* edition (Oxford, 1843), 343.

Smith's life and work were largely connected with his adoptive college, Magdalen, where he became a probationary fellow in 1663, a full fellow four years later, and Dean in 1674 after taking his B.D. Smith's interest in theology was matched by his zeal for oriental languages. Such was his oriental learning that he was known by his contemporaries in Oxford as 'the Rabbi'. Indeed, it was just that expertise that led to Smith's only absence from Oxford during his tenure as Fellow. Beginning in 1668 Smith traveled through the Mediterranean to Constantinople where for three years he was chaplain to the English ambassador, Sir Daniel Harvey. For Smith's subsequent interests and influence this trip was decisive. The three years from 1668 through 1670 gave Smith an unparalleled opportunity to acquaint himself first hand with the circumstances, practices and personalities of the Greek Orthodox Church, and to collect and study related texts and manuscripts.

The *Account of the Greek Church*

Upon his return to Oxford in 1670/1, Smith was armed with a rich supply of information and experiences about the Orthodox east to share. It took time to digest and rework it all. It was, perhaps, an incentive to Smith that during the decade of the 1670s efforts were underway to establish a Greek Church in London to serve the resident and visiting Greek community. The scheme was effectively supported by Henry Compton (1632–1713) who had been made Bishop of Oxford for a brief space in 1674 before moving to the see of London early in the following year. There are no details about Smith's exact relationship with Compton nor any information about his direct involvement in Compton's initiatives which resulted in the creation of St. Mary's Greek Orthodox Church in Soho in 1677.[6] But Smith's first attempts to present in literary form the results of his sojourn among the Orthodox in two Latin *epistolae* were presented to Compton. One was an account of the state of the seven churches of Asia Minor, a work that gave Smith ample scope to comment upon the relationship between the Greeks and their Ottoman rulers. The second, a larger and more important work, was a description of the Greek Orthodox Church, *De Graecae Ecclesiae Hodierno Statu Epistola*, published in Oxford in 1676. This second Latin treatise was then translated by Smith himself for publication in English as *An Account of the Greek Church as to its doctrine and rites of worship: with several historical remarks interspersed, relating thereunto*. It was published in 1680 and dedicated (once again) to Compton in recognition of his efforts on behalf of the Greek community in London.

Smith's roughly 250 page account follows a rationale appropriate for a western Christian's introduction to the Orthodox Church. Thus, experience and expertise are brought together. 'I have taken', Smith says in his preface 'To the Reader',

> all imaginable care to represent things truly as I found them, and relate nothing but what is confirmed by the Offices used in the Service of that Church, and other Ecclesiastical Writings, as Confessions, and Catechisms, and the like.[7]

---

6   On Compton see Edward Carpenter, *The Protestant Bishop* (London, 1956). His chapter 'The Greek Orthodox Church' (pp. 357–364) recounts the story of both the Greek parish and the Greek college efforts.

7   Smith, *Account,* a3.

He then goes on, in a work that is fully indexed, to describe for his readers the services of the Orthodox Church, the architectural setting of its worship, its episcopal structure and sees, the monastic tradition, the eucharistic liturgy, the credal basis of the Greek Church, and its views on controversial points. The appendix includes texts of several liturgical hymns.

It would be wrong to suppose, though, that Smith's purposes are simply descriptive. He writes, he describes, he comments from within a definite reformed western tradition and with an overt commitment to the doctrine and discipline of the Church of England. His *Account* is therefore both interested and appreciative yet critical at one and the same time. Behind such criticism lies Smith's subscription to Cosin's view of the Church of England: '*prisca, casta, defoecata*' (primitive, chaste, purified).[8]

But there is perhaps another reason for Smith's critical eye. In his attempts to provide what Smith himself describes as 'a Sanctuary for the poor distressed Bishops and Priests of that Communion to fly unto',[9] Bishop Compton had become embroiled in controversy with the Greek hierarchy in Constantinople. In establishing St Mary's Greek Church in Soho, Compton had laid down four requirements for the life and work of the parish: 1. No pictures or icons were allowed; 2. all officiating clergy must repudiate transubstantiation; 3. no prayers to the saints were to be said; and 4. the clergy must disown the Council of Bethlehem.[10] To some extent, then, Smith's *Account* seeks to provide substantial support for the Bishop of London's requirements.

---

8   So described in the extended title to Cosin's treatise, op. cit.
9   So in the Epistle Dedicatory of Smith's *Account*.
10 Carpenter, 360–361.

It is no surprise, therefore, that Smith's 'Epistle Dedicatory' to the Bishop of London not only applauds the bishop's attempt to provide a spiritual home for the Orthodox; it also suggests that the bishop's interests coalesce with a purpose implicit in Smith's *Account*, namely, 'to reduce [the Greeks] from those errours and corruptions, which have late crept in among them, by bringing them into a nearer and more familiar acquaintance with the Doctrin, and rites of Worship established in the Church of England.' There is, therefore, a tone of apologia for the Church of England as the branch of Christendom most worthy of emulation by the Orthodox in many aspects of its life and doctrine.

So much to introduce the work and its context. What picture of the Orthodox Church would Smith's *Account* present to an English reader of the 1680s?

Particular Points: Worship

Under the constraints of Ottoman rule the worship of Orthodox Church life stood out since in most other ways the life of the Greek Church was straitened. So Smith begins his *Account* with a description of the Orthodox services. Much of this portion of his text benefited from later study of the books which he brought back from the East. He collected, for instance, a 'Menology', or church calendar, and studied it carefully, comparing and contrasting it with the calendar of the Book of Common Prayer. Whether Smith realised the hand of the monastic tradition in the liturgy of the church is unclear. Based on his first-hand experience as an observer, though, he regarded the Orthodox offices as 'long and tedious'.[11] Smith is most affirming in his comments on the services where he espies a clear resonance or actual continuity with early Christian practices which he recognised from his own study of early Christian texts. So he is in a position to make comments like this about the festival Eucharists:

> At such solemnities the holy and august Sacrament is always celebrated, and that with great pomp and ceremony: and indeed is not onely a necessary, but the principal part of the Festival. Every one strives to bring his present or gift as he is able, according to the Primitive Custom, as Bread, Wine, Oyl for the Lamp, Wax-candles, Frankincense or such like, to be made use of in the following sacred rites, or any other way as the service of the Church may require.[12].

Smith himself witnessed the Orthodox Holy Week services at least once in Constantinople and is expansive in describing the services which the Book of Common Prayer had largely abandoned. He is both impressed and repelled by what he sees. Of the Good Friday evening liturgy, for instance, he comments:

> Toward the evening of *Good Friday,* they carry an Image of our B. *Saviour* about the Church in procession with tapers and torches; and then they represent the apokalethosis, or the manner of taking our *Saviour* down from the Crosse: in which they betray a great deal of superstition and folly, this being onely to gratify a childish and gross fancy.[13]

But he is clearly impressed by the patriarchal liturgy of Easter Eve itself.

---

11   Smith, *Account* 27.
12   Ibid., 29.
13   Ibid., 43–44.

At three of the clock in the afternoon, when their Vespers begin, the devout people flock to the Church; some continue there all night, and carry with them bread, dates, and figs, and the like, to make use of upon occasion of any fainting fit. Toward the break of day they sing the Hymn which begins, *Glory in the highest.* After which the Patriarch begins that excellent Hymn, the Quire immediately following; *(a) Christ is risen from the dead, having by his death trampled upon death, and given life to those who were in their graves.* Which they repeat twelve times Together.[14]

Texts were only one resource. Smith also resorted to the local clergy for explanations of ambiguous or complex liturgical points. One such clergyman was Fr Jeremias Germanos, whom Smith probably already knew as a result of a visit to Oxford in 1668–9 when Germanos was happily entertained by men with philhellenic interests.[15]

After his overview of the liturgical life of the Orthodox, Smith turns to ecclesiastical structures. The one point of interest in this brief and factual part of the *Account* is this: Smith praises the Greeks for maintaining their episcopal system even under Turkish oppression. The Orthodox witness could be seen to undercut nonconformist abolition of episcopacy. In the years following the Restoration of King, Prayer Book and episcopacy, when a hard line was taken on non-episcopally ordained ministers, Smith's praise for the Orthodox maintenance of episcopacy under duress would have some apologetic, even polemical, force in justifying the Church of England's firmer discipline regarding non-episcopal ministers. After all, if Greek Christians could maintain episcopacy under fierce anti-Christian persecution, what reason could reformed Christians have for abandoning it? While it may have been the first, it would certainly not be the

---

14   Smith, *Account,* 44.
15   The visit is recalled by John Covel in the Preface to his *Account of the Present Greek Church* (Cambridge, 1722), i.

last time that Orthodoxy would be cited in regard to the Church of England's own issues about ministry.

The Monastic Tradition

The extent of interest in the monastic tradition displayed in Smith's *Account* suggests that he realised how central monasticism is in the religious culture of the Greeks. It is all the more interesting in light both of the absence of a monastic culture in the reformed Church of England, and of the suspicion of monasticism generally that was so typical of the Protestant religious literature of the period.[16] In any case, his descriptions of monastic life are among the most interesting passages in the *Account*. While by his own admission, Smith's is not the first description of Mt Athos in English,[17] still he recognises its importance for the Orthodox monastic world as 'The chief Seat of these Religious [...] indeed [it is] the principal Seminary of the Greek Church':[18]

---

16   Consider, for instance, the bitterly critical accounts of Nicholas Farrer's 'Arminian Nunnery' in the 1640s. Smith may have been drawn to this state of life. He is credited with an English translation of *The Life of St. Mary Magdalen of Pazzi, A Carmelite Nun*, written by the French Carmelite Père Lezin de Sainte Scholastique. The prospect is especially curious in light of Smith's sharp anti-papalist sentiments which eventually caused his ejection from Magdalen for a brief period prior to the revolution of 1688.

17   He refers to a description recently published in English by the former Archbishop of Samos, Joseph Georgirenes.

18   *Account*, 97.

I am most assurd, that Kaloirs[19] bred up here have a greater fame and reputation for piety and learning, than any others throughout the Empire. Upon which account it is known by no other name among the Greeks, then that of agion oros, or the Holy Mountain and the Turks, in way of compliance with the fame that passes generally of that place, call it Sheicher dag, or the Mountain of Priests or Religious.

Of aspects of the monastic regimen generally Smith gives us a close account.

We may justly suppose that those, who have renounced the pleasures and delicacies and vanities of the world, not to be over-curious and nice in their Diet. They never touch any kind of Flesh, or Fish that has bloud in it. Their chief food is Shell-fish, Olives, Beans and Pulse, Onions, Melons, Raisins, and what their Field and Gardens afford. With this dry diet they enjoy good health, and find the happy effect of moderate and thin feeding in a lasting and vigorous old age. Their Bread is course and hard, being usually twice baked. Thrice a week, that is, on Monday, Wednesday and Friday, they do not end their Fast till after three a clock in the afternoon. After Evening-prayers they are content with a crust of bread and a draught of water. On other days they eat the Fish that they account lawfull, and White-meats and then allow themselves to drink Wine. In the great Lenten Fast before Easter, some will eat but once in eight and forty hours; others will forebear all kind of sustenance for two or three or four entire days.[20]

It is within this description of the monasteries around Constantinople that Smith has occasion to tell a charming story which also illustrates that the relations between Islamic Turks and Christian Greeks were not always bad.

The narrative that follows, describing an occurrence near a monastery standing upon grounds belonging to the mosque of the emperor Bayazid in Constantinople, was related to

---

19   An anglicised form of the Greek term *kalogeros*.
20   *Account,* 100–101.

Smith by the hegoumenos Macarius 'acquainted with me', says Smith, 'when I was upon the place with him':

> That in the year 1661. or 1662. (for I have forgot the exact year) The present Emperour Sultan *Mohamet Chan,* hunting not far from the *Euxine,* (to which exercise he is very much addicted,) In the pursuit of his game, at last, wearied and tired, lighted to rest at a Fountain at some little distance from their Convent. Upon the news of which, they consulted, whether they should wait upon him with some poor Present or no: at last one of the pert Monks undertook it. Advancing toward the Emperour, having made his reverence after the custom of the Country, and making an excuse for the presumption he was guilty of, presented him with a little Cheese and a basket of Cherries: then which latter nothing could have been more welcome to him, being thirsty and over-heated with excessive riding, and who yet in such an extremity abhorred the least thought of Wine. After some little time he calls the poor *Kaloir,* and very calmly asked him, whether he would become a *Musulman,* out of design questionless to have preferred him. But he, no way wrought by this powerfull temptation, continued speechless in his humble posture, with his eyes fixt upon the ground. The Emperour no way displeased with his behaviour, which he looked upon as a modest denial, *Well,* said he, *I perceive you have a mind to continue as you are;* and then bidding him look up, made a half circle with his hand, telling him, he gave the grounds lying about, which he thus markt out, to the Convent; And then commanded one of his favourite attendants to give the poor man thirty pieces of Gold.[21]

Thus, despite Smith's serious scholarly purposes, he peppers his text with stories of real human interest.

---

21   Ibid., 105–106.

The Divine Liturgy

Just as Smith's narrative could be charming, so it could be critical. An instance of this arises within Smith's long commentary on the Orthodox eucharistic rite. A case in point is what Smith calls 'the second or great Introitus or Entrance or access to the Altar'.

> This seems to be, and really, is, as they order the matter, the most solemn part of the Grecian Worship, and at which they express the greatest devotion, if we may judge of it by these outward and visible signs. A practice that really gives great offence, and is wholly unjustifiable, notwithstanding all the little and trifling excuses and pretensions made by Symeon Thessalonicensis and Gabriel Severus in favour of it: as, that proskunesis signifies Adoration and Respect in general; and that the Elements, by their being blest and separated from common use, are already sanctified and dedicated to God, and so are in readiness and disposition to be consecrated and made the Body and Bloud of Christ; and that they are fit matter prepared and determined to this Sacramental end and purpose. Therefore, say they, this Adoration is justly due to them. Whereas after the Consecration, when the Symbols are exposed and shewn to the people, the Reverence is not half so great; onely a little bowing of the body, which is soon over. But the miscarriage seem'd to me, when I was present, so gross and scandalous, as that it needs no other confutation than the bare relating.[22]

Smith's positive interest in the eucharistic rite is focused on the eucharistic prayer that follows. He provides lengthy quotations from the eucharistic text of the Liturgy of St. John Chrysostom; he even manages to capture something of the dynamic dramatic quality of the rite in the interplay between priest and choir, and the priest's own use of sotto voce and full voice in the saying of the eucharistic prayer.

---

22   Ibid., 134–135.

Following the description of the liturgy as a whole, Smith turns to controversial matters relating to the Eucharist: the time of consecration, *metousiosis* (transubstantiation), the use of leavened bread, once daily celebration, the communion of children, and the reservation for use of the sick.[23] As to the first matter, 'In what moment of time the Consecration is made', Smith understands both the eucharistic prayers themselves, and the ancient commentators, to emphasise the sanctifying role of the Holy Spirit. 'As to the moment of Consecration', he says,

> 'tis certain that the Greeks, herein following the authority of several ancient Writers of their Church, do not hold this Divine Mystery to be perfected and consummated by or after the pronunciation of those words, Take, eat, this is my Body; the Change, what-ever it be, not being made, according to St. John Damascen, but by the descent and illapse of the Holy Spirit upon the Gifts or Elements placed upon the Altar. Therefore in order to the completion of this Sacrament, they adde Benediction and Prayers, in which they do explicitly implore the Divine grace of the Holy Spirit of God: the Priest, after he has recited the words of our B. Saviour in the Institution, invoking God in these words, Send thy Holy Spirit upon us, and upon these Holy Gifts lying before us; and after a little pause, having three times made the sign of the Cross, adding, (which I purposely repeat) Make this Bread the precious Body of thy Christ, and that which is in this Cup the precious Bloud of thy Christ; then, with his hand lift up, and held over them, changing them by thy Holy Spirit. These are the formall words of the Liturgies of S. Chrysostome and S. Basil now in use.[24]

In no sense does Smith question or challenge this theology of consecration. It may even be that his textual commentary contributed toward the Non-Juror commitment to the epicletic tradition in the eucharistic prayer.

23   Ibid., 136 ff.
24   Ibid., 144–145.

That same text hints at another issue which Smith takes up in detail in his *Account*, the issue of transubstantiation, or *metousiosis*. It was, of course, a polemical inheritance from the controversies with Rome in the previous century. Even among high-church divines in the Interregnum and Restoration periods it continued to be a vigorously contested point.[25] Smith's support of Bishop Compton, who forebade the Greek parish's acceptance of the doctrine of transubstantiation as taught, for instance, by the Council of Bethlehem, gave an immediate polemical edge to Smith's discussion.

In Smith's critique there are two main points. First, in keeping with English divines before him, Smith insists that there is a change in the elements which cannot and should not be defined. He gives this essential position away in his discussion of the moment of consecration. He refers to 'the Change, *whatever it may be*'.[26] Without entering into the details of scholastic metaphysics, Smith asserts that there is a change which need not, indeed, does not involve a substantial change in any technical sense.

The issue was more complex from the Orthodox side, however. Smith knew that among them the term 'transubstantiation' (*metousiosis, metabole, metapoiesis*) was evolving. He is referring to the influence of Latin scholastic categories which began to infiltrate the theology, writing, even the public documents, of Orthodoxy in this period. Given the English Church's firm opposition to transubstantiation, and with Compton's regulations in mind, it is important for Smith not just to instruct the English but to remind the Orthodox of the state of this issue from the point of view of their own

---

25   In the hands of, for example, John Bramhall, John Cosin and Herbert Thorndike.

26   *Account*, 145. (Italics mine.)

usage and theology. Smith therefore provides an extended discussion of the history and meaning of the term among Orthodox writers and documents and in their liturgies, reminding his readers, for instance, that Patriarch Jeremias of Constantinople, in writing to the Wittenburg divines about Orthodox eucharistic doctrine, asserts 'that after the Consecration the Bread is changed into the very Body of Christ, and the Wine into his very Bloud, by the Holy Spirit, without defining more particularly the nature and manner of the change'.[27]

In fact, argues Smith, Orthodox liturgy uses words which signify real change in the object of sacramental grace without meaning substantial change. He cites, for instance, the baptismal liturgy where the verb *metapoiethenai* is used of the person receiving sacramental grace. In no sense does it mean that they cease to be substantially what they are, however else they might be changed. All of this, then, should be borne in mind by a reader, English or Orthodox, who turns to the canons of the Council of Bethlehem and finds the term 'transubstantiation'. Thus, Smith's *Account* serves to legitimise Bishop Compton's insistence that the canons of Bethlehem be rejected by English and Orthodox alike as a teaching that is inconsistent with both the reformed doctrine of the Church of England as well as the historic teaching of the Greek Church.

It was less easy for Smith to disconnect Orthodox tradition from the iconographic tradition which Bishop Compton also sought to bar from London's Greek Church. While Smith explicitly intends 'onely a Narrative' and 'not a Confutation',[28] he leaves his English reader in no doubt as to the good sense of Compton's disallowance of 'Pictures [...] of our Saviour, and of the Saints' which the Orthodox count 'sacred and venerable'.[29]

---

27   Ibid., 148.
28   Ibid., 213.
29   Ibid., 211.

'These', he says, 'they reverence and honour by bowing and kissing them, and saying their prayers before them'.

> At set times the Priest, before he enters into [the chancel], makes three low Reverences before the Image of *Christ*, and as many before that of the Virgin *Mary*: and he does the like in the time of the Celebration, and oftentimes perfumes them with his Incense-pot. Upon some of the great Festivals they expose to the view of the people, upon a Desk in the middle of the Quire, a printed picture of that day's Saint done in Christendom, whither upon their approach they bow their body, and kiss it with great devotion. This practice they defend from the Authority of the Seventh general Synod.and from this vain and idle pretence, that they worship the Saint in the Image which represents him, by the help of which they presently have an *Idea* of him in their mind; and that they worship the figure and representation not with the worship of latreia but of douleia and that onely sxetikos, relatively: which is all they have to say for their gross and scandalous behaviour herein.[30]

It should be borne in mind, however, that in many of his comments about Orthodoxy Smith is concerned with the relationship between Christianity and Islam. In the matter of icons in particular he regards the 'subtil and nice distinctions' too much for the 'gross and dull' Ottomans. The net result is simply the conclusion that Christians are idolaters.

Reformed Orthodoxy

Nevertheless, Smith is clear in his fundamental approbation of the orthodoxy of the Greek Church and its share with the Church of England of the foundational twin doctrines of the Trinity and the Incarnation. At the same time, Smith wishes

---

30   Ibid., 212–213.

to see the Greek Church reformed of practices and beliefs that do not, in his view, express the faith and practice of the church of the first five centuries. This desire for a reformed Orthodoxy accounts for Smith's reverence, even adulation, for the ill-fated Patriarch Cyril Lucaris. To his *Account of the Greek Church* Smith appended a narrative entitled 'The State of the Greek Church under Cyrillus Lucaris'. To a large extend that text is polemic against the Roman Catholic Church, and fuels the long-standing English suspicion of Jesuits. Positively, though, it presents the murdered patriarch as a martyr, sacrificed for the reformed purity of the Orthodox Church. In fact, Smith, a devotee (like many in the Restoration Church) of the royal martyr, likens Lucaris' sacrifice for the church to Charles I's martyrdom on behalf of the reformed Church of England. In the hands of Smith, Lucaris represents for the English what the Greek Church as a whole might be, a partner with the Church of England in an alliance of Christian churches reformed according to the ancient catholic church.

Conclusion

It is well known that the plan for a Greek College failed. The efforts at practical support here in Oxford at the turn of the eighteenth century lapsed and were forgotten. 'The curtain', as Edward Carpenter put it, 'which separated the East from the West, although lifted for a short time, soon fell again'.[31] It is also true that Smith's sojourn in the east gave him little hope of reform in the Greek Church such as Patriarch Cyril might have promoted. 'Indeed, considering the present state

31   Carpenter, op. cit., 364.

of things, there is little sign or hope of a Reformation', he laments. 'For the misery of it is', says Smith,

> that though it is manifest to all, who understand Antiquity, how much the present Greeks have in several points of Doctrine varied from the Beliefs of their Ancestours, and have corrupted the simplicity and purity of Religion by a mixture of odd opinions and fancies, they pretend notwithstanding, that their Tenants are agreeable to the Fathers, and that they follow the Traditions of the ancient Church.[32]

Smith's remark, however true or false, reveals an emerging historical-critical perspective in which the benchmark of antiquity is critically applied. In applying this benchmark to the Greek Church Smith uses the very measure which the Interregnum and Restoration clergy fought so hard to identify, defend and apply to the Church of England itself.

The accession of James II, Smith's own brief ejection from Magdalen College, the subsequent Revolution, and the crisis of oath and allegiance that affected some royalist clergy, all took their toll on Smith. Some years before his death in 1710 he gravitated toward the Non-Juring movement. Both his theological style and his ecumenical sympathies were broadly consistent with Non-Juring ideals. It is likely that his *Account*, in the hands of friends like the aged William Sancroft and younger Non-Jurors too, provided a springboard for the contacts with the Orthodox hierarchy made during the archiepiscopate of William Wake. It is well known that their correspondence on church union was cut short by Wake's intervention. However, that eighteenth-century attempt provided rich documentation for nineteenth-century Tractarians like William Palmer and William Birkbeck who developed the ecumenical possibilities opened up by the Tractarians to

---

32   Preface.

new degrees. Smith's *Account of the Greek Church* may be said to flow as a hidden spring into those initiatives. Thus, however limited and at times even prejudiced Thomas Smith and his *Account* may seem to be to contemporary readers, they have played a part in furthering the ecumenical knowledge and commitments upon which the twentieth century so constructively built.

5. 'Incoherent Pageantry' or 'sincere Devotion': Dr John Covel (1638–1722) on the Liturgy in Constantinople

Ephrem Lash

In 1659 M. Antoine Arnauld of Port-Royal together with M. Pierre Nicole published, at the request of the nuns of the Order of the Holy Sacrament, an Office of the Holy Sacrament in two volumes, covering the fifty-two Thursdays of the year. At the request of the nuns, each office included six patristic readings on the subject of the Holy Eucharist, which thus formed a massive florilegium of 312 passages from St Ignatius of Antioch to St Thomas Aquinas. The edification of the nuns was not the only purpose of this compilation, 'La traduction des trois cents douze Leçons, extraite des Pères de l'Eglise, avoit encore un autre but. C'étoit de présenter aux hérétiques, sur le mystère qu'ils contestoient, une lumière d'autant plus efficace, qu'elle étoit moins contentieuse.'[1] As a preface to this work Arnauld and Nicole wrote a short treatise entitled *La Perpétuité de la Foi Catholique touchant l'Eucharistie*.

---

1   A. Arnauld and P. Nicole, *La Perpétuité de la foi de l'Église catholique, touchant l'Eucharistie, deffendue contre le livre du sieur Claude, etc. (Livre douzième contenant deux dissertations sur le sujet de J. Scot, et de Bertram.)* (Paris, 1777) tome 12, Préface, iii. This was first published in 1664. At least two anonymous translations were made into English in the 17th century. One was printed in Edinburgh, at Holy-Rood House, in 1687, another in London in 1710. A translation of Jean Claude's reply was printed in London in 1684.

Since this was in effect an attack on the Calvinist doctrine, it was decided not to publish it in a work, 'où l'on ne se proposoit que d'éclairer et de nourrir la piété des fidèles pour ce saint mystère.' However a few copies were made and one of these fell into the hands of M. Jean Claude of Charenton, the Calvinist minister in Paris. He immediately published a reply, which was widely circulated. This provoked from the Gentlemen of Port Royal, who were never adverse to controversy, a massive reply in three large quarto volumes, running to over two and a half thousand pages, with the same title as the original pamphlet. Later Eusèbe Renaudot wrote a *Défense de la Perpétuité*, which was, in its turn, supplemented by three more volumes totalling over two thousand pages. This was no mere patristic florilegium, but a massive work of controversy, with a particular interest in the Eastern Churches and included a great deal of material from contemporary Orthodox sources. Arnauld contacted French diplomats and others in the Levant and elsewhere to collect authenticated testimonia from Orthodox bishops and theologians. One of the most assiduous collectors was le Marquis de Nointel, a devout fellow Jansenist, a relative of Arnauld and Louis XIV's ambassador to the Sublime Porte.[2] Covel knew de Nointel well and writes of him that he was 'a man of Address and great Devotion' and

> very Courteous, Affable and Obliging to every Body; and though I had far different Sentiments from him, yet I had the Honour of his Acquaintance and frequent Conversation; and I shall not blame him

---

2   Charles-François Ollier, Marquis de Nointel, was French ambassador to the Sublime Porte from 1671 to 1678. He was famous among other things for the *affaire du sofa* and for the splendour of his *train de vie*. For a vivid impression of the semi-royal state of the ambassadors to the Porte in this period, see Philip Mansel, *Constantinople* (London, 1987), ch. 8.

for showing his Zeal for his Religion, for he would always candidly give me leave, civilly and freely to defend my own; besides he was a *Jansenist* in his own Opinion, and therefore had a peculiar respect for Mr. *Arnold* and as great a Favour for his Cause.[3]

M. Jean Claude was less fortunately placed. As he himself wrote, 'Leurs armes, je le confesse, sont bien plus luisantes, & plus pompeuses que les miennes.' So he turned to his potential allies, among them the Protestant subjects of Charles II, in similar posts in the Levant. A copy of the 'memorial' he sent to possible allies, and to which I shall return, is preserved among the papers of Dr John Covel, Fellow of Christ's College, Cambridge, who in 1670 had been appointed chaplain to Sir Daniel Harvey, ambassador of the Levant Company to the Sublime Porte.[4]

Covel was born in 1638, entered Christ's College in 1654, became a Fellow before Christmas 1659, took his M.A. in 1661 and was awarded his D.D., by royal command, in 1679. He was skilled in botany and drugs, and may have intended to take up

---

3   In an undated letter from the Marquis, but which probably dates from 1672, he writes of Covel, without naming him. 'Vous saurez que le Ministre de M. l'Ambassadeur d'Angleterre, m'étant venu me voir, je lui ai montré l'attestation synodale et plusieurs autres. Je lui ai fait lire les paroles qui concernent l'Eucharistie; et il est convenu positivement de la croyance que les Grecs ont de la présence réelle et de la Transsubstantiation. Il s'étonne même de l'opiniâtreté à disputer ce fait de la part du Ministre Claude ; et il prétend qu'il n'y a aucun mémoire venu d'Angleterre qui lui ait pu donner lieu de le faire avec quelque fondement.'

4   I do not know if M. Claude contacted Covel directly, but he certainly received a copy of the 'memorial' from James Crawford, the English chaplain to the ambassador in Venice. In a letter to Covel, dated 22 August 1674, Crawford writes, 'I have here sent you a memorial wch I brought from Monsieur Claude and which may be very useful to you in this affaire.' The underlining is Covel's. British Library, Addit. MSS. 22910.77 v°. The 'memorial' is at Addit. MSS. 22910.83.

medicine.[5] The date of his ordination is not known, but on 17 March 1669/70 he was appointed chaplain to Sir Daniel Harvey, in Constantinople.[6] He was allowed to retain his Fellowship. The King approved his appointment in May 1670. He left England on 21 September 1670 and reached Constantinople on New Year's Eve. His encounter with the customs officials was an unpropitious beginning.

> When I went to get my books and other things on shore, The Customers ript open my Trunks and boxes and searched and rifled every thing; however at last I mist nothing but Niceron's *Thaumaturgus opticus*, which I shrewdly suspect was filch't from me by one, who was <indeed> call'd a Christian, but had not <it seems> the honesty of a common Turk.[7]

He left Constantinople in April 1677 and returned to Cambridge, where he later became both Master of Christ's and Vice-Chancellor, via Mt Athos, Venice, Naples and Rome, reaching England early in 1679. During the last year of his life (he died on 19 December 1722) he published his detailed account of *The Greek Church with Reflections on their present Doctrine and Discipline*. In the preface he regrets that publication has been so delayed, but

> It has lain by me a long while, being only a successive and therefore imperfect Collection; had I been Happy after my Return to have had some mean Preferment, which would have supported me, and not Sequestered me from my Books, but settled me down to them and my Papers, I should long ago have ventured to have Published my

---

5   See W. Hunt in *DNB* 12 (1887), 355 f., and J. Peile, *Biographical Register of Christ's College, 1505–1905*, vol. 1 (Cambridge, 1910) 559–561.
6   The letter inviting him to take up this post from Sir Eliab Harvey, who says that he must preach before the Company in London, on a text of his own choosing, is preserved among his papers in the British Library. Addit. MSS. 22910.29.
7   Addit. MSS. 22912.74.

Travails and this Performance; but I have been forced to live a kind of Itinerant Life, at *York*, in *Holland* and elsewhere; and find my Self at last Chained to a perpetual College Bursar's place, which takes up at least three quarters of my time.

Both on his journeys and while resident in Constantinople he kept a copious and detailed journal, probably with a view to subsequent publication. He scrupulously recorded the details of people, places and plants; and many of his drawings of ancient Greek inscriptions are still useful. Most of this material is unpublished, but there exist two articles in which a certain amount of it is transcribed. One contains extracts from his journals on his travels in Turkey and the other a fairly full transcription of his visit to Mt Athos.[8] The journals, in two volumes, together with two large folios of correspondence, are preserved in the British Library.

To anyone who has read his book, which is a work of controversy and much of it written in the aggressive polemic style of the period, his journals are a surprise. Here he is an observer, recording, often in painstaking detail, the people and places he visits. He is more anthropologist than theologian. If in the book the adjective 'monkish' is pejorative, his account of his visit to Athos is strictly factual. In February 1676/7 he visited Nicea, where he attempted to make contact with the Orthodox community. The account in his travel journal is compassionate rather than hostile.

---

8   His account of Athos was published by F. W. Hasluck in the *Annual of the British School in Athens*, No. 17 (1910–11), 103–131, a reference which has escaped the notice of the new edition of the *Oxford Dictionary of the Christian Church*. The extracts from his journals were edited and published by J. T. Brent as *Early Voyages and Travels in the Levant* (Hakluyt Society 87, 1893), 101–287. See illustration 3.

When we came first to town I desir'd to lodge at a greek house if possible; we were at last brought to ye greek church, where ye papas hearing strangers enquiring for him ran and hid himself; but with many good words and entreatyes we at last got a lodging at a poor womans house: there are not above 10 greek familyes here now left, and about 50 armenians ye rest are all Turkes; none of the greeks know how to speak their own toung, the papas himself, who (after he was better informed and his fear was over) came to us and beg'd our excuse, could understand well enough what we spoke to him in greek, but could by no meanes answer us in the same language; they got by heart the formes of baptisme, and ye words of consecration of ye Eucharist, and some part of ye office for Buriall and the like; and severall prayers he hath by heart of their Mattins and Vespers, and with these he makes a shift to entertain his hearers, though neither he nor they understand one word in twenty. I was to here him say Vespers, and he saide the πατὴρ ἡμῶν, ye μεγάλη & μικρὴ συναπτὴ and the θεοτόκε παρθένε he could not say ten lines right; yet as to ye formality of the action he imitated that of ye rest of ye papas in other places; and where he came out to blesse and incense (perfume) ye people he always had no other words than the θεοτόκε or παρθένε; which he galloped over and over till he was many times quite out of breath; he was most miserably poor, and the saddest ignorant soul that ever I met withall in Greece.[9]

Covel explains the way in which he approaches other forms of religion in a letter to the British Consul in Naples, written from Rome during his journey back to England. The circumstances of the letter were these. On reaching Rome he heard that a rumour was abroad to the effect that an 'English minister' in Naples had been converted to Roman Catholicism. Realising that this could in all probability only refer to himself, he wrote a long letter to the Consul in Naples asking him to help scotch the rumour, which he naturally attributes to the Jesuits. In it he explains that the only thing that could

---

9   Addit. MSS. 22914.15 v°.

have given rise to this was the fact that he been present at the liquefaction of the blood of St Januarius.[10] He writes,

> It was my design when I first left England to see and understand and take an account with mine own eyes (and not be beholden to the fallible relations of others) of what was acted and believed by all people abroad where I went in my travailes. And therefore I have been in the Turkish Mosche's at Constan^ple. many and many times at their houres of prayer; I have seen their devotions and manner of worship; and I have all their prayers and functions in Arabick and in Vulgar Greek. Next I have been often and often in the Synagogues of ye Jewes and converst with them and their bookes as well as with those who are cal'd the Rabinaïms as the Karaïms which are counted set [?] by ye others, and I met with them onely at a town by Constantinople where are about 60 familyes of them.[11] Thirdly I have been to see ye Greeks say their Liturgy or Masse a hundred times and have conversed with all the Patriarches and Metropolites which were in my time. I have done the like with the Armenians and as many of the Georgians and Russians as I could meet with at Constantple. and truely of all these I think I am able to give a tolerable account especially as to their Religion and devotion. Now these Father Machievels (who ever they are) may with the same charity and as much reason say that J. Covel is in his heart, A Turk, A Jew, A Greek, an Armenian or the like because I conversed with them all, over and over again, and never scrupled to be by as a spectator of their rites and ceremonyes; I say that may as well and justly said of me, as this, that I am a Papist because I will not be ignorant of what the Churche of Rome professe and doe; if I now assert a thing of the Church of Rome, or Greece, or Armenia or ye like, or of the Turk or Jew, it shall be grounded upon the evidence of what my own eyes have seen

---

10 His journals contain an interesting account of this, in which he observes that the liquefaction could easily be explained by the fact that the vial, of which he provides a drawing, is normally kept in a cool, dark place, but is warmed by being held in the hands of the officiating bishop.

11 In the archives of Christ's there is an extremely interesting letter from Covel describing the Karaite community. I am grateful to the librarian of the college for enabling me to see this letter.

practised, and not upon the meer report of another; and I know of no reason why a man, that is by his own profession bound not onely to know but defend his own Religion, might as well not see, as read the practices of others, let them be what they will. For my part I shall say more; were I in the Indies, I would certainly enter into their idol temples, if I could, and see their blind way likewise; for I thank my God I have that true Christian liberty which St Paul speakes of; I know, saith he, that an idoll is nothing, and to him that account it as nothing (as St Paul did, and really in itself it is,) certainly it is nothing.[12]

He signs the letter, 'Worthy Sir, Your faithfull friend and a true son of ye Protestant Church. Jo: Covel.' Does he 'protest too much'? I am sure his protestations are genuine, but perhaps it was not only Jesuits who found his behaviour surprising. After all not many disinterested observers are prepared to stay through a full agrypnia, as Covel seems to have done,

I have been amongst them at their ἀγρυπνία *Vigils*, upon some great Festival following, where all have stood from the very beginning of the Vespers, during all the following Offices to the end of the Liturgy; that is from the Evening till Noon the next day, without sitting or kneeling at all.[13]

His predecessor was less of an enthusiast, remarking, 'Their offices are long and tedious. [...] I have been present for seven hours together at their service upon a Festival day from

---

12   Addit. MSS. 22910.164–165.
13   The next few lines show his care in translating. He is commenting on the Deacon's Στῶμεν καλῶς before the Anaphora, 'This Exhortation therefore of the Deacon is to stir up their Reverence and Attention in this their solemn Posture of Attention. And that admonition which I have hereafter noted, σοφία ὀρθοί, may be understood of that *standing*; as if the sense had been, σοφία, *the Gospel, attend*, ὀρθοί or *be ye Standing or Erect'*.

between four and five of the clock in the morning, till toward twelve.' In his journals and his book Covel has many detailed observations on Orthodox liturgical practices, occasionally with a somewhat sardonic humour. On the method of communicating the laity he remarks, 'So that in this point, there is this difference between the *Greeks* and the *Latins* suitable to the *Genius* of their Country; These make for their Laymen a sober feast, *a little Wafer and no Drink*, those a merry Treat, *something to Drink but nothing to Eat.*'

More importantly he was admitted into the Altar during celebrations of the Liturgy, including that of the Presanctified, both in Constantinople and on Mt Athos, something that would not normally happen today. Moreover he had been present at Liturgies in the open air, where there would have been no iconostasis.

At those Anniversary Meetings in the Fields at the Holy Fountains, or the like there is commonly but one poor Altar or Table, made up of Brick, or Stone, or Earth, and repair'd against the day, if decay'd, or any part be broken down) and that serves both for a *Prothesis* and a *Holy Table* too.

He translates in full, and comments in great detail on the *Proskomide*, noting that often only one prosphora is used, even in the patriarchal church, 'I have very often seen only one Sealed Loaf made use of for all the *Portions*, not only in small Congregations, but in the Patriarch's Church it self.' But he notes that the portions are often taken from many different loaves, 'especially in Monasteries at *Athos*, and some elsewhere.' He further observes, on the portion for the Bishop, 'I have seen (especially at Mount *Athos*) him that celebrates dig out a little piece of the Loaf for his *Portion*, as likewise for the *Founders* in the next; but for all the rest he only scrapes off little Mites with the Spear from the Crust of the Loaf.' This is clearly an eye-witness account and gives a particular interest to his comments on the placing of the portion of the Mother of God on the *diskos*. He has a diagram in which the portion of the Mother of God is on the same side as the nine ranks and he comments, 'And in all Places, where I have been, I never saw that *Portion* of the *V. M.* set otherwise than I have set it.' But he also says that his copy of the Liturgy has the usual explanation of why 'right' means 'left'. He says, with relish, '*Goar* hath here made a great blunder.'[14] His translations are scrupulous and usually accurate. For example he is aware of the Trinitarian understanding of the Trisagion in the Orthodox tradition and translates it, 'Holy God, holy (Thou that art) strong, holy (Thou that art) Immortal have mercy upon us'. His predecessor, Smith, has 'Holy God, holy and powerful, holy and immortal', a mistranslation that persists in some places today. He has a lengthy discussion of the phrase κατὰ πάντα καὶ διὰ πάντα, and arrives at what is, I believe, the correct translation, even if one may dissent from his theological conclusion. 'And the words here following, Offering to Thee, *Thine of Thine*, κατὰ πάντα καὶ διὰ πάντα, *in all things and for all things*, must signify that *all things*, whatever we offer to God, are *his Creatures*, or Gifts, or *from Him* and *for all things and purposes for which he hath order'd them to be.*' He says of Goar's note on this passage, 'He hooks in his *Transubstantiation* by this special Gloss'. This 'gloss', incidentally, is 'In sacrificio namque, nec nudus panis, neque Corpus Christi simpliciter, sed panis vere consecratus, & corpus Christi panis specie velatum, velut hostia mundi totius immolatur.' In his

---

14   His diagrams and drawings of clergy are taken from Goar. The drawing of a Patriarch in street dress, entitled in Goar *The Patriarch Bekkos,* is retitled *The Patriarch.* He is carrying what looks like a Cardinal's hat, but is probably the Byzantine *skiadion*, a broad-brimmed sun hat. Covel has mistakenly had the word Ἐπιγονάτιον written beside this, but inadvertently omitted to delete Goar's equally erroneous annotation, 'Pileum Cardinalis'.

journal he makes the interesting observation that two deacons elevate the holy gifts at this point, 'τὰ σὰ ἐκ τῶν σῶν one deacon took hold of ye discus, ye other of ye chalice wth their right hands acrosse (one over the other) and gently moved them backwards and forwards'. In the *Cheruvikon* he correctly translates the participle ὑποδεξόμενοι as a future, not a final clause, and he is aware that some texts have an Aorist.

It is important to remember that one of the objects of his book was to counter Catholic claims that the Eastern Churches believed the Latin doctrine of transubstantiation and in particular to counter this claim as defended by Goar in his *Euchologion, sive Rituale Graecorum*, as Covel's title page makes clear: 'SOME ACCOUNT of the PRESENT GREEK CHURCH, with REFLECTIONS on their Present DOCTRINE AND DISCIPLINE; Particularly in the EUCHARIST, And the Rest of their SEVEN PRETENDED SACRAMENTS, compared with JAC. GOAR's Notes upon the GREEK RITUAL, or EUCHOLOGION.' Like Goar he gives a translation of the Liturgy of St John Chrysostom followed by detailed notes by way of commentary. Although not complete, this must be one of the earliest, if not the earliest, translations of the Liturgy into English. However, since his main interest is in the doctrine of the Real Presence, he translates the Proskomidi in full, but not the Liturgy of the Catechumens, which he dismisses very briefly before coming to the Great Entrance, which he describes in detail.

But before that, there is a very long confused, incoherent Piece of Pageantry, rather than solid and severe Devotion, carried on by the Priest and the Deacon (sometimes loud, other times soft, intermixing with some Set-Prayers, many, many *Suffrages, Versicles, Responses, Repetitions*, with numerous and various Rites and Ceremonies) and by the Singers and Choir, (who carry on a Service by themselves in the mean time, and now and then in peculiar Places mix their *Responses and Suffrages* with them) in such a manner as we may justly say of the whole Service, what is said of our Service before the Reformation.

He then quotes the well-known passage from the Preface to the *Book of Common Prayer*, 'Moreover, the numbre and hardnesse of the rules, called the Pie, and the many chaungynges of the seruyce, was the cause, that to tourne the boke onely was so harde and intricate a matter, that manye tymes there was more busynesse to fynde out what shoulde be read, then to reade it when it was founde out'. He deals summarily with the Liturgy of the Word, 'In the Middle of this Theatrical Devotion comes in a Scene for reading the Epistle and Gospel.' In his journal there are some very detailed notes on a patriarchal Liturgy on the First Sunday of Lent, in the course of which he observes, 'whilst ye Ghospel was read, though there was a great murmur before, not ye least noise'.[15]

The Great Entrance, on the other hand, was of the greatest interest to him, not least because of the profound reverence displayed during it by the whole congregation from the Patriarch downwards. In the same set of notes on the Liturgy for the First Sunday of Lent he writes, 'The p. meet them, and go out 2 <or 3> steps and bowing to ye ground receive first ye br. and then ye wine (bowing again) and place them reverently on ye Table'. In the book he describes the Entrance when the Patriarch is present but not celebrating. The Entrance is made by going right through the church, in the present Greek, but not the Russian, manner. He notes,

---

15 These notes are not always easy to read, since they are full of abbreviations and page references, presumably to an *Euchologion* that Covel used when writing his notes when he returned from church. He describes the vesting of the Patriarch in detail, observing, among other things, that at a patriarchal Liturgy, the other concelebrating Hierarchs are not vested in the *Sakkos*, but in the *Phelonion* and *Omophorion*. Addit. MSS. 22914.65.

'The Pomp of this Procession, especially on High Days, or when the Patriarch celebrates, is very great'.

The Patriarch, he says, comes down a step or two from his throne, and he and all the Metropolites remove the '*outward Hood*, or Vail of their Head'. He also describes an occasion when both he and the French ambassador were present,

> 'I remember, the Illustrious *Marques de Nointel*, the French Embassador, was once with me present at the Patriarch's Church, upon a new Patriarch's Enthronement, and seeing this Adoration, he smiled upon me, and afterwards used it as an Argument for the *Latines* adoring the Host; but when I informed him that the Elements were not as yet Consecrated, he dropt the Discourse'.

This brings us back to the contemporary controversy between the Catholics and Protestants on the subject of the Eucharist with which we began. Here Covel's evidence is of the greatest interest, since he was in Constantinople in the 1670s and knew many of the key players, including Patriarch Dositheus of Jerusalem. He seems to have had a soft spot for Patriarch Methodius, referring to him as 'our Methodius'. The latter had even taken refuge at the ambassador's palace when he was deposed from the patriarchate.[16] Covel discusses the Synod in Bethlehem of 1672 at length, writing, he claims, as an objective historian, 'I would be understood to write [...] Historicorum more, *like an Historian*, that is, to give an honest and Impartial Account, to the best of my Knowledge, how matters passed in the Greek Church when I was there'. He asserts that Patriarch Dionysios had produced his declaration of 1672 under pressure and that the same was true of the Decree of the Synod of Bethlehem. Of Dionysios he writes, 'And what *Dionysius* and his *Partisans* did now, was to my knowledge done

---

16   A letter from him is preserved among Covel's papers.

with an unwilling willingness; as he hath often suggested to me, for I frequently visited him, especially after he was turned out in 1674 and whilst he was Sick and in Prison, where by God's help I recover'd him'. Of the Synod of Jerusalem he says,

> If this was a real Synod, and Matters were, as they ought, day by day leisurely debated in it, I wonder how seventy Men durst come together so often, for several days at least, and set, and closely consult under that most Suspicious and Jealous Government; The *Turks*, who have always a very watchfull Eye over any such Meetings, would certainly have made an *Avania* upon them, and have severely pincht their Purses, or chastised their Carcases. It is more likely that this *Confession* or *Apology* lay ready drawn and finished, and was so produced at the Festival, and the good Fathers Subscribed it without any farther scrutiny.

At the heart of these reservations about the various declarations of the Eastern hierarchs lies the word 'transubstantiation'. This was the main point at issue between the Jansenists and the Calvinists in France; this was the doctrine that the Catholics wanted the Orthodox to declare was part of the traditional faith of the Church. Linked to this was the question of whether it was proper to offer divine adoration, *latria*, to the consecrated elements. Pastor Jean Claude's Latin memorandum, addressed to 'the very reverend and distinguished English pastors dwelling in Eastern parts and who for their zeal for reformed Religion wish to approach Greek and other oriental Christians of better note, those that is who favour no syncretism with Romanisers [*Romanensibus*] and who are not alumni of the Roman curia nor disciples of missionaries', contains 15 questions to which answers are be sought from the Easterners. The first seven are all concerned with the doctrine of transubstantiation, eight, nine and ten with *latria*. The last five are concerned with whether the doctrine has ever been sanctioned by any Eastern council and the various recent Eastern councils and declarations between 1639 and 1642. The document is undated, but it must predate 1672, since otherwise he could hardly have failed to mention the two important Orthodox declarations of that year.[17] Clearly the debate was formulated, by both sides, in highly scholastic terms which were unfamiliar and unappealing to the Orthodox; but I think it is also the case that if asked to choose which position more nearly represented Orthodox doctrine, the Orthodox would have inclined to the Catholic rather than the Protestant. This seems to me clear from the reply of the Patriarchs to the Non-Jurors. The latter had listed among points of disagreement the doctrine of the Eucharist. They write,

> Tho' they believe a divine mystery in the Holy Eucharist, through the invocation of the Holy Spirit upon the elements, whereby the faithful do verily and indeed receive the Body and Blood of Christ; they believe it yet to be after a manner which flesh and blood cannot conceive. And seeing no sufficient ground from Scripture and Tradition to determine the manner of it, are for leaving it indefinite and undetermined; so that every one may freely according to Christ's own institution and meaning, receive the same in faith, and may also worship Christ in spirit, as verily indeed present, without being obliged to worship the sacred Symbols of His presence.

The opening of the lengthy patriarchal reply to this point leaves little doubt as to the Orthodox view,

> How can any pious person forbear trembling to hear this Blasphemy, as I may venture to term it? For, to be against worshipping the Bread, which is consecrated and changed into the Body of Christ, is to be against worshipping our Lord Jesus Christ himself our Maker and Saviour. For what else is the sacrificial Bread, after it is consecrated

---

17   A copy of this is preserved among Covel's papers. Addit. MSS. 22910.83.

and transubstantiated by the access of the Holy Spirit? Truly,
nothing less than the real Body of our Lord.

A great deal of Covel's book is concerned with the
Catholic doctrine of Transubstantiation, but he also has
chapters on the other six Sacraments and a long final one on
Images. Despite the book's title, he devotes page after page
to refuting Roman teaching, especially as exemplified by
'Bellarmine and his Myrmidons', as he calls them. Indeed, had
the book had an index nominum I suspect the most numerous
references would be to the learned Jesuit. Nevertheless, he
also compares and contrasts the doctrines and practices of the
Greeks, not infrequently commenting favourably on Orthodox practices. His comments on fasting and penance are not
without interest.

> The longest and strictest [fast] is, as our Lent, before Easter; at the
> beginning of which there are particularly appointed, by the Patri-
> archs, and Metropolites and Bishops in their several Provinces and
> Dioceses, some grave and Reverend Persons, (Men that have been
> bred up in their Monasteries to a strict and mortified Life) to go to
> their respective Cities and Towns as they are ordered, to Advise,
> Direct and Assist all good People, who will go to them, for the
> encouraging and encreasing of their Devotion, and for the better
> management of their Lives and Conversations, that they may be
> worthy to communicate at the approaching Festival. A very Pious
> and laudable Institution!

He also describes a rule of prayer which he has found in a
recent, 15th or 16th century, manuscript *Canonarium*. This
mentions a 'Rosary of 103 beads', though he himself had never
seen one, and an interesting variant on the Jesus Prayer, 'Lord
Jesus Christ, Thou Son of God, have Mercy upon me a Sinner,
through the Mother of God'.

Finally towards the end of his chapter on Images, he has a
long discussion of the sign of the Cross. This was a matter of

current debate in England, and the abolition of the rite signing the candidate with the Cross at Baptism had been one of
the demands of the Presbyterians at the Savoy Conference in
1661. Covel has an interesting passage in which he defends the
practice of making the sign of the Cross, based on his
experiences in the Levant. He is of the opinion that the early
Christians had used it as a sign of mutual recognition, and he
described how it is still so used in the East,

> when you can by no other Language be understood *this very Crossing
> your self* expresses to every one what you are; no *Turk,* or *Jew,* or
> *Heathen* will do it. Many and many times, as poor *Russian Slaves and
> others*, came Begging and Singing by in the Streets, and I could speak
> no Language to their understanding, if looking out of my Window
> upon them, *I Crost my Breast*, they would certainly do so too to shew
> me that they were *my fellow Christians*; and often Travelling in
> *Turkish Habit* (as we are Privileged to do in that Countrey) we came
> to a great Village or Town they should be afraid to give us any
> Entertainment, or say that they had any thing to sell, especially Wine
> (a very necessary Comfort upon the Road) for fear we should take
> and destroy all they had as being forbidden ware; But when *I Crost my
> self* and said εἰς τὸ ὄνομα τοῦ Πατρός, *in the name of the Father and of
> the Son and of the Holy Ghost*, and thereby only own'd my self to be a
> Christian, they would bring forth what they had, and freely let us
> have any thing which they had for our Money.

He then gives a moving account of a 'poor Greek', who had
been tricked by some Turks into reading in one of their books
the words, 'God is but one God, and Mahomet is his Prophet'.
They then forcibly circumcised him, but

> because he would not absolutely renounce his Christianity, and turn
> *Turk*, he was, after much barbarous usage, at last beheaded before his
> own door. I saw him when he was led to his Execution; (as I had
> often done before;) and all the way as he went through the Street,
> when we could not hear any thing which he said in the throng which
> prest about him, he almost continually *Crost himself* after the Greeks
> manner; publicly and stedfastly thereby professing himself to live and

die a Christian. Thus according to the very words of our Church in Baptism, *he was not ashamed to confess the Faith of Christ Crucified, and manfully to fight under his Banner, as his Faithfull Soldier and Servant to his Lives end.*

I like to think that John Covel would himself have followed the poor Greek Orthodox Martyr's example, had he been called upon to do so, for in the letter to the Consul in Naples from which I quoted earlier, he had written,

> First then I do here in ye presence of my God and with the solemne witnesse of my own conscience affirme my self to be immoveably a true Son of the Protestant Church in which I have been baptised and bread, and in which by the help of God I resolve to die; secondly I doe declare that there are many points and tenents as in matters of faith, as in discipline and practise now held and enjoyn'd by the Church of Rome, unto which I am utterly irreconcileable, and therefore I do hereby and ever did absolutely renounce both it and them, and am ready, if it should please God to call me to sacrifice my life in witness of this my affirmation and Declaration.

Appendix

In his well-known account of the Greek Church after 1453, *The Great Church in Captivity*, the late Sir Steven Runciman devotes a number of pages to the Greek College in Oxford. Towards the end he writes, 'Apart from the Jesuits' victims, the name of only one [student] has survived, Francis Prossalenos, who several years later published a friendly little book describing Dr Woodroffe's quirks and foibles'.[18] He gives no reference for this book, and the description of it in

---

18   S. Runciman, *The Great Church in Captivity* (Cambridge, 1968), 304.

the article on Woodroffe by W. P. Courtney in the *DNB* is significantly different, 'One of them, Franciscus Prossalentes, printed in 1706, the work, which was reproduced in 1862, in the Greek language exposing the paradoxes and sophisms of the principal'. Courtney's description of the book is confirmed by Eusèbe Renaudot in the fourth volume of *La Perpetuité*, where he writes in some detail about detail about the college. Renaudot describes Woodroffe as 'zélé pour la Religion Protestante, & la voulant inspirer aux Grecs'. He claims that, unlike the practice of the Greek Colleges in Rome and elsewhere, in which the Orthodox students were free to use their own prayers, offices and ceremonies, at Oxford this was not the case. He also asserts that 'le même Dosithée a écrit des lettres circulaires pour détourner les Grecs d'envoyer leurs enfants, ou d'aller en Angleterre étudier à ce Collège, menaçant même d'excommunication ceux qui mépriseront ses avis.' He gives a number of details about Francis Prossalento. He was from Corfu and had passed through Paris on his way home from Oxford.

> Il dit à diverses personnes, que le principal sujet de son retour étoit l'avis qu'il avoit reçu, que le Patriarche de Constantinople Gabriel étoit favorablement disposé pour lui ; mais que le séjour d'Oxford seroit un grand obstacle à son avancement, s'il ne se retiroit promptement d'un pays d'hérétiques.

According to Renaudot Woodroffe 'a eu très-grand soin de les catéchiser sur la Religion Anglicane, de déclamer contre la Transsubstantiation, contre l'invocation des Saints, le signe de la croix, & sur-tout contre l'autorité de la Tradition.' The young Prossalento (he was twenty-five at the time) wrote a tract entitled, Ὁ αἱρετικὸς διδάσκαλος ὑπὸ τοῦ Ὀρθοδόξου μαθητοῦ ἐλεγχόμενος. An odd title for 'a friendly little book' describing someone's 'quirks and foibles'. Renaudot concludes his paragraph as follows, 'Et dans tout le Livre, il ne traite jamais autrement son Maître Woodroff, un des grands témoins de M. Claude, que comme un hérétique. On peut voir dans la *Défense de la Perpétuité* un plus ample extrait, qui donne une juste idée de ce Collège Grec d'Oxford, & de l'horreur des Grecs pour ce qu'on voulu leur y enseigner.' Later on Renaudot comments on the general failure of attempts at mass proselytism, citing as examples the efforts of Charles I to impose episcopacy and Anglican liturgy on the Scots, the failure of the Portuguese to convert the Ethiopians and the Christians of Malabar to the Roman Church.

6. The Greek College at Oxford, 1699–1705

E. D. Tappe

Introduction

There has perhaps never been a time since the Reformation when some group in the Anglican Church has not been exploring the possibility of a rapprochement with some section of the Orthodox Church. In particular during the seventeenth century and the first quarter of the eighteenth, Anglicans showed considerable interest in the Greek Church, and this interest was reciprocated.[1] In 1616 Cyril Lucaris, then Patriarch of Alexandria, commended a young priest, Metrophanes Critopoulos, to the Archbishop of Canterbury. At his own expense the Archbishop, George Abbot, sent Metrophanes to Oxford, to study theology at Balliol. On his return to the East, Metrophanes, in spite of an adverse report from Abbot, continued to enjoy the favour of Lucaris and rose to be, in his turn, Patriarch of Alexandria. That Metrophanes was not the only Greek anxious to study in England at that time is shown, for instance, by an appeal made in 1621 to the King, the Archbishop of Canterbury and the Bishop of

Reprinted from *Oxoniensia* XIX (1954) 92–111, with the kind permission of the Oxfordshire Architectural and Historical Society.

1   This subject is fully treated in T. Spencer's book, *Fair Greece Sad Relic,* which has appeared since this article was written.

London by two others, Gregory, Archimandrite of Mace-
donia, and Kantakouzenos, who asked to be sent to Oxford to
study philosophy and theology.[2] The period of the Civil War
and the Commonwealth was as unpropitious for cultural
relations with the Greek Orthodox Church as it was for
commerce in the Levant. Nathaniel Conopius, another protégé of Lucaris, who fled from Constantinople when his
patron was murdered, was also at Balliol, and was expelled
from there by the Puritans in 1648. His chief claim on the
gratitude of Oxonians is that, according to the diarist Evelyn,
he was the first man to drink coffee in Oxford. There is a story
that the Regicides were visited by a Patriarch of the Greek
Church, sent to represent his brother Patriarchs and to pose
the question, 'By what Law either of God or Man they put
their King to Death?'[3] But perhaps he was as mythical as the
Patriarch who gave his blessing to royalists at Oxford in 1659,
and received a harangue from the Professor of Greek; this
personage was a London merchant, and the rag was organised
by the future bishop, William Lloyd.[4] After the Restoration,
when High Churchmen were in the ascendancy, relations
with the Eastern Church were resumed. Some able clergymen
took service as Chaplains of the Levant Company in the
period 1660–1710. Thomas Smith, chaplain at Constantinople
1668–1671, and his successor, John Covel, were among the
more distinguished. Smith's book on the Greek Church
appeared in Latin in 1676 and in an English version in 1680,
with an account of Cyril Lucaris appended. (Covel's book was
only published in 1722.) But Paul Rycaut, who was consul at
Smyrna in the chaplaincies of Smith and Covel, also published
a book in 1678 on the state of the Greek Church.

---

2   MS. Smith 37, ff. 25–27.
3   *Notes & Queries,* 6th ser., XI, 284.
4   A. Wood, *Life and Times,* ed. Clark, I, 282.

It is about this time when Smith's and Rycaut's books appeared that we have the first suggestion of a scheme for educating Greeks in England. Joseph Georgirenes, Archbishop of Samos, who came to England in 1676 and built a church in Soho Fields for the Greek Community of London, visited Oxford in July 1677 to raise money for the completion of that church. Anthony Wood wondered whether he was not also there in connexion with a scheme for creating a Greek College in Oxford at Gloucester Hall. 'At that time,' he says, 'there was great talk of converting Gloucester Hall into a College for the educating 20 or 30 Greeks in Academical learning.'[5] In any case, it was Georgirenes who wrote a letter to William Sancroft, Archbishop of Canterbury, apparently about 1682, in which he requests that about 12 scholars from Greece should be constantly in England, 'to be instructed and grounded in the true Doctrine of the Church of England, whereby (with the blessing of God) they may be able dispensers thereof, and so returne into Greece aforesaid to preach the same.'[6] It is to be noted that he asks for only 12 scholars at a time, and that he does not expressly mention Oxford. But he, an Orthodox Archbishop, specifically proposes instruction in the doctrine of the Church of England. Sancroft, to whom he addressed his appeal, had already shown his interest in the Greek Church by asking Covel during his Constantinople chaplaincy to enquire into the Orthodox doctrine of the Real Presence. Henry Compton, Bishop of London, to whom – as well as to the King – Sancroft was asked by Georgirenes to communicated the scheme, had already sponsored Georgirenes' appeal for building the Greek church in Soho Fields. Thus the highest levels of the Anglican hierarchy may

---

5   A. Wood, *Life and Times,* ed. Clark, II, 379.
6   MS. Tanner 33, f. 57; printed in Williams, *The Orthodox Church of the East in the Eighteenth Century,* lxvi.

well have shown sympathy for the proposal. Nothing more, however, is known of it for the next ten years.

Woodroffe's Scheme

Then early in 1692 the Scheme reappears. 'We have often the company of Dr Woodrof,' writes Edward Harley to his father.[7] 'The Doctor is indeavouring to revive an old designe of bringing over yong Greek youthes to be educated in the knowledge of the scriptures. If it take efect according as it is said, it may be of great use.' Dr Benjamin Woodroffe, Canon of Christ Church, was also rector of St Bartholomew near the Royal Exchange. For a short time in 1688 he had been Dean of Christ Church, being nominated by James II (to whom he had been chaplain twenty years before) but replaced by Dean Aldrich under William III. His interest in the Greek Church can be traced as far back as his twenties. Thus in 1668–9 he was acquainted with one Jeremias Germanos at Oxford, who told everyone that the Greek Church did not believe in Transubstantiation. When Covel sailed to Constantinople in 1670, Woodroffe commissioned him to deliver a present of books to this Greek priest.[8] It may well be that Woodroffe was behind the scheme mentioned by Anthony Wood as discussed in Oxford in 1677, for creating a Greek College at Gloucester Hall. And he may well have co-operated with Georgirenes, though if he did so, he was later disillusioned.[9]

Gloucester Hall had been for years in a state of fearful decay. Under the principalship of Dr. Byrom Eaton it had

---

7   Portland MS., Harley Papers, xvi, 30 January 1692. See illustration 4.
8   J. Covel, *Some Account of the present Greek Church* (1722), 1.
9   See Appendix A, note (*b*).

become empty of students, and its buildings had fallen into disrepair – one might say, ruin. Now, on 15 August 1692, Woodroffe was admitted as Principal. Workmen began repairs on the fabric immediately. The 15th of August was a Monday, and on the following Saturday the new Principal was writing to Harley about the Greek Scheme, wishing to interest the Levant Company in it as soon as possible and hoping that when the new Ambassador to the Porte, Lord Paget, appoints his chaplain, his choice will be a man capable of forwarding the scheme.[10] As a matter of fact, before the month of August was out, Woodroffe appeared before the Court of the Levant Company, explained the scheme, and obtained the Court's grant of free passage on the Company's ships for Greek students. And within six weeks of Woodroffe's institution, his scheme for a Greek College at the Hall is noted by Luttrell. '20 famous Grecians,' says Luttrell, 'are sent for from Antioch and Constantinople etc. to reside there.'[11] No one can accuse Woodroffe of lack of energy.

The publicity given so quickly to the scheme suggests that a printed pamphlet may already have been distributed. Indeed the printed prospectus, entitled *A Model of a College to be settled in the University for the Education of some Youths of the Greek Church*, was probably issued by Woodroffe about this time.[12] It proposes that twenty youths, who must be between the ages of 14 and 20, be trained under Woodroffe to be preachers and schoolmasters in their own country. The lines of their training and discipline are laid down. The College, it is announced, will be supported by voluntary contributions.

Such was the prospectus. Gloucester Hall was not, of course, intended to be nothing but a Greek College. Ordinary

---

10   Portland MS., Harley Papers, XVI, 21 August 1692.

11   N. Luttrell, *A Brief Historical Relation of State Affairs* (1857), II, 583.

12   See Appendix A.

Oxford undergraduates were to reside there too. From a project for the Hall which Woodroffe sent to Harley in February 1693, we see that while the Greeks were to be accommodated in one part of the Hall and the ordinary undergraduates in another, both parties were to share in the use of Hall, Chapel and Library.[13]

The Greek scheme then was off to a flying start. But after this nothing seems to have happened for a long time. A lampoon in Latin elegiac verse, contrasting Gloucester Hall with an Oxford ale-house called Rump Hall, makes fun of the fact that the Greek scheme is hanging fire and the students show no signs of coming. This is in June 1693.

> [...] *Dum pergraecatur parvae chorus ebrius aulae*
> *Ah! major Graecis indiget aula suis;*
> *Hinc ait, insultans, vulgus Rumpense 'Calendas*
> *Induet ad Graecas Graeca iuventa togam'.*[14]

In fact the first students to receive free passage from the Company did not arrive till early in 1699.

There is, however, trace of one single Greek at Gloucester Hall much earlier than that. On 23 July 1693 Woodroffe writes to Mr. John Houghton, Apothecary in St. Bartholomew's Lane near the Royal Exchange, evidently an old parishioner of his, about a certain Dionysius the Grecian who will call at his house for a letter.[15] Dionysius, who, he says, has been to Houghton's house with him in the past, is now ready to come down to Oxford. Woodroffe wants Dionysius either to come to him in Essex – the letter is dated from 'Ryse' near Bishop's Stortford – and then travel with his party to Oxford when they return, or else to let him have his address so that

---

13   Portland MS., Harley Papers, xvii, 11 February 1693.
14   Wood, *op. cit.*, iii, 426
15   Sloane MS. 4276, f. 208.

Woodroffe can announce their return to Oxford, and Dionysius come down by the 'flying Coach'. Evidently the Greek did reside at Gloucester Hall for at least the academic year 1693–1694; for on 21 June 1694 Woodroffe writes to the scholar Thomas Smith of Magdalen whom we have already had occasion to mention, asking that he may retain for another three weeks or so some books which Smith has lent him,

> there being severall things I think necessary to acquainte Dionysius the Greeke with, who is still with us here in Oxford, and having gone thorow his Studies in Mathematicks, of which he seemed to be most desirous, hath promised seriously to give me a good part of the time he yet intends to spend here, in order to the acquainting him with such Theological Authors, especially in Greek, which may make him the more usefull in his own Country at his Return.[16]

The reference to Dionysius's mathematical studies seems to show that he was not following the curriculum laid down in the *Model*. He was an older man, already in priest's orders, and had no doubt come to Oxford independently of the scheme. Woodroffe clearly encouraged foreigners to come to Gloucester Hall. His first student was a Frenchman. And in Hungary, in 1703, Edmund Chishull met a young Hungarian at Debrecen, by name Paul Gyöngyösi, who had recently resided at Gloucester Hall.[17]

While Dionysius was at Gloucester Hall, Woodroffe wrote a letter in Greek to Callinicus, Patriarch of Constantinople, explaining the scheme to him.[18] The programme of studies is now more ambitious. 'First the Latin, Greek and Hebrew tongues; then philosophy of all kinds; by turns, medicine and mathematics; further, theology, as purely set down in the Gospel, and set forth in the ancient canons and

---

16   MS. Smith 54, f. 169.
17   E. Chishull. *Travels in Turkey and back to England* (1747), 106.
18   Lambeth MS. 951, f. 1.

Greek fathers; or anything else, or in any other way, acceptable to you, we will make it our business to teach.' Possibly
Dionysius's influence is to be suspected in this extension of
the curriculum to medicine and mathematics. From this letter
and from the *Model* we can see how the whole process of
recruitment and transport was planned. The four Patriarchs
were to send twenty youths, five from each Patriarchate, or in
any other proportion they pleased, giving the names and
addresses to the Levant Company's three chaplains (Constantinople, Smyrna and Aleppo), together with particulars of how
they are to be taken to the Company's ships. In this letter a
knowledge of Syrian is added to the list of desirable quali-
fications. The Levant Company will bring the students to
London, where Woodroffe will meet them, present them to
the Bishop of London, and take them to Oxford.

The matter still moved very slowly. On 16 August 1695
Woodroffe wrote to Mr. Edward Williams, the Chaplain at
Constantinople, enclosing copies of a printed scheme and
a single copy of a letter to be communicated to all the
Patriarchs.[19] As these enclosures are not preserved, it is
impossible to tell whether the printed scheme was the same as
the *Model* which we have already discussed; the date of the
Model is not known, and we cannot be sure whether it
precedes the letter to Callinicus in 1694, or not. In this letter
to the Chaplain, Woodroffe shows his awareness of the
difficulties which are likely to arise; and to such objections he
provides answers. He foresees that the recruitment will be
hindered:

    (*a*) by the Turks, who will not wish to lose the annual poll
        tax which the students would avoid by being abroad;
    (*b*) by the youths' relations, who will not wish to lose
        wage earners;

---

19   Appendix B, 1.

(c) by the Greek ecclesiastical authorities, who will be suspicious of foreign education.

His answers to the objections are:

(a) the subscribers will pay the Turkish poll tax on behalf of the students;

(b) the education, particularly in medicine and mathematics, will make the students able to earn more;

(c) the Greek Church is less suspicious of the Church of England than of any other church.

He then proceeds to answer another objection: 'How shall they be maintained when they return?' Although such provision is unlikely to be needed, because surely the Greek hierarchy will give good preferment to those whom it has sent abroad for study, the subscribers will guarantee it where they judge it necessary. He adds that as good a provision as any might be to make presents to the Greek ecclesiastical authorities! He is confident that the English can do more for the Greek religion than the French have lately done.

He adds that he waited on Lord Paget before he left England in 1692, and that the Ambassador promised support for the scheme. 'Our earnest request,' he tells Williams,

> is that one way or another you would please [...] to take care that such a number of youths as we propose may be found out; the number is not so great, but that in several places they may be gathered up and sent on board in severall places as chance-passengers; for their countrey is not so straight a prison, but that daily many of them seek their liberty abroad and return again at their pleasure to their own homes.

He concludes by emphasising that he writes at the direction of the Bishop of London.

This letter was eventually answered by Paget himself. On 1 August 1696 he wrote to Woodroffe explaining that in the present state of the Greek Church the authorities were unable to send young Greeks abroad on their own initiative, as the Porte would never permit it. He had been told this by Dositheus, Patriarch of Jerusalem ('a discret, well-temperd man'), who had seemed to appreciate Woodroffe's good intentions; and the statement had been confirmed by the Chief Dragoman of the Porte, Alexander Mavrocordati, who suggested that the only way to get Greek students to Oxford would be to persuade individual fathers to send their sons, leaving the church out of the question. Callinicus, Patriarch of Constantinople ('a rougher man' than Dositheus), had been much less sympathetic.[20]

The original form of the scheme having thus proved impracticable, the way was open for Paget to propose an alternative. This was to approach individuals and suggest that they send their sons to Oxford, with a view to their becoming interpreters in the service of the Levant Company. He was evidently a little doubtful whether the English churchmen would approve this change, and in writing to Woodroffe and to the Bishop of London on 8 January 1697, he tactfully lays little stress on the training of interpreters, and says that his proposal in only another way of obtaining the original object. He has persuaded the Resident of the Prince of Wallachia to send his son and a near relation to Oxford.[21] The Wallachian Resident at the porte at this time appears to have been a Greek named Janachi Porfirita. Whether the two young men ever came to Oxford, and if so, whether they are identical with students whose names we already know, are questions which it seems impossible to answer.

---

20   Appendix B, 2.
21   Appendix B, 3 and 4.

The Greek College, 1699–1705

At length, on 11 September 1698, Woodroffe, writing to his former pupil, John Ellis, Under-Secretary of State, says cautiously that it is not improbable 'that we shall have Greeks sent to study here, according to our former designe for the Education of some youths of that Church, which hath hitherto been disappointed, but is likely in a short time to take effect'[22] This expectation was fulfilled; in the following February the first batch of Greek students arrived from Smyrna. We may suppose that their appearance in Oxford caused comment; for the regulations laid down that they should wear 'the gravest habit worn in their own country', and they did in fact wear it both in Oxford and elsewhere. The original batch numbered five. Early in the following year more were expected, and seem in fact to have arrived. It would be interesting to know more of their ordinary everyday life at Oxford; as it is, we hear of them chiefly in connection with scandals, the first of which is known to us only from a sentence in a letter of William Adams to Thomas Tanner (4 May 1699): 'The young Graecians are run away from Gloster Hall.'[23] I think we may guess that Woodroffe did appoint two tutors for them, as laid down in the *Model*, and that these two men were Mr. Roger Bourchier and Mr. Edward Eden. They take part in a disputation with two of the Greeks, which Woodroffe published in 1704; and Alexander Helladius, one of the later students, actually refers in his book to 'Mr. Roger Bourchier, my most reverend tutor in Mathematics and English'.[24] Bourchier and Eden both took

---

22   Add. MS. 28883, f. 151.
23   J. A. W. Bennett, 'Oxford in 1699' in *Oxoniensia*, IV (1939), 149.
24   *Status praesens Ecclesiae Graecae* (1714), 192.

their B.A. from Gloucester Hall in 1699, and were therefore just the sort of people Woodroffe would be likely to choose to teach his newly-arrived Greeks. Fifteen years later, when Gloucester Hall became Worcester College, Bourchier was one of the first fellows on the new foundation.

At what stage the Reverend Edward Stephens became interested in the Greek students, it is impossible to determine. He was originally a lawyer, became ordained at a fairly advanced age, and lodged in Oxford for a couple of years, possibly about 1701. His passionate desire for the reunion of Christendom is likely to have been regarded as eccentric by nearly all other Anglicans of his day. He persuaded Neophytus, Archbishop of Philippopolis, to admit him to communion with the Orthodox Church, and he used to celebrate the Eucharist according to the Greek rite; so he may well have been interested in the college long before we first hear of him helping two of its students. Neophytus visited Oxford to receive the honorary degree of D.D. The day of its conferment (2 September 1701) must have been a great one for Woodroffe. He delivered a speech of welcome, and we may imagine that he proudly displayed Gloucester Hall and its Greeks to the visitor. Edward Thwaites, the Anglo-Saxon scholar, wrote a glowing account of the University solemnities, but could not resist a dig at the Principal of Gloucester Hall: 'Indeed Dr. Woodroffe has exerted himself and shown us that he does understand Greek.'

An even greater day perhaps was in August 1702, when Queen Anne, stopping in Oxford on her way from Windsor to Bath, heard among the many addresses presented to her an ode in Greek hexameters spoken by the senior Greek student, Simon Homerus. The ode was printed by Woodroffe along with the disputation mentioned above.

But trouble was brewing. The scheme did not escape the notice of the Jesuits. One of them, a Greek from Crete named

Nicolaus Comnenus Papadopolus, who had been converted to the Roman Church and who taught Canon Law at the University of Padua, refers to it in the preface to his book *Praenotationes Mystagogicae*, 1697, and says that it will administer noxious draughts of heresy to the Greeks, though he charitably describes Woodroffe as 'a good man, but excessively simple'. Emissaries of the Roman Church were in contact with the Greek students. Late in 1702 or early in 1703 the brothers George and John Aptal, and another student named Stephen Constantine, ran away to Holland.[25] The ringleader was Stephen Constantine – described by Helladius as handsome, clever and rich – who had not been, like the Aptals, one of the original entry of 1699. He was tempted away by the promise of better accommodation at Paris, where Louis XIV had been persuaded to start a Greek College. The Aptal brothers seem rather to have looked forward to getting home quickly. But it is said to have been the nefarious Deacon Seraphim who, working behind the scenes, sold them to the missionaries of the Propaganda. Deacon Seraphim of Mitylene, translator of a Modern Greek version of the New Testament published in London in 1703, is portrayed by Helladius in the most lurid colours. Whether or not he was ever a member of the College, he was in Oxford in 1701 (according to Helladius, whose dating is not above suspicion), and abused the favour of Woodroffe.[26] Stephens says that the three students were approached by a person belonging to the chapel of the Portuguese Ambassador in London. Along the network of Roman agents – to put the matter in the melodramatic light in which Stephens saw it – the trio was passed

---

25   The sources for this escapade are Helladius, ch. xvi; S.P. T1/87, f. 142 (printed in *Calendar of Treasury Papers, 1702/1707,* 207); and E. Stephens, [see Appendix F].

26   Helladius, 253, 279.

on to Brussels, where the Papal Internuncio interviewed them, and was disappointed not to find among them the eldest of the Oxford Greeks, Simon Homerus. 'Homer is not here!' cried the Internuncio, and again, as he pointed at Stephen Constantine, 'That is not Homer!' After a stay of five months at the Irish College at Louvain, where an attempt was made to convert them to the Roman faith, the three students were sent to Paris, and then put on their way to Rome to be presented to the Pope. The brothers Aptal now began to lose their nerve; at Genoa they sought out the English Consul and got him to ship them back to England. Constantine, however, went on to Rome, confident that he had the whip hand of the Romans. He threatened that if they would not let him go, he would write to his stepfather at Smyrna to use his influence with the Pasha for reprisals on the Roman missionaries there. He said he was going to follow in the footsteps of his step-father, the richest merchant in Smyrna, and had not intention whatever of being ordained; and to give colour to his asser-tion, he threw himself into the pursuit of wine, women and gambling. Stephen Constantine never returned to England. But the Aptal brothers did, and in October 1703 arrived in London, where they stayed with Edward Stephens. Wood-roffe welcomed the prodigals, and wrote off to their fellow-students a letter in Greek full of rejoicing, exhortation, and dark references to 'that loathsome one' and his 'scandal of scandals', phrases which Helladius explains as referring to Seraphim. (By this time Seraphim had fled to Holland, because – according to Helladius – he had violated a small girl in London.) The Levant Company made arrangements for the Aptals to sail to Smyrna, and even paid their debt when they were arrested at Gravesend for the cost of their voyage to England from Leghorn. While they were lodging with Stephens, one of them received a letter from an acquaintance in the Greek College at Rome, delivered by a member of the

Florentine Envoy's suite. By this letter and the person who brought it, an attempt was made to persuade the recipient to go to Rome; but under Stephens's direction he wrote an answer asking some awkward questions, to which he received no reply. The Aptal brothers probably returned to Smyrna in 1704.

Meanwhile, in the spring of 1703, Lord Paget had reached England with more students in his suite, after a leisurely journey overland from Constantinople. Woodroffe wrote to him (25 April), telling him of the difficulties into which the scheme had come because it had not received adequate financial support and because the Roman church was seeking to lure the students away to Paris.[27] He refers briefly to the escapade of the three runaways, who were at the time of writing in France. Particularly interesting is his report of the progress of his students.

> The ancient Greek, which they were utter strangers to, when they came first hither, they read and understand as their Mother-Tongue; the Latin they understand so well, as to be able to discourse and dispute in that tongue. The English they speak as if they were Natives. In the Hebrew they are moderate proficients. They perform all exercises promiscuously with our Under-graduates and Batchelors of Arts, and some of them dispute with us in Divinity in the Chappel. They are well entred in all the Systems of Philosophy and in the Mathematicks, and perform all exercises indifferently either in Greek or Latin, &c.'

From this it seems that the original stipulation for Ancient Greek as an entrance qualification had been waived. Another stipulation that was waived in 1703, if not before, was the maximum age of twenty for entrants.

There seem to have been three students who came over in Lord Paget's suite. One was Francis Prossalentis of Corfu, who had his 25th birthday soon after reaching England. He

---

27   Appendix B, 5.

was accompanied by a student, junior to himself, Alexander Helladius, who calls Prossalentis his 'Praeceptor'. This precocious youth wrote an epic on the war between the Ottoman and Hapsburg Empires and on his own Odyssey across Europe; when he wished to submit it to the Oxford University Press, Prossalentis forbade him. In later life he was to publish a chatty little book called *Status Praesens Ecclesiae Graecae*, which yields a great deal of information about Greek students in Western Europe in the early eighteenth century. The third Greek, Eustathius Placicus, a doctor, must have joined the party at Bucharest, where Paget in his progress across Europe was received with great honour by Constantine Brâncoveanu, the reigning Prince of Wallachia. Placicus was one of Brâncoveanu's court physicians.

These were probably the last students to join the College. The escapade of the three runaways had damaged its reputation; the scandal of Seraphim, though less closely connected, must also have created an unfavourable atmosphere. And at least one of the students, namely Prossalentis, complains of the scrappiness of their instruction. 'First they would learn grammar for a few days, then physics for five or six, then logic, then grammar again, then mathematics – in short, in the space of five or six months they read all branches of knowledge and exhaust none.'[28] Thus it came about that when the students found that a group of Protestants in Saxony offered them better conditions of accommodation and study, they began to leave Oxford and enrol themselves at the University of Halle. Helladius says of two friends of his, Matthew of Paros and Theodore Basilius of the Black Sea, that 'spurning Britain they made for Halle' (where they enrolled in March 1704). This sounds as though they too may have been for a while at

---

28 Prossalentis, Ὁ αἱρετικὸς διδάσκαλος ὑπο τοῦ ὀρθοδόξου μαθητοῦ ἐλεγχόμενος (1862), 11.

Gloucester Hall; Stephens speaks of students staying 'not many months' because of the unsatisfactory arrangements. Eustathius Placicus enrolled at Halle in October 1705, and Helladius himself went there in the end.

By 1704 the Greek scheme was clearly a failure. On 6 July the Levant Company told Sir Robert Sutton, Paget's successor in the Embassy, that they would not accept any more students.[29] That the Company and their Ambassadors should train 'druggermen' at Oxford was, as we have seen, Paget's idea; it was certainly not part of the conception of those who originated the scheme for a Greek college. It is strange, as Professor A. C. Wood has pointed out, that the Company throughout the 250 years of its existence never made a practice of training Englishmen to be its interpreters.[30]

Finally, in 1705, the Greek Church put a veto on students. Jeremias Xantheus, Registrar of the Greek Church at Constantinople, wrote to Stephens: 'The irregular life of some priests and laymen of the Greek Church living in London has greatly disturbed the Church. Therefore the Church has also prevented those who wish to go and study at Oxford.'[31] Was this the shadow of Seraphim's proligacy again? To put the finishing stroke to the College, Woodroffe was now in financial difficulties, difficulties which were eventually to land him in the Fleet Prison; probably, as Barker says, he was the only ex-Dean of Christ Church to suffer that fate. Neither voluntary subscriptions nor Royal bounty had ever been forthcoming in sufficient sums; he claimed only to have received £400 pounds from the Crown, and to have spent between £2,000 and £3,000 on the education and expenses of the Greeks. Some of this estimate is undoubtedly to be

---

29   S.P. 105/115, 6 July 1704.
30   *History of the Levant Company* (1935), 226–227.
31   Lambeth MS. 933, f. 49. See appendix F.

accounted for by his expenditure on a building opposite the gates of Gloucester Hall which he erected for the accommodation of Greek students. This building, according to Hearne in 1714, was of such slight construction that up to that date at least, it had never been inhabited;[32] but it was not pulled down until 1806. Nicknamed 'Woodroffe's Folly', it was for a century, as Barker says, the only memorial of the Greek scheme.

Edward Stephens made a valiant attempt to save something from the wreck in 1705, printing a leaflet in which he said: 'There is no need for a College at Oxford, nor of building a Church here, but a good House well situated, with convenient Lodgings for some Greek Clergymen and young Scholars, and a decent Oratory here in London, may be so order'd, as to serve all that is necessary and more to the Satisfaction of the Greeks.' He sent this *Proposal* to the Anglican Bishops; with the copy at Lambeth there is what appears to be a covering letter, dated 12 December 1705.[33] But the aged Stephens had not enough time left to achieve any result, for he died four months later. And so the College faded away. Prossalentis and Placicus had sailed to Holland in the summer of 1705, the former staying for some time in Amsterdam, where in the following year he published his little book, *The Heretic Teacher Cross-examined by his Orthodox Pupil*, a work in which, as Hearne says, 'he falls upon Dr. Woodroffe very smartly'. Hearne was told about the book by one of the Grecians of Gloucester Hall, so there was evidently still one in Oxford at that date (15 March 1707).[34] The solitary survivor may have been Helladius. In which case, when Helladius too departed for the Continent nothing was left of the scheme but 'Woodroffe's Folly'.

---

32   *Collections* (O.H.S.), II, 276–277; IV, 349. See illustration 6.
33   Lambeth MS. 929, f. 131.
34   Op. cit., I, 339.

Reflections on the Failure of the College

Some of the causes have already been noted; lack of financial support is clearly an important one. But how far is the fundamental cause to be found in the deficiencies of Woodroffe's own personality? Barker points out that the contemporary judgments on Woodroffe are mostly hostile, and ascribes this in great part to the dislike inspired in contemporaries by Woodroffe's self-advertisement. His intellectual ability, at any rate in languages, was not seriously denied. Was he then just a clever adventurer? If the word 'adventurer' implies superficiality and lack of principle, that seems a very unfair judgment. That he was a careerist, we may allow. And, of course, one aspect of this was certain to make him very unpopular in Oxford during the last decade of the seventeenth century and the first of the eighteenth: namely, the fact that he, the nominee of James II for the Deanery of Christ Church, should so readily accept the Glorious Revolution. In an Oxford largely Non-Juring and Jacobite, such a man was bound to be disliked. Add to this that he was making an experiment in education, and what is more, in the education of foreigners; while the mind which is most characteristic of Oxford (I speak *honoris causa*!) is sceptical of educational innovation and rightly vigilant for academic charlatans. I do not think Woodroffe was a charlatan, but he probably appeared to claim more attainments than he indisputably possessed. A man with unconventional ideas, who at the same time has a liking for being conspicuous and occasionally makes a ridiculous exhibition of himself – how little likely is one to forget Humphrey Prideaux's description of Woodroffe, when both men were students of Christ Church, standing at his window in Tom Quad all afternoon, toying with Mrs. Walcup and fanning himself with her fan! – such a man may fairly earn the name of crank, especially when like Woodroffe he lacks practical ability. (Yet Prideaux said in another letter to John Ellis that Woodroffe would make a better bishop than many people thought.) No, the Principal of Gloucester Hall was not a great administrator, nor even a passably good one. Without subscribing to the view that Woodroffe was an adventurer, I would suggest that the failure of the College was partly due to his lack of practical ability, and partly to the fact that his behaviour was such as to alienate the sympathy of those who might have given financial aid.

It seems unjust to accuse Woodroffe, as Barker has done, of a breach of faith, in that he tried to wean his Greek pupils from the doctrines of the Greek Church. The authorities of the Greek Church must have realised that the students would be instructed in Anglican doctrine; Georgirenes had asked for such instruction, and Woodroffe's *Model* had proposed instruction in the controversies between the Greek and Roman Churches, and between the Roman Church and the Protestants, which implies a knowledge of the Anglican position. Assuming that Woodroffe believed that there were doctrinal and not merely liturgical differences between the Greek Church and the Church of England, I suspect that he further believed all such differences to be Romish accretions to Orthodoxy. He may therefore have hoped to introduce his pupils as a Reforming element into the Orthodox Church. But he certainly had not intention of seducing them from their allegiance to the Patriarch; he was not acting like the Roman missionaries, who were proselytising for their Church among Orthodox believers. And in aiming at a Reformation in the Orthodox Church, he would not be guilty of treacherous conduct.

Was the College in fact the pitiful failure that it is usually held to have been? We must admit that it trained very few students, probably ten in all. We must admit too that some of the students behaved very scandalously. In that connexion, let us remember that the selection of students was not easy. The Greek ecclesiastical authorities probably did not exert themselves to choose suitable candidates, and the English diplomatic and consular officials in the Levant were tempted to send young men who would be likely to enter their service as interpreters. This practice was not likely to ensure suitable students for Woodroffe's scheme. And as for his acceptance of the infamous Seraphim, such mistakes may be made in the best academic circles; it is not easy to detect at first sight the charlatans among foreign intellectuals. Woodroffe's fancy ran riot when he pictured the future of his pupils; for proof we have the absurd scene described by Prossalentis, in which the Principal assigned to his young students the various Patriarchal thrones! Gloucester Hall produced no Patriarchs; but at least three of the Greeks – Prossalentis, Helladius, and Placicus – profited greatly by their stay in Oxford, if only because they had access to the Bodleian Library and made good use of it. The contribution of Oxford life to the development of the Greek students is something which we have no means of assessing; but it would be strange if they – and through them their fellow-countrymen – did not receive sufficient benefit for Woodroffe to feel that his efforts had not been wasted.

Alumni of the Greek College

We know for certain the names of ten students. These are: (*a*) the seven who signed the address in verse to Queen Anne, delivered by Simon Homerus on the occasion of her visit to Oxford in August 1702, and later published by Woodroffe together with the disputation about the sufficiency of the Holy Scriptures. They were: Simon Homerus, George Homerus, George Aptal, John Aptal, George Marules, Michael Damiral and Stephen Constantine. (b) The three who travelled in Lord Paget's suite. They were: Francis Prossalentis, Alexander Helladius and Eustathius Placicus.

In addition it is probable that Seraphim of Mitylene, Matthew of Paros and Theodore Basilius of the Black Sea were also at Gloucester Hall. It seems unlikely that the total of alumni exceeded fifteen.[35]

---

35   E. D. Tappe, 'Alumni of the Greek College at Oxford, 1699–1705' in *Notes and Queries*, CC (March 1955), 110–114.

7. The Non-Jurors, Peter the Great, and the Eastern Patriarchs

ANN SHUKMAN

To the memory of my uncle
Steven Runciman

Prologue

In January 1698 Peter the Great, Tsar of Russia, arrived in London on the English leg of his 'Great Embassy', the journey that was to take him through the countries of western Europe in pursuit of new technologies and new ideas. Among the dignitaries who came to greet him in Deptford was a delegation of Anglican bishops, led by Bishop Gilbert Burnet of Salisbury. Though not the most senior, Bishop Burnet was at that time the most influential of the bishops of the Church of England, a favourite at the court of the Protestant monarchs, William and Mary, and a fervent and loquacious spokesman for English Erastianism, the doctrine that the Church should be subject to the State.[1] 'Just as every soul ought to be subject to the higher powers, so I think the Church ought to be

---

1   So named after Thomas Erastus, 1524–1583, whose works became widely read in England at the end of the sixteenth century. Archbishop Thomas Cranmer had been voicing the same ideas during the reign of Henry VIII: see D. MacCulloch, *Thomas Cranmer: A Life* (New Haven: Yale University Press, 1996), 278–280.

subject to the State in everything that is not against natural equity, or the positive laws of God.'[2]

Peter was evidently intrigued by this churchman of novel type, and their relationship soon warmed. By March, Bishop Burnet reported that 'the Czar grows so fond of me that I can hardly get from him', some of their meetings lasting as long as four hours.[3] Their discussions touched on questions of doctrine: the Trinity and the *filioque*. 'I convinced him,' Burnet records, 'that the question of the Procession of the Holy Ghost was a subtilty that ought not to make a schisme in the Church.'[4] They spoke too of the veneration of saints and of icons, but what really awoke Peter's interest was the Bishop's explanation of Church–State relations in England: of the rights of monarchs to govern the Church, to appoint bishops and exact their loyalty, to dispose of ecclesiastical benefices and Church lands. Most probably such ideas were at that time new to Peter, and he certainly would not have heard them so eloquently and authoritatively expressed. Bishop Burnet for his part was flattered and moved by the great ruler's attention, and expressed his sentiments in near-Churchillian rhetoric: 'I could not but adore the depth of the providence of God, that had raised up such a furious man to so absolute authority over so great a part of the world.'

---

2   Burnet to Dodwell, quoted in T. E. S. Clarke and H. C. Foxcroft, *A Life of Gilbert Burnet* (Cambridge: Cambridge University Press, 1907), 453–454.

3   Burnet to Dr Fall, 19 March 1698, quoted in James Cracraft, *The Church Reform of Peter the Great* (Palo Alto: Stanford University Press, 1971), 30. (Cracraft refers to the Bodleian Library's holdings of Burnet's papers, Bodl. MSS. Add. D. 23, f. 10). Peter's friendship with Burnet was also remarked on by the Austrian Resident in London at that time, Johann Philipp Hoffmann, see Cracraft, ibid.

4   Ibid. Burnet's spelling.

Significantly, perhaps, Bishop Burnet did not find so ready an ear with Peter's chaplain who seems to have been of a more typically traditional Orthodox cast of mind: 'The Czar's priest is come over,' the Bishop reported, 'who is truly a holy man, and more learned than I could have imagined, but thinks it a great piece of religion to be no wiser than his fathers, and therefore cannot bear the thought of imagining that anything among them can want amendment.'[5]

On his return to Russia after the Great Embassy Peter's energies were taken up with other matters, wars and the building of his new capital, and he made no 'amendments' to the Russian Church. In the early 1720s, however, the Tsar was in a position to impose reforms on the Russian Church, reforms which had the effect of taking away the independence of the Church and making it subservient to the State, and, for good or ill, determined the character and the organisation of the Russian Church for the next two hundred years. Bishop Burnet, however, died in 1715 and so did not live to see the fruit of his discussions.

The Non-Jurors and the Eastern Patriarchs

The Erastian ideal of the essential bond between Church and State, of which Bishop Burnet was so confident an apologist, like any ideology, had to face the realities of lived religion, of personal conscience and honest disagreement. England since the Toleration Act of 1689 had become a land of relative religious pluralism. Bishop Burnet, however, was known as the foe of all those who could not or would not share his views:

---

5   Burnet to Fall, 5 April 1698, quoted in Cracraft, *Church Reform*, 33–34.

Calvinists, Papists, High Churchmen, Puritans, and, naturally, that splinter group from the Church of England, the Non-Jurors. The Non-Juring clergy, who may have numbered as many as 600, together with the many laity who followed them, felt themselves in conscience unable in 1688 to sign the oath of allegiance to William and Mary on the grounds that they had given their pledge to the ousted Stuart king, James II. They included in their number the then Archbishop of Canterbury, William Sancroft, and the Bishop of Bath and Wells, the saintly Thomas Ken. Theirs was not a political movement, though later they may have been implicated in the Jacobite cause. They sought rather to live with integrity within the Anglican faith into which they had been born and which they continued to serve, though outside the structures of the Established Church of England.

By 1716 the Non-Jurors had lost a number of their senior members through death, and, to outward appearances at least, had become a group uncertain of their identity and riven by disagreements.[6] Their leading members, however, among whom Thomas Brett was at this time the chief, remained

6   On the Non-Jurors, see Thomas Lathbury, *A History of the Non-Jurors, their Controversies and Writings* (London, 1845); G. Williams, *The Orthodox Church of the East in the XVIIIth Century, being the Correspondence between the Eastern Patriarchs and the Nonjuring Bishops* (London, 1868); J. H. Overton, *The Non-Jurors: Their Lives, Principles and Writings* (London, 1902). On the Non-Jurors and the Greek Church, see Steven Runciman, *The Great Church in Captivity: A Study of the Patriarchate of Constantinople from the Eve of the Turkish Conquest to the Greek War of Independence* (Cambridge: Cambridge University Press, 1968), ch. 7: 'The Church and the Churches: the Anglican Experiment', especially 310–318. On the Non-Jurors and the Russian Church, see Steven Runciman, 'The British Non-Jurors and the Russian Church', in Andrew Blane, ed., *The Ecumenical World of Orthodox Civilization. Russia and Orthodoxy: volume III. Essays in Honor of Georges Florovsky* (The Hague: Mouton, 1973), 155–161.

serious in their adherence to what they regarded as the Tradition. Like their now departed leader, Thomas Ken, they saw themselves as heirs to the Undivided Church, when East and West were one. They looked back to the roots of the Church in Britain before the Reformation, and 'before ever they were made subject to the Bishop of Rome and that Church', in fact to the Christian Tradition they had received, so they believed, 'from such as came forth from the Church of Jerusalem'; this was the faith 'deliver'd by the Apostles, and explain'd in the Councils of Nice and Constantinople'. Seeking affirmation of their identity they opened negotiations with the Greek Orthodox Church, believing that it was to this faith that they, 'the Catholick remnant of the British Churches', should be united 'as part of the Catholick Church in communion with the Apostles, with the holy Fathers of those Councils, and with their Successors.'[7]

Negotiations were opened through the mediation of Arsenios, Metropolitan of the Thebaid, who had come to London in 1714[8] to raise money for the Patriarchate of Alexandria. In August 1716 the Non-Jurors composed a set of proposals to the four Eastern Patriarchs (Constantinople, Antioch, Jerusalem and Alexandria) outlining what was needed, and what they would be prepared to do, to come to a concordat with the Eastern Church, a concordat being a temporary measure until such time as 'a full and perfect union' could be achieved.[9]

The proposals are of abiding interest for a number of reasons: they summarise the practices and beliefs of the High

---

7   'Proposals of the Nonjurors', London, 18 August 1716, quoted in Williams, *Orthodox Church*, 5–6. All spelling as in the original.

8   See Runciman, *The Great Church*, 311.

9   Ibid. On the group who formulated the proposals, see Runciman, *The Great Church*, 312; Thomas Brett's summary account, together with his description of the ensuing disagreements among the Non-Jurors, is to be found in Williams, *Orthodox Church*, 3–4.

Church of that time; they demonstrate considerable knowledge of Orthodoxy and of the doctrinal differences between
Orthodoxy and Anglicanism, though probably not of the lived
reality of the Church under Ottoman rule; they raise points
about elements of practical church-life – liturgy, prayers and
other practices. Above all they are written not as an intellectual exercise but in the tone of a serious quest to explore
the possibilities of union with another Church, in a 'spirit of
honest simplicity and manly independence' as one commentator has expressed it.[10]

There were 29 points in all. The first twelve are concerned with the general ordering of the Church Universal and
the Non-Jurors' place in it:

> 1. That the Church in Jerusalem be acknowledge as the true
> mother Church whence all other churches have derived.
> 2. That the Bishop of Jerusalem be therefore placed in order
> above all other Christian bishops.
> 3. That the Churches of Antioch, Alexandria and Constantinople,
> with their Bishops be recognised in all their ancient canonical rights,
> privileges and pre-eminences.
> 4. That the Bishop and Patriarch of Constantinople be granted
> equal honour with the Bishop of Rome.
> 5. That the 'Catholick remnant of the British churches' be
> reciprocally acknowledged as part of the Catholic Church in com-
> munion with the Apostles, with the Holy Fathers of the Councils,
> and with their successors.

The next five proposals list what the British 'remnant' would
undertake to do:

> 6. To revive the 'ancient godly discipline of the Church' – which
> they claim to have actually begun to do.
> 7. To establish conformity of worship, in so far as local custom
> and circumstances allow.

---

10   Williams, *Orthodox Church*, xxxv.

8. To restore 'the most ancient English liturgy'.

9. To make translations of the Homilies of St John Chrysostom and other Fathers to be read in our holy assemblies.

10. To pray during public worship for the Bishop of Jerusalem and the other Patriarchs.

The last two points of this first section were:

11. To request the prayers of the Eastern Church for themselves.

12. To request an exchange of letters in order to confirm these acts and agreements.

The curious opening proposal to give primacy to Jerusalem may perhaps be explained by the Non-Jurors' concern with origins, their longing for a return to the Church of the Apostles as a way out of the crisis of identity which their situation had forced on to them. The points about reviving the ancient discipline may refer to the attempt by some but by no means all of the Non-Jurors to live by the liturgical year with its saints days and fast days;[11] while the reference to 'the most ancient English liturgy' could be a reference to the new Communion office which the Non-Jurors had recently composed: this was based on the 1549 Prayer Book and included prayers at the offertory from the liturgy of St Basil, as well as items from the liturgy of St James.[12]

---

11 See for instance the prayer book of Thomas Deacon, *A Complete Collection of Devotions, both Publick and Private Taken from the Apostolic Constitutions, the Ancient Liturgies, and the Common Prayer Book of the Church of England,* 1734.

12 See Henry Broxap, *A Biography of Thomas Deacon* (Manchester: Manchester University Press, 1911), 41–45. Thomas Rattray, who helped translate the Non-Jurors' letter to the Patriarchs into Greek, was later to restore the Liturgy of St James to the Episcopal Church in Scotland, of which he became Primus in 1739. See A. M. Allchin, 'Thomas Rattray: The Eucharist and Unity', *Revista Teologica* (Sibiu, Romania) nos. 3/4, July/December 1996, 144–161.

Then followed twelve points of doctrinal agreement:

1. The twelve articles of the Creed (without the accretions brought in by the Latin Church).
2. The consubstantiality of the Holy Ghost with the Father and the Son.
3. The procession of the Holy Ghost sent forth by the Son from the Father.

To this, however, a rider was added: 'When they [i.e. the Non-Jurors] say in any of their confessions that He is sent forth or proceedeth from the Son, they mean no more than what is, and always has been confessed by the Orthodox Oriental Church, that is from the Father by the Son.'[13]

4. The Holy Ghost did truly speak by the prophets and apostles and is the genuine author of all Scripture.
5. The Holy Ghost assists the Church in right judgement in matters of Faith, as in the Orthodox Councils.
6. The nature and number of the Charismata of the Spirit.
7. There is no other foundation of the Church but Christ alone.
8. Christ alone is the Head of the Church. Since this is so the title 'Head of the Church' should not be assumed by anyone, least of all by any secular person. Bishops under Him have a vicarious headship, 'being thence subject in spirituals to no temporal power upon earth'.

This was of course a crucial point for the Non-Jurors who had broken away from the Established Church on account of its subservience to the monarch. They expressed the hope therefore that the Patriarchs of the Oriental Church would be pleased to signify, 'that they own the independency of the Church in spirituals upon all lay powers, and consequently declare against all lay deprivation'.[14]

---

13   Williams, *Orthodox Church*, 7.
14   Ibid., 7–8.

9. Every Christian should be subject to the Church.

10. The Sacrament should be administered in both kinds.

11. Baptism is necessary for salvation, but the other holy mysteries, though they should be revived and celebrated with reverence, are not so generally necessary.

12. There is no proper Purgatorial Fire. Yet 'none do immediately ascend into the heaven of heavens, but do remain until the resurrection in certain inferior mansions [...] joining in the prayers and praises of the militant Church upon earth, offer'd up in faith."[15]

Finally came the five points 'wherein they cannot, at present, so perfectly agree':[16]

1. Though holding the ancient general Councils in reverence, the canons of the Councils cannot carry the same authority as Scripture.

2. Though the Mother of Our Lord is indeed blessed and highly exalted, being a creature, she should not receive the glory due to God; rather God should be blessed and magnified for the grace and honour He bestowed on her.

3. Though the angels and saints unite with us in our prayers, they should not be directly invoked lest this detract from the Mediation of Jesus Christ.

4. As regards the Eucharist, a divine mystery does indeed take place through the Invocation of the Holy Spirit, and the faithful do indeed receive the Body and Blood of Christ. But how this mystery comes about should be left 'indefinite and undetermined'.

5. As regards images, the writers expressed the fear that the ignorant might be drawn into idolatry, and that the Jews and Mahomedans be offended.

After presenting these five thorny problems the letter ended on an optimistic note: if a concordat could be achieved, then a church, to be named Concordia, should be built in London, under the jurisdiction of the Patriarch of Alexandria. With the Patriarch's approval the 'British Catholics' might

---

15   Williams, *Orthodox Church*, 8–9.

16   Ibid., 9–10.

sometimes hold their services in English. On the other hand, 'if it shall please God to restore the suffering Church of this island and her Bishops to her and their just rights'[17] (a reference perhaps to the hope for a Jacobite restoration), then they would use their best endeavours to ensure that leave be granted for the Greek Bishop to celebrate the Greek rite in St Paul's Cathedral. Best of all would be if one common liturgy could be agreed upon, for 'nothing can more conduce to the establishing of a Union and Communion betwixt both parties on catholick terms.'[18] Finally all endeavours should be made on both sides 'to heal the breaches of Christendom, and to promote and propagate Christian Unanimity and Peace.'[19]

The letter was dated 18 August 1716. The Eastern Patriarchs, meeting in Synod in Constantinople, composed a lively, lengthy but adamant reply, richly larded with Biblical quotations, which, though dated April 1718, was not received in London until the autumn of 1721.[20] The delay was caused by the fact that the Non-Jurors' intermediary, Metropolitan Arsenios, had by this time, after a meeting with Tsar Peter in Holland in 1717, moved to Russia.

The reply was composed by Patriarch Chrysanthos of Jerusalem and signed as well by the Ecumenical Patriarch Jeremias, Patriarch Samuel of Alexandria, and the bishops and clergy assembled in Synod. The answer was courteous but firm:

On the order of the Patriarchates: There could be no change in order of precedence of the Patriarchs. If the British felt drawn to Jerusalem, then let them place themselves directly under the jurisdiction of the Patriarch of Jerusalem.

---

17   Williams, *Orthodox Church,* 10–11.
18   Ibid., 11.
19   Ibid., 11.
20   The Patriarchs' answers to the proposals are printed in Ibid., 15–67.

On the procession of the Holy Ghost: There could be no concession about the procession of the Holy Ghost, Who proceeds
from the Father Alone.

On the question of the Real Presence in the Eucharist: the
Patriarchs gave a lengthy exposition of the doctrine of Transubstantiation.

*On the veneration of the Mother of God, on icons, prayer to the saints
and angels:* the British were simply failing to make the distinction between *latria* – the worship due to God alone, and *dulia*
– the veneration of the creature through whom prayers rise to
the Godhead.

On the liturgy: it should be those of St John Chrysostom and St
Basil.

On the question of the headship of the Church: the Patriarchs
agreed that Christ is the Supreme Head, and that priests and
bishops have power under Him in matters spiritual and ecclesiastical. However the Patriarchs acknowledged the rights of
the secular powers in civil matters of right and wrong, and of
Kings to have supreme power over all their subjects to judge
and punish with justice those who are delinquent, unless it be
in spiritual matters, in which cases the right lies with the
Ecclesiastical Council.

The Orthodox faith, they declared, was pure and unsul-
lied and had remained so from the time of the Apostles and
Holy Fathers. Papists as well as 'Luthero-Calvinists' were
heretics, and the so-called *Confession* of Cyril Lucaris, former
Patriarch of Constantinople, which admitted some Protestant
thinking, was roundly declared to be a forgery.[21] As for their
correspondents, the Non-Jurors, the Patriarchs declared that
'being born and educated in the principles of the Luthero-
Calvinists, and possessed by their prejudices, they tenaciously

---

21   Williams, *Orthodox Church,* 15–22. On Lucaris's *Confession,* ibid. 19–20;
      Runciman, *Great Church,* 276 ff.

adhere to them, like ivy to a tree, and are hardly drawn off. So paint of a deep colour sinking into a garment is almost indelible.'[22]

To strengthen their arguments the Patriarchs appended a copy of the 1672 *Synodical Answer to the Question, What are the Sentiments of the Oriental Church of the Grecian Orthodox; sent to the Lovers of the Greek Church in Britain*,[23] and a further memorandum on the Holy Eucharist dated 1691.[24] However the sentiments expressed at the end of the letter echoed those of the Non-Jurors: they wrote of their 'spiritual joy and exultation' at the prospect of public services in St Paul's Cathedral, and 'we rejoice and leap for joy, and are exceedingly transported, when we see your eager desire to unite and agree with the pious Oriental Church'.[25]

The Non-Jurors responded in May 1722. The tone of the letter was conciliatory though not subservient. In most things they agreed with the Orthodox Patriarchs, but there remained two areas of disagreement: the invocation of saints and angels and the worship of images, and the doctrine of transubstantiation. On these points they offered long and learned arguments with many Patristic references. The letter concludes:

> And thus having represented the Differences between us, we are now to suggest a Temper, and offer a Compromise. If therefore, our Liberty is left us in the instances above-mentioned; If the Oriental Patriarchs, Bishops &c. will authentically declare us not obliged to the Invocation of Saints and Angels, the worship of Images, nor the Adoration of the Host; If they please publickly and authoritatively by an Instrument signed by them, to pronounce us perfectly disengaged in these particulars; disengaged we say, at home and abroad, in

---

22 Williams, *Orthodox Church*, 48.
23 Ibid., 67–76. Original spelling.
24 Ibid., 76–83.
25 Ibid., 65–66.

their Churches and in our own: These relaxing concessions allow'd, we hope may answer the Overtures on both sides, and conciliate an Union.[26]

The response from the Orthodox came in 1723. It was terse and uncompromising: the British should submit on all points 'with sincerity and obedience, and without any scruple or dispute. And this is a sufficient Answer to what you have written'.[27] The letter included extracts from the authoritative Confession of Dositheus ratified at the Synod of Bethlehem of 1672.[28]

A year later the Archbishop of Canterbury, William Wake, got wind of the negotiations going on between the Non-Jurors and the Eastern Patriarchs and wrote to Patriarch Chrysanthos of Jerusalem denouncing the Non-Jurors as schismatics who were in no way representative of the Church of England. The correspondence with the Eastern Patriarchs thus came abruptly to an end. But that was not quite the end of the story.

Epilogue

In 1717 Metropolitan Arsenios of the Thebaid, who had expedited the sending of the Non-Jurors' first letter to the Orthodox Patriarchs the year before, left London for Holland to seek an interview with Peter the Great who was on his way home from a state visit to Paris. His chief purpose was to request funds from the Tsar for the building of a Greek

26   Williams, *Orthodox Church*, 100–101.
27   Ibid., 119.
28   On the *Confession of Dositheus,* see Runciman, *Great Church,* 350–353.

church in London; however it is likely that he also spoke to the Tsar about the British 'Catholick remnant' who were seeking a concordat with the Orthodox Church,[29] for in the autumn of the same year the Non-Jurors wrote to Tsar Peter, presumably on Arsenios's advice, seeking the Tsar's help in the matter of a union.[30] The letter was taken to Russia by Arsenios's attendant, the Proto-Syncellos James, who seems to have been charged with the arrangements for Arsenios's stay in that country. At any rate by 1721 Arsenios was living in St Petersburg, and this was the reason why the reply of the Patriarchs to the Non-Jurors had taken nearly three years to arrive back in London, having travelled via Russia.[31]

The Patriarchs' first response had been received in London together with a covering letter from Arsenios, to whom the Non-Jurors immediately responded with their gratitude, adding:

> Our Hopes of a happy Conclusion in this Affair are encreased by the generous Encouragement which, we are glad to understand, His Imperial Majesty [i.e. Tsar Peter] is graciously pleased to give it, and which will redound to the immortalising of his Name. And we are

---

29   Runciman, 'The British Non-Jurors', 157.

30   Williams, *Orthodox Church*, 12.

31   The messenger was the Proto-Syncellos James who arrived in Constantinople in 1717 and set off on his return journey with the Patriarchs' answer in October 1718 via Smyrna. He eventually arrived back in Holland in April 1719, having survived shipwreck and piratical attacks. In July he followed Arsenios to Russia where he stayed until 1721. ('Kratkaia Tserkovnaia Letopis', sostavlennaia po khraniashchimsia arkhivnym dannym i chernovym zapisiam, ostavlennym byvshim nastoiatelem o. Ioannom Leliukhinym' ['Brief Church Chronicle', compiled from archive material and notes by the former Rector, Fr Ioann Leliukhin], typescript extract sent to Steven Runciman by Igor Vinogradoff, with accompanying letter, 24 January 1966).

very sensible, that we owe his Majesty's being rightly apprised of this Affair to your faithfull Representation of it to him. [32]

On the same day, 30 May 1722, the Non-Jurors despatched a letter to the Governing Synod of the Church in Russia, asking them to forward a copy of their response to the Patriarchs, and to beg the Tsar to lend his authority, and assist financially, in the transmission of the document. The following day they wrote to the Chancellor of Russia asking him to continue to grant them his favour. On 9 September the messenger carrying these letters, the Proto-Syncellos James, wrote to report his safe arrival in St Petersburg. By November Metropolitan Arsenios had received the letter in Moscow, but reported that the Tsar was away in Astrakhan. Eventually in August 1723 Arsenios wrote to describe the joy with which the correspondence had been received by Tsar and Synod:

> How much his most Sacred Majesty's Joy was augmented, after his Return from Persia, and how acceptable this Matter was to him, I suppose the Governing Council [Synod] has told you in their Letters,[33] and acquainted you that his Majesty has freely promised to promote the Affair, that it may have the wished for Conclusion.[34]

Arsenios, however, added the request that two representatives of the Non-Jurors should travel to Russia in order to finalise the agreement. The same request came from the Synod in February 1724. The Non-Jurors did indeed select two of their number to go to Russia, but wrote in July 1724 to Arsenios, to the Chancellor, and to the Synod to explain that for personal reasons the visit would have to be postponed

---

32   Williams, *Orthodox Church*, 103–104.
33   Letter from the Holy Synod to the Non-Jurors, dated February 1723, Williams, *Orthodox Church*, 114–116.
34   Ibid., 112. For the correspondence with Russia, see Ibid., 102–132.

until the following summer.[35] The delay was fatal to their cause.

What did the Non-Jurors hope to gain from dealing with the Russians? Perhaps they thought the Russian Church authorities would be less intransigent than the Greek Patriarchs; perhaps their warm relations with Metropolitan Arsenios, his encouragement to them, and his evident position of influence in Russia, seemed to offer fruitful possibilities for negotiations. What were Peter the Great's motives in pursuing a possibility of union with a small group of Anglicans? Perhaps the answer to this question lies in the political and diplomatic relations between England and Russia at that period. Peter was opposed to King George I, but needed to trade with England. Possibly he identified the Non-Jurors as a Jacobite group, and, as Runciman has suggested, by encouraging the Non-Jurors, 'Tsar Peter clearly believed that he would be able to show sympathy to an important group in British religious circles while at the same time embarrassing King George's government.'[36] There is no doubt too that Peter was intrigued by the idea of a foothold in London in the form of an Orthodox Church, especially a church to which some Britishers might belong.[37] Perhaps in

---

35   Ibid., 123–128.
36   Runciman, 'The British Non-Jurors', 159.
37   'The Russian Orthodox Church in London was founded in the reign of Peter the Great. Services were held already in 1721. There is some evidence that Peter commanded a church to be built in London "appropriate to the greatness of Russia" but his will was not fulfilled in his lifetime.' 'Brief Church Chronicle', 1. In 1716, according to the 'Chronicle', Prince Kurakin came to London as Russian ambassador. When he learned from Metropolitan Arsenios that the English wanted to build a church where services would be held in three languages (English, Greek and Russian) and which would be under the protection of the Russian Emperor, Kurakin advised Metropolitan Arsenios to go to Holland to meet Tsar Peter, which he did.

this affair we are witnessing another example of Peter's wish to control and manage Church affairs.

What did the Non-Jurors know of the momentous changes which had taken place in the Russian Church in these years? Did they realise that the 'Holy Governing Synod' (established by Peter's *Ecclesiastical Regulation* of 1721) was, in spite of its ecclesiastical-sounding title, a newly formed instrument of the bureaucracy, a ministry for religions, that it was headed by one of Peter's guards officers, Colonel I. V. Boltin, as Procurator-General, and that all of its members, in spite of their resonant ecclesiastical titles, were the personal appointees of the Tsar, chosen for their compliance in his modernising and 'Erastian' policies?[38]

History has many ironies. Perhaps we may be grateful that the Non-Jurors were spared further acquaintance with the realities of the Russian Church by the death of Peter in January 1725 and the indifference of his successor, his widow Catherine, to all matters of Church union: for with Peter's death the negotiations came finally to an end.

Peter ordered Arsenios to come to Russia, while Archimandrite Gennadios, Arsenios's companion, was sent back to England with the promise of a salary of 500 roubles. ('Chronicle', 2). Vinogradoff notes in his accompanying letter: 'The Church inventory of 1749 mentions several English church books (some of them translated from the Greek) a creed in Greek and English for use of "Greeks and *'non-jurors'*" (English word inserted in ms) who wish to join the Greek church.' (Vinogradoff to Runciman, 24 January 1966).

38 See Cracraft, *Church Reform*, passim.

8. 'The Reverence of God's House': The Temple of Solomon and the Architectural Setting for the 'Unbloody Sacrifice'

PETER M. DOLL

The building of a church in Soho for Greek Orthodox inhabitants of London coincided with a time of serious engagement by Anglican scholars with the buildings of the early Greek church. Nevertheless, there is no sign that this new building inspired any particular interest on the part of Anglican architects and liturgical theologians. Rather, as John Barron has shown (see chapter 3), the potential use of the church was constrained by London's paranoid preoccupation with the threat posed by the Popish Plot in 1678. Any Orthodox practice which might be thought to smack of Popery, such as the use of icons or of prayers to the saints, was summarily forbidden. While it is pleasant to think that freedom of worship for the Greeks might have inspired a wider appreciation of Orthodox liturgy and spirituality, it is perhaps more likely that its foreignness would have impeded rather than enhanced such understanding. Whatever might have happened, the failure of Archbishop Georgirenes' project marks a missed opportunity for Anglicans and Orthodox Christians to recognise the extent to which their liturgical and architectural theologies coincided with one another. They shared with one another a deep attachment to the eucharistic theology of the Church Fathers; both located the origin of Christian worship in that of the Temple in Jerusalem and expressed that conviction in the design and use of their church buildings. Although the visual culture of Anglicans was different from that of the Orthodox, it nevertheless expressed theological convictions the two held in common.

Because the character of the Orthodox tradition is more visibly one of unbroken continuity with the early Church, it is appropriate to begin a comparison here. As Alexander Schmemann said in an address to American Episcopalian liturgists, 'It is true that the great names of St Basil and St John Chrysostom are not to be *discovered* in our tradition. They are there. Our liturgy is still deeply "patristic".'[1] The liturgy, together with the Bible 'is the primary source and manifestation of the life of the church and the revelation of eternal truth.'[2] The typological exegesis of the Bible is central to an understanding of the liturgy; the literal and spiritual meanings of the rite are equally important and equally real.

The sense of continuity in Orthodox worship not just with the early Church but also with the Jewish worship in the Temple is especially evident in the design and use of the Byzantine church building.[3] The building is not called a 'church' (*ekklesia*, derived from *synagogi*, gathering) but a 'temple' (*naos*). Its architecture mimics that of the Temple, providing for a gradual access to the focal holy place of the sanctuary. As the Temple was surrounded by courtyards providing increasingly limited access until one reached the

1   Alexander Schmemann, 'The Liturgical Revival and the Orthodox Church' in Massey Hamilton Shepherd, Jr. (ed.) *The Eucharist & Liturgical Renewal* (New York: Oxford University Press, 1960), 118.

2   Paul Meyendorff, 'Eastern Liturgical Theology' in Bernard McGinn and John Meyendorff (eds) *Christian Spirituality* vol. 1 (New York: Crossroad, 1993), 361.

3   This discussion below is based on the lecture '"For the Remission of Sins": Eucharist and Atonement' by Bishop Basil (Osborne) of Sergievo. The Constantinople Lecture, 25 November 2004.

heikhal, the Temple proper, and saw the curtain that separated the *heikhal* from the *dvir*, the Holy of Holies itself, so in the Byzantine church, after proceeding through the narthex and nave, one comes to the icon screen, separating the nave from the sanctuary and the altar and with a curtain that recalls the veil of the Temple. The Temple altar was outdoors because of the blood, flames and smoke of the sacrifices, but the Byzantine altar is inside the sanctuary because the Church's sacrifice is (according to the Orthodox liturgy) a 'reasonable and unbloody worship'.[4] The *menorah* of the Temple is present in the seven-branched candlestick behind the Byzantine altar (cf. Rev. 4.2–5, Is. 11.2), here seen through the filter of St John's vision of the heavenly sanctuary (Rev. 1.12f.). The 'table of shewbread' or of 'the bread of the Presence' (in LXX Exod. 39.36, *tin trapezan tis protheseos*) becomes the *prothesis* or table of preparation.[5] Bishop Basil affirms that the connection between the Liturgy of the Eucharist and the furnishings of the Temple were part of the Eastern tradition at least from the beginning of the third century.

Appropriately enough, it is the Epistle to the Hebrews that provides a crucial link between the worship of the Temple and that of the Church. According to the author of Hebrews, Christ at his Ascension entered the heavenly tabernacle, the same as that revealed by the Lord to Moses on Sinai (Exod. 24–25): 'For Christ did not enter a sanctuary made by human hands, a mere copy of the true one, but he entered into heaven itself, now to appear in the presence of

---

4   *The Orthodox Liturgy, being the Divine Liturgy of S. John Chrysostom and S. Basil the Great.* (London: S.P.C.K. for the Fellowship of SS. Alban and Sergius, 1939), 72.

5   Bishop Basil points out that Origen connected the bread of the Presence with the self-sacrifice of Christ and its commemoration in the Eucharist (*Hom. in Lev.* 13.3, 5).

God on our behalf' (Heb. 9.24). In the Byzantine tradition, the church building represents Christ's bearing our humanity into the heavenly places. As Maximus the Confessor explains in his explication of the Divine Liturgy, the church building is 'an image of the perceptible world as a whole, since it possesses the divine sanctuary as heaven and the beauty of the nave as earth' (*Mystagogia* 3). According to Hebrews, Christ has entered the heavenly sanctuary as great high priest with his own blood to win eternal redemption for his people (Heb. 9.11–14). He pleads his own sacrifice at the heavenly altar. The eucharistic offering of the church on earth is united by God's grace with Christ's heavenly offering; as it is attended by God's people on earth, so it is by his angels in heaven (*Mystagogia* 1). This is the same point as is made by the liturgy's reference to its 'reasonable and unbloody worship' – that through Christ the earthly and the heavenly are united.[6] For the Orthodox Christian, to move in worship from the nave to the sanctuary is to move from the visible to the invisible world and into the heavenly tabernacle.

While it is not possible to include here a full exposition of Orthodox eucharistic theology, it is important to mention some major points of comparison with its Anglican counterpart. The Eastern Church in its understanding of the eucharistic prayer and consecration does not focus simply on the words of institution, as was the case in the Tridentine Roman Catholic Church. Rather it sees the three main sections of the prayer – Thanksgiving, *Anamnesis*, and *Epiclesis* – as parts of an indivisible whole, so that the whole prayer is consecratory, and not any moment within it. The Orthodox

---

6   For a full explication of this important theme, see Kenneth Stevenson, '"The Unbloody Sacrifice": The Origins and Development of a Description of the Eucharist' in Gerard Austin, ed. *Fountain of Life: In Memory of Niels K. Rasmussen, O.P.* (Washington, D.C.: Pastoral Press, 1991), 103–130.

Church also affirms the *reality* of the presence of Christ in the consecrated elements of bread and wine without seeking to explain the *manner* of the change. Finally, the Orthodox believe the Eucharist to be a sacrifice – not as a new sacrifice nor as a repetition of that made by Christ on Calvary, but as a participation in that once-for-all sacrifice. 'The events of Christ's sacrifice – the Incarnation, the Last Supper, the Crucifixion, the Resurrection, the Ascension – are not repeated in the Eucharist, but they are *made present*.'[7] This is not the bloody sacrifice of the old covenant, but the 'unbloody' offering of the new. In these important respects, the Orthodox maintained the teaching of the early Church on the Eucharist, holding on to treasures that much of the Western Church would rediscover only in the Liturgical Movement of the late twentieth century.

While the Orthodox Church has been reckoned to be faithful to its traditions even under oppression, the Anglican Church of the late seventeenth and eighteenth centuries was until recently generally regarded as faithful to nothing more than rationalism, laxity, and Protestant aridity. This facile dismissal, however, has not stood up to the scrutiny of scholarship over the past twenty years.[8] The many reassessments of Georgian Church which acknowledge its vitality and strength have pointed to the significance of an ethos, theology, and polity marked by a powerful sense of identity with the 'primitive' Christian church. As the Roman Catholic historian Eamon Duffy has observed,

---

7   Timothy Ware, *The Orthodox Church* (Harmondsworth: Penguin Books, 1972), 290–294.

8   See, for example, the important summary of recent scholarship in the introduction to John Walsh, Colin Haydon, and Stephen Taylor, eds. *The Church of England c.1689–c.1822: From Toleration to Tractarianism* (Cambridge: Cambridge University Press, 1993).

The magisterial work of Ussher and Pearson on the Ignatian epistles, of Pearson and Fell on Cyprian, and of Bull on the ante-Nicene fathers, each contributed to a deepening sense of the continuity of the church of England with the catholic church of the first centuries. More and more the appeal to antiquity became the criterion of orthodoxy, and in that antiquity Anglicanism found not merely its origins, but, occasionally and increasingly, a mirror image of itself.[9]

This 'patristic mind' in Anglicanism was reflected both in scholarly studies like Joseph Bingham's monumental *Origines Ecclesiasticae; or the Antiquities of the Christian Church* (10 v., 1708–1722)[10] and in popular works for a wider audience, most notably Charles Wheatly's definitive liturgical commentary, *A Rational Illustration of the Book of Common Prayer* (1722). If the Orthodox maintained their strong sense of identity with the early church by means of an unbroken tradition, the Anglican patristic identity was no less powerful for being the fruit of rediscovery.

While Anglican churches of the period have usually been dismissed as mere preaching boxes,[11] architectural historians are slowly beginning to recognise that theological reference to Christian and Jewish antiquity was also mirrored in the

---

9   Eamon Duffy, 'Primitive Christianity Revived; Religious Renewal in Augustan England' in Derek Baker (ed.), *Studies in Church History* 14 (Oxford: Blackwell, 1977), 287–8.

10   John Glen King, an Anglican priest who published a landmark work on the Russian Church in 1772, reported that 'Our learned countryman Bingham is very greatly esteemed by the Russian clergy, and indeed it is astonishing that he should have been able to penetrate so far, by mere dint of reading.' *The Rites and Ceremonies of the Greek Church, Russia, Containing an Account of its Doctrine, Worship, and Discipline.* (London, 1772), x.

11   For a recent example of this fallacy, see James Stevens Curl, *Georgian Architecture* (Newton Abbot: David & Charles, 1993). See also John Summerson, *Georgian London* (Harmondsworth: Penguin Books, 1962), 97.

preoccupations and designs of seventeenth- and eighteenth-century architects. Nigel Yates has pointed out the extent to which architects like Inigo Jones, Wren, James Gibbs and Nicholas Hawksmoor modelled their churches on the form of early Christian basilicas.[12] In a ground-breaking work combining architectural expertise with an open theological sensibility, Pierre du Prey has demonstrated the deep influence that Anglican patristic scholarship had on the architecture of Hawksmoor's London churches.[13] Wren's churches were famously designed as 'auditories', not as auditoriums for the ministry of the word alone, but in the sense that the people were to be able to hear the *whole* service, from pulpit and altar alike.

The Georgian church, then, so long dismissed under the influence of the Gothic and Tractarian revivals, is now being recognised as an object worthy of liturgical as well as architectural study. Indeed these buildings could not have emerged from the sort of liturgical vacuum the eighteenth-century church was long presumed to be. On the contrary, the patristic mind of eighteenth-century Anglicanism was profoundly present in its liturgical scholarship and practice.

---

12   Nigel Yates, *Buildings, Faith, and Worship. The Liturgical Arrangement of Anglican Churches 1600–1900* (Oxford: Clarendon Press, 1991), 4. See also G. W. O. Addleshaw and Frederick Etchells, *The Architectural Setting of Anglican Worship. An Inquiry into the Arrangements for Public Worship in the Church of England from the Reformation to the Present Day* (London: Faber and Faber, 1948), 249. For a more extensive treatment of many of the themes in this essay, see Peter Doll, *After the Primitive Christians: The Eighteenth-Century Anglican Eucharist in its Architectural Setting* (Alcuin Club and the Group for Renewal of Worship Joint Liturgical Study 37. Cambridge: Grove Books, 1997).

13   Pierre de la Ruffinière du Prey, *Hawksmoor's London Churches: Architecture and Theology* (Chicago: University of Chicago Press, 2000).

Anglican interest in early liturgies was keen and discriminating. Their study of the Orthodox liturgies and of the so-called Clementine liturgy of the Eighth Book of the *Apostolic Constitutions* had a critical effect on their interpretation of the communion office of the Book of Common Prayer and bore fruit in the Nonjurors' liturgies of 1718 and 1734 and in the Scottish liturgy of 1764 and its many descendants.[14] Even in the established Church of England, where substantial deviation from the 1662 Prayer Book was not possible, popular devotional manuals and Prayer Book commentaries expounded a sacramental theology drawn from the teaching of the early church. This theology and piety, sharing the patristic mind of Orthodoxy, is most movingly captured in the eucharistic liturgy to be celebrated on the last day of this conference, Bishop Thomas Rattray's *Office for the Sacrifice of the Holy Eucharist* based on the Liturgy of St James of Jerusalem. This liturgy, at once plainly Anglican yet also deeply Orthodox, exemplifies the Anglican yearning for a concrete expression of the unity of the faith of the whole Church.

The classical Anglican eucharistic doctrine which developed in the seventeenth century looked to the early church for its doctrines of eucharistic presence, consecration, and sacrifice and for the model of its worship.[15] The basis of

---

14   See W. Jardine Grisbrooke, *Anglican Liturgies of the Seventeenth and Eighteenth Centuries*. Alcuin Club Collections No. XL (London: S.P.C.K., 1958). See also Kenneth Stevenson, *Covenant of Grace Renewed. A Vision of the Eucharist in the Seventeenth Century* (London: Darton, Longman & Todd, 1994).

15   For an admirable summary of the development of Anglican eucharistic doctrine, see Byron D. Stuhlman, *Eucharistic Celebration 1789–1989* (New York: Church Hymnal Corporation, 1988), chap. 1. For a more detailed approach, see Darwell Stone, *A History of the Doctrine of the Holy Eucharist* vol. ii (London: Longman, Green and Co., 1909); C. W. Dugmore, *Eucharistic Doctrine in England from Hooker to Waterland* (London: S.P.C.K., 1942); Edward P. Echlin S.J.,

interpretation of Cranmer's rite of 1552 was not Cranmer's intentions nor even Reformation theology as such. Just as the Reformation intended to restore the primitive purity of the church, so the basis of interpretation came to be the theology of the early church. Without substantially altering the text of the 1552 rite, the exponents of the developed eucharistic doctrine read into the rite an understanding of the Eucharist inconsistent with Cranmer's intentions and much closer to that of the much-admired rite of 1549.[16] Stuhlman observes, 'The Church of England began to develop a eucharistic theology which was at variance with, though not in absolute contradiction to, its eucharistic liturgy.'[17]

Two principal schools of eucharistic thought are commonly held to have developed. The first and more moderate school, derived from Cranmer, Laud, Jeremy Taylor, Ralph Cudworth, and Daniel Waterland, found no 'proper or material sacrifice in the eucharist', rather what Waterland called 'symbolic feast upon a sacrifice, that is to say, upon the grand sacrifice itself, commemorated under certain symbols'.[18]

The Anglican Eucharist in Ecumenical Perspective. Doctrine and Rite from Cranmer to Seabury (New York: Seabury Press, 1968); and Stevenson, Covenant of Grace Renewed.

16   Samuel Johnson recalled hearing his father say that when he was young in the book trade, 'king Edward the Sixth's first liturgy was much enquired for, and fetched a great price'; but once Thomas Brett published the whole communion office in A Collection of the Principal Liturgies, Used by the Christian Church in the Celebration of the Holy Eucharist (London, 1720), the price of the 1549 Prayer Book was reduced 'to that of a common book'. J. C. D. Clark, Samuel Johnson. Literature, Religion and English Cultural Politics from the Restoration to Romanticism (Cambridge: Cambridge University Press, 1994), 113.

17   Stuhlman, Eucharistic Celebration, 11.

18   Richard Sharp, 'New Perspectives on the High Church Tradition: historical background 1730–1781' in Geoffrey Rowell, ed., Tradition

The second, derived from Lancelot Andrewes, Joseph Mead, John Overall, Peter Heylin, and Herbert Thorndike and their use of the liturgies of the Eastern Church, was summed up in *The Unbloody Sacrifice* of John Johnson of Cranbrook.[19] 'This second tradition emphasised the continuity of the Eucharist with the material sacrifices of the Old Testament as described in Leviticus 24 and Malachi 1.1–10, and contended that Christ was offered in every Eucharist, not hypostatically, as the Tridentine Church of Rome supposed, but representatively and really, "in mystery and effect".[20] Each school had its own influential advocates and popularisers.

While the two schools disagreed about the nature of the sacrifice, each upheld Christ's real presence in the Eucharist. Ideas about the 'reality' of the presence have tended to be ambiguous because of the different ways in which 'real' may be understood. To the early Reformers 'real' was understood in a narrowly philosophical sense. Thus when the Black Rubric was restored and revised in 1662, 'real' was replaced with 'corporal'. But through the influence of Calvin and the Swiss theologians who followed him, real presence came to be understood in the broader sense of 'true' by both Puritan and high Anglican alike. Calvin 'strove earnestly to guard against an expression of eucharistic doctrine which seemed to reduce

    Renewed: Oxford Movement Conference Papers (London: Darton, Longman & Todd, 1986), 11.

19   (Johnson's title is worth citing in full as a summary of his eucharistic theology.) *The Unbloody Sacrifice, and Altar, Unvailed and Supported, in which the nature of the Eucharist is explained according to the sentiments of the Christian Church in the first four centuries; Proving, That the Eucharist is a proper material Sacrifice, That it is both Eucharistic and propitiatory, That it is to be offered by proper officers, That the Oblation is to be made on a proper Altar, That it is properly consumed by manducation* [...] (1704) Library of Anglo-Catholic Theology (Oxford: John Henry Parker, 1847), 321–322.

20   Ibid., 11–12.

Christ's presence to a merely subjective reality dependent on the faith of the communicant.'[21] Thus the first part of the homily concerning the sacrament (1571) contended,

> Thus much we must be sure to hold, that in the Supper of the Lord there is no vain ceremony, no bare sign, no untrue figure of a thing absent; – but the Communion of the body and blood of the Lord in a marvellous incorporation, which by the operation of the Holy Ghost – is through faith wrought in the souls of the faithful,

who therefore (the catechism maintains) 'verily and indeed take and receive the body and blood of Christ in the Lord's Supper'.[22] William Nicholson, the Restoration bishop of Gloucester, argued how this might be in *A Plain but Full Exposition of the Catechism of the Church of England* (1655):

> We believe Christ to be present in the Eucharist Divinely after a special manner, Spiritually in the hearts of communicants, Sacramentally or relatively in the elements. And this presence of his is real [...], for he is truly and effectually there present, though not corporally, bodily, carnally, locally.[23]

Real presence was affirmed, but (as in the Orthodox Church) as a mystery the manner of which cannot be precisely defined.

Given these explanations of eucharistic presence, the question arises how Christ is made present in the sacrament – the doctrine of consecration. Contemporary theologians

---

21   Stuhlman, *Eucharistic Celebration* 12.

22   Both citations are from Charles Wheatly, *A Rational Illustration of the Book of Common Prayer of the Church of England* (1722) (Oxford: Oxford University Press, 1846), ch. II, sect. xxxi, 278–279. 'Of the Protestation'.

23   Paul Elmer More and Frank Leslie Cross (eds), *Anglicanism. The Thought and Practice of the Church of England, Illustrated from the Religious Literature of the Seventeenth Century* (London: S.P.C.K., 1951), no. 204, 470–471.

worried that the logic of the 1552 rite demands the conclusion that the words of Christ spoken by the celebrant consecrate, for there is no epiklesis or invocation of the Spirit in this liturgy.[24] Both Calvin and the Eastern church held that the consecration was effected by the epiklesis; indeed this was Puritan doctrine according to the Westminster Directory, the standard of worship under the Commonwealth.[25] The great patristic scholar Bishop George Bull tried to work around this stumbling block in *The Corruptions of the Church of Rome*, attempting to conform an invocation of the Spirit model to the Prayer Book rite. Citing Justin and Irenaeus, Bull argued,

> By or upon the sacerdotal benediction, the Spirit of Christ, or a divine virtue of Christ descends upon the elements, and accompanies them to all faithful communicants and [...] therefore they are said to be and are the Body and Blood of Christ; the same divinity which is hypostatically united to the Body of Christ in heaven, being virtually united to the elements of Bread and Wine upon the earth. Which also seems to be the meaning of all the ancient liturgies, in which it is prayed, 'that God would send down His Spirit upon the bread and wine in the Eucharist'.[26]

Johnson also emphasised the importance of the role of the Spirit, but he was also careful to distinguish between the primitive doctrine and what he perceived as the contemporary Roman emphasis on 'words of consecration' and an Eastern insistence on the invocation as consecratory. Johnson

---

24   Cranmer himself wanted to avoid any indication of a 'moment' of consecration. See Colin Buchanan, *What did Cranmer think he was doing?* (Grove Liturgical Study 7, Bramcote, 1976) 23–25; cf. Diarmaid McCulloch, *Thomas Cranmer* (New Haven: Yale University Press, 1996), 502.

25   Stuhlman, *Eucharistic Celebration*, 17.

26   Cited in Stone, *A History* ii, 448.

insisted on the necessity of both – that the consecration is the corporate act of the whole community of the faithful. As Jeremy Taylor noted in *Holy Living*, 'the people are sacrificers too in their manner: for besides that, by saying *Amen*, they join in the act of him that ministers, and make it also their own.'[27]

Because the epiklesis was of the utmost importance to these theologians, its lack in the 1662 Prayer Book was of deep concern. Wheatly strains to conjure up an epiklesis upon the elements in this rite:

> There was always inserted in the primitive forms a particular petition for the descent of the Holy Ghost upon the Sacramental Elements, which was also continued in the first liturgy of King Edw. VI, in very express and open terms ... [with thy holy Spirite & Word, vouchsafe to bl✠esse and sanc✠tifie these thy gifts ...]. This upon the scruples of Bucer, (whom I am sorry I have so often occasion to name,) was left out at the review in the fifth of king Edward; and the following sentence, which he was pleased to allow of, inserted in its stead [grant that we receiving thy creatures ...]. In these words, it is true, the sense of the former is still implied, and consequently by these the elements are now consecrated, and so become the body and blood of our Saviour Christ.[28]

Because of the importance they attached to the epiklesis upon the elements, Johnson, Wheatly and others of that tradition preferred the 1549 and 1637 rites to those of 1552 and 1662. Johnson's influence was central to the liturgies of the Non-Jurors (who put his principles into practice) and thus to the Scottish rite of 1764 and the various Anglican liturgies

---

27 Cited in H. B. Porter, *Jeremy Taylor – Liturgist* (London: Alcuin Club, 1979), 61–62.

28 Wheatly, *Rational Illustration*, ch. VI, sect. xxii, §2, pp. 254–255. Wheatly is not ascribing consecration to the epiclesis alone; he affirms that it is by 'the prayer of the Church'.

(particularly of the American Episcopal Church) descended from it.[29]

Closely related to consecration is the doctrine of eucharistic sacrifice. The condemnation in Article xxxi of the Roman sacrifice of masses as 'blasphemous fables, and dangerous deceits' arose from the reformers' desire to avoid any notion of an independent sacrifice in each eucharistic oblation. Like the Orthodox, Anglicans turned to the Epistle to the Hebrews to express an understanding of the church's sacrifice united to that of Christ in heaven. Jeremy Taylor used the Christology of Hebrews 9 and 10 to describe Christ as high priest after the order of Melchizedek pleading his sacrifice in the heavenly sanctuary even as the priest pleads it in the church's Eucharist.[30] Thus, with a vision strikingly like that of Maximus the Confessor, Taylor writes,

> The church being the image of heaven, the priest, the minister of Christ; the holy table being the copy of the celestial altar, and the eternal sacrifice of the lamb slain from the beginning of the world being always the same; it bleeds no more after the finishing of it on the cross, but it is wonderfully represented in heaven, and graciously

---

29   Grisbrooke, *Anglican Liturgies*, 71. See also James David Smith, *The Eucharistic Doctrine of the Later Nonjurors: A Revisionist View of the Eighteenth-Century Usages Controversy*. (The Alcuin Club and the Group for the Renewal of Worship Joint Liturgical Studies 46. Cambridge: Grove Books, 2000).

30   Although Grisbrooke, *Anglican Liturgies* p. 27, argues that Taylor was the first Anglican to articulate this theology, William Forbes does the same; see *Anglicanism* no. 205, 471–473. On Forbes, see Stevenson, *Covenant* 77–83. Wheatly argued that the burnt offerings of the Temple, 'being types of the great sacrifice which Christ the Lamb of God was to offer up for the sins of the world, [were] sacrificed at the same hours wherein his death was begun and finished.' *Rational Illustration*, ch. II, Introduction, 69.

represented here; by Christ's action there, by his commandment here.[31]

This doctrine of the eucharistic sacrifice was given full liturgical expression in the 'tremendous and unbloody sacrifice' of Rattray's *Liturgy of St James* and full visual expression in the frontispiece to Wheatly's *Rational Illustration* (illustration 7). Here Christ the Great High Priest in the presence of the cherubim offers the sweet-smelling savour of his oblation of himself to the Father even as the church on earth participates in the offering of the Eucharist. Heaven and earth are united in one.[32]

Those concerned to emphasise the sacrificial nature of the Eucharist also stressed the significance of the oblation of the elements, the offering back to God what he has already given us, that he might transform them. As Johnson expressed it (effortlessly blending images of the old and new covenants),

---

31   Jeremy Taylor, *The Worthy Communicant* (1660), cited in Dugmore, *Eucharistic Doctrine*, 102.

32   This Hebrews-influenced theology was most eloquently expressed in the eucharistic hymns of Charles Wesley, though his expression of it tended to emphasise its 'bloody' rather than its 'unbloody' character. See Donald Allchin's treatment of Wesley's theology in his conference address below, 'Orthodox and Anglican: An Uneasy but Enduring Relationship'. Also, Daniel B. Stevick, *The Altar's Fire. Charles Wesley's Hymns on the Lord's Supper, 1745. Introduction and Exposition* (Epworth Press, 2004).

Edward Stephens, one of the most enthusiastic of the supporters of the Greek College, was also a liturgist keen to promote understanding of the 'unbloody sacrifice', publishing liturgies that include this petition at the end of the anamnesis: 'that this our Unbloody, Reasonable and Spiritual Sacrifice may be acceptable [...]'. He taught 'That this One *Unbloody Sacrifice*, or Holy Rite of the *Blessed Eucharist*, doth succeed as an *Antitype* and *Memorial* in the Christian Church'. See Grisbrooke, *Anglican Liturgies*, 227 and 241 for the liturgies, and 47 for commentary.

the bread and wine are that 'upon which God, at the prayers of the Priests and people, sends down His peculiar spiritual benediction, by which it becomes a Sacrifice of a sweet-smelling savour, as being therefore fully consecrated into the spiritual Body and Blood of Christ, and therefore fit with which to propitiate the Divine mercy.'[33] The prayer of oblation which followed the words of institution in the 1549 Prayer Book by 1552 had been dislocated and become a post-communion prayer. This caused much distress to sacrificially-minded Anglicans. Lancelot Andrewes privately recited his own prayer of oblation from Eastern sources.[34] Wheatly appeals to the example of Bishop John Overall (1560–1619), whose practice it was to use the prayer of oblation 'between the Consecration and Administering, even when it was otherwise ordered by the public Liturgy'.[35]

Following on this primitive understanding of oblation, it was appropriate that contemporary Anglicans should, after the manner of the early church, move the liturgical action from the nave to the sanctuary. Unlike the early church and the Orthodox, however, all the communicants accompanied the priest to 'draw near with faith' and gather around the altar. As Wheatly describes it, following the exhortation, 'The feast being now ready, and the guests prepared with due instruction, the Priest (who is the steward of those mysteries) invites them to *draw near*; thereby putting them in mind, that they are now invited into Christ's more special presence, to sit down with him at his own table.'[36] Joseph Bingham explicitly links this movement within the structure of the

---

33   Johnson, *Unbloody Sacrifice* i, 304–305.
34   Stuhlman, *Eucharistic Celebration*, 23–25.
35   Wheatly, *Rational Illustration*, ch. VI, sect. xxii, §3, 257–258. This was the practice also of Overall's chaplain John Cosin. According to Stevenson (*Covenant*, 94), others adopted this pattern as well.
36   Wheatly, *Rational Illustration*, ch. VI, sect. xiv, 247.

early Eucharist to Anglican practice by calling the *missa cate-chumenorum* 'the Ante-Communion Service on the *Lord's Day*' held in the nave, and the *missa fidelium* the 'Communion Service' celebrated at the altar.[37]

One churchman, Sir George Wheler, after experience of the Eastern church, went so far as to suggest that this division of the service might be an effective way to reintegrate into the Church of England 'Penitents & those Dissenting on grounds of Discipline & Form of Worship' yet who would be willing to hear the scriptures and sermons. Wheler argued that cathedrals and churches could be rearranged on a primitive pattern to serve such a ministry, with the pulpit moved to the place of the throne behind the altar, the clergy within the sanctuary, the Faithful (segregated by sex) within the choir, and the Dissenters in the aisles.[38]

Thus, while the Anglican liturgy was not so full of movement as the Orthodox, the congregational movement that did take place reflected that sense that Anglicans and Orthodox shared of the Eucharist as the offering of the whole church, priest and people together. As the historian of worship Horton Davies has observed, 'Moving to the chancel for the Communion service seemed to give the Sacrament a special sacredness, which has been strongly emphasised through most of Anglican history; the chancel screen helped to separate the liturgy of the catechumens from the liturgy of the faithful,

---

37   Bingham, *Orig. Eccles.*, bk. XIV, ch. V, sect. xii–xiii, and bk. XV, ch. III, sect. v.

38   Sir George Wheler, *An Account of the Churches, or Places of Assembly, of the Primitive Christians; From the Churches of Tyre, Jerusalem, and Constantinople, Described by Eusebius. And Ocular Observations of Several very Ancient Edifices of Churches yet Extant in those Parts. With a Seasonable Application.* (London, 1689) 110–115.

thus imparting to the climax of worship a sense of deep mystery.'[39]

For Anglicans as for Orthodox, the form of the church building and its decoration were of great importance, serving to shape the offering of worship and to express the theology underlying its practice. The requirements of the Anglican canons were rudimentary: Canon LXXXVII demanded that the Holy Table be placed where it was most convenient for celebration, be covered with a decent carpet or covering, and that the tables of the Decalogue be set up at the east end. In the late seventeenth and eighteenth centuries, however, the setting tended to be much more elaborate. The importance of the Eucharist was emphasised in a number of ways – the division between nave and chancel, normally with a chancel screen; the altar being railed off and raised up one or more steps; the painting of the chancel ceiling or the area above the altar; the presence of a ciborium or a painted canopy over the altar; the presence of a reredos or large east window above the altar; and the rich furnishing of the table itself with a cloth, communion plate, and sometimes candles. The eighteenth-century church valued its chancels and enriched them.

As the icon screen is one of the most significant furnishings in an Orthodox church, so the chancel screen remained a significant if not universal presence in Anglican churches. Queen Elizabeth's Order of October 1561 made it clear that screens (without roods or lofts) were to remain in churches, and the practice of building churches with screened chancels remained common. The main exceptions to this rule were Wren's churches in London. While Wren preferred to build single-cell churches, at the insistence of the then rector William Beveridge (eminent patristic scholar and future

---

39   Horton Davies, *Worship and Theology in England. From Cranmer to Hooker 1534–1603* (Princeton: Princeton University Press, 1970), 365.

bishop of St Asaph), St Peter's Cornhill (1681) was given a
chancel and chancel screen. Beveridge explained his rationale
at the church's opening:

> The Sacrament of the Lord's Supper being the highest mystery in all
> our religion, as representing the death of the Son of God to us, hence
> that place where this Sacrament is administered was always made and
> reputed the highest place in the church. And therefore, also, it was
> wont to be separated from the rest of the church by a screen or parti-
> tion of network, in Latin *cancelli*, and that so generally, that from
> thence the place itself is called the 'Chancel'. [...] I mention it at
> present, only because some perhaps may wonder why this should be
> observed in our church rather than in all the other churches which
> have lately been built in this city. Whereas they should rather
> wonder, why it was not observed in all others as well as this. For,
> besides our obligations to conform, as much as may be, to the prac-
> tice of the universal Church, and to avoid novelty and singularity in
> all things relating to the worship of God, it cannot be easily imagined
> that the Catholick Church, in all ages and places, for thirteen or
> fourteen hundred years together, should observe such a custom as
> this, except there were great reasons for it.
> 　　[...] It may be sufficient to observe at present, that the Chancel in
> our Christian churches was always looked upon as answerable to the
> Holy of Holies in the Temple; which, you know, was separated from
> the sanctuary or body of the Temple, by the command of God
> Himself.[40]

Here again we see that Anglican concern for concrete expressions of unity with the whole Church. Not only the universal
practice of the Church but also the example of the Temple of
Solomon demanded that the holiest place in the church
building should be distinguished as such.

------

40 William Beveridge, 'The Excellence and Usefulness of the Common
    Prayer: Preached at the Opening of the Parish Church of St Peter's,
    Cornhill, the 27th of November 1681', *The Theological Works of
    William Beveridge*, 12 vols. (Oxford: Library of Anglo-Catholic
    Theology, 1842–1846), vi, 388

Architects and theologians of the period were intensely interested in the Temple.[41] Du Prey lists no fewer than twelve representations of the Temple by English scholars (including Isaac Newton) between 1627 and 1741.[42] This interest was a natural consequence of their concern both for fidelity to the witness of the early church and for the example of classical antiquity. As we shall see, much of the visual vocabulary of Anglican churches was also based on Jewish precedent, in one stroke demonstrating their adherence to a typological understanding of Scripture (as in the writing of the Church Fathers) and avoiding the kind of symbolism associated with the mediæval church and Counter-Reformation Catholicism.

The earliest of these Temple scholars was Joseph Mede, the Cambridge Hebraist and polymath. In his discourse, *Churches*, he affirmed the modern church's dependence on the worship of the old and new covenants: 'Because [the early Christians] had before their eyes an example and pattern in the Proseuchais and Synagogues of the Iews, from whom their Religion had its beginning [...] Who can beleeve, that such a pattern should not invite the Christian to an imitation of the

---

41   For a thorough treatment of this subject, see du Prey, *Hawksmoor's London Churches* ch. 1 and appendix 1. For the links between Temple, synagogue and church in the primitive period, see Louis Bouyer, *Liturgy and Architecture* (Notre Dame: University of Notre Dame Press, 1967), and Lee I. Levine, *The Ancient Synagogue: The First Thousand Years* (New Haven: Yale University Press, 2000).

       It is not coincidental that the Ode of the scholars of the Greek College to Queen Anne should be addressed to her as to a latter-day Solomon: ' 'Tis He's thy pattern both in Church and State, / Doubt not but his too is thy happy Fate, / The Temple Thou with Him esteem'st so Dear, / Void of its blessing cannot leave thy Care.' See Appendix C.

42   Du Prey, appendix 1.

same?'[43] Mede's sermon on 'The Reverence of God's House' insists that God's presence with his people is as real in church as it was in the Temple. He speaks of the Old Testament sacrifices as memorials, rites of remembrance 'whereby the Name of God was commemorated or recorded, and his Covenant with men renewed and testified.' Against any would-be Marcionites in the congregation Mede insisted on the continuing significance of the Jewish witness:

> You will say, What is all this to us, now in the time of the Gospell? I answer, Yes. For did not Christ ordaine the holy Eucharist to be the Memoriall of his Name in the New Testament? [...] And what if I should affirme, that Christ is as much present here, as the Lord was upon the Mercy-seat between the Cherubins? Why should not then the Place of this Memoriall under the Gospell have some semblable sanctitie to that, where the Name of God was recorded in the Law?
>
> In a word, all those sacred Memorialls of the Jewish Temple are both comprehended and excelled in this One of the Christians, the *Sacrifices, Shewbread,* and *Ark of the Covenant*; Christ's Bodie and Bloud in the Eucharist being all these unto us in the New Testament, agreeably to that of the Apostle, *Rom.* 3.25. '*God hath set forth Iesus Christ to be our* ʹλαστηριον *through faith in his bloud*', that is, our *Propitiatory* or *Mercy seat.*[44]

The Christian Eucharist is the fulfilment of the Old Testament sacrifices, and God is present to his people in the sacrament of Christ's Body and Blood just as he was enthroned in his glory upon the Ark of the Covenant. 'Where his *memoriall* is, there his *SHECINAH* or Δόξα is.'[45]

---

43   Joseph Mede, *Churches, that is, Appropriate Places for Christian Worship; both in, and ever since the Apostles Times* (London, 1638), 55.

44   Joseph Mede, *The Reverence of God's House. A Sermon preached at St. Maries in Cambridge, before the Universitie on St Matthies day. Anno 1635/6* (London, 1638), 9–11.

45   Ibid., 15.

Mede goes even further, arguing that the *shekinah* or presence of God is not confined to the sacrament. Just as he was
present in the burning bush and at Bethel, so God is present
wherever his 'traine or retinue is, where the heavenly *Guard*,
the blessed Angels keep their sacred station and rende-vous'.
As the Temple was decorated with cherubim with their faces
turned toward the Mercy-seat and as the Jews continued this
practice in their modern synagogues, so Christians from St
Paul (1 Cor. 11.10) onwards have acknowledged the presence
of the angels in the place of assembly, their eyes turned to the
Mercy-seat or altar. Whether or not the sacrament is present,
Mede assures his listeners that the Lord is in their churches,
and that these buildings are fitly called God's house.[46]

Because of the association of the altar with the Ark of the
Presence in the Temple, symbolic references to the divine
presence can usually be traced back to Temple imagery. Most
often the reredos took the form of the tables of the Decalogue. Modern observers have usually seen these as evidence
of the arid legalism of the Georgian church, when in fact they
are a reference to the true presence of God in the covenant he
made with his people. The tablets of the law were kept within
the Ark of the Covenant in the Holy of Holies; this reminder
of the old covenant is an entirely appropriate symbol to asso-
ciate with the altar and the new covenant in Christ's Blood.[47]
The altar is the new Mercy-seat for the divine presence in the
Eucharist.

The tablets of the law rarely stood on their own; usually
they appeared with other symbols related to the sanctuary of
the Temple. A particularly rich example was to be found at St

---

46   Ibid., 18–34. On the altar, see Joseph Mede, *The Name Altar, or
      ΘΥΣΙΑΣΤΗΡΙΟΝ, anciently given to the Holy Table.* (London, 1637).

47   See David H. Chaundy-Smith, 'The Moral Shecinah: The Social
      Theology of Chancel Decoration in Seventeenth Century London',
      Anglican and Episcopal History lxix, 2 (2000), 193–210.

Saviour's, Southwark (the modern-day cathedral), in the altar-piece of 1703, which was 35 feet high:

> It consists of an upper and lower part; the latter is adorned with four fluted columns, and their entablature of the Corinthian order; the inter-columns are the Commandments done in black letters, on large slabs of white and veined marble, under a glory (exhibiting the name *Jehovah*, in Hebrew characters) and the triangular pediments, between four attic pilasters, with an acroteria of the figures of seven golden candlesticks replenished with tapers; the whole is under a spacious circular pediments belonging to the Corinthian columns, which are placed between the Paternoster and Creed; each under a pediment, between small pilasters. [...] In the centre of this upper part is a glory in the shape of a dove descending within a circular group of cherubims, all very spacious and finely painted.[48]

This reredos is an overwhelming expression of the identity of earthly and heavenly worship in the Eucharist. The glory with the tetragrammaton indicates the *shekinah* and is emblematic of the real presence.[49] The seven golden candlesticks are a reminder of the *menorah* as well as of the seven golden lampstands of *Revelation* 1.12; they are comparable to the seven-branched candlestick behind the Orthodox altar.[50] The

---

48   Basil F. L. Clark, *The Building of the Eighteenth-Century Church* (London: S.P.C.K., 1963), 166, citing David Hughson, *A History and Description of London, Westminster and Southwark*, iv, 498. See also Wickham Legg, *English Church Life from the Restoration to the Tractarian Movement Considered in Some of its Neglected or Forgotten Features* (London: Longmans, Green and Co., 1914), 128, for a 1708 description of an equally impressive altarpiece at All Hallows, Lombard Street.

49   The *shekinah* often (and for the same reason) also appears on communion plate of the period. Curiously, this frequently takes a form identical to the emblem of the Society of Jesus.

50   A surviving example (from 1728) of the seven candlesticks may be found at Gayhurst, Bucks. See Mark Chatfield, *Churches the Victorians Forgot* (Moorland Publishing, 1989), 13–15.

cherubims were a part of the Ark and are also invisibly present as the church's worship is united with that of 'angels and arch-angels and all the company of heaven'. And mindful of the debates in eucharistic theology, the presence of the dove is particularly notable. We know that the early Christians and many Anglicans held that the consecration was inseparable from the epiclesis, the invocation of the Holy Spirit upon the elements, and in some early church buildings 'the Holy Ghost was represented in the effigies of a silver Dove hovering over the Altar', the *peristerion* or *columbae*.[51] The presence of the dove over the altar may be an indication of Anglican adherence to this primitive eucharistic doctrine.

The use of this visual vocabulary was not confined to the church. The same themes reappeared in illustrations to popular devotional materials. Besides the famous frontispiece to Wheatly's *Rational Illustration*, that to Parsell's Latin Prayer Book of 1713 is also worthy of note (illustration 8). It incorporates a summary of church life and worship, from the font in the foreground, to the congregation gathered in prayer around the triple-decker reading desk, to the eucharistic feast awaiting on the altar, with the cherubim and the *shekinah* marking the real presence. The frontispiece to Lancelot Addison's *The Introduction to the Sacrament* (1693) (illustration 9) incorporates candles (during the ante-communion), commandments, and ciborium over the altar as well as the *shekinah* hovering over the consecrated elements.

As this last illustration shows, various other means were used to honour the altar. Sometimes there was a ciborium, or columned canopy, over the altar. That at Hawksmoor's St

---

51   Bingham, *Orig. Eccles.*, bk. VIII, ch. VI, sect. xix. A surviving example of the dove descending may be found in the chapel of Trinity College, Oxford, and St Peter's Vere Street, St Vedast Foster Lane, St Clement Eastcheap, St Martin Ludgate, and St Mary Woolnoth, all in London.

Mary Woolnoth even has the twisted columns believed to have originated in the Temple of Solomon. A distinctive east window would focus a stream of light on the focal point of the altar, emphasising the orientation of the church toward the parousia and the rising sun of the Resurrection.[52] Another external indicator of the function of an Anglican church was the use of an apse; this too was in imitation of the early Christian basilica.[53] The altars themselves might be made of stone or wood (no significance being attached to either material), and the wooden ones could be elaborately carved with cherubs, or wheat sheaves and bunches of grapes (emblematic of the eucharistic oblation).

One criticism of these churches, casting doubt on their sacramental credentials, has been that the triple-decker pulpit and reading-desk was sometimes placed in the central aisle, interrupting the view from the door to the altar. In fact there was good patristic precedent for this practice. In the early church (as in the contemporary synagogue), the ambo, the focus of the liturgy of the word, was often in the middle of the nave. The ambo performed the same function as the reading-desk, as Bingham pointed out: 'The *Ambo* itself was what we now call the Reading-Desk, a Place made on Purpose for the Readers and Singers, and such of the Clergy as ministered in the first Service, called Missa Catechumenorum.'[54] William Beveridge, in his collection of patristic canons Συνοδικον, includes ground plans of ancient eastern

---

52 On the significance of orientation in Anglican churches, see Doll, *After the Primitive Christians,* 13–15.

53 The apse might be found on large, rich churches, like St Mary-le-Strand in London, but also on comparatively humble churches. Several small plain brick churches on the Eastern Shore of Maryland have apses in which their altars are placed, e.g. Old Trinity, Church Creek (1674), and St Luke's, Church Hill (1731).

54 Bingham, *Orig. Eccles.,* bk. VIII, ch. V, sect. iv.

churches, *Ichnographia Templorum Orientalium*, based on textual evidence from authors like Simeon of Thessalonica, the fifteenth-century Byzantine ecclesiologist. Of the ambo Beveridge writes, 'Hunc autem, et de eo prius aliqua delibimus, in medio Ecclesiæ interspeciosas & sanctas fores, & altari directè oppositum esse.' His illustration is 'fidem facit Symeon Thessalonicensis dicens, ὁ ἄμβων προ της θυρας του μνηματος ἰσταται, Ambon è conspectu parte bematis statuitur [...].'[55] Even where there was no chancel screen, the reading-desk could be an effective means of separating nave and chancel.

The Anglican sense of identity with the primitive church is architecturally nowhere more explicitly revealed than in the plans for the 'Fifty New Churches' (only twelve of which were actually built) of 1711.[56] When the commission for building the churches was formed, the commissioners sought the best advice available on how to proceed. On the one hand, Wren submitted his letter on the 'auditory church', pointing to St James's Piccadilly as beautiful, convenient and 'the cheapest of any form I could invent';[57] on the other, Sir John Vanbrugh insisted that the churches 'should not only serve for the accommodation of the inhabitants [...], but at the same time remain monuments to the Posterity of [...] Piety and Grandeur, and by Consequence become Ornaments to the Towne,

---

55   William Beveridge, Συνοδικον, *sive Pandectæ Canonum SS. Apostolorum, et Conciliorum ab Ecclesia Græca receptorum* (Oxonii, 1672) II, Annotationes, 73.

56   See du Prey's comprehensive treatment, *Hawksmoor's London Churches*, ch. 2; also E. G. W. Bill (ed.), *The Queen Anne Churches. A Catalogue of Papers in the Lambeth Palace Library of the Commission for Building Fifty New Churches in London and Westminster 1711–1759* (London: Mansell, 1979).

57   Addleshaw and Etchells, 249. Wren's letter is reproduced here as Appendix II.

and a Credit to the Nation.'[58] But a decisive submission was made by the Non-Juror George Hickes, who replied to Vanbrugh's advice in 'Observations on Mr. Vanbrugg's proposals about Buildinge the new Churches'.[59] Hickes was not a member of the commission; his name never even appears in the minutes. This is hardly surprising, given that he was deprived of the deanery of Worcester as a Non-Juror and was the Non-Juring bishop of Thetford. But the influence of his 'Observations' on both the written plans of the commission and Hawksmoor's architectural plans is clear. Hickes's involvement is evidence of the continued close identity of juring and nonjuring theology – indeed the churches influenced by the commission's plans might be seen as architectural expressions of the principles of the patristic mentality of Anglican theology.

At a meeting of 11 July 1712 a committee laid out principles for the design of the churches. Among them were the following:

> 5. One general design or form to be agreed upon for all the fifty new intended churches, where sites will admit thereof; the steeples or towers excepted.
> 8. There be at East end of each church two small rooms, one for vestments, another for vessels or other consecrated things [...].
> 10. Fonts in each church be so large as to permit Baptism by dipping when desired.
> 11. All pews be single and of equal height, so low that every person in them may be seen either kneeling or sitting, and all facing the communion table [...].
> 13. Chancel be raised three steps above nave or body of the church.[60]

---

58   *The Queen Anne Churches*, 11.
59   Printed in full in du Prey, Appendix 3, 139–142.
60   M. H. Port (ed.), *The Commissions for Building Fifty New Churches. The Minute Books, 1711–27, A Calendar* (London: London Record Society, 1986), xiv.

Hickes in his 'Observations' called for vestries at the east end of the church 'for keeping sacerdotal Robes, and holy Vessels'; for a baptistry at the west end with a font 'large and deep enough for immersion';[61] for an ascent of three steps between nave and chancel; and for the east–west orientation of the churches. The careful provision of vestries (no. 8), the attention given to the font (no. 10), the orientation of the low pews toward the holy table (no. 11), and the raising up of the chancel above the nave (no. 13) all reveal the sacramental bias of the design. These instructions envisaged a church on the primitive basilican model, a church which would also conform to Vanbrugh's stress on 'the most Solemn & Awfull Appearance both without and within'.[62]

In response to these recommendations, Nicholas Hawksmoor produced a proposed design for a site in Bethnal Green which the commissioners in the end did not build. Tellingly, he entitled the design 'The Basilica after the Primitive Christians' with reference to the 'purest times of Christianity' in the fourth century (illustration 10). It is a plan clearly in tune with the ecclesiological preoccupations of the time. It is part historical reconstruction, part ideal model, and, as Downes points out, 'each of [its] functions is considered both ecclesiologically and architecturally.'[63] This plan is keyed to – even expands upon – Hickes's recommendations: vestries (D), a 'place for the font for ye Converts which was in ye Porch—&

---

61   The requirement for fonts deep enough to accommodate infant baptism by dipping rather than infusion also reflects the influence of the early church, where baptism by immersion was the norm. John Johnson, that enthusiast for all things primitive, went so far as to install in his church at Cranbrook a font large enough for the baptism of adults by immersion in the hope of attracting Baptists into the church. The font remains to this day.

62   Kerry Downes, *Hawksmoor* (London: Thames & Hudson, 1970), 105.

63   Downes, *Hawksmoor*, 106–107.

to be immersd' (B), east–west orientation (A), as well as an array of surrounding buildings.[64]

In the bibliography attached to his 'Observations', Hickes makes clear his debt to 'the third vol. of Mr Bingham's Ecclesiastical Antiquities'. The broad sympathy between Hickes's and Bingham's principles should already be evident, and for details regarding the furnishing and use of primitive churches Hickes and Hawksmoor would naturally have turned to the *Origines Ecclesiasticae* as a compendium of all available evidence on early churches. It is worth noting that Hawksmoor does not use the term 'basilica' in its precise architectural sense of a building with colonnaded aisles and an apse, but rather as a generic term for a church; Bingham had already noted that this was the sense in which the early church used the term.[65] Bingham also provided a variety of plans (including one Beveridge provided in his Συνοδικον) which are reflected in the planned and completed churches. Particularly notable is the provision of rooms flanking the chancel, what Hawksmoor following Hickes called 'The vestrys for ye Sacred Robes and holy Vessells'. These correspond (according to the requirements of Anglican worship) to the *Prothesis* and the *Diaconicum* to be found on either side of the bema as depicted in the *Ichnographiae Templorum Beverigij* and *Jacobi Goar* (illustration 11). The plan for the basilica after the primitive Christians found its way not only into Hawksmoor's churches, but also those of Thomas Archer and James Gibbs, whose St Martin-in-the-Fields was particularly important –

---

64   Du Prey, *Hawksmoor's London Churches*, 62–63.
65   Du Prey locates in Bingham the sources for many of Hickes's proposals, *op. cit.* 66f.

Gavin Stamp has called it 'one of the most influential and imitated buildings in architectural history'.[66]

What the Orthodox Church had maintained as an unbroken tradition from the time of the early Church, the Church of England had struggled to recover out of the turmoils of the Reformation and the Commonwealth. The rupture in the unity of the Western Church provided an opportunity for Anglicans to rediscover the witness of the undivided Church and to implement concrete liturgical and architectural expressions of their adherence to that unity. Both the Orthodox and Anglicans looked to the same sources in Scripture and in the Fathers of the Church; therefore it is unsurprising that there should be a common understanding in so many points of eucharistic theology: real presence, sacrifice, consecration, the unity of heaven and earth through participation in Christ's offering of himself to the Father. Their church buildings shared a sense of connection to the Temple and the divine presence found there. But because of the historic constraints imposed by the Book of Common Prayer, much of the common ground between Anglicans and Orthodox was implicit and hidden rather than explicit and obvious. Orthodox observers might have been hard pressed to perceive in Anglican worship any close correspondence to their own. Likewise, Anglicans found themselves so preoccupied with 'Popish' threats that they were not in a position to understand the Eastern traditions of worship with icons and prayers to the saints except through spectacles tinted by their fears of Popery.

Nevertheless, each knew that the worship of their churches on earth was united with the worship of Heaven,

---

66   Gavin Stamp, 'Church Architecture' in Robert Fermor-Hesketh (ed.), *Architecture of the British Empire* (London: Weidenfeld and Nicolson, 1986), 149.

sharing in the unbloody sacrifice of Christ's self-offering to the Father. Whether that belief was expressed through icons or the visual imagery of the Old Testament, this was a reality that united them in the fullness of God's time, even if they did not fully realise it on earth.

9. Orthodox Influences on Anglican Liturgy

GREGORY WOOLFENDEN

The history of Orthodox influence on Anglican liturgy could probably be best summed up as the 'History of the Anglican Epiklesis' – other areas of influence do exist, but this is perhaps the one where the most fruitful dialogue with the east has taken place, even if the present fruits might possibly be of variable quality.

Before we go any further, it may be useful to remind ourselves that the beginning of Cranmer's liturgical work was solidly and undeniably based in the structures of the Roman rite with which he had long been familiar, above all in its Sarum form. Some years ago, under very different circumstances, I was involved in a liturgical reconstruction of a Sarum-use High Mass in Jesus College Chapel, Cambridge. I remarked at the time that the *style* of the ceremonial reminded me more of the Byzantine rite than of the pre-Vatican II Roman. However, this was nothing to do with either the structure or text of the ritual; it was more of an atmosphere, which felt very different from the Baroque setting which had given a very different feeling to the Roman Mass as it was until the 1960s. To put it in plain words, there was nothing specifically oriental about the way Mass was celebrated in mid-sixteenth century England, and it was this medieval matrix that was the starting point for Cranmer's experiments and ultimately the Prayer Books of 1549, 1552 and later.

That is not to say that Cranmer knew nothing of the east. In his magnificent book on Cranmer, Professor Diarmaid

MacCullough has pointed out that Orthodoxy had been identified as a possible non-Roman alternative by the more conservative ecclesiastics who could however face breaking with Rome.[1] But Cranmer seemed to have been very little influenced by the Greek liturgies, which he may have known from the Greek version printed with a Latin translation in 1528.[2] He is known to have possessed Greek liturgical books or Latin translations thereof,[3] but he did not make great use of them.

One prayer was however undeniably derived from this source, the so-called 'Prayer of St Chrysostom' that first appears at the end of the 1544 Litany:

> Almighty God, who hast given us grace at this time with one accord to make our common supplications unto thee and dost promise that when two or three are gathered together in thy name, thou wilt grant their requests: [...]

In 1662 it became the prayer that concluded the so-called state prayers at Morning and Evening Prayer, and continues to be a popular way of concluding intercessions at the end of the offices to this day. Bishop Kenneth Stevenson has examined the prayer and noted especially the change to the original opening; 'O you who have granted us to pray together in harmony', which more clearly showed that the prayer was addressed to Christ.[4]

The prayer almost certainly cannot be attributed to St John Chrysostom and in the eighth century Euchologion,

1   Diarmaid MacCullough, *Thomas Cranmer* (New Haven & London: Yale University Press, 1996), 220.
2   Ibid., 415–416.
3   Geoffrey Cuming, 'Eastern Liturgies and Anglican Divines, 1510–1662' in *Studies in Church History* 13 (Oxford: Blackwell, 1976), 231–238.
4   Kenneth Stevenson, 'Cranmer's "Prayer of Chrysostom" Reconsidered', dated 1990, not published?

Barberini Gr. 336,[5] is found only in the Liturgy of St Basil, and not in that of St John Chrysostom. This is no doubt because the stational service of psalm chants and prayers that preceded the Liturgy on greater days may well have been entirely omitted on lesser days when the shorter Chrysostom liturgy was used. Bishop Kenneth felt that although the prayer functioned extremely well to conclude intercessory prayer, that was not its function in the Byzantine stational liturgy. However, Juan Mateos did conclude that its original purpose was indeed to conclude a litany and not to accompany a psalm.[6] Cranmer and his successors cannot have known this, but they certainly identified the genius of the prayer.

Cranmer and the Epiklesis

One of the very first books of liturgical history I read was a popular work by Percy Dearmer when I was a young teenager asking awkward questions. Dearmer repeated the then accepted wisdom about Cranmer's epikletic phrase praying God 'with thy holy Spirit and Word vouchsafe to bless and sanctify these thy gifts and creatures of bread and wine, that they may be unto us the body and blood of thy most dearly beloved Son Jesus Christ.'[7] Dearmer described this as effecting a reconciliation between eastern and western ideas, most especially because it placed the petition *before* the

---

5   S. Parenti and E.Velkovska (eds), *L'Eucologio Barberini gr. 336* (Rome: Edizione Liturgiche, BEL Subsidia 80), 3.

6   Juan Mateos, *La Célébration de la Parole dans la liturgie Byzantine* (Rome: *Orientalia Christiana Analecta* 191, 1971), 59.

7   William Keeling, *Liturgiae Brittanicae* (Cambridge, 1851, reprinted Farnborough: Gregg, 1969), 210.

Words of Institution, seen in Medieval theology as the moment of consecration.[8] I cite this popularising source because it may give some indication of how widespread this interpretation became.

F. E. Brightman[9] gives the Liturgy of St Basil as the source for this part of Cranmer's 1549 Eucharistic Prayer, and quotes the relevant section of the Greek anaphora. Brightman later changed his mind on this and adopted an interpretation which was to be shared by E. C. Ratcliff; that, in spite of the mention of the Holy Spirit, the phrase was an invocation of the effective word of the creator, actuated by the words of institution said shortly afterwards, and by *virtue* of the Holy Spirit. In other words, what Ratcliff saw as the traditional western theory of consecration.[10]

Ratcliff was of course defending what he thought was the traditional theory of the consecrating power of the Words of Institution. Was this what Cranmer was anxious to preserve at all cost? Whatever he was doing he was quite clearly not adopting what many still believe to be an Eastern theory of consecration by Epiklesis alone.[11] Bryan Spinks has examined the writings of other reformers to see if a connection is made between Spirit and word in a prayer for consecration. He noted the links made by Luther and Zwingli, and the importance of the Spirit in Calvin's theology, but a strong influence

---

8   Percy Dearmer, *Everyman's History of the Prayerbook* (London: Mowbray, 1912), 68.

9   F. E. Brightman, *The English Rite* (London: Rivington, 1915), II, 692.

10   A. H. Couratin and D. H. Tripp (eds), *E. C. Ratcliff: Liturgical Studies* (London: S.P.C.K., 1976), 195.

11   I do not believe that Orthodox theology at its best has any place for a 'moment of consecration' – the whole anaphora is consecratory. I will readily admit that popular devotion does tend to centre around the praying of the Epiklesis, especially where the people have been encouraged to join in the deacon's response of 'Amen'.

must have been Peter Martyr Vermigli, who expressed himself in similar terms several times. It may also be important that Martin Bucer criticised the petition, but not for its linking of the Spirit and the Word, rather that it invoked the Spirit only upon the elements and not the communicants, a point to which we shall return. This criticism and the way in which Stephen Gardiner used the petition to argue that one could thereby continue to express a doctrine of Transubstantiation probably contributed to the fact that the petition was not included in the 1552 rite.[12]

Cranmer's doctrine of 'True Presence' envisaged a spiritual presence which was the work of the Spirit uniting Christ and his people.[13] However this petition for consecration, and the institution following, could still allow for a moment at which the bread and wine were separated from profane to spiritual use as Cranmer wanted. According to Bishop Colin Buchanan, Cranmer was already moving away from any notion of consecration, hence the ease with which this petition disappears in 1552 and is not reinstated under Elizabeth or in 1662.[14]

To sum up our consideration of the 1549 petition, we can only say with Richard Buxton, that if the text of St Basil suggested the wording, that is not evidence that there was any desire to introduce or understand an Eastern theory of consecration at that time.[15] At the same time, we can give but

---

12   Bryan Spinks, "'And with thy holy Spirite and Worde": further thoughts on the source of Cranmer's petition for sanctification in the 1549 Communion Service' in Margot Johnson (ed.), *Thomas Cranmer* (Durham: Turnstone, 1990), 94–102.

13   Peter Newman Brooks, *Thomas Cranmer's Doctrine of the Eucharist* (London: Macmillan, 1965), 104.

14   Colin Buchanan, *What did Cranmer think he was doing?* (Bramcote: Grove Liturgical 7, reprinted 1982), 16–20.

15   Richard Buxton, *Eucharist and Institution Narrative* (London: Alcuin Club & Mayhew-McCrimmon, 1976), 72.

cold comfort to the followers of Ratcliff, because Cranmer quite clearly did not intend consecration in the way that, for example, Gardiner did.

Scottish Developments

Although the 1549 petition ceased to be part of the liturgy of the Church of England, it did re-appear in Scotland in the 1637 Prayer Book. If Cranmer seems to have seen no need for an explicit petition for consecration of the elements, it is noted by Donaldson that the lack of such was something that the English Puritans objected to in 1661. They were at one with the Westminster Directory's (1645) requirement 'that there should be prayer to God "to vouchsafe His gracious presence and the effectual working of His Spirit in us, and so to sanctify these elements, both of bread and wine and to bless His own ordinance, that we may receive by faith the body and blood of Jesus Christ".[16] The petition to bless with Word and Spirit was in no way at variance with the eucharistic doctrine of the Scots Confession of 1560, or of the Westminster Confession that was promulgated in 1647–1648. Although we all know the somewhat embroidered stories about the reception, or non-reception, of the 1637 book, it is worth noting that strong Presbyterians were already critical of Knox's lack of the petition and were commonly supplying it themselves.[17] On the other hand it is impossible at this point to say that there was any conscious desire to accept an eastern Orthodox influence; the dispute was entirely within the

---

16   Gordon Donaldson, *The Making of the Scottish Prayer Book of 1637* (Edinburgh: University Press, 1954), 68.

17   Ibid., 67–68.

Reformed ambit. However, some later Church of Scotland scholars also tried at least to establish a parallel with the East on this matter.[18]

A change of outlook begins to become apparent when we examine Hamon L'Estrange's *Alliance of Divine Offices*, first published in 1659. L'Estrange[19] knew the liturgy of Apostolic Constitutions, book 8, then called the 'Clementine Liturgy' and was quite clear that although the Fathers thought the Institution Narrative important 'yet were they far from imagining that the elements were sanctified any other way than by prayer.'[20] At the same period Jeremy Taylor constructed a Eucharistic Prayer which included phrases that are very close to the Orthodox ones, as a comparison with the Chrysostom liturgy will show:

[...] send thy Holy Spirit upon our hearts, and let him also descend upon these gifts, that by his good, his holy, his glorious presence, he may sanctifie and enlighten our hearts, and he may bless and sanctifie these gifts. That	[...] send down your Holy Spirit upon us and upon our gifts here set forth
this Bread may become the Holy Body of Christ. Amen. And this chalice may become the life-giving Blood of Christ. Amen.[21]	and make this bread the precious Body of your Christ, Amen. And what is in this cup the precious Blood of your Christ. Amen. Changing them by your Holy Spirit.[22]

---

18 E.g., G. W. Sprott, *The Worship and Offices of the Church of Scotland* (Edinburgh & London: Blackwood) 1882, 119–121.

19 L'Estrange was one of several 17th century Anglican divines who were well acquainted with the eastern liturgies. Cuming, 'Eastern Liturgies', 236–237.

20 Cited by Buxton, *Eucharist*, 113.

21 W. Jardine Grisbrooke, *Anglican Liturgies of the Seventeenth and Eighteenth Centuries* (London: Alcuin/S.P.C.K., 1958), 193–194.

Taylor's epiklesis however preceded rather than followed the Institution Narrative, whereas in the Byzantine anaphora this petition emerges out of the anamnesis.

Another scholar with interest in the Greek Orthodox tradition was Edward Stephens (born 1633), who was friendly with Greek students in Oxford and even claimed to have received communion in the Orthodox church.[23] Stephens designed a liturgy for possible public use that was published in 1696. The prayer of the Anaphora is lengthy and continues the 1549 petition for Word and Spirit.[24] Another liturgy intended for a private congregation is far lengthier, and much more obviously indebted to Orthodox sources. It has the epiklesis after the Institution and a lengthy and elaborate anamnesis/oblation. The prayer invokes the Spirit primarily upon the gifts of bread and wine.[25]

John Henley published another liturgy in 1726 that was uncritically accepting of the Clementine Liturgy, and the Epiklesis following the institution is solely concerned with consecrating the gifts, but Henley uses the verb 'show' to translate αποφαίνειν; whereas others, e.g. Grisbrooke, would translate it as 'make'.[26]

When we turn to the Liturgies of the Non-Jurors of the eighteenth century, we find that the Epiklesis has become, like that of Apostolic Constitutions 8, a prayer for the Spirit to come upon the sacrifice, and change the bread and wine into the Body and Blood of Christ, and this petition now

---

22   *The Divine Liturgy of our Father among the Saints, John Chrysostom* (Oxford University Press, 1995), 33–34.
23   Grisbrooke, *Anglican Liturgies*, 37–38.
24   Ibid., 214.
25   Ibid., 242.
26   Grisbrooke, *The Liturgical Portions of the Apostolic Constitutions* (Bramcote: Alcuin/GROW 13–14, 1990), 38–39.

definitely follows the Institution.[27] The Scottish Non-Jurors, the ancestors of today's Episcopalians, had in Thomas Rattray a very considerable scholar who knew the Greek liturgies well.[28] Much attracted to the Liturgy of St James, then widely believed to be much earlier in its present recension than can now be held to be the case,[29] Rattray calls for the Spirit to 'come down *upon us*, and upon these gifts which are here set forth before Thee'.[30] This is very important. Rattray identified the point that is common to all the Orthodox epikleses, that they invoke the Spirit upon *us* first, and then upon the gifts. The importance of this has been recently pointed up by the Irish Roman Catholic scholar David Power. In his discussion of the dispute between East and West about consecration he said: 'For Latins, the sanctification of gifts and the sanctification of the people are two distinct actions. Greek formulations express that the people are sanctified with and through the sanctification of their gifts.'[31]

The Scottish communion office of 1764 included the epiklesis after the institution, but failed to link the sanctification of the gifts with that of the people. One can say that by the eighteenth century, Anglican thinkers saw consecration as effected by prayer and not just by recital of the words of institution, a position that is characteristic of Orthodoxy, as for example in the work of St Nicholas Cabasilas: 'And in the same way, here in the liturgy, we believe that the Lord's words do indeed accomplish the mystery, but through the medium of the priest, *his invocation, and his prayer*. These words do not

---

27   Grisbrooke, *Anglican Liturgies*, 289 and 311
28   Ibid., 137–138.
29   See J. R. K. Fenwick, *The Anaphoras of St Basil and St James* (Rome: *Orientalia Christiana Analecta* 240, 1992).
30   Grisbrooke, *Anglican Liturgies*, 325.
31   David Power, *Sacrament: The Language of God's Giving* (New York: Crossroad, 1999), 220.

take effect simply in themselves or under any circumstances'[32] (emphasis supplied). On the other hand, only Rattray appears to have discerned the importance of the invoking the Spirit upon people and gifts in the same moment, the point which I believe Professor Power has made very clear.

As is well known, the Scottish Liturgy became the basis for that of the Episcopal Church of the United States of America from 1790.[33] The Epiklesis continued to follow the Institution and Anamnesis, but from being a petition that the gifts may become the Body and Blood of Christ, became a prayer that the gifts thus blessed might be received worthily.[34] Strangely, the importance of invoking the Spirit upon both gifts and people was also missed by the compilers of the Western rite Orthodox *St Andrew Service Book*.[35]

Nineteenth and Twentieth Century Developments

It is probably true to say that although there were Anglican scholars who learnt much from the Greek Orthodox liturgical texts in the seventeenth and eighteenth centuries, it would seem that either they had little knowledge or experience of

---

32   J. M. Hussey and P. A. McNulty (eds), *A Commentary on the Divine Liturgy* (London: S.P.C.K., 1960), 72.

33   Detailed account in Marion J. Hatchett, *Commentary on the American Prayer Book* (New York: Seabury Press, 1981), 359–360.

34   Bernard Wigan, *The Liturgy in English* (London: Oxford University Press, 1962), 58–59.

35   *St Andrew Service Book* (Englewood, N.J.: Antiochian Orthodox Christian Archdiocese of North America, 1996), 71–72, and see my discussion in 'Western Rite Orthodoxy – Some reflections on a Liturgical Question' in *St Vladimir's Theological Quarterly* 45 (2001) 163–192.

how they were actually used, or they did not feel any particular sympathy with this seemingly foreign and possibly corrupted church tradition. The Tractarian return to the Fathers greatly enriched the theology and church life of Anglicanism, and of course, drew upon Greek Fathers as much as Latin. Possibly owing to the Romantic movement's correction of extreme enlightenment views, a more sympathetic view of foreign churches became apparent. Finally, there were increasing opportunities to travel and study the Orthodox, as well as continental Roman Catholics.

An important figure for introducing Anglicans to the Orthodox church and its worship is J. M. Neale. The useful index of original first lines in the *English Hymnal* includes twenty-three Greek titles, of which eleven are Neale's translations, including such well-known and loved hymns as 'Come ye faithful, raise the strain', and 'The Day of Resurrection' (based on the opening of the Easter canon). Other translators followed where Neale led and gave us such very well-known pieces as Moultrie's version of the Cherubic Hymn for Holy Saturday and for the Liturgy of St James, 'Let all mortal flesh keep silence'. The numbers of versions of Φως ἱλαρον that are about show the enduring popularity of that ancient hymn. The *English Hymnal*'s version was derived from the *Yattendon Hymnal*, while Keble's found its way into *Hymns Ancient and Modern*. Of course the uses to which these were put could be somewhat different from their original function, so that 'Let all mortal flesh' tends to be used as a communion hymn rather than at the transfer of the gifts of bread and wine to the altar, and Moultrie's version of the Holy Week troparion 'Behold the Bridegroom cometh in the middle of the night' is an Advent hymn in *English Hymnal*.

Neale's own respect for the Orthodox church is well illustrated by the fulsome dedication of his *Essays on Liturgiology*

and Church History[36] to St Philaret (Drozdov), then Metropolitan of Moscow. This respect did not stop Neale criticising
the continued addiction to Church Slavonic in Russia,[37] but in
another essay on 'Prospects of the Oriental Church' he notes
the primitive and privileged status of the immersion in
baptism and the communion of infants. On the latter he says:
'We must always remember, while we condemn the denial of
the chalice to the laity as a great and crying corruption, that
the disuse of the communion of infants is as contrary to
primitive practice, is perhaps even more diametrically opposed
to the express words of Scripture, and is even a later "development".'[38] One cannot help but feel that it is only now that the
Anglican churches have begun to wrestle with the question of
communicating *all* the baptised.

    I would characterise Orthodox influence on Anglican
liturgy in this period as fundamentally indirect. Perhaps the
most important thing was to show that it was possible to have
a realist view of the eucharist, also seeing it as in some way
sacrificial, or to pray for the dead, without having to adopt a
characteristically Roman Catholic theology of Transubstantiation, propitiatory sacrifice, or purgatory. On the other
hand, it is clear that the views of contemporary Roman
Catholicism were in fact gaining more and more ground in the
Church of England's liturgical practice as that practice came
to emphasise the words of Institution with elevations and
bells. Anglo-Catholic devotion moved increasingly towards
adoration of the reserved mysteries in a way quite foreign to
Orthodoxy, and also became more ready to adopt modern
feasts reflecting a Roman theology, such as Corpus Christi
and the Immaculate Conception. I readily concede that most

---

36   J. M. Neale, *Essays on Liturgiology and Church History* (London, 1863).
37   Ibid., 200.
38   Ibid., 261.

of these things were found only amongst the most pro-Roman, but in many ways they had a more direct effect on Anglican worship than anything taken from Orthodoxy.

Iconography is often cited as a particular 'gift' of the Orthodox world to the churches of the West. Unfortunately, for the nineteenth century and much of the twentieth, orthodox iconography was at a low state. Much influenced by Western renaissance painting, it had become dull, lifeless and derivative; however that can be said of a great deal of ecclesiastical art at this period. The progressive revival of traditional styles of icon-painting since the second half of the twentieth century has led to a new atmosphere in Orthodox churches throughout the world, and that is often seen as very attractive by Westerners, who have often introduced icons into their churches. It must be admitted that many people still cannot find in themselves an appreciation of this kind of art, and also that the whole Orthodox theology of the icons and their veneration has not made a great impact in the West as yet.

The Epiklesis again

The nineteenth and twentieth centuries saw a great flowering of liturgical scholarship in the English speaking world. Not only Anglican scholars like A. J. Maclean, W. C. Bishop, F. E. Brightman and H. A. Wilson, but also English Roman Catholic scholars Dom R. H. Connolly and Edmond Bishop all contributed to a new and much more well-founded knowledge of the liturgical texts, their history and their theological context. An important later contributor to this scholarship was Walter Howard Frere, superior of the Community of the

Resurrection from 1916 to 1922 and then Bishop of Truro from 1923 to 1935. He is not only of great importance to our subject as a liturgiologist, but also as one who sought a new mutual understanding with Orthodoxy, not least through his warm relations with Metropolitan Evlogy in Paris.

Frere discussed the Epiklesis in his *Some Principles of Liturgical Reform*[39] and was very cautious about any reinsertion of an invocation of the Spirit. In correspondence with Bishop T. W. Drury of Ripon in 1919, Frere suggested an Epiklesis that was to follow the Institution, and invoked Word and Spirit to bless and sanctify the elements to the benefit of the communicants.[40] Drury, an Evangelical, wrote back a suggestion in which the Father was asked: '[...] send thy Holy Spirit upon us, thy humble servants, that we receiving these thy gifts of Bread and Wine...' When a revision committee discussed it, it became an invocation 'upon us and upon these thy gifts', which is getting remarkably close to the Orthodox formula.[41] However, in a letter of 23 February 1927, the Bishop of Chichester told Frere that he had been informed that the phrase 'to bless and sanctify both us and these thy gifts' would be unacceptable in an Orthodox context![42] This objection seems to have been aimed at a proposed text that simply invoked the Spirit upon gifts and people in a very general way; this was not what found its way into the proposed prayer book of 1928:

---

39   W. H. Frere, *Some Principles of Liturgical Reform* (London: John Murray, 1911), 188–189.
40   R. C. D. Jasper (ed.), *Walter Howard Frere: His Correspondence on Liturgical Revision and Construction* (London: Alcuin/S.P.C.K., 1954), 72.
41   Ibid., 75–77.
42   Ibid., 123.

Hear us, O merciful Father, we most humbly beseech thee, and with thy Holy and Life-giving Spirit vouchsafe to bless and sanctify both us and these thy gifts of Bread and Wine, that they may be unto us the Body and Blood of thy Son, our Saviour Jesus Christ, to the end that we receiving the same, may be strengthened and refreshed both in body and soul.[43]

Frere's later opposition to the proposals appears to have been caused by other areas of dispute; he had, for example, also fought for an alternative Anaphora that did not have an Epiklesis, so as to accommodate the large and very vocal constituency that held on to the theory of the exclusive consecratory value of the Institution narrative.[44] In his writings commenting on the revision process in the Church Province of South Africa, Frere defended the epiklesis and also strongly backed its being an invocation upon both people and gifts.[45] He strongly argued for a theology that explicitly involved the Spirit in the consecration of the gifts and their fruition in the communicants as being primitive, and not just eastern.[46]

I have gone into this in some little detail in order to highlight two important areas; first, that whatever eastern and Orthodox influences were running around, it was often seen as necessary to get behind them to an imagined 'primitive form of the eucharistic prayer'. And secondly, that much of the argument about this was confined to the Spirit's role in consecrating the bread and wine, and the sanctification of the participants was a separate and distinct moment in the eucharistic action.

---

43 *The Book of Common Prayer with the Additions and Deviations Proposed in 1928* (London: Eyre & Spottiswoode), 258.

44 R. C. D. Jasper, *The Development of the Anglican Liturgy 1662–1980* (London: S.P.C.K., 1989), 124–125.

45 See e.g., Jasper (ed.), *Frere: Correspondence*, 211.

46 Ibid., 215–216.

In order to clarify this I should like to outline what I believe to be the present scholarly understanding of the Orthodox tradition of the Epiklesis. We might usefully start with the version of the Liturgy of St Basil used by the Coptic church and identified by scholars as the liturgy that St Basil elaborated and which then became the present Byzantine Anaphora of St Basil. The section we are at present interested in reads:

> And we, sinners and unworthy and wretched, pray you, our God, in adoration that in the good pleasure of your goodness your Holy Spirit may descend upon us and upon these gifts that have been set before you, and may sanctify them and make them holy of holies. Make us worthy to partake of your holy things for sanctification of soul and body, that we may become one body and one spirit, [...]

This, a translation of a Sahidic Coptic text dating to the first half of the seventh century, is notable for the lack of any request for the Spirit to change the gifts.[47] The modern Coptic text has rather awkwardly added an indirect statement about the work of consecration; 'And this bread he makes into his holy body.'[48] The Marquess of Bute's translation is more direct.[49]

The later Byzantine Basil inserts after 'may sanctify and make', the words 'this bread the precious body [...] and this cup the precious blood [...]' and continues to pray, 'Unite with one another all of us who partake'.[50] The Chrysostom liturgy, which is no longer believed to be an abbreviation of Basil but

---

47 R. C. D. Jasper and G. Cuming (eds), *Prayers of the Eucharist: Early and Reformed,* 2nd ed. (New York: Pueblo) 1980, 67–71.

48 *Coptic Liturgies and Hymns* (Hayward, Calif.: Jonathan Center, 1995), 193–194.

49 John, Marquess of Bute, *The Coptic Morning Service for the Lord's Day* (London: Masters, 1882), 89.

50 Jasper and Cuming, 119–120.

a prayer that was at least redacted by the saint,[51] has a similar prayer for the Spirit to be sent upon 'us and on these gifts set forth'. There then follows an obvious insertion, 'and make this bread the precious body of your Christ, etc.', and then it continues: 'so that they [the gifts] may become to those who partake for vigilance of soul, for fellowship with the Holy Spirit, for the fullness of the kingdom'.[52] All this should make clear that the Orthodox tradition invokes the Holy Spirit, not just to change bread and wine, but to change the people who partake of them. Hence the constantly found order of 'us and these gifts here set forth', and the fact that the prayer is not completed by the Deacon's Amens to the petition for the change of the elements, but continues to pray for the foundational benefits of the Eucharist, union in the Spirit with each other and a proleptic entry into the Kingdom of God. Again quoting Power, 'The people are sanctified with and through the sanctification of their gifts.'[53]

It is not clear to me that this understanding has been taken at all seriously by modern western liturgical revision, and yet it is clear that at least one Roman Catholic scholar wishes that it were. We are all now used to the notion that the whole Eucharistic Prayer or Anaphora is consecratory, even if our practices, Roman Catholic, Anglican or Orthodox, do not always clearly witness to this view. I believe that there is more exploration to be done in this area that might be fruitful for all our churches.

The *Alternative Service Book* of 1980 and now *Common Worship* seem in many ways to have been influenced more by the modern Roman Catholic 'split epiklesis', largely derived

51   On this see R. F. Taft, 'The Authenticity of the Chrysostom Anaphora Revisited. Determining the Authorship of Liturgical Texts by Computer', *Orientalia Christiana Periodica* 56 (1990), 5–51.

52   Ibid., 133.

53   See above.

from the theories of Cipriano Vagaggini,[54] rather than by those who have cogently argued against such a theory. However, *Common Worship* does include a version of the Egyptian Basil, which is probably the first time that a eucharistic prayer of Eastern Orthodox provenance has been included in an official liturgical book of the Church of England. Some provinces of the Anglican Communion do already have a version of a proposed ecumenical prayer also based on the Egyptian Basil, and closely related to the fourth Eucharistic Prayer of the Missal of Pope Paul VI.

Prescinding from the unfortunate 'garden of delight' (the new Sourozh translation uses 'paradise of delight' which sounds less like a Chinese restaurant![55]), the *Common Worship* version of St Basil, prayer F, entirely fails to invoke the Spirit upon either us or the gifts, and prays only that the communicants be formed into the likeness of Christ.[56] By contrast the sixth eucharistic prayer of the *Book of Alternative Services of the Anglican Church of Canada* contains this petition:

> Father, we pray that in your goodness and mercy your Holy Spirit may descend upon us, and upon these gifts, sanctifying them and showing then to be holy gifts for your holy people, the bread of life and the cup of salvation, the body and blood of your Son Jesus Christ.
>
> Grant that all who share this bread and this cup may become one body and one spirit, a living sacrifice of Christ to the praise of your name.[57]

---

54 Cipriano Vagaggini, *The Canon of the Mass and Liturgical Reform* (Staten Island, N.Y.: Alba House, 1967).

55 *The Divine Liturgy of our Father among the Saints Basil the Great* (London: Diocese of Sourozh, 2000), 38.

56 *Common Worship* (London: Church House Publishing, 2000), 198–200.

57 *Book of Alternative Services of the Anglican Church of Canada* (Toronto: Anglican Book Centre, 1985), 209–210.

To me, this Canadian prayer shows a real interest in integrating the insights of both Egyptian Basil and its later development, while remaining true to the Anglican tradition of reticence concerning the nature of the eucharistic change. It also clearly anchors the sanctification of the people in the sanctification of the elements. All this reminds us once again that Orthodox influence on Anglican liturgy cannot be confined only to a possible Orthodox influence on the liturgy of the Church of England, even though that church has tended to dominate my present reflections.

Some Other Areas of Consideration

Turning our attention away from the Eucharistic liturgy, we should ask whether Orthodox ideas have had any influence on Anglican theology and practice of initiation. I should imagine that everybody here is well aware that the Prayer Book requires total immersion, unless the parents certify that the child be too weak – this means that the vast majority of infants born of Anglican parents are poorly and in danger of death! To be fair, quite a lot of Russians would be quite alarmed if we always insisted on *total* immersion – the continuance of the practice of pouring water over the baptisand remains a point of dispute with the Old Believers.

It seems likely, bearing in mind some early iconographic representations of the baptism of Christ,[58] and the form of some fonts, such as that at Dura Europus in Syria, that pouring water over a person standing up to ankle depth was

---

58 E.g., The Neonian Baptistery (Baptistery of the Orthodox) in Ravenna of the 5th century.

quite normal in late antiquity. Many modern writers distinguish between submersion (total) and immersion (partial), and
both appear to have been acceptable. The reaction against
(partial) immersion may well have been occasioned by the
increasingly minimalistic practices relating to *quam primum*
baptism, i.e., as soon as possible after birth. It is probably true
to say that it is only now that the Western churches have
really begun to revive the lavish use of water in baptism, and I
would think that the example of the Orthodox has probably
been influential here, especially amongst those who would not
have been convinced by the equally good example of the
Baptists!

The biggest problem in modern initiation is surely that of
infant communion. The Western churches, especially Roman
Catholic and Anglican, have the complicating problem of the
status of Confirmation. The work of scholars such as Aidan
Kavanagh has shown that the baptismal washing and the gift
of the Spirit are but two moments of the same rite.[59] This is
the traditional way in which the Orthodox church has also
regarded Baptism and Chrismation, in spite of the way the
rite has been presented in later books under Western influence. For example, the well-known and frequently misleading
Service Book of Isabel Hapgood breaks up the Baptism service
with a large heading: *The Office of Holy Chrismation,*[60] while
the authoritative Ευχολογιον το μεγα, while differentiating
the making of the catechumen and the rites eight days
after baptism from the actual rite of baptism, includes the
chrismation in the latter without further heading.[61]

---

59   Aidan Kavanagh, *The Shape of Baptism* (New York: Pueblo, 1978).
60   *The Office of Holy Chrismation* (Reprinted, Englewood, N.J.: Antiochian
     Orthodox Christian Archdiocese, 1975), 281.
61   (Venice: 1839), 143–145.

The two problems here are the desire to count exactly seven sacraments, a desire not unknown to Orthodoxy but entirely foreign to it, and the perceived problem of the role of bishops – if they do not do confirmations, have they a role? All I can say at this time is that the number of diocesan bishops in Russia has hugely increased in recent years, and there are now more dioceses than there were before the Revolution, and the bishops all do seem to have plenty to do!

The role of bishops brings me to another area where all the Western churches might like to look closely at Orthodox practice, that is ordinations to the ministry. It is my impression that much modern Western thinking and discussion tends to concentrate on promises and the content of instructions. Late medieval and Reformation–Counter-Reformation controversy tended to revolve around the very late medieval rites of *porrectio instrumentorum*[62] and anointing. The Byzantine Orthodox rites of ordination to diaconate and presbyterate have no instructional material, no promises, no anointing, and only a very limited form of *porrectio;* the deacon is given a fan to wave over the gifts, and the priest is entrusted with the consecrated lamb until it is time for the fraction.[63] The consecration of a bishop has developed an elaborate rite of profession of faith, which is really more to do with the rite of election.[64] In all cases the emphasis is on the selection of this person, and then prayer with the laying on of hands; the prayer being a general petition for the grace to undertake the particular ministry, described in quite broad terms.

It is no longer true, I hope, that bishops have no real idea of the truth of a person's vocation and that person's readiness

---

62 That is, the giving of such things as a chalice and paten to a newly ordained priest, saying certain words.

63 See Hapgood, 311–318.

64 Ibid., 323–331.

to exercise ministry before the actual ceremony. Maybe the relative abruptness of the Orthodox ordination could serve as a model for a ministry that was truly to be exercised in and of the community, rather than by somebody picked and placed over the community by ecclesiastical authority.

A similar area would be the very different concepts of Christian marriage in east and west, a difference that appears to be entirely insuperable. Traditional Orthodox rites contain no exchange of vows and the ritual emphasis is on the church's blessing and crowning of the marriage. This is in contrast to a sometimes almost Pelagian insistence on the couple's vows and intention that seems to leave relatively little room for the grace of God. On the other hand, Orthodoxy has a special rite for second marriage, which has certainly been of interest to some Anglicans, as a way of coping with the regrettable but unavoidable fact of divorce.[65]

One of the features of Orthodox worship that is attractive to some people, while alienating others, is the sense of mystery associated with dark, icon-filled churches with great screens that hide some of the action from view. Many Orthodox churches are not in fact shrines of the 'dim religious light' that many nineteenth century thinkers saw as vital for true devotion. Both in Greece and in Russia one can go into churches that are filled with light, but they all have iconostases. The idea of the iconostasis is not to act as a barrier to the sanctuary, so much as a window upon eternity. The desire to see what is going on at the altar is a misplaced one, for in a purely worldly sense nothing is going on! What is really happening is happening in heaven as we present ourselves before the unseen throne of God.[66] This appears to be a view that

---

65   The rite is in Hapgood, 302–305.
66   Gregory Woolfenden, 'Is Seeing necessarily Believing?', *Studia Liturgica* 29 (1999), 84–99.

would now be almost totally rejected in the west, with the almost complete ubiquity of the modern innovation of the altar facing the people. I would like to suggest that the Orthodox church building is not primarily concentrated on the altar and sanctuary in the same way as a Roman Catholic or Anglican church is; the principal space is congregational and the most important acts take place in that space. This is something that might be more influential in the future.

In his fascinating and amusing book *Fashions in Church Furnishings,*[67] Peter Anson tried to show how the styles of ecclesiastical vesture and decoration seemed to follow secular fashion. How he would have enjoyed post-Modernism! I seem to recollect that, somewhere in that book, he suggested that when vestments were revived in the Anglican churches, they would have been less divisive had an eastern shape been adopted rather than a western. I am not sure that heavy, stiff Russian vestments would have immediately won the hearts of doughty Protestants, but fuller vesture and more relaxed and less precise ceremonial might have caused less irritation. The Russian church in particular took the grand and spacious Byzantine ceremonial to heart and made it its own, and many non-Orthodox observers agree that it is often carried out in a far more relaxed way than is normal in many of the more ceremonial western liturgical traditions. Perhaps one of the best influences that has reached some parts of Anglicanism from Orthodoxy is that one does not have to be ceremonious and portentous in the house of God – for it is our house as well, and we can all be at home within it.

---

67   Peter Anson, *Fashions in Church Furnishings,* 2nd ed., (London: Studio Vista, 1965).

10. Greek Orthodox Compensatory Strategies towards Anglicans and the West at the Beginning of the Eighteenth Century

Vasilios N. Makrides

Introduction

It is useful to begin this paper with an overview of the entire socio-historical context under which my particular topic falls. This is because the prehistory of my topic is vital for capturing the significance of the *longue durée*-phenomenon under discussion. If one tries to consider the Eastern Byzantine world and the Western Latin world as entire cultural complexes and to discern their idiosyncrasies throughout the Middle Ages, a particular recurrent feature may be located. This has to do with the continuous mutual comparison between these two cultures and the need to establish the superiority of the one over the other. Needless to say, the progressive and growing estrangement between these two worlds at the time made this feature even stronger. If one examines, for example, the eleventh century, i.e. the period of the Great Schism of 1054, one realises that this alienation was already a fact. The same pertains especially to the period after the sacking of Constantinople by the Crusaders in 1204, which rendered the separation between the two worlds irreparable in the hearts of Orthodox Christians. Mutual perceptions between Eastern and Western Christians were afterwards marked by negative and pejorative characterisations, feelings of resentment against each other, and complete lack of understanding. Religious differences between East and West were further transformed into deep cultural and socio-political rifts. In this way, this process of comparison pertained not only to the elements supporting religious superiority (e.g., orthodoxy vs. heterodoxy and heresy), but also to the general non-religious achievements of the two worlds and their overall ways of life.

Yet, as long as the Byzantine Empire existed, it is accurate to say that most Byzantines felt superior not only to Western Christians, but to other peoples as well. Considering themselves as being the 'new Israel', i.e., the new elect people of God, the Byzantines were generally convinced of their innate superiority to every other part of mankind.[1] This superiority was founded in three distinct, but interrelated ways: ethnic; cultural, based on ancient Greek culture and their separation from the barbarians or half-barbarians (μιξοβάρβαροι); and religious, through the possession of the uncontaminated Orthodox Christian faith.[2] There exist many evidences of such Byzantine attitudes towards other peoples including Western Christians, who especially after 1204 were seen in very negative terms in the Orthodox East (cf. a characteristic Greek play on the words Ἰταλός, Italian, and ἰταμός, impudent, shameless).[3] This superiority did not pertain solely to the domain of theology, but also to that of the 'liberal arts', and other forms of secular knowledge (ἐγκύκλιος

---

1   R. Jenkins, *Byzantium and Byzantinism* (Cincinnati, 1963), 5.
2   H. Hunger, *Byzanz, eine Gesellschaft mit zwei Gesichtern*. Eine J. C. Jacobsen Gedenkvorlesung (Det Kongelige Danske Videnskabernes Selskab, Historisk-filosofiske Meddelelser 51:2) (København, 1984), 10.
3   See H. Hunger, *Graeculus perfidus* – Ἰταλὸς Ἰταμός. *Il senso dell' alterità nei rapporti Greco-Romani ed Italo-Bisantini* (Roma, 1987).

παιδεία).[4] Such differences were highlighted in disputations with Western Christians by Nikiphoros Vlemmydis and Theodoros Laskaris in the thirteenth century as well as by Nikiphoros Gregoras (in his dialogue Φλωρέντιος) in the fourteenth century.[5] It is interesting to note that this Byzantine superiority was more or less acknowledged by Western Christians, who at the time of the Great Schism either keenly realised their inferiority or tried to compensate for it in various, even aggressive ways. The rise of strong anti-Byzantine feelings at the time among the Latin religious elite is a case in point. To mention just an example: Liutprand, the bishop of Cremona, having twice visited Constantinople in 949–950 and in 968, included in his work *Legatio* many critical observations on the Byzantine way of life. Liutprand's particular reaction has been interpreted as a Latin way of compensating for the established cultural superiority of Byzantium.[6] In other words, feelings of inferiority could lead to the formation of certain compensatory mechanisms to alleviate them. Even in the period of the Great Schism the Western view of Byzantium (apart from some negative opinions for understandable reasons) did recognise openly the intellectual strength and the superiority of the Byzantines (e.g., the Greek *sapientia*).[7]

---

4   Cf. Hunger, *Byzanz, eine Gesellschaft*, 22: *Unbestritten bleibt die Überlegenheit der byzantinischen Bildung im Vergleich zum Westen während des ganzen Mittelalters.*

5   F. Tinnefeld, 'Das Niveau der abenländischen Wissenschaft aus der Sicht gebildeter Byzantiner im 13. und 14. Jh.', *Byzantinische Forschungen* 6 (1979), 241–280, here 248–261, 265–267.

6   See M. Rentschler, *Liudprand von Cremona. Eine Studie zum ost–westlichen Kulturgefälle im Mittelalter* (Frankfurt, 1981).

7   H. Hunger, *Phänomen Byzanz – aus europäischer Sicht* (= Bayerische Akademie der Wissenschaften, Phil.-Hist. Klasse, Sitzungsberichte Jg. 1984, Heft 3) (München, 1984), 18–19. For further details see also B. Ebels-Hoving, *Byzantium in westerse ogen, 1096–1204,* (Assen, 1971);

Is it, however, accurate to consider the entire Western culture of the time as being inferior to the Byzantine one? Is it perhaps better to locate the particular periods in which this was more or less true? This observation becomes useful if we examine the last 150 years of Byzantine history. In this particular period we observe an increased internal dissatisfaction among many Byzantines with the cultural, religious and socio-political foundations of their empire. This phenomenon was connected to a quest for importing fresh knowledge from abroad including – peculiarly enough – from those previously considered barbarians or half-barbarians.[8] I. Ševcenko has aptly described this period as 'the decline of Byzantium'.[9] One source for a potential renewal of Byzantium was the West itself, which from the high Middle Ages onwards was not inferior to Byzantium, as some Byzantines thought or wanted to believe. The rise of the medieval universities, of Aristotelianism, of scholasticism as well as seminal developments in science and technology are but a few examples indicating the progress made in the West. Such developments could not simply be passed over in silence. It is not accidental that some Byzantines noticed this Western progress and intended to profit from it.

In the domain of theology let me mention here the brothers Dimitrios and Prochoros Kydonis, converts to Roman Catholicism, who learned Latin, translated Latin theological works into Greek (including the *Summa contra Gentiles* and the *Summa theologica* of Thomas Aquinas) and familiarised

---

M. Rentschler, 'Griechische Kultur und Byzanz im Urteil westlicher Autoren des 10. Jahrhunderts', *Saeculum* 29 (1978), 324–355; idem, 'Griechische Kultur und Byzanz im Urteil westlicher Autoren des 11. Jahrhunderts', *Saeculum* 31 (1980), 112–156.

8   See Tinnefeld, 'Das Niveau', 262–265.

9   I. Ševcenko, 'The Decline of Byzantium Seen Through the Eyes of its Intellectuals', *Dumbarton Oaks Papers* 15 (1961), 167–186.

themselves with Western theological reasoning. It is characteristic that Aquinas opened for Dimitrios Kydonis the world
of Latin theology, who was amazed at the 'loftiness of his
thoughts, and the inevitable logic of his syllogisms'. After
having tasted the lotus (λωτοῦ δὲ γεσαύσαμενος), Kydonis
could not but continue to pursue Latin theology. His translations had shown that the Latins were able to think too and
that consequently the ancient illusion of dividing mankind
into Greeks and barbarians (including the Latins) had to
be radically revisited (πάντας ἀνθρώπους εἰς Ἕλληνας καὶ
βαρβάρους διχοτομοῦντες). Kydonis also opined that previously
there was no way to prove to his compatriots that the Latins
could think and talk about anything other than paltry,
mechanical arts. In his opinion, the long separation of the two
peoples had resulted in much ignorance of each other (τὸ γὰρ
πολὺν χρόνον ἀλλήλων διεστάναι, τὰ ἔθνη πολλὴν ἀλλήλων
ἄγνοιαν ἀμφοτέροις ἐνέθηκεν).[10]

In the domain of technical and scientific progress, let me
mention Cardinal Bessarion, another convert to Roman
Catholicism. From 1441 he lived in Italy and had the opportunity to observe various scientific and technical developments there. Around 1444 he wrote a lengthy letter to the
future last Byzantine emperor, Constantine XII Palaeologus,
when the latter was still despot of the autonomous Byzantine
province of Morea. There he asked him to send gifted Greek
students to Italy in order to profit from the new technical
developments, such as the use of water to eliminate manual

---

10   See K. M. Setton, 'The Byzantine Background to the Italian Renais-
     sance', *Proccedings of the American Philosophical Society* 100/1 (February,
     1956), 1–76, here 52–57. See also Tinnefeld, 'Das Niveau', 268–280;
     G. Podskalsky, *Theologie und Philosophie in Byzanz* (München, 1977);
     Ph. Demetracopoulos, 'Demetrius Kydones' translation of the
     Summa Theologica', *Jahrbuch der Österreichischen Byzantinistik* 32/4
     (1982), 311–319.

labour as well as new arts of weapon-making and shipbuilding. Subsequently, they could introduce this new knowledge to Byzantium and contribute to the much needed defence against the expanding threat of the Ottoman Turks. Bessarion emphasised that the Byzantines had no reason at all to feel inferior to the West because they would take some knowledge from there. In reality, they were going to take back what they had offered to the West several centuries ago.[11]

These exemplary cases make clear the ways in which the traditional Byzantine sense of superiority was challenged and called into question during this period. Such pro-Western proclivities among certain Byzantines, however, caused heated reactions from the anti-Western majority of the clergy and laity. This was because, especially after 1204, the West was seen by Orthodox Christians not only as a religious, but also as a generalised threat.[12] Some anti-Westerners even went so far as to prefer Ottoman rule over Byzantium to union with Rome.[13] Such an attitude can be observed *mutatis mutandis* later as well, when many anti-Western Orthodox bestowed upon the Ottoman domination a religious legitimacy.[14]

---

11   See S. Lambros, "Ὑπόμνημα τοῦ Καρδιναλίου Βησσαρίωνος εἰς Κωνσταντῖνον τὸν Παλαιολόγον', Νέος Ἑλληνομνήμων 3 (1906), 12–55; A. G. Keller, 'A Byzantine Admirer of "Western" Progress: Cardinal Bessarion', *The Cambridge Historical Journal* 11 (1955), 343–348; Chr. P. Baloglou, 'Προτάσεις οἰκονομικῆς καὶ κοινωνικῆς πολιτικῆς ἀπὸ τὸν Βησσαρίωνα', Βυζαντινὸς Δόμος 5–6 (1991/92), 47–73.

12   See A. Kolia-Dermitzaki, 'Die Kreuzfahrer und die Kreuzzüge im Sprachgebrauch der Byzantiner', *Jahrbuch der Österreichischen Byzantinistik* 41 (1991), 163–188; A. E. Laiou and R. P. Mottahedeh (eds), *The Crusades from the Perspective of Byzantium and the Muslim World* (Washington, D.C., 2001).

13   See H. Evert-Kappesowa, 'La tiare ou le turban', *Byzantinoslavica* 14 (1953), 245–257.

14   See R. Clogg, 'The "Dhidhaskalia Patriki" (1798): an Orthodox Reaction to French Revolutionary Propaganda', *Middle Eastern Studies* 5

What happened, then, after the fall of Byzantium to relations between East and West and the aforementioned quest for superiority? The religious and cultural confrontation between the two worlds continued to take place, but within a quite different context. Byzantium as a political institution had ceased to exist and the Eastern Christian world was for many centuries in a period of stagnation, cultural and otherwise. This was due mainly to the harsh conditions of the Ottoman domination and to the concomitant general seclusion of the East from the tremendous developments in the West. This additional separation further deepened the existing schism between East and West. At the same time, the West remained free and had the opportunity to develop at an incredible pace. A few examples can illustrate this unprecedented Western evolution from the fifteenth through the eighteenth centuries: the age of discoveries; Western overseas expansion and colonialism; the Renaissance; humanism; the Reformation; the scientific revolution; major socio-political developments concerning individual human rights and parliamentarianism; and the Enlightenment. None of these breakthroughs that radically shaped modern Europe and subsequently the whole world came out of Eastern Christian lands. In some cases, though, the East did play a catalytic role in the emergence of such developments; for instance, through the emigration of Byzantine scholars and their contribution to the Renaissance in Italy,[15] and later through some Greek humanists (Frangiskos Portos, 1511–1581, Maximos Margounios, 1549–1602, Ioannis Kottounios, 1572–1657) residing and

---

(1969), 87–115; idem, 'Anti-clericalism in pre-independence Greece c. 1750–1821', in D. Baker (ed.), *The Orthodox Churches and the West* (Oxford, 1976), 257–276, here 261–262.

15   For details see Setton, 'The Byzantine Background', passim; D. J. Geanakoplos, *Interaction of the Sibling Byzantine and Western Cultures in the Middle Ages and Italian Renaissance* (New Haven, 1976).

teaching in the West who contributed to the rise of European humanism. But these contributions were articulated and shaped in a fundamentally different socio-political and cultural environment than the East, namely in the West, where these scholars were able to live and work.

This overall situation made the gap between East and West during this period even greater and later led to the rise of various strong pro-Western currents in the East, which were keenly aware of its lack of progress and demanded wholesale Westernisation.[16] Yet, while for the pro-Westerners the West was an ideal model to imitate, the anti-Westerners considered it as the source of all evils. These opposite currents and orientations characterised the entire history of the Orthodox East throughout the modern period and are responsible for its torn identity until today. More specifically, the anti-Westerners were eager to develop various compensatory mechanisms in order to alleviate their inferiority complex, to show the vanity of the Western progress, and to demonstrate the real superiority of the Orthodox East. This will be the focus of my paper with reference to the beginning of the eighteenth century.

---

16   See L. S. Stavrianos, 'The Influence of the West on the Balkans', in
      Ch. and B. Jelavich (eds), *The Balkans in Transition*, (Berkeley/Los
      Angeles, 1963), 184–226.

East and West at the Beginning of the Eighteenth Century

Let me turn now to the period of the Greek College at the beginning of the eighteenth century. How was the situation between East and West at that time? The old enmity and confrontation between the Orthodox and the Roman Catholic Churches was still alive and well. The chaplain to the Levant Company in Constantinople and later Master of Christ's College in Cambridge, John Covel, wrote characteristically about this ecclesiastical alienation, 'It is incredible how great malice, envy and inward hatred there is between the Greek and Latin churches.'[17] To mention an example: in 1706 the Patriarch of Constantinople Gabriel III (after 20 August 1702 – 17 August 1707) sent an encyclical to the inhabitants of the island of Andros, his birthplace, in order to protect them from the Roman Catholic propaganda and its agents, the so-called Φραγγοπατέρες. His encyclical abounds in negative characterisations about the fake, perverted and novel Roman Catholic doctrines (κίβδηλα καὶ διεφθαρμένα νεωτερίσματα – ὑστερογενῆ ἐφευρήματα – φρενοβλαβῆ νεωτερίσματα) deviating from the traditional Orthodox faith. The term 'innovate' (νεωτερίζω or καινοτομῶ) has a long tradition of negative connotations in the Orthodox East since the early Byzantine times and not only in the religious domain.[18] The Patriarch considered the preservation of the Orthodox faith the highest task of every true Orthodox believer, even at the price of the believer's own life (ὥστε, ἐὰν γένηται χρεία, νὰ χύσουν καὶ τὸ

---

17   J. Covel, *Some Account of the Present Greek Church* [...], (London, 1722), lii (preface).

18   Hunger, *Byzanz, eine Gesellschaft*, 26–27.

258 *Vasilios N. Makrides*

αἷμά των, καὶ αὐτὴν ὁμοῦ τὴν ζωήν των νὰ παραδώσουν διὰ τὴν ὀρθοδοξίαν καὶ εὐσέβειαν)[19]

Yet this anti-Catholic spirit among the Orthodox did not mean there was no contact with the West as a whole. There were numerous such contacts at many levels ranging from the Greeks residing or studying in Western Europe to Greek converts, mainly to Roman Catholicism. The presence of Western diplomats and their entourages at the Sublime Porte in Constantinople as well as the commercial activities of Western companies in the Levant further facilitated this rapprochement, as did the religious differentiation of Western Europe through the appearance of the various Reformed Churches (Lutherans, Calvinists, Anglicans, etc.). In truth, the encounter of the latter with the Orthodox East was not particularly fruitful. The Orthodox still continued to view the West as a whole in religious and other terms as a threat. But the fragmentation of the Western religious landscape led unavoidably to the proliferation of contacts between East and West. After all, the Orthodox East was seen by Western Christians in general as a promising area to be exploited, not only in terms of a missionary expansion of influence, but also in terms of finding a potential ally in the wider context of the confessional disputes and wars of the day. This struggle for increased influence in the East was sometimes connected with tragic events, such as those related to the violent death of the Patriarch of Constantinople Cyril Loukaris in 1638.[20] This Western interest in the Orthodox East is also mirrored at the beginning of the eighteenth century by the story of

---

19   D. P. Paschalis, Γαβριὴλ ὁ Γ΄ Πατριάρχης Κωνπόλεως (1702–1707)', Ἐπετηρὶς Ἑταιρείας Βυζαντινῶν Σπουδῶν 10 (1933), 304–320, here 308–312.

20   See G. Hering, *Ökumenisches Patriarchat und europäische Politik 1620–1638* (Wiesbaden, 1968). There is a Greek translation of an updated edition with additions, Athens, 1992.

the Greek College in Oxford (1699–1705), the subsequent *Collegium Orientale Theologicum* in Halle (1703–1707),[21] and the Roman Catholic attempts to stop this growing Anglican and Pietistic influence in the East.[22] After all, the Roman Catholics were the ones who had initiated similar endeavours. The *Collegio San Atanasio* in Rome had been founded by Pope Gregory XIII in 1573 to educate ex-Orthodox Greek students and to use them later to infiltrate the Orthodox East.[23]

Be this as it may, it is also worth noting that at the beginning of the eighteenth century the West was for many Greek Orthodox a place from which they could learn and profit. This period preceded the better-known era of the so-called 'Neohellenic Enlightenment' (1774–1821), when a more systematic effort was undertaken to bridge the gap between East and West through a process of Westernisation[24] such as that undertaken earlier by Tsar Peter the Great (1689–1725) in Russia, causing him to be hailed as a seminal figure worthy of imitation in the Orthodox Balkans.[25] At the beginning of the

---

21   On this Pietistic attempt, see U. Moennig, 'Die griechischen Studenten am Hallenser Collegium orientale theologicum', in J. Wallmann and U. Sträter, Hrsg., *Halle und Osteuropa. Zur europäischen Ausstrahlung des hallischen Pietismus* (Tübingen 1998), 299–329.

22   Cf. the reaction of a Cretan convert to Roman Catholicism, Nicholas Comnenus Papadopoli (1655–1740): A. Pippidi, 'On Wallachia's Relations with Padua', *Revue des Études Sud-Est Européennes* 26 (1988), 267–270, here 269–270.

23   See Z. Tsirpanlis, Τὸ Ἑλληνικὸ Κολλέγιο τῆς Ρώμης καὶ οἱ μαθητές του *(1576–1700)*. Συμβολὴ στὴ μελέτη τῆς μορφωτικῆς πολιτικῆς τοῦ Βατικανοῦ (Thessaloniki, 1980).

24   See indicatively P. M. Kitromilides, Νεοελληνικὸς Διαφωτισμός Οἱ πολιτικὲς καὶ κοινωνικὲς ἰδέες (Athens, 1996).

25   See P. Cernovodeanu, 'Pierre le Grand dans l'historiographie roumaine et balkanique du XVIIIe siècle', *Revue des Études Sud-Est Européennes* 13 (1975), 77–95; Ath. E. Karathanassis, 'Pierre le Grand et l'intelligentsia grecque (1685–1740)', in *Les relations Gréco-Russes*

eighteenth century many Greeks had already realised the progress made by the West in many areas and intended to profit from it. They were aware of the inability of their own culture to provide them with the latest standards of learning, therefore they looked for any possibility to move to the West and to study there. The students attracted by the Greek College and later by the *Collegium Orientale Theologicum* fit into this pattern, even though many of them later complained about the quality of learning offered to them in the West.

Benjamin Woodroffe, the initiator of the Greek College, had made clear in his treatise *A Model of a College to be settled in the University for the Education of some Youths of the Greek Church* that the young Greeks could profit greatly from the rich curriculum at Oxford which was unavailable in their country under Ottoman rule.[26] In his letter to the Patriarch of Constantinople Kallinikos II (1688, 1689–1693, 1694–1702) in order to familiarise him with the whole project, Woodroffe spoke warmly of the debt owed by England to the contributions of earlier Greeks to the arts, the sciences and theology. The foundation of the Greek College at the famous academy of Oxford, which was comparable to the ancient one in classical Athens, was portrayed as a way of repaying this debt.[27] By writing these lines Woodroffe appeared fully convinced of Western superiority in education, whereas in his view Greece was mainly relying upon the glory of earlier times. The same image was conveyed by the Greek students

---

      pendant la domination turque et la guerre d'indépendance grecque. Premier
      colloque organisé à Thessalonique (23–25 Septembre 1981), (Thessaloniki,
      1983), 43–52.

26   See E. D. Tappe, 'The Greek College at Oxford, 1699–1705',
      Oxoniensia 19 (1954), 92–111, and above.

27   S. Runciman, *The Great Church in Captivity. A Study of the Patriarchate*
      of Constantinople from the Eve of the Turkish Conquest to the Greek War of
      Independence (Cambridge, 1968), 301.

themselves in their ode in Greek hexameters to Queen Anne in August 1702 when she passed on her way from Windsor to Bath via Oxford. These Greek students made reference to the lost ancient wisdom that had motivated them to come to England in order to study and repossess it (οἱ μὲν δεξάμενοι πάλιν, ἥν ποτ᾽ ὄλεσσαν, / ᾽Αρχαίην σοφίην).[28] Needless to say, this is hardly the sole evidence of such a mentality among the Greeks at the time.[29]

Although the big gap in knowledge and progress between East and West was undeniable at that time and the inferiority complex of the East vis-à-vis the West was increasing, there were also some notable exceptions. These show that Greek culture was still in a position to contribute in some cases to general progress. I am referring here specifically to the contributions of two Greek physicians, Emmanuel Timonis from Chios and Iakovos Pylarinos (1659–1718) from Cephalonia. They had studied medicine in Padua and were the first to familiarise Western Europeans with the practice of smallpox inoculation or variolation in a scientific way.[30] They

---

28 This verse address was printed in Greek (28–29) with an English translation (30–32) in: Ἡ τῶν ᾽Αγίων Γραφῶν αὐτάρκεια ἐν δυσὶ διαλέξεσιν ἀποδειχθεῖσα Γεωργίου ᾽Απτάλ, καὶ Γεωργίου Μαρούλου τὸν λόγον ἐναλλὰξ ὑπεχόντων, Πρυτανεύοντος Βενιαμὶν Οὐωδρῶφ τοῦ Ἱεροδιδασκάλου, καὶ τῶν Ἑλλήνων παίδων περὶ τὰς Μαθήσεις ἐν ᾽Οξονίᾳ (Oxford, 1704). See Appendix C below.

29 See three characteristic letters in 1631 by the Archmandrites Grigorios Kantakouzinos and Grigorios Makedonios to King Charles I, to the Bishop of London and to the Archbishop of Canterbury, who asked for help in order to study at Oxford and described in negative colours the overall situation in Greece under Ottoman rule: A. Tillyrides, ''Ανέκδοτος ἀλληλογραφία ἐκ τῶν ἐν ᾽Αγγλίᾳ ἐπιδημησάντων Ἑλλήνων τινῶν τοῦ 17ου αἰῶνος', Θεολογία 45 (1974), 659–709, here 682–684.

30 See Chr. G. Jöcher (Hrsg.), *Allgemeines Gelehrten-Lexicon*, Volume III (Leipzig, 1751) col. 1566 (s.v. Pilarino).

characterised it as a traditional Byzantine and Greek practice and their observations were reported in the *Philosophical Transactions* of the Royal Society in 1714 and in 1716 respectively as well as in separate scholarly publications.[31] This practice had been also observed in the East by Lady Mary Wortley Montagu, the wife of the British ambassador to the Sublime Porte,[32] who in 1721 introduced it for the first time to England. The practice of variolation spread rapidly to other parts of the world and was further succeeded by the vaccination propagated much later by Edward Jenner (1749–1823). Yet it was these two Greek doctors who for the first time had elevated this traditional empirical practice to a scientific level.

One could mention several other examples from that period, such as the large number of Greek physicians at the court of Peter the Great in Russia[33] or other Greeks who had made a name for themselves in the West. The latter included Anastasios Michail from Naousa (died 1725), a man of wide and remarkable erudition, who became a member of the *Berliner Sozietät (Akademie) der Wissenchaften*,[34] and Damianos Paraskevas from Sinope, who published three philosophical treatises in Germany and supported Chr. Wolff's philosophy in the late 1720s.[35] Yet, there exists a crucial element here

---

31 See S. Geroulanos, 'Iakovos Pylarinos (1659–1718) und sein Beitrag zur Variolation', *Gesnerus* 35 (1978), 264–275.

32 See her description of this practice in her letter to Sarah Chiswell from Adrianople (1 April 1717), R. Halsband (ed.), *The Complete Letters of Lady Mary Wortley Montagu*,v.i (1708–1720) (Oxford, 1965), 337–340.

33 See V. N. Makrides, Στοιχεῖα γιὰ τὶς σχέσεις τοῦ ᾿Αλεξάνδρου ῾Ελλαδίου μὲ τὴ Ρωσία″, Μνήμων 19 (1997), 9–39.

34 See V. Beneševic, 'Anastasios Nausios', *Byzantinisch-Neugriechische Jahrbücher* 10 (1932–34), 351–368, here 360.

35 See Damianus Sinopeus, *Meditationes Academicae de cognitione humana* [...] (Weimar, 1728); idem, *Tractatio methodica de libertate cogitandi* [...]

demonstrating the real inferiority of the East and the superiority of the West. Western culture played a vital role in the formation of these Greek scholars. In other words, all of them had been first educated in the West and later were in a position to make significant contributions. The potential of Greek scholarship at the time seemed therefore to depend upon the Western intellectual foundations. This makes the gap between the two worlds more evident.

Concerning the observed stagnation of the Greek world at the time and the concomitant inferiority complex towards the West, these can be attributed to various, sometimes interrelated, reasons. Firstly, the Ottoman domination of the Greek world raised, at least at the beginning, a serious barrier to the free development of a more fruitful interaction with the West. The Orthodox Greeks did not at the time feel part of 'civilised' Europe, therefore the identification of the West with Europe is usual in the Greek sources of this period. Secondly, the Orthodox Church through its anti-Western policies acted very often as a power that kept the divide between the two worlds alive. Thirdly, the Greek inferiority complex was enhanced by the huge discrepancy between the tremendous accomplishments of the ancient Greeks and the scarcity of modern Greek achievements. While Western Europeans considered themselves as worthy heirs to the ancient Greek heritage by maintaining it successfully, modern Greeks were seen as unable to produce anything of universal significance and value. Such a comparison was devastating to modern Greeks, even though many of them invented various ways to appropriate the heritage of their ancestors in an exclusive way.

(Weimar, 1728); idem, *Defensio Philosophiae Wolffianae* [...] (Eisenach, 1729). Later he published a medical book entitled *Parerga medica* (St Petersburg, 1734).

Greek Orthodox Compensatory
Strategies against Western Progress

It is appropriate now to examine more closely the various
compensatory strategies that were used by Orthodox Greeks
in order to demonstrate the superiority of the East vis-à-vis
the West and to minimise the achievements of the latter.
Throughout the period of the Ottoman domination we encounter a large variety of such strategies and related arguments. One such widespread argument was to claim that the
birthplace of all knowledge was ancient Greece and that
the modern West had simply walked in the footsteps of the
ancients by borrowing and even stealing from them. In other
words, modern developments would never have been possible
if the ancient Greeks had not first opened the way. This
argument was expounded in the fifteenth century by Michael
Apostolis (1422–1480),[36] in the seventeenth century by the
Patriarch of Jerusalem Nektarios (1602–1676),[37] and in the
early nineteenth century by Luigi Sotiris in his book Ἀπολογία
ἱστορικοκριτική, published in modern Greek by the priest Anastasios from Ambelakia in 1814 in Trieste.[38] By contrast, the
Greek bearers of the Enlightenment (e.g., Iosipos Moisiodax)

---

36   See V. Laourdas, 'Μιχαὴλ Ἀποστόλη, Λόγος περὶ Ἑλλάδος καὶ
      Εὐρώπης', Ἐπετηρὶς Ἑταιρείας Βυζαντινῶν Σπουδῶν 19 (1949), 235–
      244; D. J. Geanakoplos, 'A Byzantine Looks at the Renaissance. The
      Attitude of Michael Apostolis Toward the Rise of Italy to Cultural
      Eminence', *Greek and Byzantine Studies* 1 (1958), 157–162; idem, *Greek
      Scholars in Venice. Studies in the Dissemination of Greek Learning from
      Byzantium to Western Europe* (Cambridge, Mass., 1962), 108–111.
37   See I. Sakkelion, 'Διονυσίου Πατριάρχου Κωνσταντινουπόλεως καὶ
      Νεκταρίου πρώην Ἱεροσολύμων ἔγγραφα', Ἐκκλησιαστικὴ Ἀλήθεια 1
      (1881), 86–91 and 104–107.
38   See V. N. Makrides, *Die religiöse Kritik am kopernikanischen Weltbild in
      Griechenland zwischen 1794 und 1821* (Frankfurt a. M., 1995), 453–455.

tried to show that the moderns surpassed the ancients in many domains.[39]

In the present paper I will concentrate on examining such strategies of comparison and the quest for superiority at the beginning of the eighteenth century by mentioning a few examples pertaining to the Anglicans and more broadly to Western Christians. These cases present some peculiarities, because they were underscored by the particular needs of the day. By 'compensatory mechanisms' I mean the efforts on the part of certain Greek Orthodox to offer persuasive counter-arguments to various Western challenges. The main objective of these arguments was to show the incomparable value of the Greek Orthodox culture and to devalue or to minimise the importance of Western progress by totally rejecting or only partially accepting it. It is particularly interesting that such strategies were not confined to those who were in general critically disposed towards the West and were reluctant to acknowledge the decline of Greek learning. They can even be found among those who saw the West more positively, were more open and intended to profit from Western knowledge. All in all, these are nativistic strategies of defence in which the elements of the indigenous culture are used against the adulterating influences coming from abroad. This whole compensatory process reveals, albeit indirectly, that the inferiority complex under discussion was real and tangible at the time.

---

39 P. M. Kitromilides, 'The Last Battle of the Ancients and the Moderns: Ancient Greece and Modern Europe in the Neohellenic Revival', *Modern Greek Studies Yearbook* 1 (1985), 79–91.

The Incomparable Value of Orthodoxy as a Criterion of Superiority

The most widespread compensatory strategy against the
West, found throughout the period of Ottoman domination,
set new criteria for establishing superiority. According to
many Greek Orthodox, this comparison should not be made
on the basis of Western criteria and arguments. On the contrary, one had to pay more attention to the 'most important'
criteria in order to evaluate the evolution and the achievements of the two worlds. As a result, it did not much matter
whether the West was making astounding progress in the
fields of the arts, sciences and technology. From the Orthodox point of view, these were simple advances in secular
domains which were erroneously considered instrumental in
establishing the Western superiority. Far more important
than these were the religious criteria connected to the unaltered preservation of the original and authentic Christian
faith. Seen from this viewpoint, the Orthodox East, despite
its temporary and transient problems due to the Ottoman
domination, was far superior to the West. It could claim true
adherence to the original Christian faith without any alteration. The history of the West was, on the other hand, full of
arbitrary modifications and innovations in the original Christian faith. The Roman Catholic Church had started this
process in the first place, culminating later in the numerous
Christian groups that appeared in the wake of the Reformation (Lutherans, Calvinists, Anglicans). Thus, the religious
history of the West was full of deviations and heresies which
had not only altered significantly the inherited common
Christian faith but were also posing a serious threat to the
Orthodox East as well.

The Orthodox side considered this to be the most
serious and important criterion in the ongoing comparison
between the two worlds. To put it differently, the alleged

superiority of the West was superficially based on shaky foundations and had no real value. The Orthodox East, through the meticulous preservation of the true faith of the Apostles, the Ecumenical Councils and the Fathers of the Church, was therefore far superior to the West. The advance of this religious argument by the Orthodox had another dimension. The progress made by the West in mundane matters was minimised because it was thought to be of no use for the salvation of the soul and in many cases it was even considered to be detrimental to it. The extreme preoccupation with mundane things and the vain curiosity to explore the mysteries of the world could lead to the neglect of Christian duties and priorities as well as to an exclusive and dangerous preoccupation with earthly concerns. By contrast, the unaltered preservation of Orthodoxy and belief in the one true faith were seen as basic prerequisites for attaining salvation. This privilege was reserved to the Orthodox alone, and thus constituted the reason for their legitimate pride and sense of superiority.

As mentioned above, this argument was the most widespread in the period of Ottoman domination. It was expressed in various ways from the early contacts of Patriarch Jeremias II with the Lutherans in the sixteenth century[40] and the monk Anastasios Gordios (1654/5–1729)[41] up to the fierce opponent of the 'Neohellenic Enlightenment', Athanasios

---

40 See D. Wendebourg, *Reformation und Orthodoxie. Der ökumenische Briefwechsel zwischen der Leitung der Württembergischen Kirche und Patriarch Jeremias II. von Konstantinopel in den Jahren 1573–1581* (Göttingen, 1986).

41 See Anastasios Gordios, *Sur Mahomet et contre les Latins*. Édition critique accompagnée d'une introduction et de notes par Astérios Argyriou (Athènes, 1983), 392–395.

Parios (ca. 1721–1813).[42] At the beginning of the eighteenth century, we find it among Greek Orthodox in several contexts. First of all, we can observe it in the refutation of B. Woodroffe, the initiator of the Greek College, by a Greek member of it, the Corfiote hierodeacon Frangiskos Pros(s)alentis (1679–1728). He arrived in England in April 1703 in the escort of Lord William Paget, the English ambassador to the Sublime Porte, and was enrolled at Oxford. But after contacting Woodroffe and other Anglicans and reading the book Ἡ τῶν Ἁγίων Γραφῶν αὐτάρκεια *(The Self-sufficiency of the Holy Writ)* (Oxford, 1704), published under the instruction and supervision of Woodroffe and with the involvement of some Orthodox students of the Greek College, Pros(s)alentis turned against his hosts. Fearing the loss of the Orthodox faith among the students of the Greek College through growing Anglican influences, he left England for Holland in June 1705, where he published a refutation in 1706 entitled Ὁ αἱρετικὸς διδάσκαλος ὑπὸ τοῦ Ὀρθοδόξου μαθητοῦ ἐλεγχόμενος *(The Heretical Teacher Cross-examined by his Orthodox Pupil)* (Amsterdam, 1706; second edition, Athens, 1862).

In this work he intended to bring to light Woodroffe's fallacies (σοφίσματα)[43] as well as the motives behind the foundation of the Greek College. He claimed that Woodroffe's long-term intention was the control of the Orthodox

---

42   See his indicative work Ἀντιφώνησις πρὸς τὸν παράλογον ζῆλον, τῶν ἀπὸ τῆς Εὐρώπης ἐρχομένων φιλοσόφων, δεικνύσα ὅτι μάταιος, καὶ ἀνόητος ὁ ταλανισμὸς ὁποῦ κάνουσι τοῦ γένους μας, καὶ διδάσκουσα ποία εἶναι ἡ ὄντως καὶ ἀληθινὴ Φιλοσοφία (Trieste, 1802). See also Ath. Th. Photopoulos, «Ἔλεγχος τοῦ ψευδοταλανισμοῦ τῆς Ἑλλάδος». Ὀρθόδοξη ἀπάντηση στὴ Δυτικὴ πρόκληση περὶ τὰ τέλη τοῦ ΙΗ΄ αἰώνά', Μνημοσύνη 11 (1988/90), 302–364; Makrides, *Die religiöse Kritik*, 152–171.

43   See F. Pros(s)alentis, Ὁ αἱρετικὸς διδάσκαλος ὑπὸ τοῦ Ὀρθοδόξου μαθητοῦ ἐλεγχόμενος [...], Second edition (Athens, 1862), 8.

Patriarchates in the East through the future appointment of graduates of the Greek College there. This could be brought about through the financial intervention of Queen Anne and the British ambassador to the Sublime Porte.[44] Pros(s)alentis dedicated his refutation to the aforementioned Patriarch Gabriel III, who had been particularly sensitive to Roman Catholic and Anglican infiltration in the Orthodox East.[45] In 1704 Gabriel III officially condemned the translation of the New Testament into demotic, vulgar Greek (London, 1703; second ed., 1705) by the hieromonk Seraphim of Mitylene, a member of the Greek College, and financed by the Society for the Propagation of the Gospel in Foreign Parts with the help of German Pietist H. W. Ludolf.[46] Pros(s)alentis was aware that the glorious days of the Greek nation belonged to a distant past and that the nation was ruled by misery (τὰ νῦν μὲν δυστυχοῦς, πρότερον δὲ εὐτυχοῦς τῶν Ἑλλήνων γένους).[47] Yet in compensation there was still the Orthodox faith, possessed only by the Orthodox. For Pros(s)alentis there was nothing more valuable in life than the right faith in God (οὐδὲν γὰρ τῆς ὀρθῆς πρὸς Θεὸν πίστεως τιμιώτερον).[48] Therefore, in order to defend Orthodoxy and his nation (ὅθεν ὅλον ἐμαυτὸν τῇ Ἐκκλησίᾳ δοὺς καὶ παντὶ τρόπῳ ὑπὲρ τοῦ [...] τῶν Ἑλλήνων γένους),[49] he set out from an Orthodox point of view to refute systematically Woodroffe's ideas. He thus defended the written and unwritten ecclesiastical tradition (the Church Fathers, the Holy Synods, the sign of the cross, the veneration of the

---

44 Ibid., 9–10.
45 Ibid., 1–3.
46 See D. L. Brunner, *Halle Pietists in England: Anthony William Boehm and the Society for Promoting Christian Knowledge* (Göttingen, 1993), 157–158.
47 Pros(s)alentis, Ὁ αἱρετικὸς διδάσκαλος, 8.
48 Ibid., 2.
49 Ibid., 8.

saints and the icons, fasting practices, the veneration of the Virgin Mary), which he argued had been rejected by Woodroffe as a superstitious product of the Roman Catholic Church.

A similar attitude not only towards to the Anglicans but also towards the West as a whole was maintained by his close friend, Alexander Helladius (1686–?) from Larissa in Thessaly,[50] who had also come to England in the escort of Lord Paget and studied at the Greek College. Helladius called Pros(s)alentis his teacher (*praeceptor*),[51] indicating the ideological affinities between the two. He also commented positively on Pros(s)alentis' attempt to refute Woodroffe. Helladius published in 1714 in Altdorf a long book entitled *Status Praesens Ecclesiae Graecae: in quo etiam causae exponuntur cur Graeci moderni Novi Testamenti editiones in Graeco-barbara lingua factas acceptare recusent,* which he dedicated to Tsar Peter the Great as a great defender of Orthodoxy.[52] It is obvious from the title and especially from the last five chapters of his book that Helladius' intention was to criticise the Anglican (1703 and 1705) and the later Pietistic (1710) attempts to render the New Testament into demotic Greek.[53] In addition, his book is a valuable source of first-hand information about life in the Greek College at Oxford and in the *Collegium Orientale Theologicum* in Halle.

More importantly, Helladius undertook the task of defending Orthodoxy and the Greek nation against various partial and inimical presentations of it made by various

---

50   On Helladius and his world see V. N. Makrides (ed.), *Proceedings of the International Conference 'Alexander Helladius the Larissaean'* (Larissa, 4–5 September 1999) (Thessaloniki, 2002).

51   A. Helladius, *Status praesens Ecclesiae Graecea: in quo etiam causae exponuntur cur Graeci moderni Novi Testamenti editiones in Graeco-barbara lingua factas acceptare recusent* [...], ([Altdorf], 1714) 206, 255.

52   See Makrides, 'Στοιχεῖα', 9–13.

53   Helladius, *Status*, 226–371.

Western observers (e.g., by Thomas Smith, Paul Rycaut, Johann Fecht, Johann M. Heinecce) who had written lengthy books and reports about the Greeks and the Orthodox Church. Helladius' book thus had not only an apologetic but also an aggressive character, using compensatory strategies to show the religious and cultural achievements of the Greek world and the incomparable value of Orthodoxy. Having lived and studied in various European places (Oxford, London, Amsterdam, Halle, Prague, Altdorf) and known the Western world from the inside, Helladius attempted a thorough account of it. He wrote characteristically about his Greek origins and his overall apologetic objective: '*Quicquid sit! Illud omnibus et singulis notum facio: me Graecum esse natum, de Parentibus non multum gloriabor, ast pro Patria genteque mea, praesertim vero, cum injusta ratione tantas injurias illam pati videam, neque propriis Parentibus quidem, nedum illis, quibus calumniae in Graeciam, et Graecorum diffamatio maxime conducit, ad propriumque interesse vergit, ullo modo parcam; Ita tempora, non ingenia Graecorum mutata sunt!*'[54] At the same time, Helladius tried to raise the estimation of Greek learning in the world by providing data which regrettably were in many cases exaggerated and unreliable.[55] In this way, he also hoped to minimise the Western achievements, which he had of course partially acknowledged, and to show the overall potential of his compatriots. His very critical book, however, caused heated reactions in the West, as the long refutation of it by Johann Matthias Gesner (1691–1761) in 1716 clearly demonstrates.[56]

---

54 Ibid., 329.
55 See for example ibid., 1–67, where he discusses the educational level of his compatriots at the time.
56 See J. M. Gesner, 'Observatio XXX. De Eruditione Graecorum, qui hodie vivunt, contra Alexandrum Helladium, nat. Graecum', in *Miscellanea Lipsiensia ad incrementum rei litterariae edita*, tomus II

Yet Helladius did receive some spiritual support from his country in his continuous struggles to defend Orthodoxy and Hellenism within an inimical Western environment. His former teacher, Mark Porphyropoul(l)os of Cyprus, wrote him an interesting letter around 1714/1715 from Bucharest.[57] This letter furnishes the clearest evidence of the Greek compensatory strategy. Mark was well informed about the many controversies that Helladius had had in the West over many years and he offered him words of comfort in his difficult task. In his letter he gave a clear evaluation of the two worlds, East and West. He began by criticising the Western sophists who loved to debate (φιλερίδων σοφιστῶν) and to blame the Orthodox Christians (τῶν φιλούντων διασύρειν τὰ ἡμέτερα) for great ignorance, lack of order (ἀμάθειάν τε ἐσχάτην καὶ ἀτασθαλίαν ἡμῶν καταψηφιζόντων), analphabetism, bad morals (ὡς ἀναλφαβήτους καὶ φαυλοήθεις διακωδωνίζουσιν) and many other evil things. Instead of loving and admiring the Orthodox Christians who were forced to live under the harsh conditions of the Ottoman domination and still kept the Orthodox faith intact, these Western materialists (οἱ ὅλως σάρκες ὄντες) attacked and criticised the Orthodox in an unfair way.[58] In Mark's opinion, the Orthodox need not feel inferior at all because of Ottoman domination or the lack of progress in mundane matters. The Orthodox were aware that they possessed the most important thing, namely the Orthodox faith. By contrast, Western Christians were enemies of the truth and arrogant innovators (καινοτόμοι καὶ ἀγέρωχοι), because they had altered radically the original and authentic

---

(Lipsiae, 1716) 397–452; idem, 'Observatione L. Παραλιπόμενα quaedam Observationis XXX. Completa', ibid., 712–719.

57   See Angeliki Nikolopoulou, 'Ἐπιστολὴ Μάρκου τοῦ Κυπρίου πρὸς τὸν Ἀλέξανδρον Ἑλλάδιον' Ἐπετηρὶς Ἑταιρείας Βυζαντινῶν Σπουδῶν 44 (1979/80) 331–344.

58   Ibid., 339,

Christian tradition. Therefore they had no idea of their own ignorance and of their inferior status vis-à-vis the Orthodox (οὐκ ἔγνωσαν, οὔτε συνῆκαν τίνα τε λέγουσιν οὐδὲ περὶ τίνων διαβεβαιοῦνται).[59] The only criterion for establishing the superiority of the one world over the other was the preservation of the true Christian faith, whereas the progress in mundane matters had no real significance in the present context. Mark concluded by saying that the alleged barbaric and uneducated Orthodox had no need at all to delve deep into the secular knowledge or to observe the stars (ἀστροθεάμονες) and the things in heaven (μετεωρολέσχαι) like Western Christians did.[60] Under the harsh conditions of the Ottoman domination they needed only to keep the Orthodox faith intact (διατηροῦμεν ἀκέραια, ἀμείωτα, ἀπαρεγχείρητα τὴν εὐαγγελικὴν θεηγορίαν, τὸ ἀποστολικὸν κήρυγμα, τὴν πατρικὴν διδασκαλίαν καὶ πᾶν ὁτιοῦν σωτηριῶδες μάθημα) and they would be richly rewarded by God. After all, secular knowledge such as science and technology was not needed for the salvation of the soul. Therefore, the Orthodox had no particular interest in or need of such vain, mundane wisdom (οὐ χρεία ἡμῖν τῆς περιττῆς καὶ κοσμικῆς σοφίας).[61] Even so, the East was not totally deprived at that time of such wisdom (ἔτι σώζεται ἐν τῇ Ἑλλάδι ἴχνος σοφίας, οὐ παντάπασιν ἐγκαταλέλοιπεν ἡμᾶς ἡ θεία καὶ συνετίζουσα χάρις), as the educational and the intellectual situation in Wallachia at the time clearly showed.[62] Here we encounter another argument in favour of the self-sufficiency of the Greek Orthodox world vis-à-vis the West, which will be dealt with later in more detail.

---

59 Ibid.
60 Ibid., 341.
61 Ibid., 342.
62 Ibid., 343–344.

*Modern Greeks as the Sole Legitimate Custodians
of the Ancient Greek Heritage*

A second strategy of establishing the superiority of the East
vis-à-vis the West can be found in the particular way modern
Greeks considered, appropriated and evaluated the ancient
Greek heritage. Their cultural and linguistic continuity with
their ancestors was thought to render them unique custodians
and exclusive interpreters of the ancient Greek culture. Given
that Greek letters had been especially valued and cultivated
in the West from the period of the Renaissance and the
humanists onwards, this naturally raised the issue of the
correct appropriation of this rich Greek heritage. Who had
the greater claim to it? Whose interpretations and theories
were more pertinent and authoritative? The rise of classical
scholarship in the West and the systematic cultivation of the
two main languages, Greek and Latin, helped establish classical learning as a cornerstone of the modern Western world.
But where does this leave modern Greeks, the alleged sole
legitimate heirs to this heritage? Although they did contribute
to the spread of classical scholarship in the West through
Byzantine and post-Byzantine scholars, there are early signs of
disagreement regarding the appropriation of the ancient
Greek heritage by the West. A case in point is the introduction of the Erasmian pronunciation of ancient Greek,
established in the West up to this day. Another controverted
point is the relationship between ancient and demotic, vernacular Greek as well as their significance in modern Greek
culture. As might be expected, modern Greeks were not
willing to consider Western peoples as worthier heirs of the
classical tradition than themselves. In fact, they intended to
reserve this right to themselves alone.[63]

---

63   It is characteristic that Theodoros Laskaris already in the thirteenth
      century had prophesied that the Latins could be better stewards of

These two issues were taken up at the beginning of the eighteenth century by the most eminent student of the Greek College, the aforementioned Alexander Helladius. In his book *Status Praesens* he dealt systematically with many issues pertaining to the Greek language and its evolution as well as to the classical tradition. There are many indications that Helladius thought of himself as being a genuine successor of the unbroken classical tradition. For example, his unusual surname was not his real one, but rather a *nom de plume*[64] which he selected after he left Ottoman Greece to study abroad. He probably did this because he intended to present himself as a real heir to the ancient Greeks. In addition, he was very fond of ancient Greek literature, composed poems in ancient metric style,[65] and had tried to imitate Homer since his childhood.[66] In such matters he was therefore reluctant to accept any advice or help from the West. His familiarity with the ancient Greek language was something for which he was particularly noted in the West and that helped him establish some good contacts there (especially at the University of Altdorf).

In 1712 Helladius republished in Nuremberg an older Greek grammar by Bessarion Makris, to which he added a fictive dialogue (both in Greek and in Latin) to refute the

the ancient Greek heritage in the future and superior to its direct descendants, i.e., the Byzantines. See Tinnefeld, 'Das Niveau', 253.

64 Cf. E. D. Tappe, 'Alumni of the Greek College at Oxford, 1699–1705', *Notes and Queries for Readers and Writers, Collectors and Librarians* [Ser. 2] 200 (1955), 110–114, here 112.

65 See V. N. Makrides, "Ἕνα ποιητικὸ κείμενο τοῦ Ἀλεξάνδρου Ἑλλαδίου περὶ τῆς ψυχῆς τῶν ζώων', Θεσσαλικὸ Ἡμερολόγιο 32 (1997), 257–278. See also Makrides (ed.), *Proceedings of the International Conference 'Alexander Helladius the Larissaean'*, passim.

66 See Helladius, *Status praesens*, 205–206.

Erasmian pronunciation of ancient Greek.[67] This was anal-
ogous to Erasmus' own 1528 publication of his theory in the
form of a dialogue. Later in the *Status Praesens* Helladius tried
to refute some scholars (J. Tribbechov, J. Lang) who claimed
that modern Greek was barbaric (*barbarograeca*) and that
modern Greeks could neither use the ancient language nor
read ancient texts. Helladius argued that the vernacular,
spoken Greek language was merely a dialect and that the true
Greek language has always been the classical one. In his
opinion, Greek had not essentially changed over the centuries
and modern Greeks could without difficulty or special education read ancient Greek texts. This viewpoint also explains
his attacks against rendering the New Testament into modern
Greek. He criticised the ethnically non-Greek peoples in the
Ottoman Empire who used to speak Greek at that time and
who had contributed unwittingly to the corruption of the
classical language. Helladius sought to show the unbroken
continuity of Greek culture, so he paid little attention to the
merit of Erasmus' theoretical views. He considered the Greek
of his day from the point of view of the ancient language, and
thus neglected the various forms of Greek language in history.
It is characteristic, however, that in these matters he showed
no intention at all of learning anything from the West. On the
contrary, he wanted as a true Greek by descent to enlighten it.

---

67   See A. Helladius 'Διάλογος περὶ τῆς ἐν Εὐρώπῃ ἑλληνικῆς προφορᾶς',
     in idem, Σταχυολογία τεχνολογικὴ τῆς Ἑλλάδος φωνῆς [...] (Nürnberg,
     1712), at the beginning of the book, without pagination.

The Self-Sufficiency of the Greek Orthodox World

A third Orthodox compensatory strategy against the West was related specifically to the progress made by the West. The main question here was, Should the Greek Orthodox world profit from the achievements of Western progress or not? Although there was a general tendency to learn and to profit from the West (the Greek students studying abroad and Greek translations of Western books) there was also another opposite current. According to this viewpoint, the Greek Orthodox world, despite the problems of the day, was still in a good and satisfactory condition and could satisfy the educational needs of its members. The main objective here was to show the self-sufficiency of the Greek world, which had no particular need to import Western ideas in order to improve its overall condition. In some cases importation from the West was not altogether rejected, but was rather considered trivial and unimportant for ameliorating the Greek educational system. This particular strategy can be found in various forms throughout the Ottoman domination and reached its climax in the period of the 'Neohellenic Enlightenment'. At that time of increased contacts with the West the hieromonk Athanasios Parios tried to keep Greek students away from the West and to persuade them to satisfy themselves with the rather poor curricula offered in his school on the island of Chios.[68] This Orthodox sense of self-sufficiency had clear religious origins. The self-sufficiency in the religious domain for the Orthodox was thus extended over the domain of secular knowledge and created an often static sense of complacency and immutability.

---

68 See V. N. Makrides, "Ἡ δυσμένεια τοῦ Ἀθανασίου Παρίου πρὸς τὸν Δωρόθεο Πρώιο', Ὁ Ἐρανιστής 20 (1995), 248–255.

Such sentiments did appear at the beginning of the eighteenth century. A characteristic example may be found in the letter of the Orthodox Patriarchs to the Anglican Non-Jurors written 18 April 1718. This interesting document reveals much about the religious and cultural self-understanding of the Orthodox at the time. The Non-Jurors had submitted proposals on 18 August 1716 to the Orthodox exploring the possibility of union with them and going very far in approaching Orthodox doctrine (e.g., concerning the *filioque* and the sacraments). But in their answer the Orthodox Patriarchs left no room for compromise and considered the absolute acceptance of all Orthodox doctrines as a *sine qua non* of any future union.[69] This was a clear sign of religious superiority, self-sufficiency and complacency on the part of the Orthodox.

In the present context I am much more interested in another aspect of this contact between East and West. It concerns a certain proposal made by the Non-Jurors which was misinterpreted by the Orthodox and caused an interesting reaction. The Non-Jurors made reference in their proposal to the study and the revival of 'the ancient learning' (τὴν παλαιὰν παιδείαν ὁσίως ἀναζωπυρεῖν).[70] The Orthodox did not rightly understand what was meant by this expression. Among other things, they interpreted it as indicating that the British wanted to teach them new things that had remained hitherto unknown in the Orthodox East. Therefore, in their response the Orthodox tried to set things straight and to correct this arrogant British offer. First of all, if these new things pertained to the domain of religion, they would have been *a priori* unacceptable to the Orthodox because such

---

69   See the entire text of this answer in I. Karmiris, *Dogmatica et symbolica monumenta Orthodoxae Catholicae Ecclesiae*, Tomus II, second edition (Graz, 1968), 868–898.

70   Ibid., 876.

an innovation would imply an alteration of the Christian Orthodox tradition. The preservation of the inherited faith in an unaltered form was seen as the highest task of the Orthodox (τῆς δ᾽ ἀρχαιοπαραδότου εὐαγγελικῆς παιδείας τε καὶ διδασκαλίας ἀπρὶξ ἀνθεξόμεθα, ἕως ἂν τὸ ζῆν ἔχωμεν).[71] This was a clear sign of the religious self-sufficiency of the Orthodox usually observed in the context of such inter-Christian contacts.

Yet the Orthodox Patriarchs did not show themselves to be superior and self-sufficient in religious terms only. They were reluctant to learn from the Non-Jurors even in the non-religious, secular domain. They expounded an interesting evaluation of secular knowledge from an Orthodox point of view. Following the Apostle Paul (*Col.* 2.8; *1 Cor.* 3.19), secular knowledge (ἔξω σοφία) was seen as unimportant; it was not vital for the Orthodox to possess it (οὐ χρῄζομεν οὖν ταύτης ἀναγκαίως ἡμεῖς). If the Orthodox needed for some reason to learn about such things, they could resort to their own intellectual arsenal and schools, in which Aristotelian philosophy had traditionally been taught (ἔχομεν παρ᾽ ἡμῖν τὰς ἀριστοτελικὰς βίβλους καὶ ἄλλων σοφῶν καὶ τοὺς τούτων ὑπομνηματιστὰς καὶ ἐξηγητάς, καὶ σχολαί εἰσι παρ᾽ ἡμῖν κατὰ διαφόρους πόλεις καὶ χώρας, ἐξ ὧν δυνάμεθα πλοῦτον σοφίας οὐκ ὀλίγον ἀρύσασθαι). On the one hand they thanked the Non-Jurors for their willingness to teach them, but they also made clear that they put no particular emphasis on this issue. The main reason was that secular knowledge was not considered by the Orthodox as necessary for salvation (εἰ καὶ μὴ τοσοῦτον παρ᾽ ἡμῖν τὸ πρᾶγμα τοῦτό ἐστι ζηλωτόν, ὡς μὴ ἀναγκαῖον πρὸς σωτηρίαν).[72]

---

71 Ibid., 878.
72 Ibid., 877.

By arguing in this way the Orthodox Patriarchs intended to refute a false rumour circulating in the West at that time, namely that modern Greeks had in fact lost their rich ancestral heritage and were ignorant and uneducated (ἀλλ' οἱ καλοὶ κάγαθοὶ Βρεττανοὶ μὴ τοιαύτην ὑπόνοιαν ἐχέτωσαν περὶ ἡμῶν, ὡς δῆθεν ἀμοίρων διαμεμενηκότων παντάπασι τῆς ἀρχαίας ἐκείνης καὶ πατρίου καὶ ἐθάδος παιδείας). This was in their view completely mistaken. In reality, this heritage was still kept much better in the Orthodox East than in several other countries (ἔν τισι δὲ σὺν Θεῷ καὶ κρειττόνως ἢ παρ' ἄλλοις τισὶν εἰς ἔτι καὶ νῦν παρ' ἡμῖν διατηρουμένης). This was hardly an exaggeration or figment of their imagination (ἀλλὰ μή τις ἡμᾶς τῶν μεμψιμοίρων οἰέσθω λέγοντας ταῦτα εἰκαίως ἐγκαυχᾶσθαι· τἀληθὲς καὶ γὰρ λέγομεν). There were many schools and academies throughout the Orthodox East in which both theological (according to the Church Fathers) and secular (according to Aristotle) lessons were taught. In addition, there were many treasures (manuscripts, books) related to various branches of the secular knowledge and kept in monasteries and schools. Some of these treasures were still unknown to the West and could be made available to it in the future. But the Orthodox Patriarchs emphasised again that their contact with the Non-Jurors did not arise from a desire to grow in secular wisdom – there was already a sufficient supply of this in the East (ταῦτα γάρ παρ' ἡμῖν, ὡς προείρηται πολλάκις, ὁπωσδήπως σὺν Θεῷ εὑρίσκονται). Far more important were the real union existing among various Christians and a common adherence to authentic Christian doctrine. If these could be made real, then there would be plenty of time for mutual exchanges between East and West in other fields as well.[73]

---

73   Ibid., 878.

The Patriarchs in their response presented the Greek Orthodox world as being self-sufficient not only in terms of religious but also of secular knowledge. The West, on the other hand, was seen as lagging behind and being in a position to offer very little to the Orthodox. It is characteristic that the above arguments on the part of the Orthodox were due to a misunderstanding, which was addressed in 1722 by the Non-Jurors. These Anglicans, who were after all generally well-educated men,[74] made clear that they had no such intention of enlightening the Orthodox, and the whole matter was closed. Nonetheless, the spirit underlying the aforementioned response of the Orthodox is particularly revealing and explains much about the Orthodox self-understanding at the beginning of the eighteenth century.

In reality the Orthodox arguments about educational standards in the East are nothing but a clear proof of ignorance. It appears that these Orthodox were totally unaware of the progress made in the West in science and technology. Curiously enough, this Orthodox response was also signed by the Patriarch of Jerusalem, Chrysanthos, who had studied much earlier in Italy and France, had become familiar to a great extent with modern science, and was among the first to introduce the Copernican System in a neutral way to his homeland.[75] To illustrate the great gap between East and West, let me mention here that while the *Philosophiae naturalis principia mathematica* by Isaac Newton had been published in 1687, revolutionising the world of science, by contrast, in the East there was still a faithful adherence to the old-fashioned Aristotelian doctrines, which survived throughout the eighteenth and up to the beginning of the nineteenth century. In 1725 a Greek scholar named Methodios

---

74   See G. Rupp, *Religion in England 1688–1791* (Oxford, 1986), 5–28.
75   See Makrides, *Die religiöse Kritik*, 45–50.

Anthrakitis was reinstated after his initial condemnation on 23 August 1723 by the Patriarchal Synod for having introduced new philosophical currents to the Greek world. He was ordered to teach only Aristotelian philosophy on the basis of the neo-aristotelian commentator Theophilos Corydalleus. This system was (erroneously) thought to be totally harmless to the Orthodox faith (καὶ μηδεμιᾶς ἐξ αὐτοῦ λύμης τῇ ὀρθοδοξίᾳ προστριβομένης).[76] One can thus more easily realise the degree to which the East was completely unaware of the radical scientific developments in the West at that time. This spirit of self-sufficiency was a hindrance to fruitful interaction with the West. Religious self-sufficiency thus became the driving force behind this Orthodox defensive policy and kept the Orthodox East apart from the West for a considerable period of time.

Moderate Greek Orthodox Attitudes towards Western Progress

These cases should not, however, be considered as the sole expressions of Greek attitudes towards the West at the beginning of the eighteenth century. There were some Greeks who had studied and lived abroad and who had developed a much more balanced attitude towards their own tradition and the many forms of Western progress. These Greeks were ready to accept the latter, even in the field of classical studies, but tried simultaneously to offer a more objective estimation of the educational situation in Ottoman Greece.

---

76   See E. Pelagidis, "Ἡ συνοδικὴ ἀπόφαση γιὰ τὴν «ἀποκατάσταση» τοῦ Μεθοδίου 'Ανθρακίτη', Μακεδονικά 23 (1983), 134–147, here 137.

One such person was the aforementioned Anastasios Michail from Naousa, a very gifted scholar, who in the first decade of the eighteenth century made a name for himself in Germany and later in Russia.[77] He had no problem acknowledging openly that the muses had left Greece at that time. Greek students had emigrated to Germany in order to catch them again (τηλεδαποὶ Ἕλληνες, μουσῶν τῶν φυγάδων θηραταὶ Γερμανικοῖς Ἑλικῶσιν ἥκομεν ἐμφιλοχωρήσοντες).[78] This was a reference to the Greek students who came to Halle in 1703 to study in A. H. Francke's *Collegium Orientale Theologicum*, the Pietistic version of the Greek College at Oxford. Anastasios had no fear of accepting the advances made by Western scholars, even in the budding field of neohellenic studies. He encouraged Johannes Tribbechov's (1678–1712) 1705 comparative study of modern vernacular and ancient Greek. In a letter to Tribbechov in September 1704, in both Greek and Latin, Anastasios flattered him as a German Philhellene who had directed his attention to the historical development of the Greek language. He also gave some information about the educational situation in Ottoman Greece and explained the reasons for the corruption of the Greek language (e.g., through the broader use of it by ethnically non-Greek peoples, including the Ottomans themselves). Yet, the whole discussion of this matter took place in a conciliatory and constructive way with the intention of bringing together the mother (Greece) and the daughter (Germany) to create a new Greek–German contact and friendship (συναναστροφὴ καὶ φιλία).[79] His sentiments differed substantially from Alexander Helladius'

---

77   See Beneševic, 'Anastasios Nausios', passim.

78   Anastasios Michaelis, Σύμβολον Χρυσοῦ Κράτους [...] / *Symbolon Aurei Regni* [...] (Halle, 1707) n.p. [f. 2r].

79   'Epistola Cl. Anastasii, Greci', in Io. Tribbechovii, *Brevia linguae* Ρωμαϊκῆς *sive Graecae vulgaris elementa* (Jena, 1705) (without pagination).

sharp critique of Western scholarship in the same field only a few years later.

Anastasios later modified his attitude a little and became less apologetic about his own nation, albeit without denying altogether the potential of the West. Around 1708, he wrote a long report in the form of a letter to the *Berliner Sozietät (Akademie) der Wissenchaften* intending to deepen the relationship between Greece and philhellenic Germany. He started by giving a long account of the condition of learning among contemporary Greeks, with a clearly apologetic attitude towards his Western addressees. His intention was more to show the intellectual potential of the Greek world, which was worthy of admiration even by those in the West. He wanted to present modern Greece as an (albeit lesser) object of admiration alongside ancient Greece. In this context he did not forget to mention several examples of admiration towards contemporary Greek learning at the turn of the eighteenth century, even on the part of some British travellers. He referred specifically to three noble British men and their escort, who had visited Ioannina at the end of the seventeenth century on their way to the Ionian islands. There they were informed about Greek curricula and schools and were amazed at the works of Theophilos Corydalleus. Anastasios mentioned that they even copied one of his works to publish it later in England.[80] He also described how the British people had admired the erudition of Neophytos the Metropolitan of Philippopolis when he visited London, Oxford and Cambridge in 1701.[81]

Furthermore, Anastasios claimed that as a modern Greek he had a different and qualitatively higher understanding of the ancient Greek heritage than Western scholars. To this purpose, he offered a long refutation of the Erasmian

---

80   Anastasios Michail, Περιηγηματικόν πιττάκιον [Berlin, 1708?], 54–56.
81   Ibid., 48.

pronunciation of ancient Greek and explained the reasons for the observed corruption of the Greek language at the time. In this way, he tried to refute those 'who were whipping the Greeks' in the West and who claimed to be worthy heirs of ancient Greek culture and its correct interpreters (ὁ τῶν τινων Ἑλληνομαστίγων αὐτός τε οἴεται καὶ ουτος ἄλλους παραπείθειν πειρᾶται ὅμιλος).[82] The whole controversy returned again to the appropriation of the Greeks' ancient heritage and the necessary credentials for undertaking this task.

There were others with moderate attitudes among the Greek Orthodox at the time, and they openly acknowledged the progress made in the West in the fields of science and technology, if not in that of classical philology. Let me mention only one clear evidence of this spirit. This comes from a very flattering letter of recommendation in Latin written on 7 June 1733 by the Patriarch of Constantinople Serapheim I (from the middle of March 1733 until September 1734) for a young Greek named Georgios. The addressee of this letter was the famous Dutch physician Herman Boerhaave in Leiden, 'an extraordinary learned man, whose most honourable name has become known also in the Eastern countries among the learned people'.[83] Georgios was recommended to 'derive treasures, which are not to be disdained, from your vast store of solid learning for which you [Boerhaave] are famous everywhere, and that he will preserve then in his heart and bring them with him to his native country.'[84] Serapheim referred to an older and usual argument, namely that the West somehow owed much to the Greeks because of what they had offered to the world in ancient times. 'We know very well that the

---

82   Ibid., 63.
83   See G. A. Lindeboom (ed.), *Boerhaave's Correspondence,* Part Two (Leiden, 1964), 7.
84   Ibid.

sciences, which in olden times the Greeks lavishly distributed to foreign peoples, will not be denied to a Greek guest.'[85]

It is also interesting that Serapheim wanted Georgios to 'enter the holy of the holies of science under your guidance with more security' and to be educated in the new scientific reasoning and methods.

> We especially asked for a method of study, and a clear way, which does not wander and deviate, both with respect to skill in languages and to the apparatus of the subjects, in order that our novice will not only hunt after words with playful effort, and be clamourously sacrificed to philosophy; in short that he will not, seeking difficulties where there are none, learn to string nonsense together, but in order that he may by rational experiments be instructed in the knowledge of philosophy and the precepts of a sound medicine and gradually strongly mature into a fertile plant.[86]

Although the background of this letter and the later fortunes of the recommended Georgios are still unknown, this is an important document showing a highly positive evaluation of Western progress on the part of the highest Orthodox prelate of the day.

Conclusion

The phenomenon of inter-civilisational comparisons that I examined in this paper does not pertain only to the period of the Ottoman domination of Greece. It can be observed in

---

85   Ibid., 9.
86   Ibid., 9. On Boerhaave's fame in the East at the time see G. A. Lindeboom, *Herman Boerhaave. The Man and his Work* (London, 1968), 359–360.

various forms with varying frequency up to the present.[87] The old habit of making comparisons between various cultural complexes (here between East and West) and to look for elements of superiority has not vanished even today. As far as the Greek Orthodox side is concerned, there still exists a tendency to use the aforementioned arguments *mutatis mutandis* as compensatory mechanisms in order to validate the superiority of the Orthodox world over the West. More specifically, there exist several groups within Greek Orthodoxy, ranging from the conservative rigorists to the sophisticated intellectual Neoorthodox, who still use Orthodoxy and Hellenism in various ways as elements of superiority vis-à-vis Western and international achievements generally. Although we live nowadays in a quite different and globalised environment, the need to acknowledge Greece's own achievements and to develop nativistic strategies towards foreign and imported elements still remains particularly strong. Such inter-civilisational comparisons acquire additional importance in our days, particularly if we take into consideration the fact that some scholars (S. P. Huntington) have prophesied the coming clash of civilisations after the end of the Cold War. Such a clash might be produced through the mutual contact, the influence and, last but not least, the comparison and the quest for superiority between structurally different cultures worldwide.

---

87 See also V. N. Makrides, "Ἡ Ὀρθοδοξία ὡς μηχανισμὸς ἄμυνας καὶ ἀντιστάθμισης ἔναντι τῶν προόδων τῆς Δύσης κατὰ τὴν Τουρκοκρατία', in Λαογραφικὸ Ἱστορικὸ Μουσεῖο Λάρισας. Ἐνημερωτικὸ Δελτίο (Ἡμερίδα «Οἱ εὐρωπαϊκὲς παράμετροι τῆς νεοελληνικῆς σκέψης», Λάρισα, *13* Φεβρουαρίου *1998)*, (Larissa, 1998), 3–30.

11. The Fifth Earl of Guilford and his Secret Conversion to the Orthodox Church

KALLISTOS WARE

Some forty-five years ago, when I was undertaking research for my book on the Greek theologian Eustratios Argenti,[1] I was surprised to find that the library of the British Museum possessed a remarkably complete collection of Greek Orthodox books dating from the seventeenth and eighteenth centuries. By comparison, Greek theological literature from the 1830s onwards was far less adequately represented on the shelves of the British Museum library; its holdings in this area were meagre and erratic. The majority of the works that I consulted from the earlier period contained a bookplate with the name 'The Hon[ble] Frederic North'. Who, I asked myself, was this 'Frederic North'; why had he assembled such an extensive library on Greek Orthodoxy; and how had his books passed into the hands of the British Museum?[2]

This is a corrected and greatly expanded version of the article that originally appeared in Derek Baker (ed.), *The Orthodox Churches and the West: Papers read at the Fourteenth Summer Meeting and the Fifteenth Winter Meeting of the Ecclesiastical History Society.* Studies in Church History, vol. 13 (Oxford: Basil Blackwell, 1976), 247–256.

1   Timothy Ware, *Eustratios Argenti: A Study of the Greek Church under Turkish Rule* (Oxford: Clarendon Press, 1964; photographic reprint, Willets, Cal.: Eastern Orthodox Books, 1974).
2   They are now in the British Library, Euston Road, London NW1.

In due course I discovered the answer to all these questions. Frederic North (1766–1827)[3] was the third (and youngest

---

3   There exists as yet no full biography of Frederic North, fifth Earl of
     Guilford, and anyone attempting to write one will certainly need
     patience and energy, as his papers, for the most part still unpublished,
     are exceedingly extensive. There is abundant material in, among
     other places, the Kent County Archives Office (Maidstone), the
     British Library (London), the Library of the Corfu Reading Society
     (Kerkyra), and the Gennadius Library (Athens).
         The basic published source on North's life is A. Papadopulo
     Vreto, *Notizie biografiche-storiche su Federico Conte di Guilford Pari
     d'Ingailterra, e sulla da lui fondata Università Ionia*, text in Italian and
     Greek on opposite pages (Athens: Reale Stamperia, 1846). Andreas
     Papadopoulos-Vretos (c. 1800–1876), who was in charge of the library
     of the Ionian Academy during 1824–1830 and was a personal friend of
     North, is relatively well-informed about his patron's later years but is
     less reliable on North's early life; and, as a devoted supporter of
     North, he cannot be considered an impartial witness.
         There is a sound survey of North's life in S. and K. Vovolinis, eds,
     Μέγα Ἑλληνικὸν Βιογραφικὸν Λεξικόν 2 (Athens: Viomichaniki
     Epitheorisis, 1957), 463–482. Two important studies on North that
     have recently appeared make full use of unpublished archival
     material: Eleni Angelomati-Tsougaraki, Τὰ ταξίδια τοῦ Λόρδου
     GUILFORD στὴν Ἀνατολικὴ Μεσόγειο (Athens: Ἀκαδημία Ἀθηνῶν,
     Κέντρον Ἐρεύνης τοῦ Μεσαιωνικοῦ καὶ Νέου Ἑλληνισμοῦ, 2000),
     esp. 16–71 (on North's life, travels, archaeological interests and
     library); Vasiliki Bobou-Stamati, Ἡ Βιβλιοθήκη GUILFORD στὴν
     Κέρκυρα *(1824–30)*, included in her volume of collected studies
     Ἱστορικῆς ἐρεύνας ἀποτελέσματα. Μαρτυρίες γιὰ τὴ νεοελληνικὴ
     παιδεία καὶ ἱστορικὰ μελετήματα (16ος–19ος αι.) (Athens, 2002) 495–
     560, originally published in the periodical Ὁ Ἐρανιστής 20 (1995) 97–
     162 (with detailed references to the earlier bibliography). Neither of
     these two authors deals in any detail with North's conversion to the
     Orthodox Church.
         In English, see in particular J. M. Rigg, in *The Dictionary of
     National Biography* 41 (London: Smith, Elder & Co., 1895), 164–166;
     and Z. Duckett Ferriman, *Some English Philhellenes. VI. Lord Guilford*
     (London: The Anglo-Hellenic League, 1919), 75–109. See ill. 12.

surviving) son of the second Earl of Guilford, also named Frederic North (1732–1792), who as head of the British government during 1770–1782 failed to prevent the defection of the American colonies. After the death of his two elder brothers without male offspring, Frederic *fils* the book-collector became the fifth Earl in 1817; but he too left no direct heir, for he died unmarried ten years later. He is chiefly remembered as the first Chancellor of the Ionian Academy, which was founded on the island of Corfu in 1824, almost entirely through his efforts.[4] During the opening years of its existence, this was an institution of major importance, since until the establishment of the University of Athens in 1837 it was the only centre of higher education anywhere in the Greek world. Indeed, it may be justly called 'the first Greek university'.[5]

Frederic, fifth Earl of Guilford, is best described by the phrase: a philhellene, but not as the other philhellenes. As a British friend of Greece he is unusual, if not unique during his lifetime, by virtue of the total and all-embracing manner in which he expressed his devotion to the Hellenic tradition. His philhellenism extended not only to classical but to Christian Greece, not only to the ancient era but equally to the Byzantine Empire and the Turcocratia. He appreciated how

---

4   On the Ionian Academy, see Eleni Angelomati-Tsougaraki, Ἡ Ἰόνιος Ἀκαδημία. Τὸ χρονικὸ τῆς ἱδρυσης τοῦ πρώτου ἑλληνικοῦ Πανεπιστημίου *(1811–1824)* (Athens: Ekdoseis Ho Mikros Romios, 1998). In English, consult G. P. Henderson, *The Ionian Academy* (Edinburgh: Scottish Academic Press, 1988). This is a revised version of a work that originally appeared in Greek: Ἡ Ἰόνιος Ἀκαδημία, translated by Ph. K. Voros (Kerkyra: Κέντρον Ἐρεύνης καὶ Διεθνοῦς Ἐπικοινωνίας «Ἰόνιος Ἀκαδημία», 1980). For a detailed review of this, with much supplementary information from unpublished sources, see Protopresbyter Georgios D. Metallinos, Professor at the Theological Faculty of the University of Athens, in Παρνασσός 23 (1981) 321–375.

5   Henderson, *The Ionian Academy*, ix.

Kallistos Ware

impossible it is to understand the continuity of Greek history without taking into account the part played in it by the Orthodox Church. Nor was this all. He was not content merely to admire the Orthodox Church from a distance but himself actually became a member of it, receiving Orthodox baptism as a young man during his first visit to Greece, on Corfu during the night of 23–24 January 1791, according to the Old Calendar (3–4 February by the New Calendar).

What led him, an Anglican by upbringing, a member of the Tory aristocracy, to commit himself in this way to the Orthodox communion? At the time such a step, if not totally unprecedented, was altogether exceptional. During the seventeenth century, it is true, there were numerous contacts between Anglicans and Orthodox,[6] as there were also between Roman Catholics and Orthodox. 'We live in an age when people are much concerned with the reunion of religions', observed the French Biblical scholar Richard Simon (himself a Roman Catholic);[7] and it is salutary to remind ourselves that these words were penned, not at the end of the 'ecumenical' twentieth century, but in the 1680s. 'Reunion', for both Anglicans and Roman Catholics, meant not least reunion with the Orthodox. 'Perhaps no century', it has been claimed, 'was preoccupied with the Christian East as much as

6 These are well described by Judith Pinnington, *Anglicans and Orthodox* (Leominster: Gracewing, 2003). Compare also Arthur Middleton, *Fathers and Anglicans: The Limits of Orthodoxy* (Leominster: Gracewing, 2001).

7 Preface to Richard Simon, *Histoire critique de la créance et des coûtumes des nations du Levant* (Frankfurt: F. Arnaud, 1684). The English translation by A. Lovell, entitled *The Critical History of the Religions and Customs of the Eastern Nations* (London: H. Faithorne and J. Kersey, 1685) has a different preface.

was the seventeenth.[8] The foundation of the Greek College at Gloucester Hall, Oxford, was but one among many instances of this widespread 'preoccupation'.

During the eighteenth century, however, there was a significant change of atmosphere. Following the letter of Archbishop Wake to Patriarch Chrysanthos of Jerusalem, dated 6 September 1725,[9] which effectively brought an end to the negotiations between the Anglican Non-Jurors and the Eastern Patriarchs, there followed over a hundred years of mutual isolation and ignorance, with relatively little direct contact until William Palmer of Magdalen College, Oxford, made his visit to Russia in 1840–1841, in order to request that as an Anglican he might be admitted to holy communion at the Orthodox Liturgy. 'It will lead to nothing, I fear, sir', the President of his College, Dr Martin Routh, wisely remarked before Palmer started on his journey;[10] and so indeed matters actually turned out. But at least Palmer's visits to Russia and later to Greece reopened doors that for more than three generations had remained largely closed. Typical of the ignorance prevailing before Palmer's day was Robert Curzon's experience when calling on the Ecumenical Patriarch Gregory VI at Constantinople in 1837. Curzon was, as he puts it, 'taken

---

8   Antoine Malvy and Marcel Viller, *La Confession Orthodoxe de Pierre Moghila Métropolite de Kiev (1633–1646)*, Orientalia Christiana, vol. 10, no. 39 (Rome: Pontificium Institutum Orientalium Studiorum, 1927), lxv.

9   Given in English translation by George Williams, *The Orthodox Church of the East in the Eighteenth Century: being the Correspondence between the Eastern Patriarchs and the Nonjuring Bishops* (London: Rivingtons, 1868), lv–lviii; for the Greek and Latin versions, see Louis Petit in the continuation of J. D. Mansi, *Sacrorum Conciliorum Nova et Amplissima Collectio*, vol. 37 (Paris: Hubert Welter, 1905), cols. 591–594.

10   William Palmer, *Notes of a Visit to the Russian Church in the Years 1840, 1841*, selected and arranged by Cardinal Newman (London: Kegan Paul Trench & Co., 1882), 10.

aback sadly' to find that the Patriarch had never so much as heard of Canterbury or its archbishop.[11] Today fortunately the Phanar is somewhat better informed.

Admittedly, even in the 'dark ages' of the eighteenth century there were continuing contacts. Somewhat unexpectedly, the Orthodox were involved in the early history of Methodism. Unable to find any Anglican bishop who was prepared to ordain his candidates for the ministry, John Wesley in 1763 invited a Greek cleric resident in Amsterdam, a certain Erasmus or Gerasimus, to confer the priesthood on one of his preachers, John Jones. Erasmus claimed to be Bishop of Arcadia in Crete; it has been argued that Wesley was duped by an impostor, but it seems probable that Erasmus was in fact genuine.[12] Wesley's motives in this incident are easy to understand; he needed a bishop to perform ordinations, and he looked on Orthodoxy as a sister Church with hierarchs in the apostolic succession. What Erasmus thought he was doing is less clear. Perhaps he was short of money; but Wesley for his part would surely have refused to countenance any transaction that was tainted with simony.

---

11   Robert Curzon, *Visits to Monasteries in the Levant,* ed. D. G. Hogarth (London: Humphrey Milford, 1916), 333. Curzon's work appeared originally in 1849.

12   George Tsoumas, 'Methodism and Bishop Erasmus', in *The Greek Orthodox Theological Review* 2:2 (Brookline, Mass., 1956) 62–73, doubts Erasmus's credentials as a bishop. Among other arguments, Tsoumas points out that the Greek documents prepared by Erasmus are full of mistakes in spelling and syntax, but this is scarcely a good reason for doubting his episcopal status; during the Turcocratia many Greek hierarchs were poorly educated. For further documentation on Erasmus, see A. B. Sackett, 'John Wesley and the Greek Orthodox Bishop', *Proceedings of the Wesley Historical Society* 38 (Chester, 1971–2) 81–87, 97–102, who provides good evidence for regarding Erasmus as a genuine bishop.

Another example of continuing interest in the Orthodox East from the Anglican side was the publication, a few years later in the eighteenth century, of Dr John Glen King's substantial 500-page work *The Rites and Ceremonies of the Greek Church*.[13] King, who was Chaplain to the British Factory at St Petersburg, had a detailed knowledge of the Russian Church. His pioneering translations of Orthodox liturgical texts are stylistically elegant, although they are disfigured by some egregious misprints.[14]

Nevertheless, despite this Anglican interest in Orthodoxy during the seventeenth and even to some extent during the eighteenth century, the number of Anglicans who seriously considered joining the Orthodox Church, in the way that Frederic North chose to do in 1791, was very restricted indeed.[15] Yet, even though his decision was highly unusual, he

---

13   John Glen King, *The Rites and Ceremonies of the Greek Church, in Russia; Containing an Account of its Doctrine, Worship, and Discipline* (London: Rivington *et al.*, 1772).

14   For example, in the hymn to the Mother of God Ἄξιόν ἐστιν ('It is meet'), the adverb ἀδιαφθόρως ('without corruption') is rendered 'being incarnate', which makes nonsense of the text: 'who being incarnate brought forth God the word' (121). But elsewhere the adverb is correctly translated 'being immaculate' (75, 172).

15   It is noteworthy that in the following century John Henry Newman in his *Apologia* nowhere so much as considers the possibility that he might have chosen to join the Orthodox Church. Once he had reached the conclusion that the Church of England had lost continuity with early Christendom, in his eyes the only alternative was Rome. This is the more surprising in that his friend William Palmer of Magdalen had a close personal knowledge of the Orthodox Church, having visited Russia in 1840–1 and 1842–3. From his meetings with Palmer, Newman cannot have been ignorant of the Orthodox option, but he found it unattractive. Despite his admiration for the Greek Fathers (see Middleton, *Fathers and Anglicans*, 296–303), he had a poor opinion of the contemporary Orthodox world: see Ian Ker, *Newman*

did in fact have some precedecessors. Arsenios, Metropolitan of Thebais, who was in England around 1714–1717, makes the claim: 'Many people came to talk with me, asking me to receive them as communicants of the Orthodox Church. But I had to refuse them, since I had no church. In spite of all that, however, I did receive a few persons into Orthodoxy, all of them secretly.'[16] Unfortunately, he gives no further details. In the period after Arsenios' visit, from 1721 onwards, there was a small but steady stream of English converts who were received into Orthodoxy, through anointing with the sacrament of chrism, at the Russian Embassy Chapel in London. The best known of these was Philip Lodvel (died 1767), originally from Virginia in America, who was chrismated on 31 December 1738.[17] He translated into English the *Orthodox*

---

and the Fullness of Christianity (Edinburgh, T&T Clark, 1993), chapter 5, 'Eastern Christianity', especially 100–102.

16   Letter of 24 February 1728, in Chrysostom Papadopoulos, Ἐπιστολαὶ τοῦ Ἀρσενίου Θηβαΐδος περὶ ἀποπείρας ἑνώσεως τῶν Ἄγγλων Ἀνωμότων μετὰ τῶν Ὀρθοδόξων *(1716–1725)*, in Ἐκκλησιαστικὸς Φάρος 7 (1911), 117–144, 199–225: see p. 224. Compare Chrysostom Papadopoulos, 'An Unpublished Correspondence. Letters of Arsenius of Thebais concerning the attempted Reunion of the English Nonjurors with the Orthodox Church (1716–1725)', *Church Quarterly Review* 113 (1931) 11.

17   Following the closure of the Greek Church in Soho in 1682, there was no place of Orthodox worship in London until 1721, when a Russian chapel was opened; from 1731 onwards, when there was regular Russian diplomatic representation in London, this served also as the Russian Embassy chapel (see Steven Runciman, *The Great Church in Captivity. A Study of the Patriarchate of Constantinople from the Eve of the Turkish Conquest to the Greek War of Independence* [Cambridge: University Press, 1968], 299–300). Greek priests as well as Russian served in this chapel during the eighteenth century. The archives of the Russian Embassy chapel are to be found in the Public Record Office in London. See the Memorandum Book of the Russian chapel (PRO, RG 8/111) 158; for Lodvel's American origin, cf. the entry for 3

Confession by Peter Moghila, Metropolitan of Kiev, which had been approved by the Synod of Jassy in 1642, and by the four Eastern Patriarchs in 1643.[18]

These rare examples do not, however, alter the fact that in joining the Orthodox Church Frederic North was taking a step that was curious and surprising. What were his motives? This is not an easy question to answer. North does not seem to have kept a diary,[19] and to the best of my knowledge he never himself wrote an account of his conversion to Orthodoxy. There does, however, survive a detailed, first-hand account of his reception by his sponsor, the Corfiot George Prosalendis (1713–1795), although this was not published until long after North's death.[20]

April 1762, recording the reception of his three daughters into the Orthodox Church by chrismation (op. cit., 51). There is a further entry on 5 August 1760, stating that Lodvel had been given holy communion on that day (96). Here his name is spelt 'Ludwel'; elsewhere it appears as 'Lodvill' or 'Ludville'. For other persons received into the Orthodox Church at the Russian chapel, see the same volume (PRO RG 8/111) 157–158. Some of these, but not all, became Orthodox because of mixed marriages.

18   *The Orthodox Confession of the Catholic and Apostolic Eastern Church from the version of Peter Mogila*, edited with a preface by J. J. Overbeck and with an introductory notice by J. N. W. B. Robertson (London: Thomas Baker, 1898). Robertson states that Lodvel's translation was originally published in 1772 (the correct date is 1762).

19   See Angelomati-Tsougaraki, Τὰ ταξίδια τοῦ Λόρδου GUILFORD, 10.

20   See Georgios Prosalendis, Ἀνέκδοτα χειρόγραφα ἀφορῶντα τὴν κατὰ τὸ δόγμα τῆς Ὀρθοδόξου Ἐκκλησίας βάπτισιν τοῦ ἄγγλου φιλέλληνος Κόμητος Γυΐλφορδ, edited by Lavrentios S. Vrokinis (Kerkyra: Typ. Korais, 1879). When I first consulted the British Museum copy of this work, I found that despite its presence in the library for nearly a century the pages were for the most part still uncut. Papadopoulos-Vretos, *Notizie*, in his account of North's reception differs from Prosalendis at several points. But Papadopoulos-Vretos came to know North only some thirty years after the event, whereas Prosalendis

North's life, prior to his 1791 journey to Greece, can be briefly summarised. Born on 7 February 1766, he grew up in what seems from all accounts to have been a happy and close-knit family. He studied at Eton for a short while, but because of his delicate health he spent much of his childhood abroad at spas, thus laying the basis for his wide-ranging future knowledge of foreign languages. On 18 October 1782 he was matriculated at Christ Church, Oxford, receiving the degree of Doctor of Civil Law some eleven years later, on 5 July 1793. His keen enthusiasm for things Hellenic dated back to an early stage in his life, certainly to his time at Oxford if not to his schooldays. In the words of J. M. Rigg, 'At Oxford North became an accomplished Grecian and an enthusiastic phil-hellene.'[21]

Frederic North made his first visit to Greece early in 1791. Sailing from Venice and travelling alone, he arrived in Corfu[22] a few weeks before his twenty-fifth birthday, on 4/15 January.[23] The Ionian Islands were at this time still under

---

was an eye-witness; and so, where the two differ, Prosalendis is normally to be preferred. For further material on North's conversion to Orthodoxy, see the review of G. P. Henderson's book by Georgios Metallinos (see n. 4), Παρνασσός 23 (1981), 332–5, and also his valuable article, Ὁ Κόμης Φρειδ. – Δημήτριος Γκίλφορδ καὶ ἡ ἰδεολογικὴ θεμελίωσι τῶν θεολογικῶν σπουδῶν τῆς Ἰονίου Ἀκαδημίας, offprint from Ἐπιστημονικὴ Ἐπετηρὶς τῆς Θεολογικῆς Σχολῆς τοῦ Πανεπιστημίου Ἀθηνῶν 27 (Athens, 1986), esp. 4–10.

21   *The Dictionary of National Biography* 41, 164.
22   Following Henderson, *The Ionian Academy*, 1, n. 1, I shall use 'Corfu' in naming the island, 'Kerkyra' in naming the town situated upon it.
23   In describing events connected with North's baptism, I shall usually give dates according to both the Old (Julian) and the New (Gregorian) Calendar (Prosalendis follows the Old Calendar). There is some uncertainty about the year in which North became Orthodox. In the earlier version of this paper I argued that it should be 1792 (not 1791, as usually accepted): see Baker, *The Orthodox Churches and the West,*

Venetian rule. The citizens of Kerkyra were quick to notice that in behaviour the new visitor was very different from the usual Frankish 'milord' making the Grand Tour. First of all he was far more polite, 'courteous to all alike', in the words of George Prosalendis, an elderly member of the local Corfiot nobility who befriended him. Prosalendis was particularly impressed by North's spontaneous humility at their first meeting in the main coffee-house of the city. As soon as Prosalendis entered the room, North leapt to his feet and ran to meet him, trying to kiss his hand. This, however, Prosalendis would not allow, withdrawing his hand and kissing his new friend on the cheek.[24] Here was none of the cold haughtiness so often characteristic of the English

---

249 n. 7. Subsequent correspondence with Dr Francis R. Walton and Dr Anthony Seymour convinced me that the correct year is indeed 1791. Confusion arises because of a glaring discrepancy on the opening page of Prosalendis's narrative, where it is stated that North arrived in Venice on 2/13 December 1791, proceeded after four days to the Ionian Islands, and then reached Corfu on 4/15 January 1791 ('Ανέκδοτα χειρόγραφα, 57). Almost certainly the first date is a misprint for 2/13 December 1790. Elsewhere Prosalendis consistently gives the date of North's stay in Corfu as 1791. Moreover, he says that, while North was there, 5/16 and 12/23 January, and also 2/13 February, were Sundays (61, 68, 157), which is indeed the case in 1791, whereas in 1792 these days are Mondays.

Independent (and conclusive) confirmation of the year 1791 is provided by the manuscript profession of faith, drawn up in Italian before North's baptism and written in his own hand, which is preserved in the Greek Orthodox episcopal archives in Kerkyra: this is clearly dated at the top '23 Gennaio 1791'. (Dr Angelos Choremis kindly sent me a photograph of this in 1977, and in 2002 I looked at it personally.) Vrokinis includes the text of this profession in his introduction to Prosalendis's narrative ('Ανέκδοτα χειρόγραφα, 41–43), but omits the date at the beginning. See further, n. 57.

24 Prosalendis, 'Ανέκδοτα χειρόγραφα, 59, 65; for Prosalendis's family background, see the introduction by Vrokinis, 15–36.

aristocrat abroad. Prosalendis found him 'a complete philhellene, and fairly well acquainted with the Greek language'.[25]
'By nation I am an Englishman', North said to him, 'but in my
heart I am a Greek.' 'A philhellene', Prosalendis corrected
him. But North would not accept this, insisting twice, 'Greek,
Greek'.[26]

There were also other points in North's behaviour that
struck the Corfiots as unusual. He went constantly to church,
following the Greek services with obvious devotion. Attending the Divine Liturgy and the Blessing of the Waters on
5 January, the eve of the Feast of Theophany, he came forward
to be sprinkled with holy water at the end of the ceremony,
and received the *antidoron* or blessed bread. He also venerated
the relics of St Spyridon with marked reverence.[27] As one
observer, Nicolas Arliotis, noted in his diary for 14 January
1791:

> He speaks a little modern Greek, but with a difficult pronunciation
> different from our own. He loves our church services and is closely
> familiar with the Orthodox ritual. He has attended the Liturgy in the
> churches of the Most Holy Mother of God *Spiliotissa* and of St
> Spyridon, and he delights to hear the Constantinopolitan chanting.
> In church he repeatedly makes the sign of the cross as if he were a
> hieromonk, which is scarcely consistent with the outlook and
> character of the English.[28]

The reference here to 'the Constantinopolitan chanting' is of
interest. At most Greek Orthodox churches in Kerkyra,
North would have heard, not the monophonic Byzantine
chant preserved at Constantinople (and elsewhere), but a
bastard style of harmonised singing introduced into Orthodox

---

25   Ibid., 63.
26   Ibid., 66.
27   Ibid., 61–62.
28   Cited by Vrokinis in his introduction to Prosalendis, op. cit., 47.

worship on the Ionian Islands under Venetian influence. In expressing a preference for a purer form of Orthodox church music, North displayed a love for strict, traditional Orthodoxy.

Accompanying North to church for the Sunday Liturgy, Prosalendis observed with satisfaction the exemplary behaviour of the young *archon*, as the local Greeks called him:

> Going to the centre of the church, three times he bowed down to the ground, making the sign of the cross, and accompanied by the priest Montesanto [...] he ascended the platform in front of the icon-screen and took his place in a stall. Remaining myself in the lower part of the church, I watched him throughout the entire duration of the service, standing with exceptional reverence and marvellous attentiveness, constantly making the required bows at each point in the Liturgy; and I was truly filled with amazement, reflecting in bewilderment how this man, coming from the British nation and brought up in the perverse opinions of the Lutherocalvinists, showed towards the customs of our Church and above all towards the Divine Liturgy such reverence and attentiveness as to win the admiration and to rival the zeal of us who were born and brought up and live in Orthodoxy.[29]

It is tempting to dismiss such behaviour as the ostentatious enthusiasm of a callow neophyte. But Prosalendis for his part writes without irony and in sincere admiration.

It appears that North's interest in Orthodoxy predated his arrival at Corfu. According to Prosalendis, while North was in Venice during December 1790, prior to setting out for the Ionian Islands, he went to no other place of worship except the Greek church of St George, where he talked with the parish priest. Much of his time on the sea voyage to Corfu he spent in prayer before the icon of the Mother of God, and he refused to eat any meat, wishing to observe with rigour the

---

29   Ibid., 69.

Orthodox pre-Christmas fast. Like other English proselytes to Orthodoxy in more recent times, he was mortified to discover that the Greeks themselves were somewhat easy-going in their attitude to the rules of abstinence.[30] Prosalendis found that North was already well-versed in Orthodox teaching, possessing at home in England the standard works of Greek theologians such as St Symeon of Thessalonica, Patriarch Dositheos of Jerusalem, and Meletios Syrigos.[31] One wonders how he had come across such books, which would have been altogether unfamiliar to the average western student of the classics.

It soon became plain to Prosalendis that North's sympathy with the Greek Church went far beyond that of a detached observer. Although a layman, Prosalendis was deeply read in theology. When he began to speak to North in detail concerning the Orthodox faith, he found that he met with an eager response. The more Prosalendis told the Englishman about Orthodoxy, the more the latter insisted that this was exactly what he himself already believed. One evening in the coffee-house the conversation turned to the validity of Anglican baptism. As Prosalendis recounts:

> He asked me whether the Eastern Church accepts the baptism of the English. To this I replied with another question: 'How do the English baptise?' He answered that they dip the first three fingers of the hand in the water, and with these they moisten the forehead of the baptised, calling on the three persons of the Holy Trinity. Then I said that the form of holy baptism handed down to us is not of such a kind as this, but it is performed with three immersions.[32]

Was North accurate here in his description of Anglican practice at this time, and was it in fact normal in eighteenth-

---

30   Ibid., 58.
31   Ibid., 66.
32   Ibid., 73–74.

century England to baptise, not by affusion or pouring water on the candidate's forehead, as the 1662 Anglican Book of Common Prayer specifies, but merely by marking or moistening it with wet fingers? Prosalendis went on to add that, in cases of emergency, the Orthodox Church may permit the omission of threefold immersion and may rest content with a 'threefold pouring of water over the head'. But merely to moisten or smear the forehead, without actually pouring water over it, is altogether insufficient:

> In the case of baptism performed by the Western [i.e. Roman Catholic] Church, even though in that Church it is not customarily required of the baptised that he should be naked or clothed in a single garment, yet because the Western Church baptises the candidate with water poured over his head, accompanied by the invocation of each person of the Holy Trinity, the Eastern Church accepts and acknowledges this baptism, and so in the case of [Roman Catholic] converts to the Orthodox Church it has been decided synodically that, after making a confession of faith, such persons should merely be anointed with the holy chrism. But the use of water applied to the forehead with three fingers cannot in any way be called baptism, nor is it such.[33]

Prosalendis's words, 'It has been decided synodically', refer presumably to the decision of the Council of Constantinople in 1484, which laid down that Latin converts should be received by chrismation. He appears to know nothing of the subsequent decree issued at Constantinople in 1755, requiring all Latin and other converts to Orthodoxy to be without exception rebaptised (or more exactly 'baptised', since their original baptism was considered null and void). The 1755 decree takes a Cyprianic stand: regardless of the manner in which the non-Orthodox rite has been performed, all heterodox baptism is deemed invalid, because performed outside the

---

33   Ibid., 75.

true Church.[34] Although Corfu and the other Ionian Islands were under the jurisdiction of the Patriarchate of Constantinople, presumably the 1755 decision was not applied there at this time because of the offence that it might have given to the Venetian authorities.

In answer to Prosalendis, North went on to mention an instance, known to him personally, in which an Anglican, baptised by 'moistening' in the manner already indicated, had been received into the Roman Catholic Church without rebaptism. To this Prosalendis replied that the Roman Church might act as it wished, but the Orthodox Church took no account of that:

> The Holy Orthodox Eastern Church in no way accepts or acknowledges a 'moistening with water' as a substitute for baptism. We have rules of Ecumenical Synods which lay down that those who have been baptised by heretics, if they were baptised according to the form used by the Catholic Orthodox Church, are not to be rebaptised; but if they have been baptised in some other way, then

---

34   On the historical context of the 1484 and the 1755 decrees, see Ware, *Eustratios Argenti,* 65–107; Georgios D. Metallinos, «Ὁμολογῶ ἓν βάπτισμα ...» Ἑρμηνεία καὶ ἐφαρμογὴ τοῦ Ζ' Κανόνος τῆς Β' Οἰκουμενικῆς Συνόδου ὑπὸ τῶν Κολλυβάδων καὶ τοῦ Κων)ου Οἰκονόμου (Athens, 1983); English translation by Priestmonk Seraphim, *I Confess One Baptism ... Interpretation and Application of Canon VII of the Second Ecumenical Council by the Kollyvades and Constantine Oikonomos* (Holy Mountain, Athos: St Paul's Monastery, 1994). This contains an interesting appendix on the practice in the Ionian Islands during the nineteenth century: 81–87 (Greek); 137–141 (English, abbreviated). Here Fr Metallinos mentions several cases in which from 1824 onwards, during the period of the British protectorate, Roman Catholics converting to Orthodoxy were received through baptism. The Holy See complained about this to the British authorities, who promised to the Roman Catholic authorities that the practice 'should be prevented for the future' (Sir Frederick Adam to Lord Bathurst, 16 January 1827).

they are received by baptism, since in reality they are altogether un-baptised.[35]

From this it is clear that Prosalendis did not accept the Cyprianic stance of the 1755 decree, with its denial of validity to *all* non-Orthodox baptism. North was baptised on his entry into Orthodoxy, so it seems, not by virtue of that decree, but because of the particular defect of his Anglican baptism, which had been by 'moistening' rather than affusion. Had the water been poured, he would not in Prosalendis's view have needed rebaptism. The real reason, however, why North was received into the Orthodox Church by baptism seems rather to have been that this was what he himself requested.

Prosalendis now put a leading question to North:

> I asked him if in England a man has the right to renounce the religion of that land, and to be united with [...] the Eastern Orthodox Church. To this he answered that anyone who so wishes has freedom to do this without hindrance, but whoever renounces the religion of that land and accepts another, whatever it may be, if he belongs by birth to the ruling class (ἀξιωματικοί), forfeits his privileges and cannot accede to high office.[36]

Matters now came rapidly to a head. North asked to meet Prosalendis not as hitherto at the coffee-house but in private, and they had a prolonged discussion about Orthodox teaching.[37] Prosalendis said that, should North wish to be baptised as an Orthodox, he would count it an honour to be his godparent or sponsor (ἀνάδοχος). To this North gave no answer at the time. He made an unsuccessful attempt to sail to Sta Maura (Levkas), but was turned back by bad weather. A few days later, on 22 January / 2 February, he expressed a firm

---

35   Prosalendis, op. cit., 76.
36   Ibid., 76.
37   Described in great detail by Prosalendis, op. cit., 77–143.

and definite desire to receive Orthodox baptism, and he accepted Prosalendis's offer to act as his sponsor.[38] Prosalendis now referred the matter to the most senior priest on the island, the *protopapas* Dimitrios Petrettinos.[39] The Venetians did not allow the Orthodox to maintain a bishop on the island of Corfu, his place being taken by a senior married priest, elected for a five-year period, who was styled 'protopope' and exercised episcopal jurisdiction, while lacking of course the sacramental power to ordain.

In requesting baptism, North laid down one condition: the ceremony was to be performed in strict secrecy. As he explained somewhat naively to the protopope:

> For many years I have been convinced, through my study of the Old and New Testaments, the Holy Ecumenical Councils and the Holy Fathers, that I find myself in error. But the social and economic circumstances of myself and my family have led me to shrink back. Eventually I decided to travel round the world, in the hope that the Lord would show me some way of giving my soul to him, while still retaining the civil status of my family. [...] I desire my baptism to be secret, because of the social and economic commitments of my family.[40]

Prosalendis and the protopope were far from happy about this request for concealment but eventually they consented, seeing it as no more than a short-term arrangement. Prosalendis describes the agreement that they reached with North:

---

38 Ibid., 142–145.
39 Petrettinos (1722–1795) was elected protopope in 1784, and was reelected in 1789 and 1794, holding office until his death. In North's manuscript profession of faith (see n. 23), the Greek note on the final page spells his name 'Petretinos'. In S. N. Avouris, Σύντομος Ἱστορία τῆς Ἐκκλησίας τῶν Ἰονίων Νήσων (Athens, 1966) 16, it is given as 'Petretis'.
40 Introduction by Vrokinis to Prosalendis, op. cit., 11–12.

This is to be regarded as a temporary concession, until he himself shall indicate that the proper moment has come for making the matter public. Firmly committing his conscience, he promises that he will indeed announce it at the appropriate time. He further promises, binding himself by an oath before God, that, since for the time being for reasons of expediency he does not wish to confess the truth until the right moment shall come, he will feign ignorance when others question him out of curiosity, but under no circumstances will he actually deny the truth.[41]

It was decided that the baptism should take place privately at the protopope's residence in the late evening of 23 January / 3 February. On the previous day, with Prosalendis's help, North had drawn up a profession of faith, written in Italian in his own hand; the original, with many corrections made by North himself, is preserved in the episcopal archives at Kerkyra.[42] In the profession he expresses his acceptance of the Creed, the seven Ecumenical Councils, the seven sacraments, and of various points of eucharistic teaching and practice, such as the doctrine of the real presence (using the terminology of substance and accidents, but not the actual word 'transubstantiation'), consecration through the epiclesis of the Holy Spirit, and the employment of leavened bread. The profession also refers to the Orthodox teaching concerning the invocation of the saints, the perpetual virginity of the Blessed Virgin Mary, and the veneration of icons; but surprisingly there is no direct allusion to the *Filioque* or the Papal claims.

North prepared himself carefully for his reception: although not specifically required to do so, he asked to make his confession,[43] and when Prosalendis called at his lodgings in the evening of 22 January / 2 February, he found him praying

---

41   Ibid., 148.
42   See n. 23; also Prosalendis, op. cit., 41–43.
43   Prosalendis, op. cit., 150.

in the dark in an inner room, his face flushed with weeping.[44] At the baptism on 23 January / 3 February there were only four others present, apart from North: the priest Spyridon Monte-santo, in whose company North had travelled from Venice to Corfu, and to whom he had made his confession (it was he that was deputed to perform the actual ceremony); the protopope and Prosalendis, who acted jointly as sponsors; and a deacon. Prosalendis describes the service:

> The doors of both the outer and the inner rooms were closed, and the nobleman withdrew to the inner bedroom, where the curtains were drawn. Here he removed his outer garments and emerged clothed only in his shirt, as the rubrics prescribe. At once, Fr Montesanto began the service, with the protopope standing on the nobleman's right and myself on the left. First the exorcisms were read, and then the questions about renouncing the devil and accep-ting Christ; the nobleman gave the answers himself and recited the Creed three times. The protopope named him by his own name 'Frederic', and I by the other name that he wished to receive (as Fr Montesanto had told me), 'Dimitrios'. Then, with the two of us as sponsors holding him by the arms and with the priest going in front, he was led unshod to the holy font, and the sacrament of baptism was administered to him. After this he received the seal of the gift of the Holy Spirit through anointing with the holy chrism (μύρον), and all the ceremonies were performed exactly as prescribed by the service book and by the tradition of the Holy Orthodox Eastern Church. Throughout the service from start to finish he was irradiated with marvellous devotion. [...] Afterwards we had a short talk, at which it was said that this holy action must be kept secret from everyone apart from the five of us.[45]

---

44   Ibid., 151.
45   Ibid., 153–154. There is a discrepancy here between Prosalendis and Papadopoulos-Vretos, *Notizie*, 10, 13: the latter states that the baptism took place 'publicly' in the church of the Mother of God *Mandrakina* at Kerkyra, but gives no further details. The eye-witness testimony of Prosalendis is surely more trustworthy.

On the wall of the house where the baptism was cele-brated, at the south end of Capodistrias Street, there is a plaque stating in Greek:

In this house there took place
The baptism according to the Orthodox dogma
Of the great Philhellene
Guilford
Founder of the Ionian Academy.[46]

Prosalendis told North that, after the baptism, during the night he should read in full the service in preparation for holy communion. Very early next morning, still with every precaution to preserve secrecy, the newly-baptised received communion at a Liturgy specially celebrated in one of the local churches. Later in the day he was given a written baptis-mal certificate by the protopope.[47] North continued to assure Prosalendis that 'he would keep the matter secret for the time being, but under no circumstances would he actually deny it'. Prosalendis expressed the hope that the moment for public disclosure would quickly arrive.[48] He also dreamt of an Ortho-dox movement within the English aristocracy, with North at its head: 'Through the collaboration of this nobleman with other peers of the realm who have become secretly Orthodox, there will be an increase of Orthodoxy in that kingdom.'[49]

North left Corfu eleven days after the baptism, on 3/14 February 1791,[50] not revisiting the island until nearly thirty

---

46   Henderson, *The Ionian Academy*, 12 n. 1.
47   Prosalendis, op. cit., 156–7.
48   Ibid., 160.
49   Ibid., 149.
50   This is the date given by Prosalendis, op. cit., 160. Writing to his sister Anne from Sta Maura (Levkas) on 16/27 February 1791, North states that he has arrived there on that same day, after spending fifteen days at Preveza (see E. Angelomati-Tsougaraki, Τὰ Ταξίδια

years later. He spent Lent 1791 in the monastery of St John the Baptist on the island of Sta Maura (Levkas), observing the fast (according to Prosalendis) with exemplary severity, and even persuading the monks to celebrate the Presanctified Liturgy daily, not merely on Wednesdays and Fridays according to the usual custom. He received communion at the start of Lent.[51] Writing at this time to his sister Anne, however, North himself gives no hint of his religious devotions at the monastery, stating only that he has come to the monastery 'for a few days to rest and to fast for the gout had a great mind to come to town last week'. He calls the monastery 'rather a dismal habitation', but adds: 'I am lodged in a very decent cell. You have no idea how much I am delighted with my residence.' He was, however, unimpressed by the educational level of the monks: 'These worthy fathers are by no means luminaries of the Church. They can all read, but there is not one of them who understands antient Greek.' He was also somewhat critical of the Archbishop of Sta Maura: 'one of the weakest pillars of Orthodoxy [...] much troubled with flatulency'.[52]

After Easter North moved to Ithaca, where he seems to have stayed for about a year;[53] certainly he was still there on 5/16 August 1791, when he wrote from Ithaca to Pietro Bulgari.[54] He felt a particular affection for this island, and it was here that he originally proposed that the Ionian Academy

---

τοῦ Λόρδου GUILFORD, 89); this implies that he left Corfu on or around 1/12 February.

51   Prosalendis, op. cit., 161–164.
52   Letter to Anne North from Sta Maura, 15 March 1791, N. S. (Angelomati-Tsougaraki, op. cit., 94–95). Here he expresses the intention of staying on the island for only 'three or four days longer'.
53   Angelomati-Tsougaraki, op. cit., 21.
54   Papadopoulos-Vretos, *Notizie*, 6, 8, 9.

should be established.[55] After Ithaca he spent some time in Cephalonia and Zante.[56] Perhaps he preferred the other Ionian Islands to Corfu, because in them the Venetian influence was less dominant, and he could feel himself to be in an environment more authentically Greek, and thus more genuinely Orthodox. He left the Ionian Islands in the early summer of 1792, on receiving news of his father's illness, and he arrived in London shortly before his father died on 5 August 1792.[57]

Everything had happened with striking rapidity: North's baptism took place no more than nineteen days after his first arrival in Corfu. But long before he had actually set foot on Greek soil it seems that he already felt strongly attracted to Orthodoxy. This is confirmed by his conduct in Venice and on the voyage, by his previous interest in Greek theological writings, and above all by his avowal to the protopope, 'For many years I have been convinced [...] that I find myself in error'. In all probability his mind had been more or less made up long before, and he came to the Ionian Islands looking only for a convenient opportunity to realise what was already his firm intention. Friendship with Prosalendis provided him with exactly the opening that he sought, but the Corfiot

---

55   Henderson, *The Ionian Academy*, 13 (in a memorandum presented in April 1820).
56   Prosalendis, op. cit., 164–165.
57   Prosalendis, op. cit., 167–168. The details given above about North's movements in 1791–2 make it clear that his arrival in Corfu and his baptism must have taken place in January 1791, not 1792 (see above, n. 23). This is confirmed by the dating of his letters sent from Corfu and Sta Maura to his sister Anne (Angelomati-Tsougaraki, op. cit., 87–97). If he had arrived in Corfu only in January 1792, this leaves insufficient time for his prolonged visits to other islands, prior to his return to London in August of that year.

layman did not so much convert him as confirm his existing convictions.

It would be interesting to discover what it was that first drew Frederic North to the Orthodox Church. Admiration for classical Hellas, compassion for the oppressed Greeks under Turkish domination – these were common enough feelings among men of North's background; but why in his case did this sympathy also extend, in such a specific way, to the Greek Orthodox faith? Unfortunately, evidence is lacking to resolve the question. North's profession of faith, drawn up before his baptism, is a formal statement, not referring to his inner sentiments. To balance Prosalendis's narrative, we need a personal account of his conversion by North himself. But until now no such document has come to light.

Nor is this altogether surprising. For, contrary to the hopes of Prosalendis and the protopope of Corfu, he did not in fact make his Orthodox allegiance public after his return to England. Did he, one wonders, inform even the members of his immediate family, and in particular his father? Certainly, in the four letters sent by North to his sister Anne from Corfu and Sta Maura, between 23 January / 3 February and 8/19 March – at exactly the period of his reception into Orthodoxy – he gives no hint of any special contacts with the Orthodox Church, apart from the fact that he has been staying at a Greek monastery. This is the more remarkable, in that the first of these letters was written on the very day when he was baptised, 23 January / 3 February; but all he says here is that he is 'in a town not only Christianlike but Orthodox'.[58]

It is, however, fully understandable that North should have chosen in this way not to mention such a delicate matter in correspondence, preferring to wait until he could speak with his family face to face after his return home. He must

---

58   Angelomati-Tsougaraki, op. cit., 87.

have anticipated that his parents' reaction would be astonishment and dismay. But, even when he was back in England, did he in fact tell anyone? Not a scrap of evidence has yet been discovered to suggest that he did. On the contrary, from 1792 he pursued the normal type of career open to one of his background, and his contemporaries seem to have noticed nothing unusual in his religious position.

During 1792–1794 he sat as Member of Parliament for Banbury; this town was close to the family residence at Wroxton Abbey, and the parliamentary seat was regularly held by different Norths, who were elected unopposed. Under the terms of the Test Act, at this time unrepealed, only members of the Church of England could sit in Parliament; had it been generally known that North had renounced Anglicanism, there would surely have been objections to his taking up his seat.[59] During his seven years as a not-very-successful Governor of Ceylon (1798–1805), there is no indication of any Orthodox chaplain in his retinue. He returned to Greece and the Near East for a three-year journey in 1810–1813, visiting Mount Athos and Jerusalem among many other places; but in his voluminous surviving correspondence from this time he said nothing to suggest that he was a practising Orthodox.[60] Had North regularly worshipped and openly received the sacraments at the Russian Embassy chapel in London – the sole Orthodox place of worship in the capital until the establishment of a Greek chapel at 9 Finsbury Circus in 1837 – this

---

59   To the best of my knowledge, the only other Orthodox who has sat in Parliament (long after the repeal of the Test Act) was the Greek Pandely Thomas Ralli (1845–1928), Member of Parliament for Bridport (1875–1880) and for Wallingford (1880–1885). G. E. H. Palmer (1904–1984) was Member of Parliament for Winchester during 1935–1945, but this was prior to his reception into the Russian Orthodox Church in Exile in 1950.

60   Angelomati-Tsougaraki, op. cit., 97–327.

would surely have aroused comment.[61] Even when, from 1815 until his death in 1827, he made frequent visits to Corfu – at this time under British rule – often spending the greater part of the year there, there is no record of his publicly receiving Orthodox communion.

To the British and Greek public of the time the fifth Earl of Guilford was not seen as an adherent of the Orthodox Church, but simply as one among a number of British phil-hellenes. His contemporaries knew of him as an admirer of the Greek people, who liked to express opinions such as the following (in a letter dating from 1810):

> To be sure I am partial, but I consider the Greeks of the nineteenth century as far superior to those of the fifteenth, and within these twenty years the advance they have made in science, navigation, trade and independence of spirit are inconceivable. The idea entertained of them in the West is a very false and imperfect one and I do not believe that any other nation in the world could have done so much for itself under so long and severe a bondage.[62]

His contemporaries knew of North likewise as the author of a Pindaric ode honouring the Empress Catherine of Russia,[63] as president of the English branch of the 'Society

---

61   See Michael Constantinides, *The Greek Orthodox Church in London* (Oxford: University Press, 1933), 18–33. In 1849–1850 the Greek community in London moved to the Church of the Saviour, Winchester Street, London Wall, and in 1879 to the present Church (now Cathedral) of the Holy Wisdom, Moscow Road, Bayswater.

62   Letter of North to Sylvester Douglas, Lord Glenbervie (husband of North's sister Catherine Anne), dated 1 June 1810, in Angelomati-Tsougaraki, op. cit., 101.

63   Entitled Αἰκατερίνη Εἰρηνοποιῷ, this was written by North in Greece during 1791–1792. Its appeal to Catherine not to abandon the Greeks suggests that it was composed shortly after the preliminary truce of Galatz (11 August 1791) and before news had arrived of the Treaty of Jassy (9 January 1792), after which such a plea would have lost most

of the Friends of the Muses' ('Εταιρεία τῶν Φιλομούσων), founded at Athens in 1814,[64] and as an indefatigable collector of books and manuscripts: as he once remarked to his librarian Papadopoulos-Vretos, 'Ah! my child, if I were not the Earl of Guilford I would have liked to be a librarian.'[65] Writing to his cousin Lord Bathurst in 1825, he calls his library 'this favourite child of my old age'.[66] His contemporaries knew of him above all as an ever-munificent patron of Greek letters, as benefactor to a host of Greek students in western universities, and as Chancellor of the Ionian Academy, which formed the consuming interest of his last years. Although the Academy declined in importance after North's death, failing to realise the early hopes that he and others had placed in it,

---

of its point. Prosalendis, Ἀνέκδοτα χειρόγραφα, 166, gives Zante as the place of writing; according to Papadopoulos-Vretos, *Notizie*, 8, 9, it was written in Ithaca, and this seems to be correct, since the copy of the poem in the Gennadius Library, Athens, bears on its title page the inscription in North's hand, 'Written in the island of Ithaca'. It was first published with a Latin translation (no place or date of publication), probably at Vienna by the printing house of Baumeister in 1792. Vienna is Prosalendis's suggestion (167); he tells us that North spent twenty days here *en route* for England in summer 1792. The text and translation were reissued with an introduction by Papadopoulos-Vretos (Athens, 1846), who suggests less convincingly that the first edition was printed at Leipzig.

64 North's letter in Attic Greek, accepting nomination to this office, is given by Papadopoulos-Vretos, *Notizie*, 27–29. Georgios D. Metallinos, Γκίλφορδ-Βάμβας καὶ ἕνα ἱστορικὸ Γράμμα, in Παρνασσός 23 (1983) 500–509, shows that this letter was drafted by the theologian Neophytos Vamvas (1770–1855). North, however, made several revisions; above all, in the signature at the end of the letter, where Vamvas proposed the anodyne phrase ὁ ὑμέτερος ἑταῖρος, 'your colleague', North substituted the much more expressive words πολίτης Ἀθηναῖος, 'citizen of Athens'.

65 Introduction to the 1846 reissue of Αἰκατερίνη Εἰρηνοποιῷ, 4.

66 Bobou-Stamati, Ἡ Βιβλιοθήκη GUILFORD, 515.

and although after the foundation of the University of Athens in 1837 it was inevitably overshadowed, yet for a brief but crucial period in the 1820s, during the initial years of the War of Independence, it formed for Greeks everywhere a cultural rallying-point, a promise of future spiritual renewal.

Such, then, was the picture that the public had of Frederic North: a man of letters, a philhellene, but not specifically a representative of Eastern Orthodoxy. There are repeated references to his kindness and good nature; not without reason C. M. Woodhouse calls him 'the most lovable and sincere of all the philhellenes'.[67] He was known as a man of great courtesy, 'genial and witty', in the words of Papadopoulos-Vretos,[68] consistently generous to those in need. Politeness and amiability had, indeed, marked him from his early years: Sir Gilbert Elliott in his diary for 1788 describes him as 'the only pleasant son of the family, and he is remarkably so'.[69] Even Sir Thomas Maitland, Lord High Commissioner for the Ionian Islands during 1815–1824, who doggedly obstructed North's plans for the Ionian Academy, recognised his integrity and generosity. His fault in Maitland's eyes was that he too easily believed good of others, and so was often cheated. 'He always supposes that every man is actuated by the same honourable principles as himself', Maitland wrote of North, adding that he was 'the weakest of human beings when he comes to deal with men'.[70]

---

67   Woodhouse, *The Philhellenes* (London: Hodder & Stoughton, 1969), 142.

68   Papadopoulos-Vretos, *Notizie*, xxiv.

69   Ferriman, *Some English Philhellenes*, 77.

70   Cyril Willis Dixon, *The Colonial Administrations of Sir Thomas Maitland* (London: Longman, Green & Co., 1939), 227 n. 2. Maitland succeeded North as Governor of Ceylon in 1805, and had a poor opinion of his predecessor's competence.

Polite and amiable North may certainly have been, but his acquaintances also found him decidedly eccentric. 'The most illustrious humbug of his age and country', Byron said of him.[71] His friends considered his passion for books and education altogether excessive. As Captain Robert Spencer remarked, 'I am a friend of the Earl of Guilford and I respect him, but in my opinion his great desire to support so many professors and students amounts to madness.'[72] 'A queer fish, but very pleasant', commented Sir Charles James Napier after meeting him at a dinner party in 1819; and, alluding to Guilford's linguistic versatility, he described him as 'addressing every person in a different language, and always in that which the person addressed did not understand'. His reputation for oddity was enhanced by his practice of wearing what he believed to be the garb of classical Greece: 'He goes about', protested Napier, 'dressed up like Plato, with a gold band around his mad pate and flowing drapery of a purple hue.'[73] James Emerson Tennent, visiting North some two years before his death, found him seated before a blazing fire, surrounded by books and papers, 'his mantle pendant from his shoulder by a golden clasp, and his head bound by a fillet embroidered with the olive and owl of Athens'.[74] What is more, North insisted that the professors and students of the Ionian Academy should dress in similar clothing, a requirement that cannot have been universally popular.

Had his English contemporaries known that North had joined the Greek Church, surely this would have been mentioned as a further and most striking example of his

---

71 Angelomati-Tsougaraki, Τὰ ταξίδια τοῦ Λόρδου GUILFORD, 125 n. 2.
72 Papadopoulos-Vretos, *Notizie*, 86, 93.
73 Ferriman, op. cit., 94–95.
74 James Emerson, *A Picture of Greece in 1825* (London: J. Colburn) 1826, i, 10.

eccentricity;[75] yet Napier, Emerson and the others seem to know nothing about his Orthodoxy. Moreover, Dr Eleni Angelomati-Tsougaraki, who has worked extensively on North's unpublished papers, points out that they contain nowhere any explicit reference to his Orthodox baptism at Kerkyra in 1791 and to his continuing membership of the Orthodox Church; and so she doubts whether he was ever actually received into Orthodoxy.[76] But another expert on North, Dr Vasiliki Bobou-Stamati, takes a different view. She believes that he did indeed join the Orthodox Church in 1791; the absence of any reference to this in his surviving papers is sufficiently explained by his wish to keep the matter secret from the members of his family and from the English public in general.[77]

I agree with Dr Bobou-Stamati. It seems to be intrinsically improbable that the account of Prosalendis, containing so much circumstantial detail that is *prima facie* convincing, is no more than a work of fiction. Two people who were personally acquainted with North in his later years – Andreas Papadopoulos-Vretos, who was librarian at the Ionian Academy during 1824–1830, and Georgios Typaldos Iakovatos, whose brother Konstantinos taught at the Academy during 1826–1839 – were familiar with the work of Prosalendis and accepted its authenticity.[78] As a confirmation of Prosalendis's narrative, there exists also North's autograph confession of

---

75   I remember how, shortly before I myself joined the Orthodox Church in 1958, an Anglican friend warned me: 'You will be a lifelong eccentric.'
76   Angelomati-Tsougaraki, Ἡ Ἰόνιος Ἀκαδημία, 216–217; Τὰ ταξίδια τοῦ Λόρδου GUILFORD, 22.
77   Bobou-Stamati, Ἡ Βιβλιοθήκη GUILFORD, 499–500, nn. 11 and 12.
78   Metallinos, in Παρνασσός 23 (1981), 332–333.

faith,[79] which to the best of my knowledge no one has shown to be a forgery.

There remain, however, two other possibilities. First, it has been suggested that North did indeed become Orthodox in 1791, but his action was not sincere; it was his purpose to act as a spy and as the member of a 'fifth column', surreptitiously corrupting the Orthodox Church from the inside with 'Lutherocalvinist' errors. Rumours to this effect circulated in the Ecumenical Patriarchate during the 1830s.[80] Twentieth-century English converts to Orthodoxy, including myself, have been subjected to similar accusations by Greek chauvinists. In North's case, the *canard* is convincingly refuted by Fr Georgios Metallinos, who shows that, during the years when North had responsibility for educational matters in the Ionian Islands (1815–1827), he was careful to uphold the purity of Orthodox teaching, resisting all forms of western infiltration, whether from Protestant or from Roman Catholic sources.[81]

More convincingly, it could in the second place be argued that, while North in full sincerity entered the Orthodox Church in 1791, yet in his later life he abandoned the practice of the Orthodox faith. May he not have come to regard his baptism at Kerkyra as a youthful indiscretion, best quietly forgotten? There is, however, evidence to suggest that, right up to the time of his death, he did in fact continue to adhere to Orthodoxy. The well-known priest and theologian Theoklitos Pharmakidis (1784–1860), who taught briefly at the Ionian Academy in 1824–1825, stated that North's membership of the Orthodox Church was a matter of common

---

79   See above, nn. 23 and 42.
80   See Bobou-Stamati, op. cit., 500, n. 12.
81   See Metallinos, Ὁ Κόμης Φρειδ. – Δημήτριος Γκίλφορδ (n. 20) *passim*.

knowledge in Kerkyra during his time as Chancellor.[82] This seems to be an exaggeration; but clearly Pharmakidis himself suspected that North was an Orthodox, and perhaps other professors in the Academy did as well.

Andreas Papadopoulos-Vretos claimed, more specifically, that immediately before his death North received Orthodox communion. In 1827, the last year of his life, he left Corfu on 16 June and journeyed slowly through Europe, reaching London at the end of August or the beginning of September.[83] Already his state of health was giving his friends cause for serious anxiety,[84] when a fall from his carriage[85] brought on a fatal illness. He died on 14 October. Papadopoulos-Vretos – who, however, was not with North in London at the time but in Kerkyra – states in explicit terms:

> Perceiving that the last moment of his life was near at hand, he repeatedly asked for the chaplain of the Russian Embassy chapel, his old friend Fr Smirnov, and from his hands he received communion, to the great displeasure of his relatives, and especially of his nephew the Earl of Sheffield, in whose house he died. The Earl of Sheffield

---

82   See Pharmakidis, 'Απολογία (Athens: Typ. Angelos Angelidis) 1840, 125, cited by Papadopoulos-Vretos, *Notizie*, 15, and by Vrokinis in Prosalendis, 'Ανέκδοτα χειρόγραφα, iii and 38. To North's disappoint-ment, Pharmakidis stayed at the Ionian Academy only for one year. The immediate reason for his departure was that he requested a substantial increase in salary, which North felt unable to grant, as it would have meant that Pharmakidis was paid far more than any of the other professors (see Bobou-Stamati, op. cit., 538 n. 102).

83   See Bobou-Stamati, op. cit., 524, 536–537.

84   See the letters of Koliadis (31 July 1827) and Capodistrias (3 September 1827) in the Kerkyra archive, Φ VII 36 and Φ VIII 5: Dafni I. D. Kyriaki, Κερκυραϊκὸ 'Αρχεῖον GUILFORD, Special Issue of the 'Αναγνωστικὴ 'Εταιρεία Κερκύρας (Kerkyra, 1984) 117–118, 128.

85   Papadopoulos-Vretos, *Notizie*, 134, 143.

tried in every way to prevent him receiving the ministrations of a priest of a foreign dogma contrary to that of his forefathers.[86]

He received communion, Papadopoulos-Vretos adds, in the presence of two Greeks, his personal physician Rocco Pilarino from Cephalonia, and his valet Gianni Cacciotti (Katsiotis) from Parga; presumably it was from one or both of these that Papadopoulos-Vretos gained his information.

The Earl of Sheffield to whom Papadopoulos-Vretos refers was North's nephew and heir, George Augustus Frederick Holroyd-Baker; he was the second Earl and was the son of North's sister Anne. Papadopoulos-Vretos is correct in stating that North died in Sheffield's house at 20 Portland Place; he stayed there throughout his last visit to London during 1827 because his own house at 24 St James Place had been sold not long before. The Fr Smirnov who is said to have given communion to North was Archpriest Yakov Smirnov, chaplain of the Russian Embassy in London for some sixty years (1780–1840).[87] He and North were already acquainted, for the copy of North's Pindaric ode to the Empress Catherine of Russia preserved in the British Library bears the dedicatory inscription 'Reverend J. Smirnove, with the Author's most affectionate Respects', but unfortunately there is no indication of date.[88] Papadopoulos-Vretos may well be correct in supposing that Sheffield disapproved of his uncle's church allegiance and tried to hinder Fr Smirnov's visit; for, as subsequent events were to prove, Sheffield certainly felt no sympathy for North's philhellenism and his educational work in Kerkyra.

---

86   Ibid., 134, 145.
87   See A. G. Cross, 'Yakov Smirnov: a Russian priest of many parts', *Oxford Slavonic Papers*, New Series 8 (1975), 37–52.
88   On the ode to Catherine, see n. 63.

How far can we trust the information provided here by Papadopoulos-Vretos? Some have questioned his reliability. Being himself a Greek and a fervent admirer of North, he would naturally have wished to present his patron as a faithful member of the Orthodox Church. May not Papadopoulos-Vretos, then, have invented the story about North's last communion? Alternatively, was the story perhaps made up by one or other of the two Greek servants, who then told Papadopoulos-Vretos?

Fortunately, however, the account by Papadopoulos-Vretos is fully confirmed by independent evidence. In the Memorandum Book of the Russian Embassy chapel covering the year 1827, preserved at the Public Record Office in London, there survives a letter – not bound into the Memorandum Book but loosely inserted – written by North's sister Anne, Countess Dowager of Sheffield, widow of the first Earl, and addressed to Fr Yakov Smirnov:

Saturday

Revd Smurnove
32 Welbeck Street

My dear Sir,
It is with great concern I write to say that my dear Brother is most dangerously ill and he wishes to see you as soon as you can possibly be so good as to come to him and he begs you will bring whatever is necessary for him to take the sacrament with you. I am my dear Sir very sincerely yours

Sheffield

Thus, even if her son obstructed Fr Smirnov's visit, it is evident that North's sister did what she could to ensure that he received Orthodox communion before he died. On the Countess of Sheffield's letter another hand, clearly that of Fr Smirnov himself, has entered in Russian the exact date,

'1/13 October 1827', precisely one day before North's death. On the reverse of the letter, and also in the actual text of the Memorandum Book, there is a note, likewise in Russian, in Smirnov's hand confirming that he did indeed visit North, and also referring to the latter's Orthodox baptism in 1792 (*sic*) and to his death on 14 October.[89]

Anne North's letter therefore makes it certain beyond all reasonable doubt that her brother Frederic, the fifth Earl of Guilford, died within the communion of the Orthodox Church. How far he practised his faith, in the thirty-six years between his baptism in 1791 and his death in 1827, we do not know. But on his death-bed he certainly received the sacrament of holy communion from an Orthodox priest.

North's death was a grievous blow for the Ionian Academy in Kerkyra. In a codicil to his will, signed on 13 October 1827, one day before his death, he bequeathed his magnificent library to the Ionian Academy: most of his books were already there, but some were still in the process of being transported from London. He also specified that all the students at the Academy for whom he was personally providing bursaries should continue for the next four years to receive from his estate one half of their current stipend. Unwisely he added a condition: the Government of the Ionian Republic was required to assign to the Academy an annual sum of £3500, and also to pay the other half of the students' bursaries for the coming four years.

North's heir, Lord Sheffield, viewed with grave disapproval the massive scale on which North had used his inherited wealth to subsidise the Ionian Academy. Claiming

---

89 PRO RG 8/115, 27. The correct date of North's baptism is almost certainly 1791 (see n. 23). North's mind on his death-bed may have been confused, and perhaps inadvertently he told Smirnov the wrong year.

that the government of the Ionian Republic had not fulfilled
the conditions laid down in the codicil of 13 October, he had
North's library withdrawn from the Academy and sent back
to London, where it was dispersed – along with the books not
yet sent out to Kerkyra – in a series of auctions held during
1828–1835. According to Papadopoulos-Vretos, the total
collection that was put up for sale amounted to 3000
manuscripts and 15,000 books.[90]

One of the most interesting items is no. 1795 in the sale
beginning on 9 November 1835: 'Bibliotheca Graeco-Neo-
terica. A very Curious, Valuable and Extensive Collection of
Books in the Modern Greek Language [...] in all 627 vol.' The
auctioneer rightly appreciated the importance of this item,
stating in the sale catalogue: 'This is the most Extensive
Assemblage of Modern Greek Books ever submitted to
Public Sale.' The collection was bought by the bookseller
Thomas Rodd for £137. Almost all of the books he subsequently resold to the British Museum. This, then, was the
reason why I found the British Museum to be so well supplied
with Greek theological works of the seventeenth and
eighteenth centuries when I was undertaking research on
Eustratios Argenti. But not all of North's books ended up in
the British Museum. In 1988 I acquired from a second-hand
bookseller in London a work on the Council of Florence,
issued by the Printing Press of the Propaganda at Rome in
1628, which bears North's bookplate.[91] There is no evidence
that this was ever part of the library of the British Museum.

---

90   See Bobou-Stamati, Ἡ Βιβλιοθήκη GUILFORD, 549 n. 126. She
     discusses in detail the question of North's will and the dispersal of his
     library on 542–560; for the text of the codicil of 13 November, see 543.
91   The book is entitled Ἑρμηνεία τῶν Πέντε Κεφαλαίων, ὅπου περιέχει
     ἡ ἀπόφασις τῆς ἁγίας καὶ οἰκουμενικῆς συνόδου τῆς Φλωρεντίας: see
     Emile Legrand, *Bibliothèque Hellénique [...] au dix-septième siècle*, vol. 1
     (Paris: A. Picard, 1894), § 181, pp. 259–261. The British Library does

Undoubtedly the removal of North's library was a severe loss to the Ionian Academy. But there is a small compensation. Had it remained in Kerkyra, it would almost certainly have been reduced to ashes during the German bombardment of the city on 14 September 1943, when the building that had once housed the Ionian Academy, and where the Public Library of Kerkyra was subsequently located, was entirely gutted with the total destruction of its contents.

Papadopoulos-Vretos alleges that Sheffield, as well as depriving the Ionian Academy of North's Library, also did his utmost to suppress all evidence of his uncle's conversion to Orthodoxy. He states that North's nephew, on learning of the eyewitness account written by George Prosalendis, paid £400 to the owner of the manuscript, Doria Prosalendis, on the understanding that it should not be published.[92] There is a certain improbability here. Before parting with so large a sum of money, Sheffield might have been expected actually to secure possession of the manuscript. This he did not do, and the work eventually appeared in print in 1879. Papadopoulos-Vretos is in any case far from being an unprejudiced witness. As librarian of the Ionian Academy he bitterly resented the

---

not have a copy of this, but it does have a much shorter brochure on the Synod of Florence, also issued by the Propaganda in 1628 (Legrand, § 186, 264–265). Almost certainly this once belonged to North, even though in its present form it does not contain his bookplate; but this may have been discarded when the book was rebound in 1996. A work bearing a similar, but not identical, title appears in the manuscript list of North's books, drawn up soon after they entered the British Museum library.

The British Library is preparing a full catalogue of the Guilford manuscripts in its possession, and this will also include North's Greek printed books. I am grateful to Mr Chris Michaelides for information about this project (due to be completed in 2004), and for his help in other ways.

92 Papadopoulos-Vretos, *Notizie*, 12, 13.

way in which Sheffield, exploiting a loophole in North's will, had appropriated the latter's books and manuscripts and lined his pockets with the proceeds from their sale.

While we may be confident that Frederic North, fifth Earl of Guilford, died as a member of the Orthodox Church, there are many points in his religious biography that still remain obscure. As we have noted, it is not clear what initially attracted him to Orthodoxy before he arrived in Corfu in 1791, nor how active he was in his observance of his Orthodox faith during the decades that followed. Yet, even though he never made public the fact of his conversion – thus disappointing the expectations of his Corfiot friends that he would initiate an English Orthodox movement – he none the less personally continued faithful to his Orthodox allegiance up to the end of his life. His conversion indicates the striking attraction that the Christian East has never ceased to exercise in the Occident, even over members of the eighteenth-century Tory aristocracy.

PART 2:

Anglican Reflections on Orthodox Relations

12. Orthodox and Anglican: An Uneasy but Enduring Relationship

A. M. ALLCHIN

The title of this article which I first proposed to Peter Doll is one which has continued to make problems for me as I have thought more about it. 'Orthodox and Anglican: An Uneasy but Enduring Relationship'. As you may have guessed it is the word 'uneasy' which has been a cause of unease. What did I really intend by it? Would 'difficult' have been better? Or perhaps 'problematic', or even 'fragile'; or, in a more hopeful mood, would 'unexpected' or even 'unpredictable' have been preferable? 'Enduring' I am happy with; the more we look into the history of the question the more we see that it is true; but how to characterise the recurring tendency to setback, failure, frustration, which seems to accompany it? This is a question built in to the very substance of our gathering. We are celebrating the project of Benjamin Woodroffe, a project which, as the conference statement points out, 'was not a success in its own time'. But of course the initial statement of the purpose of our meeting goes further than that. The plan for a Greek College at Gloucester Hall is rightly affirmed as 'a noble vision of ecumenical understanding [...], the culmination of many contacts between Orthodoxy and Oxford over nearly a century'. Furthermore it is suggested that the plan 'anticipated the growing understanding and fellowship that exists between the two traditions at the present time.' Who knows? Perhaps at the end of our conference together we may begin to see the plan for

Gloucester Hall as the first tentative and fumbling move towards the establishment three centuries later of an Orthodox Theological Institute in Cambridge. That surely is a development of the greatest importance ecumenically, not only for this country, but for the English-speaking world.

I

This article falls into three parts. In the first I shall look back through the history of Christianity here in Britain to try to discern something of the roots of the enduring quality of the relationship which, I would maintain, exists between Anglicans and Eastern Orthodox Christians. In the second part I shall think of some of the unexpected ways in which, in our own lifetime, the Orthodox faith has been making itself known in this country. In the third part I shall turn towards two great figures of the eighteenth century, men who belong to the generation after Benjamin Woodroffe whose name we commemorate in our meeting, both of whom were surprisingly much involved in Anglican–Orthodox interaction.

As I approached the subject, I had a sudden memory of Archbishop Michael Ramsey, speaking here in Oxford in March, 1962, at a day conference organised by the Fellowship of St Alban and St Sergius, on the theme 'Dialogue East and West in Christendom.' It was a conference which gathered together speakers of the calibre of Metropolitan Anthony, Bishop of Sergieveo as he then was; Dr John Marsh, Principal of Mansfield College; and Father Bernard Leeming, S.J., Professor of Dogmatic Theology at Heythrop College. It was a moment when the whole ecumenical process seemed to be gathering momentum. In the autumn of the previous year there had been a Pan-Orthodox Conference at Rhodes, which seemed to suggest that more cooperation between Orthodox churches in the communist and non-communist world was about to become possible. So two months later at New Delhi, at the General Assembly of the World Council of Churches, the Russian Orthodox Church and the Orthodox churches of the other Soviet bloc countries, became for the first time members of the World Council of Churches. Only a few months off was the beginning of the first session of the Second Vatican Council, though at that moment none of us knew exactly what it might bring forth.

In such a moment in which he himself had great hopes for the resumption of an official international Anglican–Orthodox dialogue, Archbishop Michael Ramsey was moved at the end of his lecture to stress the unexpected, the unpredictable character of the whole movement towards Christian unity.

> One of the biggest changes that has come over all talk, thought and action about unity in quite recent years, has been this. It always used to be assumed that if a person was pursuing unity in one direction, he was automatically shrinking from it or doing damage in another direction. As you know, the Church of England is thought of roughly as having a centre, a right and a left, and the assumption was that if you pursued unity on the right it followed that someone on the left was being cold-shouldered or some damage was being done; or that if you pursued unity on the left it followed that something would be injured on the right. I believe that that has become totally altered. We have in ecumenical work all found ourselves to be so much wrapped up in a bundle that any genuine and sincere action in the service of Christ and Christ's unity in one direction will be helpful in other directions as well. Thus the relation between East and West is no monopoly in this country of Anglicanism, still less the monopoly of any particular party, or any particular sort of theology, because all those who are baptised into Christ are bidden by him to seek the fulfilment of the prayer that he makes unceasingly for all of them, for their growth in unity truth and holiness.[1]

---

1   A. M. Allchin (ed.), *'The Dialogue of East and West in Christendom'. Lectures delivered at a Conference arranged by the Fellowship of St Alban*

We need to see our subject in the widest possible context, to see its many-layered, many-sided character, to avoid at all costs timid conventional ecclesiastical stereotypes which too easily limit our vision and paralyse our capacity for action. There is a specific tradition of Anglican–Orthodox encounter and exchange, and Archbishop Michael valued it highly, but it had no monopoly of East–West relations, and we need always to be aware of the possibilities of the unexpected and the unpredictable.

Under the impact of such a statement as that I find myself looking yet again at the title of this article, 'Orthodox and Anglican: An Uneasy but Enduring Relationship'. Perhaps the other two opening items of the title also need to be considered again? 'Orthodox, Eastern', surely that is clear and evident in its meaning? We have only to change the word Eastern to Oriental to have a sudden change of perspective and understanding. The Eastern Christian world is made up not of one but of two ancient families of churches. Certainly the greater part consists of the churches in communion with Constantinople, but not to be ignored are the churches which have never accepted Chalcedon and which at a canonical level have been out of communion with the rest of Christendom for fifteen hundred years, which yet at another, deeper level are still so evidently part of the one, Holy, Catholic and Apostolic Church. Their theologians are sometimes people with whom an Anglican may feel a very deep affinity, whether one thinks of a great Armenian teacher of the twelfth century, like St Nerses Shnorhali, reflecting on the theme of Christian unity while confronted by the two great churches of Rome and Constantinople, both of which claim to be the whole; or whether one thinks of an ecumenical leader of the twentieth century, such as

Metropolitan Paulos Mar Gregorios with the constantly unexpected quality of his Indian insights into questions about Christian unity.

But if the word Orthodox proves itself less clearly self-evident than one would have expected, what about the word Anglican? The word 'Anglicanism' we know is a largely nineteenth century coinage. 'Anglican' itself goes back much further. But one only has to begin to become sensitive to the different historic peoples who share our two islands, Ireland and Britain, to see how strange it is that a man like Thomas Rattray, a great and in many ways typical eighteenth-century Scotsman, should be called an *Anglican,* as strange as it is in our own century to consider a man like Archbishop Henry MacAdoo, or Archbishop Rowan Williams, as *Anglicans,* when one is so evidently Irish and the other Welsh.

Of course, in thinking of Anglican–Orthodox relations we are usually thinking primarily of Anglican–Orthodox relations in the centuries since the break between Canterbury and Rome. But insofar as one of the basic definitions of an Anglican from the time of that sixteenth-century schism till today has been that an Anglican is one who does not and will not recognise that his Church begins at the time of the schism, it is essential also to recognise that this dating of Anglicanism from the sixteenth century can never be more than highly provisional and conditional.

For what is even more significant in our particular Anglican–Orthodox context is that an Anglican not only refuses to believe that his Church begins with the Reformation, he also refuses to believe that it began with the earlier split between Rome and Constantinople which took place in the eleventh century when the Hildebrandine Reform was making so many fundamental changes in the character of Western Christendom. This is a Church which goes back deep into the first Christian Millennium, whose greatest early leader was Theodore, a Greek of Tarsus, and whose history goes back before his day, before the fall of the Roman Empire to the church whose bishops attended the Council of Arles in 314, and whose martyrs suffered for the faith, Alban at Verulamium, Aaron and Julius at Caerleon very possibly at the beginning of the third century rather than the fourth. The churches in Roman Britain seem to have relied greatly on the larger and more developed churches in Roman Gaul. In particular the see of Lyons seems to have played a crucial role. Perhaps it was the thinking of Irenaeus, which was of vital importance to them.

When one thinks of the way in which other parts of northern Europe, Scandinavia and the Baltic countries for instance, received the gospel round about the eleventh or twelfth centuries, it is strange to reflect that in this island we have a Christian history which goes back before the Roman armies withdrew in 410, before the Anglo-Saxon invaders began to occupy and control the eastern side of our island. Living and working in Wales one cannot but be aware of living in a Church whose life goes back in unbroken continuity into this period before the Roman Legions left. Here are the roots of a deep and enduring relationship, not only with Rome, but with Constantinople, with Jerusalem and Alexandria, and perhaps above all particularly with the communities of the Egyptian desert, with whom the earliest monasteries of Wales no less than those of Ireland felt an intimate connection.

How important these very early memories are for the enduring relationship between the Churches in Britain and the Churches in the lands of the Eastern Mediterranean is a question which different people will judge differently. It seems at least important to notice how vitally significant they were for the man who was called to preside over the See of Canterbury at the moment when Mary Tudor died and her sister Elizabeth succeeded to the throne, Archbishop Matthew Parker. 1558 was a year of discontinuity indeed, and it is therefore striking to see how much care the Archbishop took at that particular moment to assure and build up the continuities which remained, through his collection of pre-Reformation manuscripts, through his promotion of Anglo-Saxon studies and his contacts with Richard Davies, Bishop of St Davids. The explicitly dogmatic and theological appeal to the Fathers of the first five centuries initiated by Bishop John Jewel at the same time, and then worked out systematically at the end of the sixteenth century and the beginning of the seventeenth by theologians of the calibre of Richard Hooker and Lancelot Andrewes, that key element in the whole development of the classical Anglican position, was accompanied by this other appeal to less well-known saints, to less articulate voices, the saints of the first generations of the Church in these islands. There too perhaps we may find the roots of this enduring relationship.

II

We have been looking back very briefly into the centuries of the first millennium in Britain and Ireland, to the centuries in which the Church in these two islands was an integral if remote part of the communion of Christendom, East and West, united in its cultural diversity, Celtic, Anglo-Saxon, Latin, Greek, Coptic, Syriac, Ethiopian.

I want now again briefly to look at some of the contemporary factors which have been at work in building up this enduring but uneasy relationship between Orthodox and Anglicans in the life of the older of us. It has been a time of hopes and disappointments, of unforeseen difficulties, and unforeseen gifts. If we look back to the time when the Anglican–Orthodox International Commission began its work in Oxford in 1973, we shall see on both sides hopes of an advance towards visible unity which today look somewhat unreal. It is not that the members of the Commission were excessively naive, but that they had not always taken full measure of the differences of approach and method which marked their two traditions. Scarcely anyone on the Orthodox side was aware of the kind of theological ferment which had been revealing itself in our Anglican world in the 1960s. Scarcely anyone on the Anglican side was aware of the depth and intransigence with which some at least of our Orthodox colleagues held to their conviction that the Orthodox Church alone was the one true Church of Christ, a Church which if true to itself could not recognise any of the separated Churches as genuine sister Churches at all.

Our progress at first was slow, and remembering the depths of incomprehension, existing on both sides of the divide, I think it was remarkable that by 1976 we had been able to arrive at the Moscow Agreed Statement, and by 1984 at the Dublin Agreed Statement. But by that time developments within the Churches of the Anglican Communion, particularly in the matter of the ordination of women, had brought the whole future of the Commission into question. Would the Orthodox Church ask for the conversations to be broken off altogether? Surely what is remarkable is that that did not happen. The relationship, if at times uneasy and fragile, was not broken. The work of the International Commission, even if it went on more slowly, went on. We await with interest the publication of new statements of consensus, and are the more eager to have them since we know that theologians of the calibre of Metropolitan John Zizioulas on the one side and Archbishop Rowan Williams on the other, have been taking part in their elaboration.

If the official conversations between Anglicans and Orthodox have known difficulties during these years, so too, on a much larger scale, have the official conversations between

Orthodoxy and Rome. What is more, the last decade or so, the years since the fall of the Communist regimes in Eastern Europe, have revealed to Christians in the West something of the deep problems which Churches which have suffered seventy years of pressure and persecution face in learning to confront the altogether different political, social and cultural situations in which they now find themselves.

But if the past decades have revealed to us new difficulties, they have also revealed to us new opportunities. Remembering Michael Ramsey's warning not to think of Anglican–Orthodox relations in isolation, his encouragement to see them in their total context, social, cultural, intellectual and spiritual, we may well be astonished at the variety of ways in which the dialogue has progressed and developed during the late twentieth century. If official conversations have hesitated, and seemed to stop, unofficial forms of East–West dialogue in Christendom have developed beyond all expectation.

I take a number of examples almost at random. At the most basic level how little there was available and accessible in English about Orthodox theology and spirituality, history and art, half a century ago! I remember the difficulty we had in the 1950s in finding a publisher for Vladimir Lossky's *Mystical Theology of the Eastern Church*, a book which in the years that have passed has never gone out of print, and has come to be recognised as a classic. We not only found it difficult to find a publisher, we found it difficult to find reviewers who could measure up to the book. The ineptitude and ignorance revealed by some of the first reviews remains in my mind.

It is not only in the realm of books that more is available now. Think of the way in which Rublev's icon of the Trinity has spread itself apparently spontaneously across the traditions of Western Christendom, Catholic and Protestant alike, providing us with a new icon of the mystery and majesty of God, rebuking silently our inherited problems about the 'Old Man with the

beard'. Think too of the nave of Westminster Abbey, proclaiming to the thousands who enter there every day, something of
the identity and meaning of that church, as a place of Christian
worship, by the placing of two great newly painted icons on the
westernmost pillars of the nave. Those icons are the work of a
Russian iconographer but I cannot help thinking too of the
members of our Anglican churches who have entered deeply
into the Orthodox tradition of icon painting, and have themselves received that particular gift of articulating the mystery of
Christ and the Saints which is granted to those who follow that
calling. No less remarkable, and perhaps even less predictable,
has been the gift of sacred music, which has come to us in this
country in these last decades above all in the work of two
musicians, Sir John Tavener and Arvo Pärt, two outstanding
representatives of the musical aspect of the Orthodox tradition.

But the most remarkable gift of all is one which seems to
have spread itself through the various families of the Christian
world as if by spontaneous combustion, the gift of the Jesus
Prayer. Here is a way of prayer which for fourteen or more
centuries has played a central role in the life of Eastern
Christendom, which in the last sixty or seventy years has made
itself known throughout the Christian West. Already in 1930
The Way of the Pilgrim appeared in an English translation. Evelyn
Underhill through her personal contact with Orthodoxy in the
'thirties, particularly in the context of the Fellowship of St
Alban and St Sergius, came to look deeply into its meaning and
practice. She writes in her great book *Worship*, 'If the simplicity
of its form be disconcerting, the doctrine which underlies it is
profound. Orthodoxy is penetrated by the conviction of the
need and insufficiency of man, and the nearness and transforming power of God. Therefore its truest act of personal
worship will be a humble and ceaseless self-opening to that divine
transforming power, which enters with Christ into the natural

order to restore and deify the whole world.'² In this passage she has already quoted Father Sergei Bulgakov on the prayer.

> It can when needful replace the Divine Office and all other prayers; for it is of universal validity. The power of this prayer does not reside in its content, which is simple and clear (it is the prayer of the publican) but in the holy Name of Jesus. The ascetics testify that in this name there resides the power of the presence of God. Not only is God invoked in it, but he is already present in this invocation. [...] Thus the name of Jesus present in the human heart communicates to it the power of that deification which the redeemer has bestowed on us.'³

It is very striking that in this remarkable ecumenical study of Christian liturgy, already in the 1930s, Evelyn Underhill, in conjunction with Bulgakov, is able so clearly to convey the theological and God-given depth of this way of prayer.

It was in the 1950s and 1960s that the practice of the prayer began to spread like wildfire in the West, particularly through the little book of Father Lev Gillet, *On the Invocation of the Name*, first published by the Fellowship in 1950, and for twenty or more years our one constant best seller, the publication which subsidised all our other publications. In more recent years the prayer has found strong advocates among Anglican writers, I think particularly of the writings of Bishop Simon Barrington-Ward and Brother Ramon S.S.F., and in particular of their joint study of the meaning and use of the prayer, a work on which Brother Ramon was intent in the very last weeks of his life. Here in this prayer we find the coming together not only of East and West, not only of the human family, but of all creation in 'the power of that deification which the redeemer has bestowed on us.'⁴

---

2   Evelyn Underhill, *Worship* (London, 1936) 270.
3   Ibid.
4   Br. Ramon and Simon Barrington-Ward, *Praying the Jesus Prayer Together* (Oxford: The Bible Reading Fellowship, 2001).

III

In this last part of the article I intend to take up two major
works of eighteenth-century Anglican theology and spirituality,
both directly intended to assist and strengthen the development
of the Church's eucharistic life. They are both works which in
very different ways, reveal how deeply the thought and devotion
of the time was influenced by patristic models, though they are
both works whose authors can hardly be considered altogether
typical representatives of the Church of England in the
mid-eighteenth century. The first is Bishop Thomas Rattray's
edition of the liturgy of St James, a work first published in 1744,
the year after the Bishop's death, the rite which on Sunday
morning we shall celebrate in the course of our conference. The
second is the collection of eucharistic hymns published in 1745
by the Wesley brothers together, but almost entirely the work
of Charles Wesley at the height of his powers as a hymn-writer.
This collection, *Hymns on the Lord's Supper,* is itself based on
a seventeenth-century treatise, the work of Daniel Brevint,
entitled *The Christian Sacrament and Sacrifice.*

That book is the work of a man from the Channel Islands
whose theological education was partly in Oxford, partly in the
Protestant Academy at Saumur, where Brevint became familiar
with the most deeply sacramental elements in the teaching of
Calvin. This is not the only occasion on which Charles Wesley
wrote a collection of hymns on the basis of a work of theology
whose contents he admired, but it is a particularly interesting
one since Brevint himself was, as we shall see, a fine writer in
prose, even if not in verse, and a theologian who can represent
both English and continental theological traditions of his time
at their most impressive.

I turn now to Thomas Rattray's book on the liturgy of St
James, a remarkable volume on any showing. It is made up of

two parts, the first a scholarly edition of the text of the rite, making use of all the resources of eighteenth century scholarship, the second an edition of the text evidently intended for use by congregations in Scotland, *An Office for the Sacrifice of the Holy Eucharist, being the Ancient Liturgy of the Church of Jerusalem to which proper rubrics are added for direction* [...]. How far the rite was ever used in eighteenth-century Scotland, particularly in the years of turmoil and persecution which followed the rising of 1745, is not known. It cannot have been used widely, and certainly not in public. But there are indications that the text was actually used liturgically from time to time, possibly in private chapels, possibly in clandestine Episcopalian gatherings. Then for two centuries it was virtually forgotten. When Dr Jardine Grisbrooke re-edited the text in 1958 in his invaluable collection *Anglican Liturgies of the Seventeenth and Eighteenth Centuries*, he commented on it, 'Of all the rites considered in this book Rattray's is probably the most satisfactory, even as it is certainly the most scholarly.'[5]

But Rattray was not only a careful and learned historian of early Christian worship. He was also a man who reflected deeply on the nature of God's revelation of himself in Christ, and of the way in which that revelation is conveyed to us across the centuries. In an essay published posthumously in 1748, 'Of the necessity of a Positive Revelation and that God herein deals with us in a rational way [...]', we find him involved in a struggle on two fronts. On the one side he is fighting against the almost overwhelming pressures of eighteenth-century thinking towards deism, towards a generalised religion of benevolence and goodwill, which dispenses with any specific revelation of God's purposes anchored in history. But on the other hand he is also

---

5   W. Jardine Grisbrooke, *Anglican Liturgies of the Seventeenth and Eighteenth Centuries* (London, 1958) 136. For the text of the rite, see below, Appendix G.

fighting against any kind of fideist position which simply appeals to a blind act of faith in the Gospel of Christ, maintaining that God in his dealings with his human creatures deals with them in a way which acknowledges their rational capacities. He does this by arguing that the revelation of God must not only be attested by a written document, but that the document itself must be understood and interpreted within a continuous and growing tradition of commentary exposition and use.

Thus Rattray sees his enquiries into the liturgical practices and beliefs of the first Christian centuries, the period immediately after that of the New Testament writers, as providing a primary way of approach to the understanding of the Bible itself and to the problem of discerning its central message and purpose. In a way which is remarkable for a man of the first half of the eighteenth century, he sees the necessary interplay between scripture and tradition, and thus seems almost to anticipate attitudes and procedures which are more characteristic of our century than his.

Rattray as a liturgist is of course a man of his time. Like many of his contemporaries, he tends to overestimate the nearness to the age of the Apostles of the text of the liturgy of St James which he is establishing; he also tends seriously to underestimate the variety of liturgical forms which existed in the early Christian centuries. In this way he tends to attribute to the rite a greater authority than it can bear. Granted these limitations, however, his book remains a daring and imaginative piece of work, particularly in his proposal that this particular rite should be adapted for the use of congregations in his own day. Let us see some of the characteristics of the rite which he particularly admires and which particularly attract his attention.

First Rattray's vision of the sacrament is through and through eucharistic and doxological; it is a matter of praise and thanksgiving. Characteristically he refers to the eucharistic prayer as the 'Hymn of Thanksgiving' and in one of his sermons he explains to his congregation that the word eucharist simply means thanksgiving. 'Accordingly in all the ancient liturgies we have a long act of thanksgiving in which the more signal instances of the goodness and mercy of God in the creation and preservation of the world and especially in our redemption by Jesus Christ are enumerated.' But Rattray is vividly aware that the eucharistic action involves not only giving thanks for, but also blessing. So he employs the word eucharistise to convey this double meaning of the verb. 'As Christ's blessing or eucharistising the loaves and fishes was by prayer, that the divine power might so multiply them as that they might be sufficient to feed several thousands; so here the blessing or eucharistising the bread and cup imports likewise a prayer for the descent of the Holy Ghost upon them, to make them his spiritual body and blood.' Thus his vision of the eucharist is Trinitarian through and through. He stresses the action of the Holy Spirit as completing and complementing the action of Christ, in the act of consecration. As he notes in reference to a passage of Cyril of Jerusalem, 'As to the words of institution, the primitive Church always thought them necessary for the consecration of the eucharistic elements, though they did not think them sufficient alone without the prayer of invocation of the descent of the Holy Spirit upon them.'[6]

If at the heart of the eucharist there is the invocation of the Holy Spirit, thus making the Trinitarian nature of the prayer explicit and clear, something which was not at all evident in the 1552 rite of Archbishop Thomas Cranmer, the context or setting of the eucharistic action is for Rattray nothing less than the whole created order, and the motifs of God's work in creation and redemption are woven together in his understanding of the rite. Commenting on the prayer itself, he points out that we praise and thank God 'As the creator and governor of the world,

---

6   Ibid., 141.

and the author of bread and of all other fruits of the earth, for his making such plentiful provision of good things for the use of man; and for the signal instance of his providence, towards the Jewish nation in particular [...] and towards all mankind also in general, especially for their redemption by his own death.'

So at the very beginning of the hymn of thanksgiving he points out that we offer our praise and adoration to God 'the maker of all creatures, visible and invisible, the treasurer of all good things, the fountain of life and immortality, the God and governor of the universe, to whom the heaven and the heaven of heavens sing praise with all their hosts, the sun and moon and the whole choir of stars, the earth and sea and all things that are in them, the angels, archangels, thrones, dominions, princi-palities, authorities and tremendous powers.'[7]

As the eucharist is seen in this truly universal setting, so it is also seen as including the departed as well as the living. Heaven and earth, time and eternity, come together in this mystery. Here again the contrast with the silence of Thomas Cranmer's rite is particularly striking. Commenting on a passage of St Cyril of Jerusalem, on the prayers of the saints which are offered on our behalf, Rattray writes,

> As for that expression in him, 'that God through their prayers and supplication would receive our petitions' he does not seem to have taken it from the liturgy but has added it only to shown one great design of this commemoration, viz, that we may reap the benefit of their prayers and supplications for us; as he immediately after says that the dead are also greatly benefited by our prayers at the altar for them; and these two, viz, their prayers for us and ours for them, are undoubtedly the two great branches of the communion of saints.[8]

---

7   Ibid., 323.
8   Thomas Rattray, *The Ancient Liturgy of the Church of Jerusalem*, (London, 1744), 51–52.

In another place he speaks at some length about the closeness of union between Christ as the head of the body and all the members of the body both living and departed. And this insistence on our concorporeality with Christ leads us to discover again at a deeper level the Trinitarian nature of the Eucharist, which we have already considered. Speaking of communion in the mystery of Christ's body and blood Rattray says,

> By this partaking of the sacrifice of Christ we have a title to all the benefits purchased by it [...]; and by eating and drinking his body and blood we are made one body and one spirit with him (it being the Spirit of Christ, descending upon and united to the bread and wine which makes them his body and blood) and thereby our bodies, as united to and nourished by his body, have a title to a glorious resurrection, being quickened by the Holy Spirit which thus dwelleth in us. And thus we have union and communion with the Father and the Son in the Holy Spirit (as the bond of this mystical unity) and with one another also, even all our fellow members of Christ's mystical body the Holy Catholic Church.[9]

There is surely something truly remarkable and admirable in this careful and balanced restatement of the patristic understanding of the Eucharist in its fully Catholic dimensions, a vision which includes the whole creation as well as human kind, and which lifts up humanity into a participation in the life of the Trinity, making our human nature partaker of the divine nature.

In making such a statement Rattray was following the footsteps of his seventeenth-century predecessors, in particular of two outstanding bishop theologians and liturgists, Lancelot Andrewes and Jeremy Taylor, who were particularly aware of the Eastern understanding of the eucharistic mystery. But Rattray was making this affirmation in the midst of a

---

9   Grisbrooke, 143.

century very different from theirs, in the midst of eighteenth-century Edinburgh, the city of David Hume. Here at the western end of the old Christian world, at the heart of Calvinist Scotland, we have a bishop publishing a version of the liturgy of St James for the use of his people, justifying his work and giving it credibility by making use of the best historical scholarship available to him, and articulating its meaning from his intimate knowledge of the teaching of the Fathers of the early centuries. He is insisting in his own period on the all-inclusive Godward direction of the Eucharist, at the very moment when the newly united kingdom of Great Britain is beginning to develop its worldwide imperial pretensions and more and more turning its attention to military and commercial concerns, at a moment when the whole tendency of the life of his society, intellectual, political and cultural alike, was moving in altogether different directions.

Such is the rite we shall celebrate on Sunday morning, a rite prepared for us by a learned bishop of our Church two and a half centuries ago. It is a rite which perhaps in our new century we can now feel free to adopt and adapt in ways which Anglicans have not felt free to do before, recognising that at its heart there is the Church's astonished and amazed affirmation of the taking of the manhood into God, which is the very core and conclusion of the mystery of Christ's coming in the flesh.

Rattray's liturgy of St James was published in 1744. In the following year a very different work, also intended to stimulate and strengthen the eucharistic worship of the Church, was published by John and Charles Wesley, *Hymns on the Lord's Supper*. Here we find a typical and powerful expression of the great revival of popular religion which the Wesley brothers set in motion in the middle and second half of the eighteenth century. If Rattray's liturgical work was forgotten, the same cannot be said of Charles Wesley's work as a hymn-writer. On the contrary it became one of the foundation stones of the whole Methodist movement. But if that is true of Wesley's hymns as a whole it is not altogether true of the hymns for the Lord's Supper. For though the hymns were frequently re-published during the Wesleys' lifetime, this did not altogether remain the case after their death. There are certainly some items in this collection of more than a hundred and fifty hymns which have become familiar sometimes in Methodist and sometimes in Anglican worship, and sometimes in both. But those who read the collection carefully may well feel that there are many hymns here whose worth has never been fully appreciated either on the Anglican or on the Methodist side of the division which sprang up so quickly after John Wesley's death. Here too a more ecumenical assessment of the hymns, indeed a more ecumenical usage of the hymns might bring them into more frequent and general use, and thus strengthen and deepen the sacramental understanding of the churches today.

As has already been said, Charles Wesley uses as a jumping-off place for his work the seventeenth-century treatise of Daniel Brevint, *The Christian Sacrament and Sacrifice*. One of the outstanding features of Brevint's work is the way in which it develops the theology of the Eucharist as our present participation in the once-for-all sacrifice of Christ, and the way in which it sees that once-for-all offering as happening 'both in the fullness of time, and in the midst of the habitable world which is properly Christ's great temple.' Not only humankind but the whole world of time and space is bought back, redeemed, by the sacrifice of the cross, the fulfilment in the New Testament of the whole history of the worship of the Temple in the Old Testament, the great redeeming and inte-grating moment in the history of the world, which even now brings together time and eternity, earth and heaven, human and divine, in a single offering of praise and thanksgiving.

This victim having been offered up both in the fullness of time and in the midst of the habitable world, which properly is Christ's great temple, and thence being carried up to heaven, which is his proper sanctuary, thence spreads all about us salvation, as the burnt offering did its smoke, as the golden altar did its perfumes and as the burning candlestick its lights. And thus Christ's body and blood have everywhere, but especially at the Holy Communion, a most true and *real presence*. When he offered himself upon earth, the vapour of his atonement went up and darkened the very sun; and by rending the great veil, it clearly showed he had made a way into heaven.

Now since he has gone up to heaven, thence he sends down on earth the graces that spring continually both from his everlasting sacrifice, and from the continual intercession which attends it. So that it is vain to say who will go up into heaven? Since without either ascending or descending, this sacred body of Jesus fills with atonement and blessing the remotest parts of this temple.[10]

We see at once how such a paragraph lies behind and articulates one of the greatest and best-known of Charles Wesley's hymns for the eucharist.

> 1. Victim divine, thy grace we claim
> While thus thy precious death we show;
> Once offered up, a spotless lamb,
> In thy great temple here below,
> Thou didst for all mankind atone,
> And standest now before the throne.
>
> 2. Thou standest in the holiest place,
> As now for guilty sinners slain;
> Thy blood of sprinkling speaks, and prays,
> All-prevalent for helpless man;
> Thy blood is still our ransom found,
> And spreads salvation all around. [...]

---

10   Quoted in Kenneth Stevenson, *The Covenant of Grace Renewed* (London, 1994) 102, a book which contains a valuable account of Brevint's work.

> 5. We need not now go up to heaven,
> To bring the long-sought saviour down;
> Thou art to all already given,
> Thou dost even now thy banquet crown;
> To every faithful soul appear,
> And show thy real presence here.[11]

Here, though in a very different idiom and in a somewhat different perspective, the inclusive scope of the Eucharist is affirmed, the gathering in of all creation, the lifting up of human to divine, no less than it is in Rattray's rendering of St James.

To do any justice to the richness of this collection of hymns would require far more space than is available here. I choose one particular strand in Charles Wesley's fabric, his jubilant sense of our present participation in the joys of heaven, in the life of the resurrection, through our share in the eucharistic feast. Here again we seem to have an unconscious reaction to the sombre colouring, not only of Cranmer's rite for Holy Communion but of much of the eucharistic practice and devotion of the sixteenth century, a practice concentrated so unilaterally on the sacrament as a showing forth of Christ's death, its meaning focused almost exclusively on the forgiveness of sins.

Brevint speaks of the sacrament as 'a pledge of heaven'. Charles Wesley expands that with ardour and daring. In our participation in Christ's sacramental body we are already anticipating the fulfilment of our life in heaven, already beginning to discover that resurrection of the body which shall be ours thereafter. Not only is the heart full of the light of life, the 'house of clay' itself is overwhelmed with the anticipation of eternity.

---

11   Hymn 133, *A Rapture of Praise: Hymns of John and Charles Wesley*, ed. H. A. Hodges and A. M. Allchin (London, 1966) 150–151. This selection contains twenty-two of the hymns on the Lord's Supper.

1. How glorious is the life above,
Which in this ordinance we *taste;*
That fullness of celestial love,
That joy which shall forever last.

2. That heavenly life in Christ concealed
These earthen vessels could not bear;
The part which now we find revealed
No tongue of angels can declare.

3. The light of life eternal darts
Into our souls a dazzling ray,
A drop of heaven o'er flows our hearts,
And deluges the house of clay.

4. Sure pledge of ecstasies unknown
Shall this divine communion be;
The ray shall rise into a sun,
The drops shall swell into a sea.[12]

Neither John nor Charles Wesley had of course ever taken part in a celebration of the Orthodox liturgy, and thus known that affirmation of resurrection life which is made at the heart of the that rite, not least when the choir sings after communion,

We have seen the true light,
We have received the heavenly spirit,
We have found the true faith,
We worship the undivided trinity,
For the same hath saved us.

But this same tone of assured rejoicing is taken up again by Charles Wesley in one of the greatest of his hymns of thanksgiving for our share in the sacrament. We can only surmise what would be the result if we let the Wesleys' expression of praise and thanksgiving come into closer contact with the celebration of the Eucharist in its Eastern Orthodox form.

---

12   Ibid., Hymn 131, 148–149.

1. Sons of God, triumphant rise,
Shout the accomplished sacrifice.
Shout your sins in Christ forgiven,
Sons of God and heirs of heaven.

2. Ye that round our altars throng,
Listening angels join the song:
Sing with us, ye heavenly powers,
Pardon, grace and glory ours.

3. Love's mysterious work is done.
Greet we now the accepted son,
Healed and quickened by his blood,
Joined to Christ and one with God.

6. Grace our every thought controls,
Heaven is opened in our souls,
Everlasting life is won,
Glory is on earth begun.

7. Christ in us, in him we see
Fullness of the Deity.
Beam of the Eternal beam;
Life divine we taste in him.

8. Him we only taste below;
Mightier joys ordained to know,
Him when fully ours we prove,
Ours the heaven of perfect love.[13]

IV

At the beginning of this essay I quoted from Archbishop Michael Ramsey's opening lecture given at a day conference held in Oxford in March 1962 on the subject of the dialogue of East and West and Christendom, in which he insisted on the

---

13   Ibid., Hymn 140, 155–156.

importance of seeing Anglican–Orthodox relations in the widest possible context, a context which would gather in the whole people of the baptised, indeed the whole world in which and on behalf of which they are baptised.

The last speaker on that occasion was the Methodist liturgical scholar and theologian, Marcus Ward. He told us how his own discovery of Orthodoxy had begun with a prize essay which he wrote when a graduate student, on 'the Byzantine Church', under the supervision of a noted Baptist scholar, Norman Baynes. Through this work he had begun to come into contact with the whole tradition of Eastern Orthodox spirituality, 'That great tradition unbroken from the New Testament through the Fathers and on, carried on by Ephrem the Syrian, Evagrius, Barsanuphius, Dorotheus, Theodore and especially the Hesychasts of whom we have heard too little. [...] I learned that the capacity of man made free to love and make sacrifices, is not bound.' What a wonderful Methodist expression of the Orthodox vision of theosis that is! 'The doctrine of perfection, consisting in charity and in the adoration which expresses it; the relation of liturgical piety to Christian belief and practice, liturgy as the background on which all aspects and details of Christian living and doing combine and cohere.'[14]

The speaker went on to tell us how later in life, when he went to teach in a theological college in South India, he had found all these things present and living in the Christians of the Syrian Mar Thoma tradition. 'I found in them and in their praying and their living and their friendship something of what I had been reading about in history. It is not something you can put into words, this spirituality, this piety, but it is there and you know it. And one thing is quite sure: at the centre there is an

---

14   *Dialogue*, 42–43.

utterly vivid realisation of the resurrection. The whole life is pervaded by the spirit of the Easter Greeting, "Christ is risen."[15]

Marcus Ward was a prominent member of the group which produced the first eucharistic rite for the use of the Church of South India, which itself had come together in 1947. Already in 1950 this group had drawn up a rite for use on occasions when Christians from the different traditions which had united in that Church needed to have a new, common form for celebrating the sacrament. 'We of Anglican, Congregationalist, Methodist, Presbyterian and Reformed traditions – we found our oneness, our nodal point, there in the Holy Kurbana of the ancient Indian Church, the liturgy of St James.' And Marcus Ward takes us briefly through the main moments in the rite, 'to that tremendous moment when the whole congregation rises to join in the great utterance, "Thy death O Lord we commemorate, thy resurrection we confess, thy second coming we await; glory be to thee O Christ."'[16] As Kenneth Stevenson remarks in a study of this rite, where he places it in relation to other essays in liturgical form from this period, 'Looking back on it now it seems amazing that by 1950 a united liturgy could have been agreed upon that has a clear structure and that also brings together the *riches* of the traditions that went into the union.'[17]

Perhaps here we can see Orthodoxy functioning as 'the miraculous glue' which can join together the broken fragments of Western Christendom.[18] Unquestionably here in the presence of the Christ who has come and who comes, of the name of Jesus, present in the human heart and present in the heart of the gathering of his Church in worship, we can see, in the words

15   Ibid., 43.

16   Ibid., 44.

17   Kenneth Stevenson, *Eucharist and Offering* (New York, 1986) 195.

18   Orthodoxy as 'the miraculous glue' is an expression of D. J. Chitty, author of *The Desert a City* and Editor of Barsanuphius and John: in himself an embodiment of Anglican–Orthodox unity.

of Sergei Bulgakov, taken up by Evelyn Underhill, 'the power of that deification which the redeemer has bestowed upon us', that deification for which our world was made in the beginning.

Here in the face of this awe-inspiring affirmation of the taking of the manhood into God, the human into the divine, we may see something of the deeper roots of that humble and tentative, yet enduring and assured relationship of the different elements of Orthodox East and Anglican West within the one Holy Catholic Church of Christ.

13. Derwas Chitty as an Ecumenist

Edward Every

Father Derwas Chitty was born in 1901. As a clergyman of the Church of England, he became a Deacon in 1928 and was ordained priest in 1929. He was the Rector of Upton, near Blewbury in Berkshire, from 1931 to 1968, and was a Chaplain in the Navy for several years during the Second World War. After he retired, he worked in Wales, where he died in an accident in 1971.

He was my teacher and was a close friend from 1928 onwards. In a recent lecture Canon Donald Allchin described Derwas Chitty as 'a scholar, a priest and a prophet'. In this short paper I shall not attempt to deal with his work as a scholar in the history of Christian monastic life, embodied in his books. I am concerned here with the aspects of his thought which I regard as prophetic.

On 8 November 1928, in Cairo, at a meeting of the 'Fellowship of Unity', consisting of Western Christian missionaries and Egyptian Christians belonging to the Greek Orthodox and Coptic Churches, he read a paper entitled, 'The Spirit of Eastern Christianity'. It was published with that title in *The Christian East* in the winter number for 1929–1930 (vol. x, no. 4). After his death in 1971, it was re-published by the Fellowship of St Alban and St Sergius in *Sobornost* (ser. 6, no. 3) with the title, 'The Spirit of Orthodox Christianity'. It began with an account of the meaning of the Greek word *orthodoxia*.

> Both in Russian and in Syriac, 'Orthodoxy' is translated, not 'right opinion' but 'right glory' – right worship. The sense given is incomplete, but significant. For it means that here the criterion is not the head, but the heart. But the heart is not thought of as the seat of the emotions. It is the seat of intellectual vision; the head can work out our understanding, but only the heart can give us material for understanding. [...] The work of Orthodoxy is to bring our minds down from the lofty throne of the head, into the humility of the heart, where Reality is to be found.
>
> The humility of the heart – for the heart is in abasement before the vastness of God: at the same time the historic facts of Christ are seen with intense realism in the intimacy of the Holy Spirit by which the heart finds in these facts its own royal freedom. [...] In Orthodoxy, doctrine and worship and life are one.[1]

Here the quotation ends and it seems to me to need explanation.

Intellectual vision is, in Greek, *Noetike Theoria*, the seeing of the *Nous*. In Derwas Chitty's use of words, head-knowledge is natural science, including the scientific study of history. Our brains devise hypotheses from the experience of our senses, primarily in order that we may control our environment.

Heart-knowledge, on the other hand, is that activity of the whole human person, mind and body, by which we know the personal realities which we love and value and glorify. This heart-knowledge cannot be expressed completely in words and conceptions belonging to human language; but it has an unchanging certainty. This is not 'wishful thinking'; we may wish not to know it. Derwas Chitty saw all knowledge as a gift of God, as God wishes us to know the truth, and he saw all that happened to him as capable of being regarded as God-given. He regarded the 'supernatural' as the 'most natural', the opposite of the 'unnatural'.

---

1   Derwas Chitty, 'The Spirit of Orthodox Christianity'. *Sobornost* ser. vi, no. 3, 147.

Sometime between 1931 and 1943, in circumstances unknown to me, Derwas Chitty typed, but did not publish, a statement headed with the words, 'Draft of a Common Confession of Faith'. This included a passage about the Bible, which expressed clearly his rejection of what is called by the name of Fundamentalism, as well as of some forms of Modernism.

> We believe that we receive of the Holy Spirit, in the Faith of Christ, a knowledge of our salvation wrought through history which no investigation or discovery of human science can overthrow; but that on the level of human science the Holy Spirit converts and employs the human understanding and does not replace it, even as the Lord assumed the condition of a human mind for its salvation. So we believe that the Holy Scriptures were not dictated from heaven to men passive as in a trance, but were written by men under the normal conditions of human understanding, capable of error on the level of human science which passes away, but protected and corrected from error and inspired to insight of truth, on the level of the things which do not pass away; and we believe that, on the level of human science, the books of Holy Scripture and the events of our Creation and Redemption are subject to all such methods of scientific criticism and investigation as can rightly be used in any region of being or experience (provided always that the limitations of such methods are recognised, as they can attain to probabilities, but not to knowledge) but that the scientific probabilities so appearing to it cannot upset in any way the knowledge that we have of the Christian Faith; and that no appearance of contradictory results can entitle us to cease to assert the facts of that Faith, though also we must not avoid the apparent implications of science, but trust to God that apparent contradictions may be resolved.

A footnote adds,

> Thus it is of the essence of the Faith that the Incarnation and resurrection of the Son of God are historical events. But the exact way in which the supernatural here breaks into the natural is necessarily above the methods and powers of scientific investigation. It

has to be remembered that even the beginning of each human life is a mystery which science cannot penetrate. Nevertheless, recognising that, since the dogmas of the Faith were defined on the upper level of human understanding when science, on the lower level, was still in its infancy, and since then scientific discovery has brought a deep revolution in human thought on that level, we suspect that the Church in future times may have more to say on the relation between the two levels. Only we believe that, as the prophets of the Old Testament prophesied without knowing just how their prophesies would be fulfilled, so the dogmatic definitions of the Church have been prophetic, not behind, but ahead of all scientific discovery or philosophical speculation. Not the Faith, but our understanding, lags behind the truth.

This last sentence may be explained by an illustration, which Derwas Chitty liked to use. He would remark that each individual begins by thinking of his or her human self as the centre of the world and for thousands of years pagan religion and immature science regarded the earth as the body around which the heavens revolve. But even then the prophets told us that the earth and the sun, the moon and the stars were like specks of dust in the infinity of the universe. Pagan thought regarded the world as eternal, but the prophets spoke of creation in past time and judgment in a future time. Now the most modern science tells us about the physical world both that it has no real centre and that it had a beginning and moves towards an end. The most wonderful fact is that human beings can think rationally about the universe. Could they do so if God were not one who seeks union with Himself for His creatures?

The only dogmatic definitions made by the whole Church were concerned with the Trinity and the Incarnation. When Derwas Chitty wrote of dogmatic definitions being prophetic, he had in mind what he expounded in his paper on 'The Spirit of Orthodox Christianity'. From this I quote what follows:

[St. Athanasius said] He became Man that we might become God. The West is afraid of saying this. But it is the essence of the matter, the only fulfilment of the Incarnation for the East. The Spirit makes us literally members of Christ. In us the Incarnation is continued and the Resurrection extends its sphere. And He giveth not the Spirit by measure. As in the Incarnation, so in the Gift of the Spirit. [...] He entrusts himself utterly to us, and that is why he is our judge.

If we would understand the staggering absoluteness of the Christian Faith, we do well to remember our Lord's Baptism in Jordan. [...] To the East it is the greatest revelation of the Trinity. What is happening here? About the person of Jesus is breaking out into man's sight, not a picture of the Trinity, but the very fact of it. That Father's voice proclaiming Him, that pure dove-embodied Spirit of the Father's love and Hallowing which now descends upon Him, is no new thing. Unseen it has been happening all through his life. More than that, present before us is the fact which *is* before Abraham was, before the world began to be created. Here in a point of time is the pure act which contains and transcends all time, and a man is the focus of its manifestation. All that God is, is revealed in immediate reality upon the man Jesus.

Think on and you find that this is always the Spirit's work. When the Spirit brooded on the face of the waters, when the Spirit spoke by the Prophets, when the Spirit overshadowed Mary, always the Son remained the goal of the Spirit's work. The Spirit's work in creation is always the framing and hallowing of the Incarnation. And afterwards it continues so. When the Spirit descended upon the Apostles, the Spirit was not merely sent by a Christ remaining aloof. The descent of the Spirit brought Christ again to the Apostles by forming him in them and making them his body. And upon this body, as in Jordan, all that God is, is shown forth to man. Here is the astounding fact that just as our Eucharist is a real partaking in the actual Last Supper, so the Baptism of each one of us is the real Baptism of our Lord in Jordan, extended to us, and by the revelation through and upon us of all that God is, our very human nature is really made divine. So always in Christ's life, which we share in the Church, we know the Holy Spirit descending, not from an aloof Christ upon us, but from the Father upon Christ being made incarnate in us.[2]

---

2   Chitty, 'Spirit', *Sobornost* ser. vi, no. 3, 152–153.

This passage signifies the theological basis of the opposition of Derwas Chitty to the Anglican use of the Filioque clause in the Nicene Creed. This requires some explanation.

The completed form of the Creed of the Council of Nicea (323), traditionally ascribed to the Council of Constantinople (381), was regarded as the One Symbol of the Undivided Church. The paragraph in it relating to the Holy Spirit and the Church may be translated thus:

> And in the Holy Spirit, the Lord, the life-giver, proceeding from the Father, with the Father and the Son worshipped together and glorified together, having spoken through the prophets, in One Catholic and Apostolic Church.

Into the Latin version of this part of the Symbol two insertions were made at various times in various parts of the Western Church. One of these was the subject of controversy; it placed the word *filioque* (meaning 'and from the Son') after the word *Patre*, so that the Holy Spirit was stated to be 'proceeding from the Father and the Son'. It was to this addition to the Symbol made in the West without the agreement of the East that the Eastern Orthodox Church has objected since 800. It seems to have originated in Spain. Its popular use in Germany and France seems to be due to the influence of Charlemagne who believed that he was reviving the true Roman Empire and wanted the Creed used in his dominions to be more complete than the Creed used in Constantinople. He failed to persuade the Church of Rome to adopt it, for Rome valued her unity with Eastern Christendom. When in the eleventh century Rome accepted the *filioque*, its theological meaning came to be defined in controversy. Western Councils declared that the Holy Spirit proceeds from the Father and the Son eternally and that the Father and the Son are conjointly the origin of the Holy Spirit. Thus the West claimed to treat as an essential article of the Catholic Faith an opinion that was contrary to the Eastern Christian theological tradition.

The Eastern view is that the Symbol is unalterable, the work of the Councils of the Whole Church. It cannot be altered by part of the Church. Moreover, the verb, which in Latin is translated by *procedere* is the verb used in John 15.26, where our Lord says that the Holy Spirit proceeds from the Father. The Symbol is, at this point, based on the words of Jesus Christ who in the same discourse says that the Father and the Son will send the Holy Spirit to the Apostles. The sending is future, while the proceeding is present. During the earthly life of our Lord, the Spirit is revealed proceeding from the Father and resting upon the Son. This is the revelation in the historical Incarnation of the eternal Trinity.

Thus from 1929 onwards, Derwas Chitty was unable to regard the words, 'and the Son', as part of the Nicene Creed in any sense. He recognised that most Anglicans understood it as merely a statement of events after the Ascension of Christ, arousing no controversy. But he thought that to be due to ignorance of church history and disregard of the need of unity between Eastern and Western Christians. It makes the Creed sound like a condemnation of those who believe as the Eastern Orthodox believe.

There is a second Western addition to the Oecumenical Symbol. It aroused no controversy and in fact Derwas Chitty did not omit it. But I think that it is significant. The words *et credo* were inserted in the Latin version between the word signifying the prophets and the description of the Church. In printed editions of the Greek and Slavonic versions there is a comma, commanding a pause at this point. Thus it can be said that in all versions the clergy and laity, after saying that they believe in the Trinity, pause and say that they also believe in One, Holy, Catholic and Apostolic Church. But punctuation marks do not belong to the original text and, if they are disregarded, it results that the Eastern version reads, I believe in the Holy Spirit [...] having spoken by the prophets to One, Holy, Catholic and Apostolic Church'. In Eastern theology, no statement is the doctrine of the Church if it is not inspired by the Holy Spirit, and the final authority in the Church is the consensus of the clergy and the laity.

Derwas Chitty was not alone in holding that the decisions of the undivided Church have an authority which no denominational decisions can have. That was a common Anglican view. But at the end of the time he spent in Jerusalem after finishing his studies at Oxford, he felt that his picture of the Christian Faith had been profoundly changed by his friendships among the Eastern Orthodox. Twenty years later he wrote in his pamphlet 'Orthodoxy and Conversion of England' (published in 1947 and re-published with other essays in 1988, in both instances by the Fellowship of St Alban and St Sergius) this account of his experience in 1925–1927.

> I found myself in Jerusalem with, as it were, scales falling from my eyes. It was as if I had, without noticing it, unlearned everything that I had known before, and started as a child to learn it again. The truths I now saw were the same truths, but a new light bound them together and interpreted them differently, explaining apparent contradictions and leading in many ways to implications hitherto unnoticed. At the same time I had a deep conviction that therein the simpler faith of my country-rectory boyhood was being vindicated against the stern voices with which Oxford had, to some extent, confused it.

The one remark I venture to make about this is that in Oxford, or any other University, what is studied as theology easily becomes a series of distinct propositions to be defended against attacks, whereas in a Christian home or in the Holy Places, the believer receives what Derwas Chitty called heart-knowledge, in personal relationships with God and with the brethren. And Eastern Orthodox theology brings together in one picture creation, redemption and judgment.

On his second and third visits to Jerusalem, in 1928 and 1929, Derwas Chitty began to consider whether it might be his vocation to remain there. He was still engaged in excavations and was not on the staff of the Anglican Bishopric. But he became involved in meetings between teachers in the Anglican missionary school and English-speaking Russian members of the Orthodox Church about practical questions relating to religious education. The effect of the Russian revolution had been to abolish the schools for the Palestinian Orthodox Christians, which had been supplied and financed by Russians. People educated in those schools were sending their own children to Anglican schools. Derwas Chitty felt very strongly that the Anglican Church ought to encourage Eastern Orthodox Children to be faithful to their own Church. He was supported by several Anglican teachers, who wanted to know more about Eastern Orthodoxy for practical reasons connected with education. But, he was opposed by some missionaries who regarded Eastern Orthodoxy as akin to Roman Catholicism as opposed to Evangelical teaching. In the autumn of 1929 he began to wonder whether it might be his vocation to move from the Anglican Church to the Orthodox Church of Jerusalem, in order to serve unity and remain in the East. To avoid an immediate decision, he went to Egypt. There Bishop Gwynne, the Anglican Bishop in Egypt, was very kind to him and gave him work as a priest in the English congregation in Alexandria. Bishop Gwynne was an Evangelical, as were practically all the Anglican clergy of Egypt. But he and the Anglican Archdeacon in Cyprus who corresponded with Chitty thought that by becoming Eastern Orthodox, although leaving the Church of England, he might be useful to her and promote unity. Derwas Chitty hoped that, whether he remained Anglican or became Eastern Orthodox, he could serve both Churches spiritually. But in 1930 he waited for God's guidance in Egypt. Towards the end of 1930 he was offered the charge of an English parish and accepted it.

He then returned to England. Early in 1931 he met the Bishop of Oxford, Thomas Strong, and had a long conversation at which the theological views which he had reached were fully expounded. A few weeks later the Bishop of Oxford appointed him as Rector of Upton, near Blewbury in Berkshire. After his induction there he became aware that the Bishop had not realised, in their conversation, that he intended to omit the *filioque* in public worship. He wrote to the Bishop of Oxford, stating that intention clearly and offering to resign the Rectory if the Bishop should ask him to do so in writing. He received no reply to his question about resignation. The Bishop, while assuming that he would stay at Upton, did not give him, indeed could not give him, leave to depart from the Book of Common Prayer. He remained the Rector of Upton for 37 years until he retired in 1968. When there was a new Bishop of Oxford he repeated the letter he had written offering his resignation, with the same result. During the War he left Upton to be a Naval Chaplain and in that capacity served in the Far East and in India, Ceylon, Ethiopia and Greece between 1941 and 1944. On his retirement he lived in Wales, where he died in 1971. From the Anglican point of view he was in the strict sense of the word, a 'Non-conformist'. I regard his 'Non-conformity' in the Symbol as a piece of prophetic symbolism.

14. The Role of the Apokrisarios in Modern Anglican–Orthodox Relations

CHAD COUSSMAKER

This morning, Father Gregory studiously avoided being anecdotal. This afternoon, I shall be unashamedly anecdotal, as I know of no better way of illustrating the work of an apokrisarios.

In the middle of November 1967, my wife and I spent our last night in Greece at Alexandroupolis, prior to driving into Turkey. We visited the Cathedral, and I got into one of those tri-lingual conversations with an Archimandrite, in which he asked me what my job was as an Anglican priest; I explained that I was on my way to take up my position as Chaplain in Istanbul, and Apokrisarios of the Archbishop of Canterbury to the Ecumenical Patriarch of Constantinople. 'But you are so young, Father,' he commented. 'I am thirty-three!' I replied, to which he answered, 'Ah, thirty-three. Yes, a good age. Our Blessed Lord died at thirty-three.' Believe me, I'm not superstitious – but I was rather relieved to reach my thirty-fourth birthday!

A slightly sobering introduction to my new appointment: next morning we drove the short distance to the Turkish frontier, noting the large number of Greek tanks deployed on and alongside the road, all with their guns pointing towards Turkey. After a long and ponderous time with the Turkish customs, who were trying to prove that we were going to Turkey to work, while our stated intention was as 'tourists'

(I never did get a work permit in four years, but that is perhaps another story) – they even found the mass of coat hangers which we had put in the car at the last moment, and accused us of being variety artistes! Finally we drove on, noting all the Turkish tanks deployed on and alongside the road, all with their guns pointing towards Greece. 'It must be a NATO exercise,' said my wife, quite seriously. I suspected otherwise, and when we arrived at the British Consulate-General in Istanbul, we were greeted by the Consul-General saying, 'Well, I don't know why you've come – we have a frigate standing by to evacuate the British population if there is a war.'

So started our stay in the city of Constantinople, New Rome: a unique chaplaincy, with two churches in Europe (St Helena's, in the grounds of the British consulate, and Christ Church, built as a memorial to those who died in the Crimean War, a huge building designed by G. E. Street, only used then on special occasions), and All Saints, Moda, in the suburb of Kadiköy or Chalcedon, on the Asian side of the Bosphorus. For four years I was the only Anglican priest to celebrate the Liturgy regularly in two continents on the same Sunday – 8.25 a.m. in Asia and 10 a.m. in Europe! And this was before the Bosphorus Bridge was open!

The threat of war when we arrived was quite real – a group of fourteen Turkish Cypriots had been shot by Greek Cypriot police on the demarcation line in Cyprus, and local Turks were sufficiently angry that a group delivered a huge wreath at the Phanar, with the damning inscription: 'Athenagoras, you are the murderer!' Interesting that after so many years in Ataturk's republic, they still regarded the Patriarch as 'Milletbasi', head of the Greek nation, just as the Ottomans had seen Patriarch Gregorios in 1821, when they hung him from the gateway of the Phanar.

As Apokrisarios, I was able to call in my first few days on His All-Holiness Athenagoras I, who immediately 'adopted' Jean and myself into his family: 'Father Piper [my predecessor] was my son – you are too young for that – you shall be my grandson, and [to Jean] you shall be my grand-daughter.' So began a unique relationship – and when we left, four and a half years later, His All-Holiness remembered it, saying, 'You came here as my grandson – you have become my son, and my father, and my confessor.'

The apokrisarios is a personal ambassador of the Archbishop – the word was used in Byzantium for ambassador, but is literally 'the man who gives the answer'. His more obvious and public function is largely in bringing personal greetings to the Patriarch on great feasts such as Christmas and Easter, but the relationship grows into much more than that, and I found myself visiting the Phanar about fortnightly for one reason or another, and on many occasions to attend the Holy Liturgy. I was generally given a place in the stalls opposite the Patriarch, and was therefore in a good position to descend and receive the antidoron from him at the end of the service. I then tried to edge behind him and watch his incredible pastoral concern as he gave the bread to the congregation, naming the many he knew personally, and asking, 'Where is Maria? Is she well?', or saying 'How good it is to see you this morning.' I learned more pastoralia from Athenagoras than I ever learned in theological college.

Making a routine call one morning, I was greeted in turn by three separate metropolitans, and then by the Patriarch himself with the words, 'Ah, Father, you are just the person we need this morning.' This was slightly alarming, as I was not used to such popularity. It soon transpired that they were awaiting, the following day, the formal visit of the Abouna of Ethiopia. The First Secretary had prepared a long speech of welcome in very flowery Byzantine Greek, but they wanted to present the Abouna with a translation of this in reasonable English. A first draft had been prepared – would I please check it over? One glance sufficed to show that this was an extremely long and complex job, and my limited Greek was of little assistance to me. Eventually, I was accompanied to my home by the Metropolitans Gabriel of Colonia and Chrysostomos of Myra, who sat on either side of me as I ponderously typed out the final version, saying on one side: 'No, Eminence, you cannot say that in English', and on the other, 'No, Eminence, that might be Byzantine English, but it is not correct modern English.' After three hours the job was finished, six quarto pages, and the metropolitans left, saying, 'Thank you, Father. Six copies, please, for 10 a.m. tomorrow!'

I was due out half an hour later for a dinner party. I returned about 11 to my desk, where I typed the speech twice, with two carbon copies each time – this was before photocopiers were in common use! Finished about 3 a.m., and to the Phanar for the Liturgy at 10. My reward was to be the only ecumenical representative at the Liturgy and subsequent lunch and to meet again after many years the Metropolitan of Aksum, whom I had known as Archimandrite Methodios Fouyas, and whose absence at this conference I greatly regret.

Although I was apokrisarios only to Patriarch Athenagoras, I had a similar, if less formal, relationship with the Armenian Patriarch Snork. He was always gracious and welcoming, and I remember taking my elderly mother to visit him on one occasion. She asked the meaning of his name. He became quite embarrassed and pointed out that the name in their tradition was given by the ordaining bishop at the time of ordination, without prior notice. He also explained that the name was used in English as a girl's name, but in Armenian it was quite usual for a boy and that it meant 'Grace'. He claimed that his bishop had chosen it because Snork himself was much in need of grace.

Few at the Armenian Patriarchate had much command of English. I was therefore extremely surprised one day when the Consulate telephonist saw me pass his office and rushed out, saying, 'Father, Father! The Armenian Patriarchate want you!' 'What language?' I asked, expecting that he would have to translate for me, and he replied, 'English'. So I took up the phone, and a deep voice asked, 'Is that Father Coussmaker? The Patriarch speaks!' It was almost like that incredible moment in the Armenian Liturgy when the Deacon, about to read the Gospel, intones the words, 'Asé Asdvadz' (God speaks). The request was a familiar one – to perfect the English of a very formal letter, of such confidentiality that the Patriarch's driver would bring it to me at the Consulate and wait for the result. It made for a rather disturbing hour and a half, especially as I knew that the driver was normally armed, and I thought that no one in the Consulate suspected this! On another occasion, waiting for a ferry on a dark evening to come back across the Bosphorus, the same driver came up behind me, asking, 'What are you doing here, Father?' I explained that I was on my way home, and he was most keen to take me home safely. It was quite hard to convince him that I actually had my car in the queue and had left it only to buy a sandwich!

Memories of just over four years in the city, and of very happy contacts. Anecdotes, yes – but my point in recounting them this afternoon is to emphasise that the role of apokrisarios today is based almost entirely on personal contacts and on bringing the churches closer together by such means. So much harm can be done by misunderstandings, and much repair of misunderstandings can be achieved only by a 'man who gives the answers'. Metropolitan Gabriel, then Chief Secretary of the Holy Synod, had a friend in England who regularly sent him the *Church Times*. Fortunately, my copy would arrive before his, and I would have notice of some of the extraordinary actions of the English clergy before he could challenge me. A picture of motorcycles being blessed in front of the altar brought an inevitable 'We do not do this sort of thing in our church'. I admit that I had not expected his horror when it was reported that a local vicar had taken the part of the devil in a mystery play in his church. 'That a Holy Priest should dress up as the Devil' was incomprehensible – and perhaps he was right.

In January 1972, my bishop needed the archetypal 'young married man with family' for a chaplaincy in Malta. This was followed by many years in Antwerp, and it was at our Diocesan Synod in 1992 that the Chaplain in Helsinki – who visited Moscow monthly, subject to visas – and the Lay Reader-Churchwarden in Moscow both outlined the need for a resident chaplain there. My wife was at Synod that year, and I went over to her, saying, 'I think I have gone mad.' 'Moscow. Yes, so have I,' she replied. So we went to the bishop, and he said, 'You're mad.' I said, 'You know that. You have known me for a quarter of a century!' And so started our preparations to move to Moscow, where my theoretical parish consisted of the whole of the former U.S.S.R., excluding the Baltic Republics, but including Mongolia. This probably covers a sixth of the world's surface, though the Anglican population is not high, and we have no ministry to bears, brown or polar!

Our arrival in Istanbul had been in politically troubled times; our arrival in Moscow was in ecumenically troubled times, overshadowed by the ordination of women to the priesthood in the Church of England. Patriarch Alexii II of Moscow and All Russia had visited the Archbishop of Canterbury personally in October 1991, specifically begging the Church of England not to take this step. The decision was taken at General Synod on November 1992, and the first ordination had taken place before my arrival in Moscow. It is interesting that the Patriarch and the Russian Synod were vastly more upset by this than they had been by the American Episcopal decision several years previously. I suppose it is a compliment to the Church of England that they still consider it the formative centre of the Anglican Communion! But initial contacts were, to say the least of it, frosty. An extremely difficult first meeting with my principal contact in the Department for External Relations, Fr Victor Petluchenko, became friendly only when we found that we were both married and had a son and daughter of similar ages! On such fragile foundations do friendships grow. I never met his children, nor he mine, but it was our initial link.

In due course I met the Patriarch. He was always kind and welcoming, though much more formal than my beloved Athenagoras. I saw it as my absolute duty to be present for the great Liturgies at Christmas and Easter and used the moments after these to present the Archbishop's formal greetings. These were 'ticket-only' functions, and I spent many hours beforehand making contact with the Patriarch's priest-secretary and picking up my tickets. At the end of the Liturgy, Fr Matthai, who was Dean of the Cathedral of the Epiphany where the Liturgy was celebrated, would come over to me to take me behind the ikonostasis to deliver my letter. After four years in New York, Fr Matthai's English was fluent but a little eccentric, and his invitation, 'You will stay for a cup of tea, Father?', was not quite an introduction to a seven-course meal, lasting from 3.30 a.m. to nearly 6.00, washed down with copious glasses of vodka! After one such meal, on a Sunday morning, I had to return to celebrate our Anglican Eucharist at 10 a.m., and all understood perfectly when I began my sermon with the words, 'This morning, I breakfasted with the Patriarch!'

In my first years, the Roman Catholic Bishop for Western Russia was always present with one or more of his clergy. Latterly they were notably absent, and I got a message that he was greatly offended that he did not receive invitations or tickets. I replied a little sharply, saying that *I* never *received* such tickets. I had to go and ask for them. I think this typifies a great deal of what is necessary with our dealing with the Orthodox Churches and with their hierarchs. We need always to make the running. This demands not only humility but also a lot of hard work.

In my first months in Moscow, I had often passed the building site in Red Square where work was proceeding on the rebuilding of the Cathedral of the Mother of God of Kazan. The original seventeenth-century church had been demolished by Stalin in 1936 and the site used for a public lavatory. The first stone of the new building had been blessed on the Feast of the Kazan Ikon on 4 November 1991, and the rebuilt Cathedral was ready for consecration exactly two years later. I was determined to be present but was finally told that there would be no ecumenical representatives. I would receive a ticket for the formal dinner and reception at the Hotel Rossiya. I replied that I had been to plenty of receptions, thank you, but that I wanted to be at the service. Finally, at two days' notice, I was given tickets for both the consecration and the reception and felt that honour was satisfied! Patriarch Alexii entered with the two former members of the City Council who had been present when the first stone was blessed; they were now President of the Russian Federation, Boris Yeltsin, and Mayor of Moscow, Yuri Lushkov. The Patriarch was obviously in very good spirits, and I later learned that, as they walked across Red Square from the Kremlin, Yeltsin had told him that the two great ikons in the Tretyakov Gallery, the Rublev Holy Trinity and the twelfth-century Vladimir Ikon of the Mother of God, were to be returned to the ownership of the Church.

For the Gospel of the Liturgy, the same passage was used as for the Feast of the Dormition of Our Lady, in which words applying to another Mary are appropriated to the Mother of God. The Archdeacon's voice rose higher and higher, increasing in volume as well as pitch. When, in this church in which the ikon of the Mother of God was again held up for veneration, the climax came with the words: 'Martha, Martha: Mary has chosen the better place, and that place shall never be taken away from her', we all wept. Mary had come home.

Later, returning from the reception in the early snow, I saw the crowds waiting to visit the new cathedral on the first day of its consecration. They were marshalled by the police behind crowd barriers which previously had controlled the crowds waiting to visit Lenin in his Mausoleum. A businessman passed on his way home, put down his briefcase in the snow, took off his hat and crossed himself, bowing to the new church. Lenin is dead, Christ is risen!

My apokrisarial duties were not confined to Moscow. I was also the representative to Patriarch Ilya of Georgia and to the Catholicos-Patriarch of Armenia – initially the elderly Vasgen, and later Karekin I. Visits to the Caucasian republics were always complicated, with overcrowded aircraft and long delays. The war between Armenia and Azerbaijan also made travel more difficult, though it became easier when I found that I could use the small aircraft of the United Nations Food Programme between Tblisi and Yerevan. This was more reliable when it had a South African pilot; his successor was a Lithuanian who would take limited visibility or high winds as an excuse for not flying – most inconvenient!

Patriarch-Catholicos Ilya of the Church of Georgia emerged as the great hero of the brief struggle against the Soviet forces in 1991, and many remember seeing him standing between the Georgians and the Russians, thereby minimising the loss of life. He is a former vice-president of the World Council of Churches, but he has been held back from recent ecumenical participation, and the Georgian

Church has withdrawn from the WCC at a time when
Georgian church life is being affected by very vociferous
supporters of the ultra-conservative Old Calendarists from
Greece. These are of the group who protest in Greece about
the 'Number of the Beast' in the Apocalypse, placarding
monasteries with posters denouncing 666.

It was of great value to the Patriarch's standing that in
May 1993, Archbishop Carey made his formal visit to Tblisi.
This was a few weeks before my move to Moscow, but I was
invited to accompany the visit. It turned out to be the only
VIP visit to Georgia, religious or secular, in the whole of 1993,
and we were very well received. The return visit to London
came in June 1995. A long-term link between Georgia and the
Church of St James, Piccadilly, accounted for the slightly
unexpected choice of the latter for a 'Liturgy of Welcome' for
His Holiness, and I had the pleasure of assisting the Patriarch
from his car, as I was one of the few present who knew him.
Unfortunately, the service had to be totally politically correct,
and I hoped that our Georgian visitors would not completely
understand the reason for the adaptations to the first hymn,
which was sung as

> Praise to the Lord, the Almighty,
> The *Source* of creation;   (*King* is sexist, of course)
> O my soul, praise God
> For God is thy health and salvation. (*him* or *he* is sexist)

It was during this visit that Patriarch Ilya 'let it be
known' that the gift he would most appreciate from the Archbishop of Canterbury would be a mate for his Rottweiler,
Tobias. This was eventually obtained at some difficulty and
considerable cost, and flown to Tblisi by courtesy of Shell Oil.
The puppy, which had a long pedigree name, was immediately
named 'Mees Carey' in the Patriarchate. In due course, I was
told rather confidentially, 'Mees Carey is now Meeses Carey',

and a fine litter of pups was born. I was under strict instructions from Lambeth Palace that I was not, under any circumstances, to accept a gift of one of them for the Archbishop. The problems of importation would have made the problems of exportation of the mother seem child's play!

During my sixteen years as chaplain in Antwep, the local Armenian community had used our church for their services two or three times a year. My third apokrisarial appointment to the Catholicos-Patriarch of Armenia, therefore, gave me great pleasure, though tinged with sorrow at the sickness and death of the Catholicos Vasgen I. I had first met him in Antwerp days, when I travelled down to Paris to visit him on one of his trips to the West. This was long before perestroika, and he gave me a clear, if guarded, account of his difficult relationships with the Communist authorities. The close identity between the Armenian Church and the Armenian people certainly eased the problems of the Church in the newly independent Republic of Armenia, and the interest of the President, Leon Ter Petrossian, in Church affairs was very apparent. Indeed, he had made a translation of the Psalms into Armenian some years before independence, and this translation was used in services in Etchmiadzine.

My visit in August 1994 was for the funeral of the Catholicos. The journey itself was unforgettable, the pilot of the huge Ilyushin-86 objecting strongly that there were ten more passengers than shown on the manifest, while I estimated that there were more likely fifty standing. I was seated with Bishop Theophan of the Romanian Orthodox Church – travelling on a Romanian diplomatic passport – and he was extremely uneasy at the realisation that the emergency doors immediately in front of us were completely blocked with piles of cabin baggage, including a vast floral cross at least 1½ metres high, destined for the funeral. We finally arrived safely soon after midnight, only two hours late, and were met by representatives of the Catholicate. The funeral, two days later, was notable for the presence of virtually all the Armenian bishops world-wide, the Patriarch of the Armenian Catholics from Beirut (most resplendent in a scarlet Greek-style kamilávka and veil), and several ministers of the Armenian Evangelical Church. Their leader, from the United States, was in dark suit, clerical collar and a scarlet shirt which would have graced any cardinal! Apart from the dignity of the occasion and the tribute to Catholicos Vasgen personally, there could have been no better sign of the unity of the nation under the Catholicos of *all* Armenians.

I had met Catholicos Karekin II of Antilas previously, at the consecration of the new Armenian Church in Brussels. In due course, he was elected as Catholicos Karekin I of Etchmiadzine, where I subsequently visited him several times. The most memorable of these visits was in September 1996, when I not only had the privilege of being present at the blessing of the Holy Oil but was also the only ecumenical representative at the unique ceremonies held the previous day, for the burial of the mortal remains of the Catholicos Horen I. This was the Catholicos who had been murdered by members of the Armenian Communist Party in 1938. His body had been buried in several locations and finally in the Cathedral of St Guyane, which is about 1½ kms from the central monastery church of the Holy Cross in Etchmiadzine. I had persuaded my long-term friend David Miller, Ambassador in Armenia, that invitations were not issued by the Armenian church for funerals – an odd snippet of information which I had gained from the funeral of Catholicos Vasgen. The ambassador was therefore also present for the funeral and for the Liturgy preceding it in St Guyane, from which we all walked to Holy Cross. I went with the Armenian clergy; great silent crowds lined the route and watched as this sad chapter of Armenia's history was finally closed. 'The blood of the martyrs is the seed of the church', but the Armenian people may query why they have been called upon to provide so many of the seeds.

The following day, Sunday, we came again to Etch-miadzine, for the blessing of the Holy Oil. Normally this is done every seven years, but the Catholicos chose to have the ceremony only five years after the last blessing by Catholicos Vasgen, so that the next occasion, seven years on, would coincide with the 1700th anniversary of the Conversion of the Kingdom of Armenia. Perhaps, also, Catholicos Karekin I had some premonition that he would not be there for those celebrations; he died from cancer in 1999 and has been succeeded by Karekin II, formerly Bishop of Ararat.

Three immense cauldrons of oil had been prepared. The Catholicos explained that the quantity was necessary with the very large number of baptisms anticipated in the immediate future. During the blessing, a distillate of aromatic herbs, which had been prepared over the previous forty days, was added: bitter herbs, symbolising the sufferings of the Armenian peoples throughout the ages; then a small quantity of oil blessed on the previous occasion, thus keeping continuity right back to the fourth century and St Gregory the Illuminator; and finally oil blessed a few months earlier by the Catholicos of Antilas, symbolising the somewhat tenuous unity between the two Catholicates. During the blessing, the oil is stirred with holy relics, including the Lance which pierced the Body of Christ at the Crucifixion, and the great silver reliquary holding the arm of St Gregory the Illuminator himself. The whole history of the Armenian Church is represented, and the oil is distributed to every Armenian Church world-wide.

I had on one occasion the opportunity of discussing with Catholicos Karekin I the ancient legend that Christianity had first been brought to Armenia by St Thaddeus in the first century. I then mentioned that in Baku, the Rabbi of the Mountain Jews there claimed that his community was 2,500 years old. I suggested that it might have been possible for St Thaddeus to have visited Armenia and other diaspora communities when the first Christians were forced to leave Jerusalem. The Catholicos immediately agreed and suggested that 'Judea' in Acts ii, 9, was an ancient error for 'Armenia' (which would fit much better geographically), and quoted Tertullian in the third century in support of this theory.

This paper has been a somewhat anecdotal attempt to describe the very varied duties and privileges of 'the man who gives the answer'. It is difficult to define the apokrisarial role more precisely, and I would hate to try to formulate a job description. Perhaps I may just be allowed to parody that lovely prayer which was printed in the *Priest's Book of Private Devotions* which asked, 'O sacerdos, quid es tu?', and then declined the responses. And so I would ask, 'O Apokrisarios, quid es tu? – Nihil et omnia.'

15. The Anglican–Orthodox Dialogue and its Future

William B. Green

No Archbishop of Canterbury in recent times has been as devoted to overcoming the schism between East and West as the 100th Archbishop, Arthur Michael Ramsey. From his days as a theological student at Cuddesdon he was involved in the Fellowship of St Alban and St Sergius. After becoming Archbishop of York, he made visits to Churches of the East and counted as friends many of its bishops and theologians. As a result in part of his own initiative, the Anglican/Orthodox Dialogue was reconstituted and enjoyed his enthusiastic support.

Ramsey maintained that the initial schism between East and West was the parent of later divisions in the Christian world and that the healing of that division was a mission in which the Anglican Church had a unique role to play. He discovered that there were lessons to be learned by Western Christians from their Eastern brothers and sisters and that the richness of the Church cannot be realised as long as East and West are separate. His biographer observed that Ramsey 'valued the Orthodox tradition, studied its classical documents, used its liturgies, respected its monastic ideals and wanted its insights to be understood and used by the members of his Church.'[1] The vision

The writer wishes to acknowledge his indebtedness and express his appreciation to The Rt Revd Maxwell M. Thomas, a senior Anglican member of the Dialogue, for his helpful suggestions.

1   Owen Chadwick, *Michael Ramsey,* 312.

of the universality of the messianic banquet where 'people come from the east and west, from the north and the south to sit at table in the Kingdom of God' was Ramsey's vision and is the inspiration for our continuing dialogue.

Following talks in 1962 between the Ecumenical Patriarch, His All Holiness Athenagoras I, and Dr Ramsey, then Archbishop of Canterbury, the Primates of the Anglican Communion proposed the establishment of a Joint Commission which would examine agreements and differences in matters of doctrine between Anglican and Orthodox Churches. In 1964, the Third Pan-Orthodox Conference held on the island of Rhodes decided unanimously to resume theological discussions with the Anglican Communion. During a preparatory period (1966–1972) in which the two commissions met separately, agreement was reached on an agenda for the Joint Discussions and answers were prepared on each side to questions proposed by the other.

The first full meeting of the Joint Commission took place at Hertford College, Oxford, in July of 1973. There followed a series of theological exchanges in which representatives of all the Orthodox Churches and the whole Anglican Communion took part. After three years the Commission produced the *Moscow Agreed Statement* of 1976.

The *Moscow Statement* brings together documents drafted by the three sub-commissions in 1974 and 1975. It reflects the agreement in principle reached by the summer of 1976 on the Knowledge of God, Authority of Holy Scripture, Scripture and Tradition, the Authority of the Councils, the Church as Eucharistic Community, Invocation of the Holy Spirit in the Eucharist, and the Filioque Clause. On the latter, which had become the focus of serious theological differences between Eastern and Western ways of expressing the experience of God as Trinity, the Anglicans agreed to omit the Filioque Clause from the Nicene Creed since it was not part of the basic text of that Creed as formulated at the Second Ecumenical Council (381). They also accepted that the Filioque fails to make a distinction between the Holy Spirit as cause and as mediator.

There was no discussion of a topic that was to become a major stumbling block, the ordination of women to the priesthood. However, a resolution was passed and attached to the press communiqué in which the Orthodox warned that 'if the Anglican Churches proceed to the ordination of women to the priesthood and episcopate, this will create a very serious obstacle to [...] our relations in the future'.[2] Since the Anglican members were divided on this issue, 'it must not be assumed that this was a resolution passed by Orthodox members alone, aimed at the Anglican world without any regard for those Anglicans present at Moscow. In fact, the text of the resolution was drafted by an Anglican delegate in consultation with an Orthodox delegate.'[3] That issue did in fact create a furore at the Commission's meeting in 1977 when the Orthodox members realised that the ordination of women was 'no longer simply a question for discussion but an actual event in the life of some of the Anglican churches'.[4] They asked themselves how the dialogue could continue and what meaning it would have under these circumstances. Some Orthodox members wished to terminate the dialogue then and there, since from their point of view agreement leading to unity was no longer possible. However, the Anglican co-chairman, Robert Runcie, then Bishop of St. Albans, devoted his sabbatical in 1978 to visiting heads of Orthodox churches encouraging them to continue discussions. As a consequence, it was agreed that the Dialogue should continue.

An important turning point was reached following the 1978 Lambeth Conference Resolution 21 on 'Women in the Priest-

---

2   *Moscow Agreed Statement*, 76.
3   Ibid.
4   *Dublin Agreed Statement* 1984, 2.

hood' in which it was recognised that four churches in the Anglican Communion 'have admitted women to the presbyterate, and that eight other members have now either agreed or approved in principle that there are either no fundamental or no theological objections to the ordination of women to the historic threefold ministry of the Church.'[5] In response, the Orthodox co-chairman of the Anglican–Orthodox Joint Doctrinal Discussion (A/OJDD), Archbishop Athenagoras, expressed his desire that 'the theological dialogue continue, although now simply as an academic and informative exercise, and no longer as an ecclesial endeavour aiming at the union of the two churches'.[6] While many of the Western churches, including the Roman Catholics, had accepted the concept of growing together by stages toward visible unity, the Orthodox found it difficult to imagine any intermediate stage in ecclesial relations. They recognised unity and sacramental communion only when there was doctrinal agreement. So agreement leading to union was no longer possible. That view prevailed, and in July 1979, the Steering Committee decided that the Full Commission should continue its work. The Committee further concluded that:

> The ultimate aim remains the unity of the two Churches. But the method may need to change in order to emphasise the pastoral and practical dimensions of the subjects of theological discussions. Our conversations are concerned with the search for a unity in faith. They are not negotiations for immediate full communion. When this is understood the discovery of differences on various matters, though distressing, will be seen as a necessary step on the long road toward that unity which God wills for His Church.[7]

---

5   *Lambeth 1978* 21:1.
6   *Dublin*, 3.
7   *Dublin*, 3–4.

The Commission convened at St. Michael's College, Llandaff, in July 1980 and welcomed as its new co-chairmen Bishop Henry Hill of Ontario, Canada (replacing the Rt Revd Robert Runcie who had been appointed Archbishop of Canterbury) and Archbishop Methodios Fouyas, formerly of Aksum, then of Thyateria and Great Britain (following the death of Archbishop Athenagoras). This second series of meetings concluded with the *Dublin Agreed Statement* of 1984 which reported a measure of agreement in three general areas: the mystery of the Church; faith in the Trinity, prayer and holiness; and worship and tradition. One knowledgeable ecumenical leader observed that

> in each of these areas, the rich theology of the Eastern tradition infuses and enriches the Western tradition of Anglicanism: for example, what is said in the section on the mystery of the Church about leadership and oversight in the Church, and what is suggested about the possible shape of a visibly united Church. Emerging from this section is a picture of the goal of unity which suggests that eventual 'full communion' will be expressed in structures and ministries which go further than simply recognising each other, or enjoy a degree of interchangeability of ministries. There will rather be one ministry, symbolised in a universal ministry of primacy or seniority.[8]

An 'Epilogue' to the *Dublin Statement* summarised the points on which agreement had been reached, those on which there was disagreement, and those which required further discussion. Throughout this series of meetings two matters reoccurred that were of particular concern to the Orthodox members: theological liberalism in Anglicanism as evidenced by statements of the Bishop of Durham, the Rt Revd David Jenkins, and the ordination of women to the priesthood. The Dialogue went through a tense and fractious period for about five years. The Orthodox

---

8   Mary Tanner, 'Anglican–Roman Catholic–Orthodox Relations' *Sobornost* 19:2, 17.

co-chairman at the time, Archbishop Methodios, was quoted as saying: 'There were a lot of disagreements in the A/O Dialogue; and of course, my attitude towards them was not very pleasant to the Anglicans.'[9]

In September of 1986, the Executive Committee of A/OJDD met to determine the future of the Dialogue. The meeting was to have been in New York and hosted by the Episcopal Church together with the Standing Conference of Orthodox Bishops in America (SCOBA). Because SCOBA was unable to share in the expense of the meeting, and the Episcopal Church thought that hospitality should be shared as planned, the meeting was relocated. At the invitation of the Bishop of Leicester, the Rt Revd Richard Rutt, who was a member of the Anglican delegation, the Committee met September 29 to October 2 at Launde Abbey, an Elizabethan Manor House built on the site of an Augustinian Priory founded in 1119. The Abbey with its estate of 400 acres of pasture and woodland had been given to the Diocese of Leicester for a retreat house.

There were seven Anglican and eleven Orthodox participants. After several highly contentious exchanges having to do with 'theological liberalism' as represented by the Bishop of Durham and the ordination of women by some churches in the Anglican Communion, civility was restored. It was decided that the Dialogue should continue as part of the process leading to the eventual union of Anglican and Orthodox Churches. Therefore an invitation to meet in September of 1987 at the Monastery of Kalavrita, Greece was accepted and topics and authors of papers to be presented at that meeting were agreed upon. It was also decided that work should continue in three sub-commissions. However, due to Church/State tensions in Greece, it became necessary to find another venue. Financial

---

9   *The Independent,* 2 April 1988.

assistance from the Ministry of Culture required to meet conference expenses had not been forthcoming.

Five years (1984–1989) were to pass between plenary sessions of A/OJDD. During this period the Commissions were reconstituted and reduced in size from twenty-eight to fourteen. Also a new Orthodox co-chairman was appointed by the Ecumenical Patriarch, Demetrios I, who was soon to die. His successor, Bartholomew I, in his enthronement address on 2 November 1991 expressed esteem for the Archbishop of Canterbury and the entire Anglican Communion. He also voiced his intention 'to continue with faithfulness the long tradition of fraternal relations with the Anglican Church [...] and [his] desire to promote our theological dialogue until we achieve the unity of faith.'[10] The new Orthodox co-chairman was to be Metropolitan John Zizioulas of Pergamon, who has lived and taught in the West and was at the time Visiting Professor of Christian Doctrine at King's College, London, and Professor of Dogmatic Theology in Salonika. In addition he was a member of the Orthodox–Roman Catholic Dialogue and co-chairman of the Orthodox dialogue with the non-Chalcedonian Oriental Orthodox Churches. This appointment was seen as indicative of the Ecumenical Patriarch's determination to continue the Dialogue and make it productive. Anglican members welcomed a leader who understood and could interpret to the Orthodox the ways of Western thought.

The Lambeth Conference of 1988 passed a Resolution on 'Anglican–Orthodox Relations' which welcomed the resumption of the Anglican–Orthodox Joint Doctrinal Discussions and

> encouraged the work of the Commission towards the restoration of that unity for which Christ prayed, particularly noting its intention to address the question of ecclesiology which it is hoped will include the increasingly significant concept of 'reception', the issue of ecclesial

---

10   Bartholomew I, 'Enthronement Address', 7, English translation.

diversity and the inter-relationship between faith and the culture in which it is expressed, believing that these are pressing issues which affect both our Communions.[11]

In May of 1989, a letter went out to the members of the Anglican–Orthodox Joint Doctrinal Discussions from the two co-chairmen, Bishop Hill and Metropolitan John, announcing that the next meeting would take place in June at the New Valamo Monastery in Finland. In light of the important changes that had taken place, this meeting was devoted to a review of the work previously done by the Commission and to the charting of a new course. Metropolitan John referred to the 'Epilogue' to the *Dublin Statement* as a useful summary of the Commission's accomplishments, and on behalf of the two co-chairmen offered a proposal of enquiry for the next stage of the Dialogue.

The study would begin with a consideration of the Mystery of the Church in light of faith in the Trinitarian God, then move on to explore the Mystery of the Church in relation to Christology, Pneumatology, anthropology and eschatology. A second group of topics to be studied related to Church structure and organisation: the nature and authority of the episcopate; the question of conciliarity and primacy; and the issue of the ordination of women to the presbyterate and episcopate. A third set of ecclesiological questions includes: What constitutes heresy in the technical sense? What constitutes schism in the church? Metropolitan John reaffirmed the need to make use of what the Commission had produced in the *Moscow* and *Dublin Agreed Statements*, cited as constituting 'a mine of theological reflection which shows the extent to which the two Churches share a common faith in spite of their differences on many points.' It was also proposed that because of the reduction in size the Commission should do its work in plenary sessions rather than

---

11   'Resolution 6:4' in R. Coleman, *Resolutions of the Twelve Lambeth Conferences, 1867–1988*, 200–201.

in sub-commissions as previously. And at New Valamo the Dialogue was given a new name, 'The International Commission of the Anglican–Orthodox Dialogue' replacing 'The Anglican–Orthodox Joint Doctrinal Discussions'.

Since 1989, the Dialogue has met six times, the most recent being in February of 2000 in Greece. The work of the Commission has followed closely the programme adopted at New Valamo. At Toronto in 1991, the opening session was chaired by Bishop Hill, who was retiring as Anglican co-chairman and who was honoured at a dinner hosted by the Primate of the Anglican Church of Canada and attended by members of the Commission. He introduced the new Anglican co-chairman, the Rt Revd Mark Dyer, Bishop of Bethlehem, Pennsylvania, chosen by the Archbishop of Canterbury and the Primates of the Anglican Communion. Bishop Dyer had joined the Commission at its 1990 meeting at New Valamo, and he paid tribute to the Revd (now Archdeacon) Joy Tetley, the first woman member of the Commission. It was suggested that because of the expense involved, the Commission meet in plenary sessions every eighteen months. A smaller 'steering committee' would meet, together with the authors of papers, between the plenaries.

The discussion focused on the Holy Trinity as the source of the Church. Consideration was given to the language used in relation to the Trinity. At the request of an Orthodox member, a paper by Dr Tetley dealt with the wide range of imagery – including feminine imagery – used of God in the Bible and the tradition of the Church. In response several Orthodox members argued that sexual images are not helpful, and one maintained that 'human and divine fatherhood are two absolutely incomparable realities'.[12] It was agreed that Christian language about God acquires significance only in the context of belonging to a

---

12   C. Scouteris, 'Image, Symbol and Language in Relation to the Holy Trinity'.

community which gives it meaning. After a discussion following two papers on 'The Holy Trinity as Communion', the authors prepared a synthesis indicating ten areas of common understanding. One of the two papers on 'The *Filioque* and the Immanent Trinity' called for a way of understanding the Spirit in the immanent Trinity which avoided the extremes of 'crude filioquism' on the one hand and a theology of single procession which 'can drive a wedge between the Spirit as actually encountered and the Spirit in the inner life of the Trinity.' The other paper insisted on a distinction between God's 'being' and God's 'life'. 'The life which God imparts in the economy is not the same as the life of God in the Trinity. God does not give us his being, he gives us his life.'

The Drafting Committee met 31 May–1 June 1994 in Oxford to draft an agreed statement incorporating the papers and discussions at Toronto for amendment and approval at the next plenary session. That would come in October when the Dialogue met at the Orthodox Centre in Chambesy, Switzerland. The first order of business at that meeting was an examination and revision of the Oxford text submitted by the Drafting Committee. A final version entitled 'The Trinitarian Basis of Ecclesiology' was studied by the Commission.

The main task at this meeting was to study the doctrine of the Person of Christ as it relates to the doctrine of the Church. A paper reviewing contemporary developments in Anglican Christology was presented and discussed. Then Professor John Macquarrie, invited as a consultant, delivered a paper drawing on the Bonhoeffer question 'Who is Jesus Christ for us Today?' in which he developed a 'Christology from below' balanced by a 'Christology from above'. He followed this with a brief summary of 'Current Trends in Anglican Christology'. Discussion of the Christological papers was lively and instructive. It was noted that contemporary Anglican Christology as represented in these papers is highly academic and divorced from an ecclesial context. It was unclear how this kind of theology could be incorporated into the service of the church. Furthermore, these papers presented Christology in a narrowly English Anglican matrix. Additional papers on 'Christ and Culture' and 'Christ and the Spirit: Towards a Pneumatological Christ' were presented and discussed at a serious level and with a genuine desire to understand one another. Once again consideration was given to the statement on 'The Trinitarian Basis of Ecclesiology'. Because a consensus could not be reached on the meaning of 'fatherhood' and 'sonship' as symbols of God, the issue was referred to the Drafting Committee.

That Committee met twice after Chambesy: first, at the Phanar in Istanbul to deal with difficulties in the statement on 'The Trinitarian Basis of Ecclesiology', and later in London to prepare the draft of an agreed statement on 'Christ and the Spirit.' As the basis of this paper, the committee adapted a chapter by Bishop Rowan Williams which appeared in 'We Believe in the Holy Spirit' (1991), a report by the Doctrine Commission of the Church of England.

When the plenary met in Llandaff, Wales, in June of 1996, its first order of business was to approve the final draft of the statement on 'Trinitarian Ecclesiology' and to discuss and accept the statement on 'Christ and the Spirit'. It then moved to a discussion of 'Christ and Culture', on the basis of papers prepared by Anglican and Orthodox members which disclosed a wide measure of agreement. Although the Church has both embraced and criticised the culture in which it lives, there was agreement that human culture is to be transformed along with every other aspect of human reality. A paper on 'Christ, Creation and Humanity', summarising earlier papers and discussions, was also presented and followed by discussion. The Commission decided that a report should be drawn up for the bishops attending the Lambeth Conference in July/August of 1998. This Interim Statement included agreed statements on 'the Trinity and the Church', 'Christ, the Spirit and the Church' and 'Christ, Humanity and the Church – Parts I and II'.

The International Commission did not meet again until June, 1998, in Bucharest at the invitation of His Beatitude Teoctist, Patriarch of the Romanian Orthodox Church. The Dialogue was held in what had been the Grand National Assembly building which housed the Romanian Parliament. Built on land taken from the Church, it had now been returned and renamed the Palace of the Patriarchate.

The opening session was attended by His Beatitude Teoctist as well as the bishops and theologians of the Romanian Orthodox Church. After welcoming remarks by His Beatitude and a response by Metropolitan John, the Commission heard and received one of two papers on 'The Risen Christ and the Church'. In response to this paper, an exception was taken by two bishops from the Middle East to the use of 'Israel' as a theological symbol which would be understood by their constituents to mean only the modern state of Israel which oppresses Arabs.

Since the last plenary meeting in 1996, the Drafting Committee had prepared a draft agreed statement on 'Christ, Humanity and the Church – Part II' which took account of previous papers on 'Christ and Culture'. That draft was presented, amended and received. In subsequent sessions papers on 'Christ: Sovereign Over All' and 'Priesthood and Identity in Christ' were read and discussed. The discussion focused on the nature and exercise of Christian ministry, which topic the Commission intends to explore more fully at its next meeting. The document on 'Christ, Humanity and the Church, Part I', drafted at the Phanar, which incorporates papers dealing with the use of gender language in theology, particularly with reference to the

Incarnation, was then discussed; some changes were accepted and the statement adopted.

In October of 1999 the Commission met again in plenary session at Sarum College in Salisbury. Only nine out of fourteen Orthodox churches were represented at this meeting. Three Anglican members were absent and one had resigned. At this meeting work was continued on the doctrine of the Church by considering the nature and authority of Episcopal ministry and the question of conciliarity and primacy. Four papers on these topics were presented by Anglican and Orthodox members. These were followed by extensive and helpful discussions from which emerged a convergence of Anglican and Orthodox views on these fundamental ecclesiological issues. The Commission also reviewed an agreed statement by the Second Anglican/ Roman Catholic International Commission on 'The Gift of Authority'. The members of the Commission welcomed this statement as a significant contribution to ecumenical dialogue. On the basis of an initial reading, the Commission raised six points on which they would be grateful for elucidation. The questions are being referred to the Inter-Anglican Standing Commission on Ecumenical Relations, which promotes consistency across all international dialogues.

The most recent meeting of the International Commission was held in Volos, Greece, in February of 2001. An agreed statement on 'Episcope, Episcopos and Primacy', summarising the papers and discussions at Salisbury, was presented and approved. The Commission then heard and discussed two papers dealing with ministry in the Church. The first considered ordained ministry in relation to the unique high priesthood of Christ and the royal priesthood of the whole Christian community. The second paper addressed the difference between the ministry of the ordained and the unordained. It was seen that between a priest and a lay person there is no legal distinction 'but precisely what may be called a charismatic distribution'.[13] The teaching that the grace of ordination imposes an 'indelible mark' which can never be removed or surrendered was seen as absolutising and isolating the individual from the ecclesial community by and for which he exists as a priest. The understanding presented here is beyond an 'ontological' or 'functional' definition.

The Commission then agreed on a schedule of work necessary in order to complete the final document in three years. Also the future work of the 'Drafting Committee' was outlined and the topics for discussion in plenary presented. Among the topics yet to be discussed are the ordination of women to the priesthood, the reception and development of doctrine, as well as what constitutes schism and heresy. That question is relevant to the issue which has plagued the Dialogue since 1977, namely the ordination of women to the priesthood and episcopate. Most Anglicans now regard this as a legitimate development of tradition, and the Orthodox members recognise the urgent need to discuss it.

Now that the conclusion of this phase of the International Anglican/Orthodox Dialogue is in sight, there are some things that should be said for the record. From the beginning the Orthodox conviction that the Orthodox Church is the one true Church, that Orthodoxy contains the truth in so far as it can be known and is therefore the criterion by which other Christian traditions are to be evaluated, has always been a factor in the Dialogue.[14] In the discussions of leadership preceding the

---

13   Cf. 'The Final Report' of the Anglican/Roman Catholic Commission, 1982, 36: 'Ordained ministry is not an extension of the common Christian priesthood but belongs to another realm of the gifts of the Spirit.'

14   Cf. The discussion of this claim by Professor John Meyendorff and Bishop David Jenkins in response to 'The New Valamo Report: The ecumenical nature of the Orthodox witness', 24–30 September 1977.

Moscow and *Dublin Agreed Statements* the Anglicans were reminded from time to time that unity would be achieved when they agreed with the Orthodox. That attitude, also characteristic of the early stages of the Anglican and Orthodox Dialogues with Roman Catholics, has created serious difficulties. In recent years, that certitude has been less of an obstacle. The atmosphere has been more collegial as the Orthodox seem ready to recognise Anglicans baptised with water in the name of the Trinity as brothers and sisters in Christ who with them are seeking the unity of all Christians in the one true Church.

Since New Valamo there has been a dramatic change in the atmosphere/methodology of the Dialogue. Heretofore it was, as Bishop Max Thomas has said, 'as if each side had its massive filing system and when asked questions of one another, each goes into the relevant file and reveals its contents to the other.'[15] In the post-1989 era the two groups have worked together, 'no longer scoring points, and clandestinely claiming superiority but listening and learning from one another'. As one Anglican member put it,

> Now it is a conversation of delight and illumination. Like all true conversations, it has had its moments of surprise and strangeness. [...] But then it is good to be drawn into a conversation which engages in profound and sustained reflection on what it is that makes the Church the Church and to affirm, against all the appearances and signs of the old age, the hidden life of the Trinity at the heart of our communities, its life-giving and empowering, renewing and creative gracious outpouring in our Eucharistic fellowship.[16]

The significance of this Report and Consultation is sufficiently important to warrant closer examination.

15   M. M. Thomas, Email to William B. Green, 12 April 2001.
16   John Riches, 'Christ, Creation and Humanity', Llandaff, June 1996.

16. Reflections on the Greek College Conference

RICHARD CHARTRES

After a day of significant contributions to our theme of 'Anglicanism and Orthodoxy 300 years after the Greek College in Oxford', I must, I suppose, embrace the role of aperitif before the Conference Dinner. Although I come as a 'specialist generalist', not daring to pretend to minute scholarship or original views, I do come with a full heart, conscious of the significance of our theme especially for contemporary Europe in the way indicated by the Prince of Wales in his greeting to the Conference.

As a small part of the engagement between the Anglican Communion as a whole and the Orthodox Churches, described by Canon Green, the Archbishop of Canterbury has charged me with the responsibility for relations between the Church of England and our Orthodox partners in the gospel. It is naturally from this perspective that I shall be speaking. My formal duties, however, are just one expression of the nearly forty years in which, like so many reformed Catholics in these islands, and not least bishops like Thomas Rattray about whom Father Donald has already spoken and whom we shall honour tomorrow, I have felt a special affinity with Orthodox Christians. Any early sense of the exotic has faded and now there is a sense of being at home, in a place where a common tradition can be celebrated, where archaeological interest can yield to the simple prayer of the mind in the heart.

It is also good to honour my predecessor Henry Compton, the 108th Bishop of London, whose role in the establishment of the first Greek Church in London has been described by Professor Barron. The plaque on the wall of St Mary's, Charing Cross Road until it was demolished in the 1930's read,

> In the year of salvation MDCLXXVII, This temple was erected for the nation of the Greeks, in the reign of the most serene Charles II, the Lord James being heir apparent. The Very Reverend Lord Henry Compton, Bishop. At the cost of the above named and the Bishops and nobles and with the assistance of Joseph of Samos, Metropolitan of that island.

Dryden in 'Absalom and Achitophel' summed up Compton as, 'Of hospitable soul and noble stem'. He was certainly hospitable to the numerous religious asylum seekers of his own day and had a lively interest in their beliefs. I have here his own copy of the Reverend Thomas Smith's *Account of the Greek Church* published in this second edition the year after the foundation of St Mary's. Dr Miller has already helped us to appreciate Smith's significance in 'Educating the English about Orthodoxy'.

St Mary's did not survive long in Greek hands but eventually became an important London centre for the Oxford Movement. Today Old Compton Street and Greek Street in Soho lie comfortably close together as a reminder of that seventeenth-century alliance.

I owe my own introduction to the Orthodox tradition to Sir Steven Runciman and it is surely just in a conference of this character and distinction to pay tribute to the part he played in opening up the Byzantine world for occidocentric students of history like myself.

I see him now in my mind's eye as he was in the early 'sixties after a college feast in another place, holding a knot of undergraduates entranced with his reminiscences. 'I was visiting a sabbat in Northern Ireland with Dame Margaret Murray', he said with his eyes half closed. 'When she came out she said – Steven, goats aren't what they were in my young day.'

More seriously, he taught a whole generation to see Byzantium with new eyes and was revered in Greece and on Athos itself as a friend and champion. One of his last acts was to secure the restoration of one of the monastic buildings on the Holy Mountain. Give rest, O Christ, to thy servant with thy saints: where sorrow and pain are no more; neither sighing but life everlasting.

To return to my broader canvas, the relations and the affinity between the Church in England and the Orthodox tradition. The story begins in the period in which the English Church received the shape which it preserves to our own day.

The seventh century was one of disaster and trauma for the whole Christian world. We are perhaps more sensitive to climactic influences than historians of previous generations, and Irish bog oak studies suggest that the political disasters of the seventh century may indeed have been preceded by extreme climatic turbulence. Certainly the eruption of the plague played a part in lowering the resistance of the Empire of East Rome to an ecologically highly destructive Persian invasion. Then came the Arabs and the advance of Islam. The cities of the civilised Eastern Mediterranean disintegrated and a host of monks and scholars were dispersed over the globe. It was our good fortune that one of them, Theodore, a Greek of Tarsus, was consecrated by the Pope as Archbishop of Canterbury in 668 when he was already past pensionable age. For the next 22 years, he was head of the English Church, extending the episcopate and bringing about greater doctrinal unity. According to Henry Chadwick he also played a significant role internationally in holding the line against Monotheletism, which was finally condemned at the Council of Constantinople in 681.

It is good that we should begin our survey in the undivided church, a state to which we intend to advance in obedience to the motto of the Diocese of London, 'Back to the future'.

The subsequent story of the mediaeval estrangement between East and West is well known. Steven Runciman helped to clear our vision about the rights and wrongs of this conflict, and the Fourth Crusade in particular has few apologists these days. As Bishop Kallistos has written,

> What shocked the Greeks more than anything else was the wanton and systematic sacrilege of the Crusaders. As the Byzantines watched the Crusaders tear to pieces the altar and icon screen in the Church of Holy Wisdom and set prostitutes on the Patriarch's throne, they must have felt that those that did such things were not Christians in the same sense as themselves.

We cannot change the past but we are responsible not only for remembering it aright with penitence where appropriate, but also for fortifying ourselves with more hopeful memories. This Conference is one such exercise in right and hopeful remembering.

I hope that you were able to see the small but interesting exhibition at the Courtauld of icons from St Catherine's in the Sinai. The evident Western influences in the double-sided icon in the centre of the exhibition (usually kept in the storeroom so that even Father Justin, the guardian of the exhibition on the day I went, had never seen it) reminds us that Latin monks were resident in Sinai long after the symbolic date of 1054. In this and in so many other ways I believe that the Monastery of the Burning Bush is a potent sign of hope for our own time.

In England, however, the sixteenth century saw a re-engagement with the churches and spiritual tradition of the East. Reformation debates led to an anxious re-examination of the patristic corpus. In the preface to the first Book of Common Prayer, Cranmer appeals to the authority of the 'auncient fathers' to establish the mind of the church on liturgical matters. Dr Woolfenden has already dealt with this theme and I shall not labour it.

This Prayer Book appeal to patristic authority has continued to be characteristic of Anglicanism. The title page of Bishop Jewel's Challenge Sermon, the classic statement of Anglican doctrine, preached at Paul's Cross just ten years after the publication of the first Prayer Book, bears a clause from the sixth Canon of the Council of Nicaea – 'let the ancient customs prevail or be maintained.'

It is possible to draw a rather facile contrast between openness to tradition and the need for the church to be relevant, and to proclaim the truth 'afresh' in each generation. In truth, there is no necessary opposition between memory and mission. If we are simply preoccupied with the conditions of the present moment and resort directly to the New Testament moment without keeping company with those who have read the scriptures before us, then it is very doubtful whether our analysis of the contemporary situation will be very profound or our understanding of the witness of the New Testament really adequate. There will be too much temptation to read the scriptures in the light of a somewhat superficial grasp of contemporary issues.

I am not pleading for an abundance of learned lumber from the patristic muniment room but I do believe that the Church always needs to be in touch with the patristic mind and have a lively sense of tradition, the Spirit-filled continuity of its life in time. The Fathers were faithful to scripture and showed a marked reluctance to go beyond the language of scripture and to define in areas where there was little scriptural guidance. Their approach to Scripture was exegetical, historical and mystical rather than systematic.

But they were not simply content to repeat old formulations in the very different cultural circumstances in which they found themselves. To have developed a patristic mind is to have acquired a capacity to discern the signs of the times and to use or discard the categories of contemporary discourse in the service of the gospel. The Cappadocians for example struggled with Arianism, having identified it as the most profound threat to New Testament understandings of Christ, and in their writings they exploited the potential of the highly developed contemporary philosophical categories of Neo-Platonism. But at the same time, and this is crucial, patristic theology was generated within the believing and worshipping community. The eucharistic community nourished theologians who, while not afraid to reason, were not ashamed to adore.

An appeal to this patristic tradition is characteristic of the English Reformation. The year after the publication of the first Prayer Book, Cranmer issued formal articles of enquiry into his Cathedral to elicit whether there was at Canterbury 'a library within this church and in the same St Augustine's works, Basil, Gregory Nazianzen, Hierome, Ambrose, Chrysostom, Cyprian, Theophylact'. The full range of patristic sources came to be published and disseminated only in the first half of the sixteenth century, and Cranmer's use of the sources that were available to him does not approach the scholarly sophistication which was possible for those who came after, but his method, which gives to the patristic sources such a privileged role in the interpretation of scripture, is of continuing significance. It is also clearly a method which makes judgements which are inherently revisable in the light of further research.

Most important of all, however, Cranmer quotes Nazianzen to affirm that progress in theology is not made on the basis of mere erudition and intellect but in proportion to the spiritual development of the theologian. 'Therefore the fear of God must be the first beginning and as it were an ABC of an introduction to all them that shall enter to the very sure and most fruitful knowledge of holy scriptures.'

Rather later in the sixteenth century the expansion of overseas trade re-established direct personal contact between Eastern and Western Christians. Trading relations with Russia were opened up for the first time in the reign of Edward VI and a few years later Tsar Ivan the Terrible sent an offer of marriage to Queen Elizabeth I. There was theological dialogue also from the Russian side as well as from the Greeks. Boris Godunov sent theological students to study at St John's College, Cambridge. The time of troubles which followed the Tsar's death prevented the return of these young Russians. One of them, Michail Alphery, was ordained in the Church of England and held a living in Huntingdonshire until dispossessed with the loyalist clergy under the Commonwealth.

We have heard from Colin Davey about the early seventeenth-century academic contacts between the Greek Church and this university and especially the significant visit of Metrophanes Kritopoulos, a protégé of Patriarch Cyril Lukaris and himself a future Patriarch of Alexandria. Colin Davey's excellent book *Pioneer for Unity,* describing the restrictions placed on the Greek Church under the Ottoman yoke, was one of the inspirations behind the foundation in our own day of the St Andrew's Trust. This Trust, now chaired by Lord Hurd, the former Foreign Secretary, has sought to emulate Archbishop Abbot in offering opportunities for study at Oxford and other universities to young theologians from Churches released from the Soviet yoke.

Metropolitan Makarios has traced for us the history of the Greek College itself, beginning from 1692 when Dr Benjamin Woodroffe became Principal of the somewhat dilapidated Gloucester Hall. Woodroffe was not only a Canon of Christ Church but also a City of London incumbent and once again was supported by his bishop, the long-serving Henry Compton.

We have heard how with the assistance of the Levant Company and its chaplains Woodroffe sought to open a College for twenty Greek students, five each from the four patriarchates, who would receive a general education in Oxford.

We have pondered on the reasons why this venture did not thrive. While we honour the promoters of the scheme we recognise the depth of the suspicions abroad at the turn of the seventeenth and eighteenth centuries. A Greek Jesuit commenting on the initiative feared that it would administer noxious drafts of heresy to the students but it was in fact proselytising Roman Catholics who were a more serious threat. Three students who had left Oxford in search of a better life on the *rive gauche* in Paris were kidnapped and forced to study Catholic doctrine in Louvain with a view to converting them.

Recent research, however, has also uncovered understandable fears from the side of the Patriarch of Constantinople that the Oxford students might 'go native'. The fact that such an educational venture was attempted at all in England remains signficant.

The self-understanding of the Church of England is published in its official formularies in which the Church identifies herself as 'part of the One, Holy, Catholic and Apostolic Church'. It has always seemed absurd for most Anglicans as a part of the One Church to claim a monopoly for themselves alone of Christian insight. A sense of that absurdity has grown with the expansion of the Anglican Communion and closer encounters with the orthodox tradition in its own homelands where for the most part, though not invariably, Anglicans have eschewed a proselytising strategy. This has engendered the confidence that is essential for friendship and mutual assistance.

The Gloucester Hall class of 1703, however, was the last to be sponsored by the Levant Company. The scheme collapsed and Dr Woodroffe spent some years near my present home, in the Fleet Prison for debtors, owing £2,500.

With the exception of the celebrated correspondence between the English Non-Jurors and the Greek Patriarchs, the rest of the eighteenth century saw very little meeting of minds.

The situation changed as the Romantic Revival encouraged a fresh appreciation of Orthodoxy. The story is summarised in a very pithy way by Randall Davidson, writing in 1923:

> We have centuries of intercourse. Where did the Codex Alexandrinus come from? It was a gift from the Patriarch Cyril Lucar to England so long ago as the days of Charles I. Every student of the subject knows the important correspondence which passed in the eighteenth century between the English Non-jurors and the Greek Patriarchs. Pass on a hundred years and we have to note the interest taken in the matter by the early Tractarians. The story of William Palmer's visit to Russia and his study of Eastern Church questions was republished by Mr Newman himself. Then in about 1840 or a few years later came the great book of Robert Curzon entitled *The Monasteries of the Levant*, followed by very many other books and monographs down to our own day, all bringing the Eastern Church in touch with ourselves. Then came the visit of Archbishop Lycurgus of Syra in 1870 and the great part which Bishop Christopher Wordsworth took in welcoming him with an address, or rather essay of historic importance. For myself personally I began to handle the subject at Lambeth long ago, 46 years ago though in a very subordinate capacity, so that I am able to estimate the steady growth of intercourse between then and now, and the new flood of communication between the churches of the east and ourselves.

I gave a paper on William Palmer (of Magdalen) in St Petersburg in 1989. It was for me a vivid example of the continuing possibility of suspicion and misunderstanding with a consequent need for patience when in dialogue with another thought world. Palmer at the time was merely in deacon's orders but he had his share of the confidence proper to an Oxford scholar of the Victorian period. Reading the account of his travels in Russia edited by his friend John Henry Newman, I was naïvely surprised that such a comparatively lowly representative of the Anglican Church was afforded such extraordinary opportunities to expound his ecclesiological doctrines, notably his version of the branch theory of the Church, to Orthodox leaders including hierarchs of the highest degree like Metropolitan Philaret (Drozdov). Fresh light was shone on the mystery by another participant in the Conference who revealed that the police reports on Palmer had survived the October Revolution and were to be found in the archives of the Holy Synod. Every facility had been given to Palmer on the assumption that he was a spy in the pay of the Foreign Office, bent on discerning the differences between Greek and Russian orthodoxy, so that the British could make mischief in the Balkans.

Despite these sub-plots, relations continued to develop in the nineteenth century. After the celebrations in 1888 of the 900th anniversary of the baptism of Prince St Vladimir, the Metropolitan of Kiev commented that the fraternal greeting from the Archbishop of Canterbury, Edward Benson, was the only such communication he had received from the head of a non-Orthodox Church.

When Nicholas II was crowned in 1896, my predecessor Mandell Creighton was despatched as Queen Victoria's special envoy at the tsar's coronation. He had to get the permission of the Lord Chancellor to wear his cope abroad. He got trapped in it after the service and was forced to eat his lunch still vested, but his table companion was John, now St John, of Kronstadt the thaumaturge, and they had a fascinating conversation. A full account of the visit, written in the bishop's own hand for the Queen herself, is preserved in the library at Windsor.

It is good to compose litanies rehearsing the story of the ties between Anglicans and Orthodox like the one composed by Davidson. If we do not then a Cloud of Forgetting supervenes, as to some extent I fear that it is in danger of doing in our own time.

At the end of last year after I had been to visit the Serbian Orthodox monasteries in Kosovo, I met a young Serb scholar who gave me a copy of a letter in Latin, sent by my predecessor Archibaldus [Tait] Episcopus Londinensis to the Metropolitan of Belgrade in 1862. Tait thanks the Metropolitan for his kindness to a priest from the Diocese of London who had visited Serbia and adds a prayer for unity '*ut Christi Ecclesiae partes diu sejunctas charitatis et verae fidei vinculo constringat*'. The young Serb scholar then rehearsed the story of relations between the Church of England and the Serbian Church up to the Second World War. There had been numerous academic exchanges and even a journal, entitled *Britannia*, published in Serbia by those who had studied in England.

The inter-war years drew Anglicans and Orthodox closer together than at any period before or since. The Serbian story can be paralleled in the story of relations with the ancient Patriarchates as well as the newer churches like the Romanian. The Orthodox Diaspora after the Bolshevik Revolution greatly enriched Western theology. Close friendships developed. I am thinking of Georges Florovsky's contacts with Lord Hugh Cecil and so many others, and it was particularly good that Canon Every's paper has reminded us of the role of Derwas Chitty in fostering more profound ecumenical relations. The Fellowship of St Alban and St Sergius remains as a precious legacy from this period.

Both Anglican and Orthodox Churches were prominent in the establishment of the World Council of Churches after World War II and in various other ecumenical ventures, but with the Cold War division of Europe, the diminution of Britain's role as world power and a great investment of energy on the part of the leadership of the Church of England in building up the institutions of the Anglican Communion, relations with the Orthodox did not perhaps enjoy the same priority as they had in the inter-war period. This is not to say that there have been no notable initiatives, as Canon Green has explained in his account of the Anglican–Orthodox Joint Doctrinal Commission, established after Michael Ramsey's visit to Athenagoras I in 1962.

Ramsey did of course look the patriarchal part and in- deed became at one point an exhibit in the Museum of Atheism in St Petersburg, which used to be housed in the Cathedral of Our Lady of Kazan. I watched the evolution of this fascinating institution over thirty years. In the seventies it was rather crude. Ramsey appeared in a gallery somewhat sneeringly entitled 'Some Foreign Friends of the Russian Orthodox Church'. There was a photograph of the Arch- bishop with his Canterbury cap set at a villainous angle, having seized a small primatial cross from some chaplain, he appeared to be advancing menacingly into a crowd scything to left and right.

Not long after, it became clear that the atheists were becoming more tentative about their lack of faith. The primi- tive vigour of the displays depicting monkish excesses was toned down and replaced by a rather pallid evolutionary line with much ado about Voltaire couched in a style which would not be such a shock to the susceptibilities of Western tourists. Finally the museum lost its municipal grant and closed at about the same time as the restoration of the name St Petersburg to the city.

As we have heard, the *Moscow Agreed Statement* was published in 1973. It includes a survey of the topics which have historically been at issue between our churches. This historic agenda was ventilated with the clarity and candour typical of the age when the English Ambassador Sir John Finch met the Patriarch of Constantinople in February 1679 to discuss the affairs of the Greek Church in London. They talked about icons, invocation of the saints, the use of unleavened bread in the Eucharist, the *filioque* and the possibility that the Church in London might be placed under the general jurisdiction of the Patriarch of Constantinople. The Patriarch and the five Archbishops who supported him were also asked by Sir John on the instructions of the Bishop of London to repudiate the Council of Bethlehem.

Viewed on our wide canvas it is encouraging to see how much progress has been made. On the question of the Council of Bethlehem, the Patriarch and his colleagues were able to say that 'they did not know what the import of the Council of Bethlehem was so they could say nothing about it.'

Face-to-face meetings continue to be invaluable, even in these days of more efficient communication, because the scope for misunderstanding still exists. I remember as Secretary to Archbishop Runcie, who certainly felt to the full the special Anglican affinity with Orthodoxy, paying an official visit to Patriarch Demetrios of blessed memory. The usual topics were raised with the notable addition of the ordination of women to the priesthood and the theology of the Regius Professor of Divinity at Oxford, Maurice Wiles. We were, however, rather surprised to be taxed with the existence of some destructive report on the Diaconate which had been prepared by a working party of a Board in Church House and had been shelved almost as soon as it had appeared. We were able to reply truthfully that there was less in it than met the eye. But the need to take care to explain ourselves to one another continues especially in a communications culture which uses hype to sell newspapers.

A recent unfortunate example was the Archbishop of Canterbury's Message for the Millennium, an impeccably orthodox piece of work which sensibly acknowledged the difficulty experienced by many people with a modern mind set in accepting the bodily resurrection. Sensational reports reached Greece that the Archbishop himself had raised doubts about the resurrection and a Greek friend told me that he had seen a university professor on television comprehensively refuting a heresy which of course the Archbishop had never for one moment entertained.

Beyond the misunderstanding however, substantial progress has been made. The Creed has been recited at the enthronement of the last two Archbishops of Canterbury sans *filioque* and the newly published book *Common Worship* provides for its omission on suitable occasions.

From being a matter of contention, icons and orthodox traditions of prayer have come to enrich Anglican worship both in private and public. An obvious example can be seen even in Westminster Abbey, where I had the privilege of blessing two icons, one of the Pantocrator and the other of the Mother of God, written by Sergei Federov, both of which occupy a prominent place in the church.

At the same time returning to the agenda of disputable issues tackled by Sir John Finch and the Patriarch, there is now no question about the significant role and the welcome presence of the Archbishop of Thyateira, representing the Ecumenical Patriarch in Great Britain, and other Orthodox leaders who are accepted as powerful witnesses for Christian faith, not as strangers, but as voices from within our culture.

It would be unwise, however, to be too self-congratu-
latory. Hard on the heels of the work done in the first phase
of the Joint Doctrinal Commission's work, came the first
ordinations of women in the Anglican Communion. It may
have been possible to believe that Anglicans were some
primitive survival of Celtic Christianity beyond the Roman
pale, but the move to ordain women to the presbyterate was
clear evidence that the truth was rather more complex. At this
point Bishop Runcie's personal role in keeping the channels of
communication open was vital. He became so identified with
the Orthodox that Archbishop Coggan was in the habit of
referring to him as 'Albanski'. He made no attempt of course to
perpetuate any fantasies about the nature of Anglicanism, and
Orthodox friends came to appreciate just what scope there was
in the Church of England for honest disagreement. The Bishop
was accompanied by Mrs Runcie on one notable visit to Bishop
Josif of Rimnicul Vilcea in Romania. They had a typically lively
debate at the dinner table and Bishop Josif observing them
with wonder said '*Dominus dixit et domina contradixit.*'

Now, however, strictly theological disagreement has been
greatly compounded by what has happened in Europe since
the fall of the Berlin Wall. The iron curtain may have been
breached but a new hard currency curtain has taken its place
following, in some parts of the continent, the ancient dividing
line between Eastern and Western Christians. Some Western
Christians have seized the opportunity for proselytising in
Orthodox lands supported by the kind of financial and technical resources which it is hard for the indigenous churches to
match. Unsurprisingly this has exposed the ecumenical movement to fresh strain and at times acute tension.

At the same time, Christian churches of all kinds have
found themselves caught up in struggles to re-define communal identity in a post-colonial and post-communist world.
This has been an element in the world-wide increase in

the salience of religious institutions and convictions which characterises the start of this new Millennium. There is much that is admirable in the recovery of the Christian roots of historic nations, but scripture, tradition and reason resist any too easy identification of Christ and the culture of any particular place and time. One of topics which Anglicans and Orthodox can profitably survey together with a proper sense of humility for past mistakes is the proper relation between church and society, church and nation, church and state.

One of the most heartening aspects of relations at present is the theological partnership that already exists as Anglicans and Orthodox together confront a post-modern sensibility which is prepared to admit the appeal of ancient liturgy and art but which combines such aesthetic appreci-ation with a relativistic despair about the possibility of any truth claims not sanctioned by individual taste.

Works like *Being as Communion* by Metropolitan John of Pergamum are studied by Anglicans not so much to gain insight into Orthodox doctrine but to assist them as fellow Christians 'to uphold the truth of the gospel against error'. A similar sentiment was expressed by a learned young monk I met on a deeply moving visit to the beleaguered monasteries of Kosovo. After a night spent in the monastery of Pecs, listening to the anguished cries of a mother whose daughter had just been raped and murdered by the militia of the rival ethnic group, I fell into conversation with Father Jovan who almost as an afterthought asked whether I was acquainted with the work of Catherine Pickstock, a remarkable young Anglican theologian whose very important book, *After Writing – on the liturgical consummation of philosophy*, was in process of being translated into Serbian.

All churches are being called to reinterpret their story in a world where there are no longer any emperors, where hierarchy is a suspect concept and where there are attempts to reduce the mystery of the church to the level of institutions which cater for spiritual consumers. We are partners in the gospel at a time which conforms to the pagan state that Gibbon described in his *Decline and Fall of the Roman Empire*. Paganism according to Gibbon is the state in which the philosophers regard all religions as equally false, the people regard all religions as equally true and the government regards all religions as equally useful.

As partners in the gospel Orthodox and Anglicans have not only the potential to make a modest contribution to building the unity of our continent and its peace by re-invigorating the synapses between the two hemispheres of the mind and memory of Europe but also I believe we have the resources and the responsibility to encourage one another in faithfulness in this beguiling pagan environment. One of the most significant ecumenical questions of our day is how the Orthodox Churches in particular are going to be able to present the inspiring story of the Christian martyrs of the twentieth century as a gift to all Christians. Russian efforts to tell and interpret the story of the Solovki martyrs for example is work that the Orthodox are doing for the whole Christian world. It may also be that the experience and struggles of Christians in the consumerist West could likewise come to have a value for those Christians who are confronting the challenges of consumerism rather than those of persecution.

Now is the moment to renew and rebuild friendships and to follow the example of Benjamin Woodroffe and his collaborators into new initiatives. Father Jillions's paper described one very hopeful development. Another example is the work done by the present Ecumenical Patriarch supported by the EU Commission in establishing the Symposium for Religion, Science and the Environment. This Symposium not only spans Christian confessional boundaries in the face of the ecological challenges which confront us all but also introduces working scientists in the field to representatives of all the major world faiths.

It was as a participant in the Ecumenical Patriarch's Symposium focusing on the plight of the Danube region after the Kosovo campaign that I was able to renew contact with a Bulgarian hierarch whom I had first met when he was a young monk and I a failing theological student at Cuddesdon in the dark days of the 'sixties. I had tried to teach him English and we had listened to my gramophone recordings of the 1953 Coronation. When it was time for him to go home, he said that he had learnt some very important things from me and from his time at Cuddesdon. 'What sort of things?' I asked artlessly, expecting perhaps a bouquet for tolerance and scholarship. 'It was here and from you,' he said with genuine emotion, 'that I discovered that Silvikrin Hair Shampoo is better than carbolic soap for cleaning my beard.' We must build on every opportunity no matter how unexpected.

Great disappointment follows if we fail to keep our friendships in good repair. It was also on that visit to the Danube that I fully appreciated the disappointment felt by many Orthodox in Serbia at what they perceived as the uncritical support given by Anglicans to the NATO bombing of their country and their abandonment by Anglican friends. Now, thanks to the very tangible support of the Archbishop of Canterbury, we have been able to appoint a young priest, Father Philip Warner, as Chaplain in Belgrade and as one of the apokrisarioi whose role has been so effectively described by Father Coussmaker. I am looking forward to visiting Serbia next year in company with Bishop Kallistos and a party of pilgrims to assess what more we can do prayerfully and practically to rebuild the partnership between the churches about which Bishop Tait wrote in his Latin letter to the Metropolitan of Belgrade, *'ut Christi Ecclesiae partes diu sejunctas charitatis et verae fidei vinculo constringat.'* Amen.

Documents

A. A Draught or Model of a Colledge or Hall to be Settled in the University for the Education of some Youths of the Greek Church [1]

Benjamin Woodroffe

The printed *Model of a College*, which is to be found in the Bodleian (Wood 276 A, f. 381) and at Lambeth (Tracts, Universities, 2), was reproduced by Ffoulkes. The manuscript *Draught* which I print here is from Portland MS., Harley Papers, 713 F, Box of letters from correspondents W–Z; it is endorsed 'Dr. Woodroffe's Proposalls about Building a Greek College'. This draft was slightly modified for the printed *Model*; for instance, the minimum age of entry was lowered from 16 to 14.

* * *

---

[1]   This was originally appended to Tappe's 'The Greek College at Oxford', chapter 6 above.

A Draught or Model of a Colledge or Hall
to be Settled in the University
for the
Education of some Youths of the Greek Church

As there is nothing is so much the distinguishing Character of a Christian as Charity, so neither is there anything whereby we can better demonstrate that Charity, than by our true compassion to those who professing the same faith with us (those of the Greek Communion I mean) have so long struggled for it, under the greatest Tyranny and Oppression of the Mahometans. It is by assisting them in such a manner as may render them capable to continue and maintain the Faith once delivered to the Saints, that this is chiefly to be done, and nothing is there whereby we can better hope to do it, than by lending them that Key of Knowledge which God hath in his great goodnesse intrusted us with, and that is by educating some of their youths in those Studies which may qualifie them for the work of that Gospell which was first preached among them, (*a*) but lyes so much neglected under their present Ignorance and Barbarity.

Which being a matter so highly for the honour of God and our Lord Jesus Christ, and so greatly for the honour and security of that Reformed Faith we profess in Opposition to the Church of Rome, (*b*) whose great design it hath long bin, and still is, to corrupt them, and so just a piece of gratitude for that knowledge, as in Religion, so in most other parts of Learning, (*c*) which hath been driv'd from those whom God hath in his Providence rais'd up in those parts to be such glorious Instruments to propagate the Truth, it is propos'd:

1. That there be a Colledge or Hall in the University, for the Education of twenty youths of the Communion, (viz) 5 out of each of the Patriarchates of Constantinople, Alexandria, Antiochia and Jerusalem, to be brought up here for the

space of 5 years, or fewer, if in lesse time they shall have gone through the course of Studies, which shall be thought necessary for them, and then without any delay or pretence whatever to the contrary, sent back into their own Countrey. It being for the Service of their own Church and Countrey that this Charity is designed.

2. That in the said Colledge or Hall, they be furnished with Lodging, Meat, Drink, Cloaths, Medicines, Books, and whatever else shall be necessary for their Support, Studies or Innocent Recreations.

3. That the Language in which they shall converse for the two first years be the Ancient Greek, and that then, or sooner, as their attainments shall be, they may be entred into Latin, making that their constant Language for 1 or 2 other years, and when sufficiently advanced in these, they may be entred in the Hebrew.

4. That, as to the Ancient Philosophy, they begin with Aristotle and the Greek Scholiasts, from thence be led on to Plato &c, and afterwards be acquainted with the new Philosophy, joining with these the study of their other ancient Authors, from thence be carried on to the Greek Fathers, at least to such of their writeings, as shall most conduce to the explaining of the Holy Bible, and thereby fit them to be Learned and able Preachers in their own countrey.

5. That they be likewise acquainted with the State of the cheifest Controversies, as between their own Church and that of Rome, so between the Protestant and the Papist.

6. That a Governour of the said Colledge or Hall and 2 Tutors (who may be provided out of any other Colledge or Hall in the University) so also the place where this Colledge or Hall shall be, may be forthwith settled.

7. That the aforesaid Youths shall be all alike habited in the gravest sort of Habit that is worn in their own countrey,

and that they wear no other either in the University or any where else.

8. That the usuall Age at which they come over be between 16 and 20, and that they may be already entred in the ancient Greek, and if there be any of them who can understand the Turkish, Arabick, Persian, Armenian or Russian Language, that as many of them as can be had, may be such.

9. That at their first arriveall their Number, Names, Age, Parents, Countrey, the Patriarchat out of which they come may be written and fixt up in a faire Table in or near the most conspicuous part of the Turky Walk upon the Royal Exchange: where, or at the Turky House (if thought more proper), they shall be solemnly deliver'd into the care of him who is to be their Governour, who having receiv'd them shall forthwith present them to the Rt. Reverend the Lord Bishop of London, and in a day or two after take them down with him to the University.

10. That the Lodgings prepar'd to receive them be so contriv'd that each Classis (for they will be divided into 2 Classis) may have their little Chambers and Studies in the View or under the Call of their respective Tutor, who shall be always ready, as to direct them in their Studies, so to be the Guardian of their manners and keep them constantly to the Language they are to converse in.

11. That the Governour of the Colledge or Hall constantly preside at all Publick Exercises, frequently visiting them in their Chambers and daily setting out and takeing an account of their Studies.

12. That the Scholars go not out of the Colledge or Hall without Leave from the Governour thereof, not without a Companion by him to be appointed, to recompense which Restraint Places for Innocent Exercises and Recreation may be allotted within themselves.

13. That there be no Vacation in the said Colledge or Hall, but only left to the Discretion of the Governour to give what Relaxations he shall see fitt.

14. That as the the time of their solemn Devotions (which shall always be in Greek), half an hour after 5 in the morning, and a Quarter after 9 at Night shall be the prefixt seasons, at each of which in their turns read a Greek Chapter out of the Holy Bible.

15. That for their better instruction in Religion, an Orthodox Catechism be compil'd in the ancient and modern Greek, as for their present use here, so to be carried with them at their Return to be distributed among the poor Christians of the Eastern Church.

16. That for the satisfaction of the University, they shall twice every Term perform Publick Exercise in the Schools by declaiming one and disputing once, as shall be directed by the Vice–chancellour.

17. That for the Satisfaction of others who may be concernd and may not have the Opportunity of taking Cognizance of what is done in the University, an account of the Progress in their Studies may from year to year, or oftner (if thought fitt), to the Rt. Reverend the Lord Bishop of London, and a Duplicate thereof at the same time sent to the Turky Company by their Governour with a particular account in writeing of the whole Progress each shall have made in his Studies in the time of his stay here, to be sent with them to the respective Patriarch to whom they belong.

18. That as to all things beside what are above mentioned relateing to good manners and Discipline & c, they be subject to the Statutes of the University.

Upon the perusal of the abovewritten Draught or Model, and in full confidence that all things shall be effectually performed as it is proposed, as also that the summes subscrib'd shall be Imploy'd by such Trustees as the Contributors

shall appoint to the uses above–mentioned, and a faithfull
account of the same be quarterly given in by the Governour of
the Said Youths, or the Officers of the said Colledge or Hall
to such person or persons as the aforesaid Trustees shall from
time to time appoint, with this farther Proviso that in case
this be not faithfully and constantly done, the Charity shall
forthwith cease.

We whose names are here underwritten do promise that
we will contribute towards the maintenance and Education of
the aforesaid Youths the Summes of
[BLANK]

Notes in Margin

(*a*)   See the great extent of it by St. Pauls preaching. Thessal.
1.1.5.6.7.8.

(*b*)   This is done in the Collegium de propaganda fide in
Rome, and in other their seminaries where they entertain
fugitive Greeks, whom having debaucht to their erroneous
Principles, they clanculary send into their own Countrey, or
imploy them otherwhere abroad to insinuate their Errours
and make the world believe that there is little or no difference
between them and the Church of Rome. Such was the Design
of the false titular Archbishop of Samos and his crew some
years since here in England.

(*c*)   Such are those who are so well known under the names of
the Greek Fathers, with their Philosophers and other famous
Writers.

B. Correspondence on the Greek College[1]

I

[These extracts from a paper endorsed 'Copy of a letter from the Rt. Rev. the Bishop of London to Mr. Edward Williams the 16ᵗʰ August 1695, received the 11 March 1696'.]

The inclosed will give you a account of a design there is among us for the service of our brethren of the Greek Communion; it is encouraged and promoted by our Governors both in church and state. ... The inclosd prints show you the intention and method in which matters will be here managed, and the letters to the Patriarchs ... we have time onely to send one single copy of what wee desire may be communicated to them all.

[Difficulties]

1. That the Turks will no suffer any of their Subjects, for whose heads they receive an annuall tax, to go out of the Countrey, and when that difficulty shall be over,

2. That the friends and relations of the Youths will not part with them, but for profit sake (their poverty tempting them to it) will themselves be apt to make some Avanias to our prejudice; and then

3. That the jealousie those of the Greek Communion watch over all others with, will make them unwilling to venture their countreymen to receive education abroad, or to receive them with that natural kindness as they show to others, at their return.

[Reply]

1. The first of these wee suppose will be sufficiently provided against, if the Tax required for such youths be engaged for to the Government, which our friends heer are willing to do. ... If wee have the youths from such places where such a tax is not required, then all this caution will be superseded.

---

1   This was originally appended to Tappe's 'The Greek College at Oxford', chapter 6 above.

2. As to the second, wee are apt to think there will be little fear from their friends, because they who are poor will be thereby eased of a great burden, in having their children bred up at the charges of others, and thereby fitted for profitable employment: which you see is particularly in our thoughts by what you read in our proposal, and in the letter to the Patriarchs, of our intentions to bring them up in the knowledge of Physick and the Mathematicks &c, which are so much desired and useful in those parts, and as to any Avanias from them, there will be little reason to apprehend that, if the Patriarchs and bishops interest themselves in this affair.

3. Wee flatter ourselves that they have the least jealousie against us of England of any part of the Christian world besides themselves. Φιλέλληνες or lovers of the Greeks, is the stile wee have always given ourselves, and, as we are informed, they still allow us. The great differerences and jealousies are between them and the church of Rome: as to what differences there are between us and them, they were never carried so high as to make a breach or Shisme. ...

[*How shall they be maintained when they return?*]

Those who propose their maintenance here, will be likewise ready to make a provision for them at their return, if that shall be judged necessary; tho we cannot imagine how those who shall be sent with the privity and good likeing of the Patriarchs, Metopolits and Bishops ... should not be very welcome to them at their return, and forthwith advanced to the best places and offices among them, for which they will be so much better qualyfied than others, who shall not have had the same advantages to improve themselves. Besides it may be as effectual to our design to make some presents to the respective Patriarchs, Metropolites and Bishops themselves, as to provide otherwise for the maintenance of the youths at their return.

We think however, the French of late may have made some figure in that court, that wee shall be able through the advantage wee have in this part of the world above them, and by our growing influence at the Port, to do them much greater service than the French have of late don for their religion. ...

... The Honourable the Turkey Company heer [have] been pleased to grant such Youths, as shall from time to time be sent hither and return'd back again, a free passage in their ships; so that what Youths shall be design'd to be transmitted to us, will there find a comfortable passage, and for the charges you or any of our friends shall be at in sending for or bringing them to the ships. Wee have herewith sent you credit, that is to say, the Honourable Turky Company have sent orders to their Agents in the severall Factories to furnish whatever mony shall be useful in this affair.

His Excellency My Lord Pagett hath likewise ben acquainted with the design, and hath promised it his Patronage. I waited on his Lordship in order thereunto, before he left England, and had the assurance of his favour herein. Only his Lordship commanded me to give him a more full account of what was desired by letter, which I hereby request you to doe; and I hope you will likewise find his Lordship prepared for what we ask by letters from Sir Henry Ashhurst and other of the Company. ... Our earnest request is that one way or other you would please ... to take care that such a number of youths as we propose, may be found out; the number is not so great, but that in several places they may be gathered up without observation and sent on board in severall places as chance-passengers; for their countrey is not so strait a prison, but that daily many of them seek their liberty abroad and return again at their pleasure to their own homes. ... What is heer written I am commissioned to let you know, comes by the particular direction of the Rt. Rev. and Rt. Honourable the Lord Bishop of London. ...

Reverend Sir,
Your most affectionate brother,
faithful friend and humble servant
Benj: Woodroffe

I presume I need not recommend it to you to take care that the youths sent over be of the most virtuous and ingenious that can be found.

The instructions with the whole design, it is desired you would particularly recommend to the Chaplains of Aleppo and Smyrna, whose assistance is earnestly asked and depended on, as there shall be occasion.

2

For Dr. Benjamin Woodroff.   Constantinople primo Augusti 1696.

If your well intended design could have had the desired success in these parts, I should not have delayed the notice of it so long. Your intentions are well meant and very good, but they are not so taken here. I have severall times used means to acquaint the Patriarchs of Constantinople and Jerusalem with yout purpose and have explained to them the advantage it might be to their church, to have young men educated under the care of an able worthy Gentleman, by whom they would be carryd on in those studies, which are proper for the service of the Greek church. The Patriarch of Jerusalem (a discret, well temperd man) received the proposition fairly, and seems to be sensible of the benefit the thing might be to them, but says – and so does Signor Mavrocordati – that they can not do, in this or many other things, what they would, because being in (and consequently under the power of) an arbitrary government, they can not send out such young men without leave from the Port, which will not be given. Signor Mavrocordati has told me also that as the affairs of the Greek Church are now, no Patriarch or Ecclesiastick Authority here has power to dispose of any young man upon any account; he says perhaps private men, Masters of Families, might be persuaded to send their children to be educated in England, but could not be induced to do so by their clergy. In short he told me plainly, that the thing, tho kindly intended by you, as they are willing and ready gratefully to acknowledge, is not practicable here, at present.

The Patriarch of Constantinople (a rougher man) was so far from likeing the offer, that he scarce received it civilly. He let me know, there were conveniences establishd here for the education of their youth, and they did not need any other. In short the Patriarch and the Ecclesiasticks of the Greek Church here are so full of passions, animosities and intrigues, to carry on their ends and manage their privat interests, that the publick is totally neglected, and the church, by that means and by the general great ignorance and distractions under which it labours, is almost irrecoverably lost. I should be too tedious, if I should enter upon a more particular relation of this poor distracted churche's circumstances; I therefore return to the matter in which, as things are, nothing can be done to answer your expectation.

The letter you sent mee was showd to the Principall men of the Profession, but after perusal they returned it to me, and giving me no encouragement to deliver it, I thought it not fit to expose the matter and the persons concernd in it to the slights it was like to receive, and therefore I keep it by mee. If you can send any directions that may make me hop my endeavours to advance your design will prove more successful then they have ben hitherto, I entreat they may be sent, for I earnestly desire that I may have means here to serve you, for I am entirely

your affectionate, humble servant

3

Dr. Woodroffe   8 January 1696/7
Reverend Sir

By my letters sent in answer to yours of the 16th August last, you will find that the Patriarch of Constantinople does not receive the kind and well intended proposition you sent hither for the education of Greek youths, so candidly as I hoped he would have don; but little better was expected from a person that does not employ himself for the benefit of his Church. I need not repeat what I have said before; only add at present that finding no good would be don that way, I have ben advised by severall considerable persons of that communion, to use the more practicable method, and receive youths from particular persons (tho not by the direction, yet with the approbation of the Patriarch) to be educated in the University under your care and direction. Accordingly I sent two persons, one the son, the other the relation, of a considerable man heer (Kehaya or Agent for the Prince of Vallachia); they are earnestly recommended to you, and the more particularly because the account they give their friends of their reception and entertainment there, may induce others to send their sons into England.

By this means the end you propose will be obtained, tho not by the way you designed; the Gospel will be advanced, and the concerns and interests of you country will be provided for, by breeding such youths as be lively and ingenious, to be Druggermen for the Nation in this place.

I need not use any motifs to persuade you to prosecute the pious charitable design you have layd for the purpose. Your just compassion for the said condition in which the Greek Church is at present, and your affection for the Nation's interests, are encouragements, which will induce you to go on with the work resolutely and cheerfully; wherein I have sent orders to my Son about contributing my assistance, and take leave to subscribe myself;

4

To the Bishop of London   Constantinople 8th January 1697
    My Lord

When by his Majesty's order (with the Honourable Levant Company's choice) I cam Ambassador hither, Dr. Woodroffe gave me propositions for the procuring from hence some young men of the Greek Communion, to be educated in Glocester Colledge under his care and direction.

Since my being heer, the Doctor has writ to the Patriarch of Constantinople concerning the same business. I have often used severall means to know how the Patriarch liked the motion, and I have ben told and know that he does not relish it, for having once sent my Chaplain to himself, he was very indifferently received; the Patriarch told him that he had settled a Scoole for the purpose, which would sufficiently serve the turn.

The Patriarch of Jerusalem received the ffer more civilly. He was sensible of the kindness intended by it, and returned thanks for it, but did not say any thing that might answer Dr. Woodroffe's expectation; and I easily observed, nothing would be had from them. So that, supposing the matter intended is a benefit to the Greek Church, I conceivd that if the end could be obtaind the manner of attaining it was indifferent. And therefore with the advice of the most learned and reasonable persons of that Church, I used this more practicable way to compass the purpose, and have prevailed with a person of note here (CapeKehaya or Resident of the Prince of Vallachia) to send his Son and a near relation of his, tho not by the Patriarch's orders, yet with their recommendations, to be educated in England. They by my son and Mr. Stephens, the bearer hereof, will be presented to Your Lordship with my humble intreaties, that they may be so disposed of by Your Lordships's favour, that the account they shall transmit to their friends from thence may encourage others to send a supply of youths henceforward, to receive the benefit that is charitably designed, and by Your Lordship's pious and generous example, encouragement and patronage will, I assure myself, be continued and promoted. Your Lordship's noble and considering mind will weigh the many benefits this may occasion, for the Honour of God and the advancement of the Gospel be the great ends; yet the advantage and interest our Countrey are like to receive, will be very considerable. Heer, the Church will not only have a supply of able Pastors, but the Ambassador the convenience of usefull and understanding Drogomen, which are extreamly wanted at present and can not well be had by other methods. These considerations encourage my taking this liberty to write to Your Lordship, and I have the more easily coplyd with my inclinations, because I have hereby an opportunity to offer my most humble respects and to assure Your Lordship that I am with great sincerite

P.S. Upon confidence that Your Lordship please to give me leave to offer my mind to the stock designed towards the carrying on so good a work, I have directed my Son to pay yearly 20 lb to such persons and by such methods as Your Lordship shall be pleased to appoint.

5

Oxford April 25, 1703

My most Honoured Lord,

[*Compliments on Paget's initiation of the project*]

... Your Lordship's application to Her Majesty, in which my Lord Bishop of London will join with you (and I have presum'd to write to his Lordship on that subject) will certainly finde a gracious Audience. What was done in this affair in his late Majestie's reign and what since her Majesty ascended the throne, my Lord of London will inform you Honour. What difficulties I have met with, I am unwilling to mention. But whilst a Fund hath been looking out for their maintenance (as his late Majesty order'd), the burden hath chiefily fell on me: and it hath been a great discouragement to the youths themselves to understand that there hath been no care taken of them by the public. Ad the advantage our Enimies of the Church of Rome hath made of it, hath been to allure them with the promise of great rewards to accept of better conditions in France: and three have already broken away form us and are now in France.

Our design for breeding the youths of the Greek Church hath raised an Emulation to do the same in France, and there is a society settled to that purpose there, as there hath been long since at rome; and how busie the Priests and Jesuits every where are, your Lordship too well knows.

As to my own part, I trust in God. Nothing will weary me from giving my best pains to serve them. As to the learning and knowledge of Religion these here have attain'd to, I hope we have no great reason to be ashamed of. Only I should be much troubled to have been whitting tools to put into the hands of the Philistins.

The Ancient Greek, which they were utter strangers to, when they came first hither, they read and understand as their Mother-Tongue; the Latin they understand so well, as to be able to discourse and dispute in that tongue. The English they speak as if they were Natives. In the Hebrew they are moderate proficients. They perform all exercises promiscuously with out Under-graduates and Batchelors of Arts, and some of them dispute with us in Divinity in the Chappel. They are well entred in all the Systems of Philosophy and in the Mathematicks, and perform all exercises indifferently either in Greek or Latin, &c.

Our discouragements therefore are the greater that, being thus in a manner fitted for every thing, (for besides this they have the French and lingua franca) we are in danger of having them every day snach't from us: though I must confess, if the corruption of human nature was not against us, I should not fear, but that they will be an over match for the subtlest of the Romish Sophisters. I know the have the knowledge of the Holy Scriptures, which will be a seed growing up in them, and Truth must prevaile.

But whilst I write this to beg your Lordship's favour in representing the affair to her Majesty in order to our obtaining a Settlement for these, who are here, and for a succession to be kept up, I would not divert your Honour from sending those to us, who as I understand are come in your retinue out the East. ...

In all faithfull Duty
Benj. Woodroffe.

C. and D. Two Publications by Students of the Greek College, translated with an introduction by COLIN DAVEY

GEORGIOS APTAL, GEORGIOS MAROULES, FRANGISKOS PROSSALENTIS

Introduction

On 25 April 1703 Dr Benjamin Woodroffe, Principal of Gloucester Hall, reported to Lord William Paget, English Ambassador to the Sublime Porte, on the progress of the students at the Greek College which he had established there in 1699.

> The Ancient Greek, which they were utter strangers to, when they came first hither, they read and understand as their Mother Tongue [...]. They perform all exercises [...] with our Under-graduates and Batchelors of Arts, and some of them dispute with us in Divinity in the Chappel.[1]

In 1704 the record of two of these Disputations was published in Oxford in Greek with the title: *The Sufficiency of the Holy Scriptures Demonstrated in two Lectures Given in turn by Georgios Aptal and Georgios Maroules Presided over by Benjamin*

---

[1] Appendix B From the Paget MSS No 5 in 'The Greek College at Oxford, 1699–1705' by E. D. Tappe, reprinted from *Oxoniensia* xix (1954) 110–111.

Woodroffe, Teacher of Divinity, and Tutor and Director of the Greek Students resident in Oxford for their Studies. This was in accordance with the original Prospectus for the Greek College in which Dr Woodroffe stated that 'the Language in which they shall converse for the first two years be the Ancient Greek'; that their studies would include 'the Greek Fathers, at least [...] such of their writeings, as shall most conduce to the explaining of the Holy Bible, and thereby fit them to be Learned and able Preachers in their own countrey'; 'that they be likewise acquainted with the State of the chiefest Controversies, as between their own Church and that of Rome, so between the Protestant and the Papist'; and 'that for the satisfaction of the University, they shall twice every Term perform Publick Exercise in the Schools by declaiming once and disputing once'.[2]

Georgios Aptal and Georgios Maroules were among the first batch of five students at the Greek College who arrived in Oxford from Smyrna in February 1699.[3] The format of each of their published Disputations follows the same sequence: the Question to be disputed; the Tutor's Introduction; the student's Lecture responding to the question, which is sub-divided into a number of further questions; quotations from the Greek Fathers in support of the argument; and then a series of replies to questions posed by the Greek College's Tutors, Edward Eden and Roger Bourchier.[4] Before concluding his lecture, Georgios Aptal also replies to 'those who argue against us [...] the "Spirituals" or "Enthusiasts" and the "Papists"'.

---

2   Ibid., Appendix A, 105–107.
3   E. D. Tappe, op. cit., 98.
4   Ibid. Eden and Bourchier both took their B.A. from Gloucester Hall in 1699.

The two Questions debated in these Disputations were 'Whether Holy Scripture contains all things necessary for Salvation?' and 'Whether Holy Scripture should be read by all?'. These were certainly among 'the chiefest Controversies, as between their own Church and that of Rome, so between the Protestant and the Papist'. Yet this was not the first time that the Orthodox had found themselves involved in debates with members of the Reformed Churches over the authority of Scripture and that of Tradition. The dialogue by correspondence over the years 1573 to 1581 between the Lutherans of Tübingen and the Patriarchate of Constantinople, based on the Augsburg Confession in Greek, was brought to a close by Patriarch Jeremias II with these words:

> We agree with you in almost all the main points of our faith. But you must not interpret any of the written words of Scripture other than in accordance with the Ecumenical Teachers and Illuminators of the Church. [...] That you do so is the sole reason for our disagreement.[5]

The crux of the matter was that the Lutherans subjected Tradition and the Church to the test of Scripture, as understood and interpreted by themselves. They could not understand why they were accused of innovating, when they thought they were simply returning to the purity of primitive Christianity. But the Orthodox subjected the teaching of the Reformers to the test of the inherited tradition of the Eastern Church, where the Fathers were seen as the authoritative interpreters of Scripture and the Canons as the authoritative rules of Church order. They simply could not understand how the Lutherans could claim doctrinal soundness, when they rejected Orthodox teaching on the sacraments, monasticism, the saints, and so on.

---

5   *Acta et Scripta Theologorum Wirtembergensium et Patriarchae Constantinopolitani D. Hieremiae* (Württemberg, 1584), 263.

A further consequence now emerged. As Chrysostom Papadopoulos wrote:

> From then on the Orthodox Church became the apple of discord between Protestantism and Catholicism. Previously she had taken no part in the Western religious conflict. But no sooner had she shown her complete doctrinal disagreement with Protestantism, than she appeared in many respects to be closer to the Latin Church. As a result the Catholics used the authority of Orthodoxy in order to attack Protestantism. [...] But when our Church quite clearly rejected Papalism, she seemed to be coming nearer to the Protestants, who also wanted to borrow her authority in their opposition to the Papacy. Both made great efforts to enlist the support of the suffering and troubled Eastern Church, which to her surprise, found that Protestants and Catholics began to woo her with flattery and with lavish offers of help and protection, which they claimed were entirely disinterested.[6]

This was the context in which the Orthodox encountered both the doctrines and the practical support and assistance of the Reformed and the Roman Catholic Churches from the late sixteenth to the early eighteenth centuries. However, far from being 'entirely disinterested', these offers of 'help and protection' were inextricably linked, not only with theological and ecclesiastical arguments, but also with the political and commercial rivalry of Protestant and Catholic countries and their Ambassadors in the Middle East. Sometimes such help took the form of supporting and financing rival Orthodox candidates for the Patriarchal throne of Constantinople. Sometimes educational opportunities were offered. For instance, the founding of the Greek College of St Athanasios in Rome in 1577 had as its ulterior motive the creation of a group of well-qualified Orthodox clergy who might be willing to work towards the corporate reunion of their Church with

---

6   C. A. Papadopoulos, Ἱστορικαί Μελέται (Jerusalem, 1906), 209–210.

Rome.[7] Similar offers from England or Holland, such as the opportunity to study at Balliol College, Oxford, which Archbishop George Abbot gave to the future Patriarch of Alexandria, Metrophanes Kritopoulos,[8] aimed to create an alliance against Rome both theological and political. And it is significant that when on 17 April 1629 the English Ambassador in Constantinople, Sir Peter Wych, sent a copy of Cyril Loukaris's Calvinistic Confession of Faith to King Charles I, his covering letter stated that

> it serveth for good authority to the doctrine of the Church, whereof your Majesty is, next and immediate under Christ, supreme head and Governor, so much denied by the Romish, who to allege antiquity for what they teach, promulge it to be the self same with the Eastern Church.[9]

Kritopoulos had spent seven years in England and one in Germany by the time he wrote his Confession of Faith for his Lutheran hosts in Helmstadt in 1625. He was able therefore to give a very careful reply to the question of the authority of the Word of God. This he divided into the 'written word of God [which] is the Holy and Inspired Scriptures' and 'the unwritten Word of God, by which is meant the oral Traditions of the Church, which the Holy Spirit delivered to it in a mystical way.' He added that the Church is the guardian and interpreter of Scripture, and that the Church's Traditions tell us how to celebrate the sacraments, how to pray, to fast, to venerate the saints and their ikons and so on. 'Each tradition, however', he emphasised, 'must be accepted for a proper reason, and none must be misused. For there is a danger alike

---

7   See Timothy Ware, *Eustratios Argenti* (Oxford, 1964), 25.
8   See Colin Davey, *Pioneer for Unity: Metrophanes Kritopouulos (1589–1639) and Relations between the Orthodox, Roman Catholic and Reformed Churches* (London, 1987), 67–8 and 71 ff.
9   Public Records Office, State Papers, Turkey, 97:14, 260 ff.

in despising or discounting tradition and in its misuse."[10] He also proposed for discussion with the Calvinist Council of Geneva in 1627 three points:

> 1. Whether or not the Word of God should decide all controversies.
> 2. When there is an obscure passage in Scripture which cannot be explained by Scripture itself, whether or not one should have recourse to the Fathers.
> 3. In the matters of rites and ceremonies, whether or not there should be a certain degree of toleration, provided there was nothing that was contrary to the Word of God and the edification of the Church.[11]

When Dr Benjamin Woodroffe proposed for debate the two questions 'Whether Holy Scripture contains all things necessary for salvation?' and 'Whether Holy Scripture should be read by all?', he will have been seeking Orthodox support for the Church of England's views on these matters, which were fiercely contested by the Roman Catholic Church. Indeed Article VI of the Thirty-nine Articles of Religion, *Of the Sufficiency of the Holy Scriptures for salvation*, declares that

> Holy Scripture containeth all things necessary to salvation: so that whatsoever is not read therein nor may be proved thereby, is not to be required of any man, that it should be believed in as an article of the Faith, or be thought requisite or necessary to salvation.

At first sight, Georgios Aptal's Lecture on this subject is a simple and straightforward answer to the question put to him, drawing on the support of the Greek Fathers for his affirmative answer to it. However, his answer to the 'Papists', rejecting their introduction of 'a number of unwritten traditions additional to Scripture', which he reaffirmed in his reply

---

10   Colin Davey, op. cit., 172–173.
11   Ibid., 260.

to the first question from Edward Eden, laid him open to the accusation that his argument against Rome could also be used against the Orthodox view of the 'unwritten Word of God'. It could also justify the Church of England's restrictions placed earlier on the proposed Greek Church in Soho in 1677,[12] as well as, according to Frangiskos Prossalentis, the refusal to allow the students at the Greek College 'to hold on to their traditional prayers or to observe any of our Eastern Church's other customs, saying that all such things are inventions of the Latin Church.'[13] For in both cases it was those in authority in the Church of England who decided what devotional or liturgical practices were 'contrary to the Word of God' and therefore not to be allowed.

It was this rejection of unwritten traditions which enraged the Greek Deacon Frangiskos Prossalentis of Kerkyra, who arrived at the Greek College in 1703,[14] and who in 1706 published, in the safety of Amsterdam, his attack on Dr Benjamin Woodroffe entitled *The Heretical Teacher Cross-Examined by his Orthodox Pupil.* In his Preface addressed 'to all Orthodox Readers' he attacks

> those who disregard our sacred traditions and refuse to accept the unwritten word of God. For if we reject these things that belong to the Church, we are deprived not only of the Holy Fathers and their venerable Synods, but also of the Canons together with the Apostolic Instructions.

In his dedication to the Ecumenical Patriarch Gabriel III he names 'remembering the faithful departed in the sacred liturgy, calling upon the Saints, and venerating their ikons' as

---

12 Judith Pinnington, *Anglicans and Orthodox: Unity and Subversion 1559–1725* (Leominster, 2003), 99–100.

13 Frangiskos Prossalentis, *The Heretical Teacher Cross-examined by his Orthodox Pupil* (Amsterdam, 1706) Preface 'To all Orthodox Readers'.

14 E. D. Tappe, op. cit., 101.

among the many unwritten commands 'that we have received from our Saviour and his Apostles and that have been preserved by the Church'. And he says that Dr Woodroffe told him that these and other beliefs and practices are things which 'belong to the Latin Church but which we think belong to ours'.

The Heretical Teacher consists of seven chapters, four of which are point by point criticisms of four of the sections of Georgios Aptal's Lecture. The other three are a defence of Tradition as the unwritten word of God and of the authority of Traditions, using both Scripture and quotations from the Greek Fathers and from the Holy Ecumenical Synods. The author's own summaries of each chapter are set out below together with his Dedicatory Letter and Preface, and part of chapter one has been included as an example of the way in which he argues his case.

The second Lecture, by Georgios Maroules, was on the question 'Whether Holy Scripture should be read by all?', and here again Dr Woodroffe sought Orthodox support for the Anglican position in another point of controversy between the Church of England and the Church of Rome, for in 1546 the Council of Trent had published the decree *De canonicis scripturis*, which had affirmed the inspiration of the whole Bible, the authority of the text of the Vulgate and the sole right of the priest to interpret it.[15]

This support is duly given, with considerable, and interesting, quotations from the Fathers. The arguments are clearly aimed at the Roman Catholic Church and its teachers, who

---

15   Émile G. Léonard, *A History of Protestantism: Volume One: The Reformation* (London, 1965) 282–3.

terrify us, thinking that only they are worthy members of the Church, and not granting Salvation of any kind to anyone else outside their own Church. So I want to ask them one question, and let them answer me: if there is so much danger in understanding the things that bring us Salvation, how great is the danger in knowing nothing at all that brings Salvation to us!

Prossalentis made no reference in *The Heretical Teacher* to this second Lecture and the question it addressed. But it may be significant that he dedicated his book to the Ecumenical Patriarch Gabriel III, who in 1704 had officially condemned the translation of the New Testament into demotic, vulgar Greek by the hieromonk Seraphim of Mitylene, a member of the Greek College, which was published in 1703 in London and financed by the Society for the Propagation of the Gospel in Foreign Parts with the help of the German Pietist H. W. Ludolf.[16] In fact, there had been an earlier translation of the New Testament into Modern Greek, begun under the auspices of Cyril Loukaris in 1629 and published in Geneva in 1638, though copies of it did not appear in Constantinople until 1645.[17] However the question of the Orthodox Church's attitude towards using the Scriptures had already been raised by the second chapter of Cyril Loukaris's Calvinistic Confession of Faith. This asserted:

> We believe the Holy Scripture to be given by God, to have no other author but the Holy Ghost. [...] We believe the authority of the Holy Scripture to be above the authority of the Church.[18]

---

16   See chapter 10, Vasilios N. Makrides, 'Greek Orthodox Compensatory Strategies Towards Anglicans and the West at the Beginning of the Eighteenth Century'.

17   Colin Davey, op. cit., 284 footnote 66a.

18   English Translation in George A. Hadjiantoniou, *Protestant Patriarch: The Life of Cyril Lucaris (1572–1638) Patriarch of Constantinople* (London, 1961), 141.

In reaction to this, the Synodical Letter from the local Synod of Constantinople called by the Ecumenical Patriarch Parthenios III in May 1642 declared:

> By accepting the Holy Scripture 'naked' and without the interpretations of the Holy Fathers of the Church, [Cyril Loukaris] attacks the inspired pronouncements of the Ecumenical Synods and rejects the traditions which have been in force successively from ancient times onwards throughout the world, without which, as St Basil says, our preaching would be a matter of words only.[19]

The later Synod of Jerusalem of 1672, which wanted to defend Cyril Loukaris by quoting from his sermons, made the observation that

> from Cyril's Sermon for the Second Sunday before Lent it is shown that he accepts the exegesis and interpretation of Holy Scripture by the Fathers of the Church.[20]

This was in fact the central issue for the Orthodox Church in relation to the reading and use of Scripture, namely whether it was to be read as interpreted by the Fathers of the Church and the Canons of the Ecumenical Synods, or as interpreted by heretics ancient or modern, and that might include members of the Roman Catholic Church or of the Reformed Churches. This issue was felt all the more strongly by those, like the Patriarch Gabriel III, who were particularly sensitive to Anglican or other infiltration or influence in the Middle East.[21]

Students of the Greek College at Oxford, like Georgios Aptal and Georgios Maroules, had undergone what Father

---

19   I. N. Karmiris, Τά Δογματικά καί Συμβολικά Μνημεία τής Ορθοδόξου Καθολικής Εκκλησίας, Τόμος Β (Athens, 1953) 578.
20   Ibid., 708.
21   Vasilios N. Makrides, op. cit.

George Florovsky termed a *pseudomorphosis*, by adopting theological categories, terminology, and forms of argument foreign to the tradition of their own Church. The question then to be answered is whether, as Bishop Kallistos has put it, 'those who used outward forms borrowed from the west none the less remained basically Orthodox in the inward substance of their thought'.[22] The two published works translated here show that Frangiskos Prossalentis correctly observed that Georgios Aptal had failed to uphold the Orthodox view of Tradition as the 'unwritten Word of God', while Georgios Maroules's arguments in favour of Holy Scripture being read by all needed to be supplemented by the Orthodox conviction that the Holy Fathers of the Church are the authoritative interpreters of it. However, Dr Woodroffe was fully in line with this when he stated in the Prospectus for the Greek College in Oxford that its syllabus would include 'the Greek Fathers, at least [...] such of their writeings, as shall most conduce to the explaining of the Holy Bible, and thereby fit them to be Learned and able Preachers in their own countrye'.[23] And he shared the hope of his students that in Oxford, 'the Athens of the British' as they described it in their Dedicatory Letter to Queen Anne, they 'might re-light & re-kindle the lamp of truth and wisdom' – the Greek double heritage of Christianity and ancient philosophy – which had been 'virtually extinguished, yet which once came from [Greece] to shine brightly upon both the British and many others as well.'[24]

* * *

22   Timothy Ware, op. cit., 7–8.
23   See footnote 2 above.
24   Dedicatory Letter to Queen Anne, below.

Η ΤΩΝ

ΑΓΙΩΝ ΓΡΑΦΩΝ ΑΥΤΑΡΚΕΙΑ

ΕΝ

ΔΥΣΙ ΔΙΑΛΕΞΕΣΙΝ

ΑΠΟΔΕΙΧΘΕΙΣΑ

ΓΕΩΡΓΙΟΥ ΑΠΤΑΛ, καὶ ΓΕΩΡΓΙΟΥ ΜΑΡΟΥΛΟΥ

Τὸν λόγον ἐναλλὰξ ὑπεχόντων,

Πρυτανεύοντος

ΒΕΝΙΑΜΙΝ ΟΥΩΑΡΩΦ τῶ Ἱεροδιδασκάλου,

ΚΑΙ

Τῶν Ἑλλήνων παίδων ἀεὶ ταῖς Μαθήσεσι ἐν ΟΞΟΝΙᾼ διατριβόντων

ΔΙΔΑΣΚΑΛΟΥ καὶ ΗΓΟΥΜΕΝΟΥ.

Ἐν ΟΞΟΝΙᾼ Ἔτει ͵αψδʹ.

THE

SUFFICIENCY OF THE HOLY SCRIPTURES

DEMONSTRATED IN

TWO LECTURES

Given in turn by

GEORGIOS APTAL and GEORGIOS MAROULES

Presided over by

BENJAMIN WOODROFFE, Teacher of Divinity,

AND

TUTOR and DIRECTOR

of the Greek Students resident in OXFORD
for their Studies.

Published in Oxford 1704

TO THE

MOST PIOUS and GOD-BELOVED

QUEEN ANNE

of ENGLAND, SCOTLAND, FRANCE and IRELAND

Peace and Salvation in the Lord.

DO not be amazed (Most Venerable Queen) that we in the East, having heard of the Wisdom and the Faith for which the people of Britain are famed throughout the world, should come here, not only to pay our respects to you, as the mighty defender of each, but also to be instructed in them both, as far as may be possible. Having learned a little, where else should we offer the first-fruits of our studies, in which, through your Royal favour, we have made progress, than at your Majesty's noble and sacred feet?

For our countrymen sent us to the famous Athens of the British, so that, as is only fair, we might re-light and re-kindle the lamp of truth and wisdom, which in these last times has, for us, been completely covered in soot, if not virtually extinguished, yet which once came from us to shine brightly upon both the British and many others as well. And will not the blessed light of your good deeds now shine together with that lamp, re-lit and re-kindled, from which the light first came?

We had heard long ago of the widespread reputation of our ancient Athens with its schools of philosophy and its academies of all other kinds; and now we have found all these here with you. We pray that Athens herself, the Mother of Wisdom, may yet again possess children of her own; but until this becomes possible, may your people adopt us and, through your kindness and friendliness make us your own sons, as even now we would sincerely desire and choose to be. [...]

Have pity on the Truth now living under tyranny; set free not us alone but also our Faith which is being ambushed wherever we go; we have the same enemies as do all the Orthodox, so give us, your Majesty, the same friends. Through You it is possible for our Country to be granted peace (and recently you granted this). Through You it is possible for our Church to be given rest and stability. Your blessed Ambassador, Lord Paget the peacemaker, famed for his wise counsel, to whose all-round virtue, devout mind, excellence in action and irreproachable zeal the people of the East bear witness, has already prepared the way. [...]

How else indeed can we, whom You have benefited so much, ever repay You, except by giving You (perhaps the greatest thing of all) our very selves. Yet through us You Yourself will also benefit, for God, the Benefactor of all, will in every way benefit You, and this is always the surest reward for philanthropy. We kneel and pray to God that He will grant You this.

The most humble G. APTAL,

The most humble G. MAROULES *and with us*

all the most humble other GREEKS.

[1]

ΔΙΑΛΕΞΙΣ ΠΡΩΤΗ.

ΠΑΤΕΡ ἡμῶν, ὁ ἐν τοῖς ἐρανοῖς, Ἁγιασθήτω τὸ ὄνομά σε, &c.

Ὁ τὸ ἐρώτημα προβάλλων, ΕΔΟΑΡΔΟΣ ὁ ἐξ ΕΔΗΝ, ΒΡΕΤΑΝΟΣ.
Ὁ λόγον ὑπέχων, ΓΕΩΡΓΙΟΣ ὁ ἐξ ΑΠΤΑΛ, ΣΜΥΡΝΑΙΟΣ.

ΤΟ ΕΡΩΤΗΜΑ.

Πότερον ἡ ἁγία Γραφὴ τὰ πάντα πρὸς σωτηρίαν ἀναγκαῖα περιέχει;

Ὁ Διδάσκαλος προοιμιαζόμενος.

Τὸ Ἐρώτημα τοῦτο (ὦ Δέσποι) ἀκούων, συνακρῶ͞ν μοι δοκῶ τὸ τε σωτῆρος, ὅτι σήμερον σωτηρία τῷ οἴκῳ τούτῳ ἐγένετο· τί γὰρ πρὸς τὴν δὲ τῆς Λυκ. ιθ´. ε´. ἁγίας Γραφῆς χρησιμώτερον, ἢ καὶ ἐνεργέστερον ἂν ἦ; Ἐστι μὲν αὐτῇ λόγος Θεῦ ζῶντος καὶ λαλοῦντος αὐτῇ, πῶς οὐκ ἐπὶ τὰ ὅσα ξηρότατα φέροιτο πνεῦμα ζωῆς; τοίοις ἡμᾶς ὁστὶς ἕως τῆδε ὁμοιωθῆναι ἐνόμιζα· τί γ᾽ ἡ Διαλεκτικὴ, ἀλ. δ´. ε´. τί τὰ ἠθικὰ, τί τὰ φυσικὰ, τί Μάθησίς τις ἄλλη, καὶ ἐπίσημη; ἀνωφελῆ μὴν καὶ νεκρὰ πάντα, ἐὰν μὴ ἐπ᾽ αὐτοῖς, ὡς εἰπεῖν, προφητεύει ἡ Θεολογία.

Ἐραυνᾶτε τὰς Γραφὰς, λέγει ὁ λέγων ἑαυτὸν τὴν ὁδὸν, καὶ τὴν ἀλήθειαν καὶ Ἰωάν. τὴν ζωὴν, ὅτι ὑμεῖς δοκεῖτε ἐν αὐταῖς ζωὴν αἰώνιον ἔχειν, καὶ ἐκεῖναί εἰσιν αἱ Ἰωάν. μαρτυροῦσαι περὶ ἐμὲ· καλῶς ἢ ποιεῖτε καὶ ὑμεῖς (ὦ ἀγαπητοὶ ἐν Κυρίῳ τέκνα) τὸ αὐτὸ φρονοῦντες· ἐπαινῶ ἢ ἐν Φιλοσοφίᾳ, ἢ ἐν τέχναις πάσαις καὶ ἐπιστήμαις προκοπὴν τῇ τῶν ἁγίων Γραφῶν σπουδῇ ἐπιτελέσαντες· ἐπρέχετε καλῶς, τίς ὑμᾶς νῦν ἀνακόψει τῇ ἀληθείᾳ μὴ ὅλως πείθεσθαι; τίς τὸ ὑμῶν ἆθλον ἀφαρπάσει, Γαλ. οἷς καὶ τὸ ἆθλον ὁ πόνος; Ἄραγε, ἀναγινώσκετε, ἐκμελετᾶτε, ἃς σήμερον ἐπα- ι. ζ. γωνίζεσθε, Γραφὰς· πλέον οὐδὲν ὑμῖν ἐπαγγέλλειν δύναμαι ἐγὼ, πὰρ ὃ ἐπαγγέλλεται αὐτὴ· ἀνοίετε τῇ Διδασκάλῳ τὴν ὅλην κυκλοπαιδείαν ὡς μάλιστα οὕτως ἐφάπαξ προσηθέντες· ὦ πόση, καὶ πόιαν Φιλοσοφίαν μία κομίζει βίβλος! λάβετε ὁμοῦ γῆς τε καὶ ἐρανὰ ἀμήχανον πλῆτιν! λάβετε Φιλοσόφων ἀξίαν, Θεολόγων ἀξιωτέραν γνῶσιν! τὰ πάντα ὑμῶν ἐστι, ὅτι ὑμῶν νιὰ αἱ ἁγίαι Γραφαὶ, καὶ μετ᾽ αὐτῶν ὁ ὑπὲρ πάντων Θεός.

Ὁ Διδάσκαλος πρὸς, ὃς λόγον ὑπεῖχε, ΓΕΩΡΓΙΟΝ ΑΠΤΑΛ.

Πρόαγε (ὦ Ἀγαπητὲ) σὺν Θεῷ καὶ ὁ Θεὸς μετὰ σε.

Ἀπόκρισις τοῦ ἐξ λόγον ὑπέχοντος.

Ἀκούω (ὦ αἰδεσιμώτατε ἐν Κυρίῳ Πάτερ) ἐξ ὑπακούω, Ἐμοὶ ἢ ἐν τῷ στόματι, τοῖς τε ἄλλοις ἐν ὠσὶ, καὶ ἡμῖν πᾶσιν ἐν καρδίαις ἡ χάρις ἔστω.

A

FIRST LECTURE

O UR FATHER, Which art in Heaven, Hallowed be thy name &c.

The Questioner: EDWARD EDEN of BRITAIN
The Responder: GEORGIOS APTAL of SMYRNA

THE QUESTION:

Whether Holy Scripture contains all things
necessary for Salvation?

The Tutor's Introduction.

When I hear this question (O excellent ones), it seems to me that we should hear also our Saviour's words, that 'Today Salvation has come to this house' (*Luke* 19.9); for what could be more useful or effective for our salvation than Holy Scripture? It is the Word of the living God; and when He speaks, how can it not bring the Spirit of Life upon the driest of bones (*Ezekiel* 37.4,6)? I have always thought that we ourselves should be likened to such bones; for what is the value of Dialectics, Ethics, Physics, or other kinds of Learning or Science? All are dead and useless, unless Theology 'prophesies upon them', so to speak.

'You search the Scriptures', says He who called himself 'the Way, the Truth and the Life' (*John* 14.6), for 'you think that in them you have eternal life, and it is they that bear witness to me' (*John* 5.39). So you too will do well (my children beloved in the Lord) if you are of the same mind. I have praise for those who make progress in Philosophy, and in all the Arts and Sciences, through their diligent study of the Holy

Scriptures. You have run well, who will now prevent you from wholly obeying the Truth (*Galatians* 5:7)? Who will take away your prize, if your prize is to struggle? Pray, read, study the Scriptures over which you struggle today; for there is nothing more that I can promise you except what they themselves promise; listen to the Teacher who once for all thus set before us a complete course of Education! How much, and what kind of Philosophy is brought to us in one book! Take the infinite wealth of heaven and earth! Take whatever Philosophers are worth, and the even greater value of what Theologians know! All this is yours, because the Scriptures are now yours, and with them is God who is over all.

The Tutor to GEORGIOS APTAL who was now to speak:

Go forth with God (O Beloved) and God be with you.

Response of the speaker:

I hear and I obey (Most Reverend Father in God) and may God's Grace be in my mouth, in your ears, and in all our hearts.

The Question is: Whether Holy Scripture contains all things necessary for Salvation?

I say, Yes, they do.

In saying 'Holy Scripture' I include all the books of the Old and New Testaments.

THE OLD TESTAMENT

1. Genesis. 2. Exodus from Egypt. 3. Leviticus. 4. Numbers.
5. Deuteronomy.   6. Joshua, Son of Nun. 7. Judges and Ruth.

8. Esther. 9. Kings I & II. 10. Kings III & IV. 11. Chronicles I & II. 12. Esdras I & II. 13. Book of 150 Psalms. 14. Proverbs of Solomon. 15. Ecclesiastes. 16. Song of Songs. 17. Job. 18. The Twelve Prophets: Hosea, Joel, Amos, Obadiah, Jonah, Micah, Nahum, Habakkuk, Zephaniah, Haggai, Zechariah, Malachi. 19.Isaiah. 20.Jeremiah & Lamentations. 21.Ezekiel. 22. Daniel.

THE NEW TESTAMENT

The Four Gospels according to Matthew, Mark, Luke and John. Acts of the Apostles. The Seven Catholic Epistles: One of James, Two of Peter, Three of John, One of Jude. The Fourteen Epistles of Paul to the Romans, Corinthians (two), Galatians, Ephesians, Philippians, Colossians, Thessalonians (two), Hebrews, Timothy (two), Titus, Philemon.

The 58th Canon of the Holy Synod gathered in Laodicea in Pakatanian Phrygia stated the following about these: 'That neither one's own Psalms nor uncanonical Books should be read in Church, but only the Canonical Books of the Old and New Testaments.'

The Revelation of John has been omitted from our list, but many other Synods, specifically Canon 24 of the Synod of Aphroi, have accepted it, as have unanimously the Holy Fathers of both East and West.

So by Old and New Testaments I understand only the Canonical Books (which the Holy Fathers called 'Covenantal'), excluding entirely the so-called Apocrypha.

The Apocryphal Books of the Old Testament are: Judith, Tobit, Esdras III & IV, Wisdom of Solomon, Wisdom of Jesus Son of Sirach or Ecclesiasticus, Baruch, Letter of Jeremiah, Prayer of Manasseh, Daniel: additions to Chapter 3 and Chapters 13 and 14 added after Chapter 12,

Maccabees I & II, and also Maccabees III which is not found in Latin.

There are no Apocryphal Books of the New Testament.

By Apocryphal is meant that part of the Books which is not found in Hebrew. In addition to this, both the time at which they were written and their authors remain obscure.

Given all this, it is now time to consider what Holy Scripture is, if it is to contain all that is necessary for Salvation.

I shall attempt to construct my response to the question by showing:
      (a) Who is the author of Holy Scripture.
      (b) Why it was written.
      (c) How it is possible to discover why it was written.
      (d) What Holy Scripture tells us about itself.
      (e) How the Holy Fathers witness together to Holy
           Scripture.
In addition, I shall reply to those who speak against this possibility; but it will be clear from what is said that Holy Scripture contains all things necessary for Salvation.

(a) Who is the author of Holy Scripture?

Who but He who is himself the Truth, namely God himself? For as we read: 'God spoke all these words' (*Exodus* 20:1), 'God commanded', 'The Lord says', 'The Lord spoke', and among the Hebrews a thousand times 'Thus says the Lord', a phrase found everywhere throughout the Prophets.

And in the New Testament, it was agreed that both Old and New are of God: 'In many and various ways God spoke of old to our fathers by the prophets, but in these last days He has spoken to us by a Son' (*Hebrews* 1:1).

For it to be spoken by God, what else does it imply other than it is the firmest and most incontrovertible thing that could be said? According to the Old Testament, 'You shall not add to the word which I command you, and you shall not subtract from it; keep the commandments of the Lord our God, all that I command you this day' (*Deuteronomy* 4.2). And 'Add not unto his words, lest he reprove thee, and thou be made a liar' (*Proverbs* 30.6). And according to the New Testament, 'We have the prophetic word made more sure' (*II Peter* 1.19). Hence therefore the whole Canon is so to speak sealed by John: 'I warn everyone who hears the word of the prophecy of this book: if anyone adds to them, God will add to him the plagues described in this book, and if anyone takes away from the words of the book of this prophecy, God will take away his share in the tree of life and in the holy city, which are described in this book' (*Revelation* 22.18- 19).

So now we can reply to anyone who speaks against Holy Scripture as Christ himself replied: 'If I bear witness to myself, my testimony is not true; there is another who bears witness to me, and I know that the testimony which he bears to me is true. For it is God who bears witness about me' (*John* 5.31 – 2).

That is our answer to the first question: Who is the author of Holy Scripture?

(b) Why was it written?

It is possible to look at this question in relation to the different parts of Holy Scripture, such as the Law and the Prophets in the Old Testament and the Gospels and the other Apostolic writings in the New Testament.

What is the purpose of the Law but the obedience of those who hear it?

What is the purpose of the Prophets, except the conviction and correction of the wicked and the comfort and encouragement of the good?

What is the purpose of the Gospels, but repentance and forgiveness of sins?

What is the purpose of the Apostolic writings, but grace and peace?

Threats or promises, mercy and patience or judgement and severity may be handed out to us here and there, yet do not these all lead to repentance, and through that, to salvation? This is good and acceptable before our God and Saviour, 'who desires that all should be saved and come to a knowledge of the Truth' (*I Timothy* 2:4).

It was for no other purpose than this that 'God has made known to us the mystery of his will, according to his purpose which he set forth in Christ' (*Ephesians* 1.9). For this reason Scripture too has been called 'the word of truth and the gospel of our salvation' (*Ephesians* 1.19). And Scripture is called 'the sacred writings which are able to instruct you for salvation through faith in Christ Jesus' (*II Timothy* 3.15–17). And all Scripture is inspired by God; see who wrote it? It was God himself. See too, for what purpose? For the writer continues, 'it is profitable for teaching, for reproof, for correction, for training in righteousness, that the man of God may be complete, equipped for every good work.'

These things belong to Scripture, which can be seen as the most excellent guide to *faith and piety*. For on these depend the only complete guarantee of eternal life, and about these I shall now speak in turn, since they together contain the whole of Holy Scripture.

(i) First, as regards *faith*: we must construct our argument that Holy Scripture is sufficient for this, since this completely clarifies everything to do with it, as far as is possible.

This is shown by the so-called Apostles' Creed, which brings together everything we must believe about God the Father, his Son Jesus Christ, and the Holy Spirit. And if anything more is added by way of interpretative explanation either in the Creed of the Holy Synod held at Nicaea, or in the so-called Creed of St Athanasios, we accept this only in so far as it in every way agrees and corresponds with Holy Scripture.

If by this we mean knowledge (a) of God as the Almighty Creator of heaven and earth, and as our most merciful Father; and (b) of Jesus Christ as his only-begotten Son, conceived by the Holy Spirit, born of the Virgin Mary, who suffered under Pontius Pilate, was crucified, dead and buried, who descended into Hades, rose from the dead on the third day, ascended into heaven, and sits at the right hand of the Father Almighty, from whence he will come to judge the living and the dead; (c) if we also mean knowledge of the Holy Spirit, and of the Catholic Church made Holy through him, and of the communion of Saints, the forgiveness of sins, the resurrection of the body and life eternal – if knowledge of all these things is provided in Holy Scripture, and nothing more is required ever from anyone from elsewhere for salvation, then none should doubt that Holy Scripture is the most complete rule of faith, for it teaches us all these things.

Are you looking for teaching about God? Begin at the beginning, for 'in the beginning God created the heaven and the earth' (*Genesis* 1.1). And as the Apostle says, 'For ever since the creation of the world his invisible nature, namely, his eternal power and deity, has been clearly perceived in the things that have been made' (*Romans* 1.20).

Are you looking for teaching about Redemption? Read this: 'And I will put enmity between you and the woman, and between your seed and her seed, and he shall watch against your head' (*Genesis* 3.15).

Read also the same promise made to Abraham: 'And in your seed shall all the nations of the earth be blessed' (*Genesis* 22.18). What seed is this? Listen to the Apostle: 'He saith not,

"And to seeds" as of many, but as of one, "And to thy seed", which is Christ' (*Galatians* 3.16).

Here is the foundation of mankind's Redemption in the first promise, here (as Holy Scripture shows) are the types, the sacrifices, the Prophecies built upon that foundation. Here too, so to speak, we find the whole Gospel built upon them; and by Gospel I mean that the whole of Scripture, Prophecy, Old and New Testaments together, are in the service of the Redemption of mankind.

Are you looking for teaching about the Holy Spirit? About his graces, gifts and powers? Are you not seeking for that which the Old Testament foretold and the New Testament fulfilled? Do not be unbelieving, for you already possess everything to do with *faith*, since Holy Scripture is the most complete guide to *faith*.

(ii) We have the same guide to *piety*. In constructing this argument, I shall ask again, how do you read the Scriptures? Is there a more complete guide to *piety* than that which the Lord our God proclaimed with his own mouth (*Exodus* 20)? Or that which he wrote with his own finger (*Exodus* 34.1)? About which our Saviour said 'Do not think that I have come to abolish the law and the prophets; I have come not to abolish them but to fulfil them' (*Matthew* 5.17).

And if the Saviour puts the law in second place, this is not to set it aside, but to strengthen it. For how does he argue this?

'You have heard that it was said to the men of old, "You shall not kill; and whoever kills shall be liable to judgment." But I say to you that every one who is angry with his brother without cause, shall be liable to judgment' (*Matthew* 5. 21–22).

And again, 'You have heard that it was said, "You shall not commit adultery." But I say to you that every one who looks at a woman lustfully has already committed adultery with her in his heart' (*Matthew* 5.27).

'It was also said, "Whoever divorces his wife, let him give her a certificate of divorce." But I say to you that every one who divorces his wife, except on the grounds of unchastity, makes her an adulteress; and whoever marries a divorced woman commits adultery' (*Matthew* 5.31–32).

'Again, you have heard that it was said to the men of old, "You shall not swear falsely, but you shall perform to the Lord what you have sworn." But I say to you, Do not swear at all' (*Matthew* 5.33–34).

'You have heard that it was said, "An eye for an eye, and a tooth for a tooth." But I say to you, Do not resist one who is evil' (*Matthew* 5.38–39).

'You have heard that it was said, "You shall love your neighbour and hate your enemy." But I say to you, Love your enemies, bless those who curse you, do good to those who hate you, and pray for those who abuse you and persecute you' (*Matthew* 5.43–44 [*Luke* 6.27–28]).

And what is all this for but to correct those who lead others astray and those who are led astray, and to bring the perverse back to the way of uprightness and truth? Thus it is that our feet will be directed in a way that assuredly will lead us to attain Salvation.

Nor let anyone think that there is any difference between this and the words of our Teacher when he said, 'You shall love the Lord your God with all your heart, and with all your soul, and with all your mind. This is the great and first commandment. And a second is like it, You shall love your neighbour as yourself. On these two commandments depend all the law and the prophets' (*Matthew* 22.37–40). For this is simply a summary and a more succinct interpretation comprising many things, as are also the words of the Apostle, 'Love is the fulfilling of the law' (*Romans* 10.10). Or again, 'For the whole law is fulfilled in one word, "You shall love your neighbour as yourself" ' (*Galatians* 5.14). This also agrees with the words of James, 'If you really fulfil the royal law, according to the Scripture, "You shall love your neighbour as yourself," you do well' (*James* 2:8).

And what more shall I say? You have the law, you have the interpretation of the law, you have collected together everything in full. Nothing is lacking in Holy Scripture for our *faith and piety*, so long as we ourselves do not neglect our pursuit of such salvation as we are offered.

That is enough of a reply to the question, *Why was Holy Scripture written by God?*

(c) How is it possible to discover why Holy Scripture was written?

In a way, this question has already been answered.

For, if we practise our faith and piety;

if we keep the royal law according to Scripture, 'You shall love your neighbour as yourself ';

if we allow that the inspired Scripture is useful to us for teaching, for cross-examination, for correction, for education in righteousness;

if we humbly accept whatever comes, severe judgment or compassionate mercy, threats or promises;

if in addition, we attain Salvation through such things as repentance and forgiveness, correction and consolation, obedience to all that the law and the gospel require, then without doubt we should be able to discern that it is for our Salvation that Holy Scripture brings us all things necessary. And without doubt also this will be possible, so long as the same Spirit who inspired the Scriptures also interprets and operates through them.

So far we have been dealing with the first three questions, namely:

(a) Who is the author of Holy Scripture?

(b) Why was it written?

(c) How is it possible to discover why it was written?

We now come to the fourth question:

(d) What does Holy Scripture tell us about itself?

What does Scripture not tell us about what is good, beneficial, and useful for bringing salvation to us? Or about what leads us to praise God for his kindness, compassion, justice, truth, power and wisdom? Or about the abundant grace of God in Christ? Or about our Redemption in him? What does Scripture not tell us about the power and the operations of the Holy Spirit, and about all the graces and charisms which he gives? Listen to some of the magnificent things it contains; just a few, but they put things very clearly indeed.

'Behold I have set before you this day life and death' (*Deuteronomy* 30.15). And 'I call both heaven and earth to witness this day against you, that I have set before you life and death, the blessing and the curse' (*Deuteronomy* 30.19). So it is written in the Law. What of elsewhere? Read the Psalms: 'The law of the Lord is perfect, converting souls; the testimony of the Lord is sure, making wise the simple. The ordinances of the Lord are right, rejoicing the heart. The commandment of the law is bright, enlightening the eyes. The fear of the Lord is pure, enduring for ever and ever. The judgments of the Lord are true, and justified altogether. More to be desired are they than gold or precious stone, sweeter also than honey or the honeycomb. And in keeping them there is great reward' (*Psalm* 19. 7–11). Or read *Psalm* 119 with its verses about law, testimonies, commandments, ordinances, judgements, instruction, and with its praises extolling the words of God.

Then there is Wisdom, which is taught so much through the Sayings of Solomon.

And read the Prophet Isaiah: 'Give heed to the law and to the testimony! Surely for this word which they speak there is no dawn, or light' (*Isaiah* 8.20). And even if the Septuagint translates this differently, reading 'gift' for 'dawn' or 'light', I simply cannot accept this. For I think that they were mistaken and confused the spelling of two Hebrew words, which, with one letter different mean 'gift' or 'dawn' or 'light' respectively.

That is all clear from the Old Testament. Similarly in the New Testament Holy Scripture is called 'The Word' (*Luke* 9. 12, 13, 15), 'The Word of God', 'The Word of Salvation' (*Acts* 13.26), 'The Word of the Gospel' (*Acts* 15.7), 'The Word of Grace' (*Acts* 20.32), 'The Word of Faith' (*Romans* 10.8), 'The Word of Wisdom and Knowledge' (*I Corinthians* 12. 8), 'The Word of Life' (*Philippians* 2.16), 'The Word of the Truth of the Gospel' (*Colossians* 1.5). What more should be added? Look again at 'the sacred writings which are able to instruct you for salvation' (*II Timothy* 3.15); add to this, 'For the word of God is living and active, sharper than any two-edged sword, piercing to the division of soul and spirit, of joints and marrow, and discerning the thoughts and intentions of the heart' (*Hebrews* 5.12). And for complete confirmation and so to speak the most unchangeable rule of all, take and hold onto the following passage: 'I warn every one who hears the words of the prophecy of this book: if anyone adds to them, God will add to him the plagues described in this book, and if anyone takes away from the words of the book of this prophecy, God will take away his share in the tree of life and in the holy city, which are described in this book' (*Revelation* 22.18-19). You see now how Holy Scripture testifies about itself as being sufficient and containing all things necessary for Salvation.

We must of course now consider:

(e) How the Holy Fathers witness together to Holy Scripture

In fact all the Eastern and Western Fathers (or the Greek and the Latin Fathers, as we might otherwise distinguish them) all say the same things one after the other. Nor, as Chrysostom says, does anyone deserve this name, who does not have the declaration of God's laws as a strict yoke and rule and guide. So let us therefore listen to them, as they sing the same song.

ATHANASIOS: 'The holy and inspired Scriptures are sufficient for the declaration of the Truth.' And again, 'For the texts of Scripture are sufficient and enough for us.'

CHRYSOSTOM: 'We shall find from there what we should learn, and what we should ignore; we shall find, too, how to show up what is false, what needs to be corrected, what needs to be learned for our consolation and encouragement, and if there is anything else that should be added' (*Homily 9 on II Timothy*).

And again, 'Do not wait for another teacher. You have the words of God, no-one will teach you as they do' (*Homily 9 on Colossians*).

And again, 'For [Scripture] is like a secure door, which forbids entry to heretics, and keeps us in safety over whatever we wish [to consider]' (*Homily 58 on St John's Gospel*).

BASIL: 'Whatever of faith is outside the inspired Scripture is sin' (*Commentary on Isaiah 2*).

'Question: Is it profitable for those who have recently come to the faith to study what the Scriptures contain straight away?

'Answer: This further question can be answered from the previous one. For it follows, and it is necessary for everyone according to their need to learn from the inspired Scripture to gather information about piety, and not to become attached to human traditions' (*Questions of Ascetics 65*).

'But those who accuse us argue that this is not their custom, and they take no notice of Scripture. What do we have to say to this? We do not think that their prevailing custom is right, to lay down a law or rule on what is correct teaching. For if custom is a strong argument for demonstrating correctness, what they say is lawful, and we should by all means follow them. So instead of that, let the inspired Scripture be our judge, and wherever doctrines agree with the divine words, they will always gain the vote of the Truth' (*Letter* 80).

CYRIL: 'We accept and understand and confess all that has been handed down to us through the Law and the Prophets and the Apostles. We look for nothing beyond these. For it is impossible to say or to conceive anything about God which goes against the things divinely spoken to us in the sacred words of the Old and New Testaments' (*On the Trinity*).

CYRIL OF JERUSALEM: 'Do not pay attention to my plausible arguments, for you could well be tricked by these. So unless you accept what the Prophets testify about each matter, and about the Virgin, do not believe what is said. Learn about place, time and manner from the Holy Scriptures, do not accept merely human testimony' (*Catechetical Instructions* 12).

'If it is possible, always keep as a seal on your mind that which has now been briefly said and summarised: the Lord will be proclaimed as far as possible through the proof provided by the Scriptures. For when speaking of the holy and divine mysteries of the faith, we must neither hand on whatever we wish without reference to the Holy Scriptures, nor simply bring forward an argument on the basis of the persuasiveness or artistry of our words. Do not simply believe me because I say these things, unless you can find proof of what is being proclaimed in the divine Scriptures. For the Salvation which our faith gives us is to be found not in plausible arguments, but in the proof which the divine Scriptures provide' (*Catechetical Instructions* 4).

EPIPHANIOS: 'We cannot find the answer to each question from one's own arguments, but from following the Scriptures' (*Against Heresies* 65).

THEODORET: 'Do not bring me human reasoning and arguments. For I am persuaded only by the Holy Scripture' (*Dialogue* 1:5).

CLEMENT OF ALEXANDRIA: 'For I would not simply pay attention to men who declare their opinions, and to whom it is equally possible to hold a contrary opinion. But if it is not enough simply to say "Glory be to God!" but we are required to believe what has been said, then we shall not be looking for testimony from men, but we shall find what we are seeking by putting our trust in the voice of the Lord, which is more trustworthy than any other proofs, or rather is the only real proof' (*Stromateis* 7).

CHRYSOSTOM: 'Do not despise our salvation, my beloved; for these things were all written for our instruction, for us upon whom the end of the ages has come.' And in addition, this most holy of the Fathers has written many many more such things, as can be seen from his *Third Homily on Lazarus*, and in his 'At your right hand stands the Queen' (*Psalm* 45.10), and similarly in a thousand other places.

I could say how not only Chrysostom but others praise the divine Scriptures using similes and parables, but I shall use just this one from Dionysios the Areopagite:

'Indeed these divine and spiritual oracles are likened to dew, water, milk, wine and honey. Their life-giving power is like that of water. They make us grow, as milk does. They revive us, as wine does. Like honey, they purge and protect us. These things the Divine Wisdom gives to those who come to her, and she produces an overflowing stream of abundant and endless festivities (that is what a true celebration means). That is why she is hymned as the life-giving, effective, renewing and nurturing one.'

That is what the testimony of the Holy Fathers tells us.

Now we must reply, as far as we can, to those who argue against us. We have two main groups of opponents, the 'Spirituals' or 'Enthusiasts' and the 'Papists'. One of these introduces a number of unwritten traditions additional to Scripture, the other literally disregards Scripture completely. Both argue against us in vain.

(a) And first about the 'Spirituals'. For is not that which they claim for themselves about the Spirit something which has been promised to all of us? 'When the Spirit of truth comes, he will guide you into all truth' (*John* 16.13). And again, 'How much more will the heavenly Father give the Holy Spirit to those who ask him' (*Luke* 11.13). Similarly, 'And they shall all be taught by God' (*John* 6.45). 'The Spirit helps us in our weaknesses' (*Romans* 8.26).

It may be that 'the written code kills, but the Spirit gives life' (*II Corinthians* 3.6), but that is why we are called 'ministers of a new covenant, not in a written code, but in the Spirit'.

How they are deceived, those who think that Scripture is of no use to them, when it is the Spirit who is at work in Scripture; when Scripture is so useful as an instrument, as a complete and full guide and rule; but no instrument or guide ever used itself, but they are there to be used by others. Holy Scripture contains all things necessary for salvation, including whatever within it are the things of the Spirit, who promises to provide these equally to all who seek them. If this is the case, what is so special about the 'Spirituals' or the 'Enthusiasts'?

(b) Those who introduce a number of unwritten traditions additional to Scripture are no more convincing. For what is meant by 'I handed on', by 'tradition', by 'I received', by 'handed down' and so on (*I Corinthians* 11.2 and 23; *II Thessalonians* 2.15 and 3.6), except the things handed down in Holy Scripture? This can never mean unwritten things.

As for unwritten things, who would dare to add any such things, after the rule sealed up in *Revelation* 22.18–19? For any addition is either necessary or unnecessary. If someone is wanting to introduce something thought to be necessary, let him listen to St Paul: 'But even if we, or an angel from heaven, should preach to you a gospel contrary to that which we preached to you, let him be accursed. As we have said before, so now I say again, If anyone is preaching to you a gospel contrary to that which you received, let him be accursed' (*Galatians* 1.8–9). But if an addition is not necessary, then it is nothing to do with us, for we are only talking here about additions thought to be necessary.

There the matter ends, so pay attention to all that I have said.

Our Question is:
*Whether Holy Scripture contains
all things necessary for Salvation?*

In order to respond to the charge, it was first necessary to establish 'What is Holy Scripture?'. This I sought to do by answering the following five questions:

(a) *Who is the author of Holy Scripture?*
(b) *Why was it written?*
(c) *How is it possible to discover why it was written?*
(d) *What does Holy Scripture tell us about itself?*
(e) *How do the Holy Fathers witness together to Holy Scripture?*

I then replied briefly, as far as was possible, to those who opposed my views. From all this it is clear that *Holy Scripture contains all things necessary for Salvation.*

We would summarise this as follows:

Its contents are, as God knows well, those things which above all are necessary for salvation, and it was written by God as that which is necessary for this.

Its contents are to do with mankind's salvation, and it was for this that it was written.

Its contents are about how we can attain salvation. (And the same testimony to Scripture is given both by the Holy and Inspired Scripture itself and, for good measure, by the Holy Fathers.)

Its contents contain all things necessary for Salvation.

Holy Scripture certainly contains all these things too.

Therefore indeed Holy Scripture contains all things necessary for Salvation.

Q.E.D.

Having demonstrated this to the best of my ability, I, your humble servant, present all this information with reverence and respect, through the certain proof and power given by the Blessed Spirit who himself also inspired the Holy Scripture.

Georgios Aptal

Questions and Answers

Question 1: According to *II Thessalonians* 2.15, 3.6 and *I Corinthians* 11.2 and 23 traditions are necessary in addition to Holy Scripture.

Answer: The speaker has already answered this point in his reply (b) to the 'Papists' above.

Question 2: Colossians 4.16 shows that some books of Holy Scripture have been lost. Some of the things that are necessary seem to have been lost with them, and so need to be supplied from traditions alone.

Answer: It is not clear that we have lost any of the Canonical Books – and these are what we are discussing. Nor is it clear that the letter from Laodicea, to which the Question refers, is any other than *I Timothy*, which was written before *Colossians*. For it is said to have been written from Laodicea, as can be seen from the end of the letter. When St Paul says: 'When this letter has been read among you, have it read also in the church of the Laodiceans; and see that you read also the letter from Laodicea', all that he wishes is that they should share the letter written to them with those in the church of the Laodiceans, and also that the one from Laodicea should in return be shared with them.

Question 3: According to *John* 16.12 Jesus did not pass on to his disciples all that was necessary: 'I have yet many things to say to you, but you cannot bear them now.' Should not those things which he left out be supplied, as I said earlier, from traditions alone?

Answer: This has nothing to do with traditions. For what he still had to say, which they could not yet bear, they were able both to hear and to bear when the Spirit of Truth spoke these same things to them and strengthened them. And this is promised clearly to them in the words which follow: 'When the Spirit of Truth comes, he will guide you into all the truth; for he will not speak on his own authority, but whatever he hears he will speak, and he will declare to you the things that are to come.' Similarly, as he said earlier, 'But the Counsellor, the Holy Spirit, whom the Father will send in my name, he will teach you all things, and bring to your remembrance all that I have said to you' (*John* 14.26). This he did,

(a) by bringing to their minds all that he had spoken to them: hence the Gospels;

(b) by teaching them all things: hence the teachings, namely the precepts of faith and piety written in the

Canonical Books, as they are called, the Letters of the Apostles, and in other Writings.

(c) by declaring the things to come, here and there in other Writings, but expressly or rather deliberately and one after another in the Revelation *par excellence*, in which the Canon is confirmed and completely sealed, in the words of *Revelation* 22.18–19. There is nothing more to be said about tradition.

Question 4: Holy Scripture teaches nothing at all about the Salvation of the Gentiles.

Answer: It teaches the same about them as it does about us; for we were once Gentiles, 'separated from Christ, alienated from the commonwealth of Israel, and strangers to the covenants of promise, having no hope and without God in the world' (*Ephesians* 2.11–12).

The Questioner: 'But now in Christ Jesus we who were once far off have been brought near in the blood of Christ' (*Ephesians* 2.13).

Answer: So with them, when they will be called.

The Questioner: I want to ask about those who are called. What does Holy Scripture teach about their Salvation?

Answer: The same as about the others, namely that 'there is Salvation in no-one else' but in Christ Jesus, 'for there is no other name under heaven given among men by which we must be saved' (*Acts* 4.12).

The Questioner: True, but what about those to whom that name is not given, as we read in *Romans* 10.14: 'How are they to believe in him of whom they have never heard? And how are they to hear without a preacher?'

Answer: Although all the Gentiles have not yet heard, they will in time, for it is said: 'as the lightning flashes and lights up the sky from one side to the other, so will the Son of Man be in his day' (*Luke* 17.24). And 'the Gentiles will glorify

God, as it is written, "Therefore I will praise thee among the Gentiles" ' (*Romans* 15.9 and 10–12).

The Questioner: But what has this to do with people now alive?

Answer: It is indisputable that God can communicate himself, his truth and his grace – but in what way we do not know, and it is not up to us to determine whether he does this. 'The secret things belong to the Lord our God, but the things that are revealed belong to us and to our children for ever, to do all the words of this law' (*Deuteronomy* 29.29). The argument I am putting forward should be sufficient, namely that Holy Scripture contains all things necessary for salvation for those to whom it is revealed; but it is not necessary that it should be revealed before the appropriate time.

Question 5: If Holy Scripture contains all things necessary for salvation, does it do so when we take it as a whole, or when we look at each part?

Answer: It is the same thing, we agree, whether Holy Scripture is taken as a whole or in part.

The Questioner: But if Holy Scripture, taken in part, contains all things necessary for salvation, then is not the rest quite superfluous?

Answer: No. For some things were given at one time only or in one place, such as most of the things in the Old Testament; some things were given to some people, but 'everyone to whom much is given, of him will much be required' (*Luke* 12.48). Nor must the same word be given each time, as one person will be given one talent and another five talents. And there are some things which are, so to speak, primarily and chiefly necessary for salvation, while other things are secondarily and to a certain extent so. Those things which are primarily and chiefly necessary are those which are necessary for the salvation of simply anyone whoever they are; those which are secondarily and to some extent necessary are those which in any way contribute towards the manifestation of the truth, the wisdom and the power of God, such as those mystical, symbolic, historical or political things, which are not necessarily accompanied by saving grace or saving faith.

Question 6: Before Salvation (such as that of the Patriarchs) came to men, it [Scripture] did not contain all things necessary for Salvation; but Salvation came to men before Scripture did.

Answer: Not at all; for Scripture was contemporary with the first promise about 'the woman's seed' (*Genesis* 3.15). Here we must make a distinction: for by Scripture we mean either that which is made of paper and ink or that of which this is a symbol, that is to say that which it signifies. Now Salvation is older than that which is made of paper and ink (which is the outward or material form of Scripture, and this was not written down before Moses). It is different however with that of which it is a symbol, namely the promise and the grace which comes through this, for Salvation always accompanies these whenever and in whatever way these are provided. In accordance with which Jesus Christ (who was himself 'the promised seed'), 'the pioneer and perfecter of our faith' (*Hebrews* 12.2) is 'the same yesterday and today and for ever' (*Hebrews* 13.8).

Question 7: Scripture leads to our destruction, according to *II Peter* 3.16, for in it 'there are some things hard to understand, which the ignorant and unstable twist to their own destruction, as they do the other scriptures'.

Answer: It is they themselves, not the Holy Scriptures, that lead them to destruction. For this does not happen to such readers because of what they read, but because of how they twist the Scriptures. If this happens to the ignorant and unstable, the reason that they are ignorant and unstable lies in themselves, not in Holy Scripture. Unless perhaps their greater keenness in other matters (alas for those who do this) makes them ignorant and unstable in this matter.

Question 8: The holy sacraments, both baptism and the eucharist (and these are both necessary for salvation) are not adequately described [in Holy Scripture]. Baptism is inadequately described in *Matthew* 28.19 because children are not mentioned. The instructions about the eucharist in *Matthew* 26.26–29 and in *Luke* 22.19–20 are obscure and difficult to understand. How great a danger is there because of this? 'For anyone who eats and drinks unworthily without discerning the body of the Lord eats and drinks judgment upon himself' (*I Corinthians* 11.29).

Answer (a): The same thing is said about the baptism of children as is said about the baptism of others, for no distinction is to be made by us between those between whom the Lawgiver made none. Nor indeed did any of the Apostles ever make a distinction between them: Paul baptized the household of Stephanas (*I Corinthians* 1.15). The jailer and all his family were baptized (*Acts* 16.33), and, it is said, 'the whole family believed in God' (*Acts* 16.34). Lydia and her household were also baptized (*Acts* 16.15). And on the day of Pentecost, there came about the fulfilment of that which the Baptist prophesied: 'He will baptize you with the Holy Spirit and with fire' (*Matthew* 3.11); and this is what was also spoken of by the prophet Joel: 'And in the last days it shall be, God declares, that I will pour out my Spirit upon all flesh' (*Acts* 2.17). And to those who asked him 'What shall we do?', Peter replied: 'Repent, and be baptized every one of you, for the promise is to you and to your children and to all that are far off' (*Acts* 3.37–39). By 'those that are far off' he meant the Gentiles; for according to *Isaiah* 33.13 and 57.19 and *Ephesians* 2.13 the Gentiles are 'those who are far off'. So this confirms that the promise is 'to you and to your children' whether they are Jews or Gentiles.

Nor should anyone look down on children as if they were without experience of faith and repentance (without which it is not possible to be baptized). For if they had been, our Saviour would not have said 'Let the children come to me, and do not hinder them; for to such belongs the kingdom of heaven' (*Matthew* 19.14). But how do they possess faith or repentance? Paul said: 'Your children are holy' (*I Corinthians* 7.14). Through what holiness? Through that which has already, so to speak, been agreed, namely through the holiness of their parents, in whom they have been sanctified. And what is there to prevent the baptism of those who are holy, whether they are children or adults?

Answer (b): My reply is as follows to your statement, my dear fellow, that the instructions given about the Holy Sacrament of the eucharist are obscure and difficult to understand: They are not so obscure and incomprehensible that each of us cannot be convinced in our own minds what we should do. For our Lord's words, 'This is my body, this is my blood', are a simple statement, they are not obscure or difficult. Anyone who hears them understands clearly what is meant by body and blood: is it not equally clear that the bread is the body and the wine is the blood?

Let us examine how this should be understood. The Saviour said, 'Take, eat, drink'. He did not say, 'Take, eat, drink that which is not present'. Nor did he say, 'Take, eat, drink myself, who am present with you'. The disciples would not have understood it if that was what he had said.

Nor did he tell them to take something other than what he himself took. He himself took the bread and the wine, and he said of the bread, 'This is my body', and of the wine, 'This is my blood'.

What was the body, what was the blood? The body in which he himself then lived? The blood which was then carried about in his body? Would any of his disciples have dared to ask that? And would any of them have dared to eat, if he had given them that body? Would any of them have dared to drink, if he had offered them that blood? I do not think so.

But this is what he said: 'This is my body given for you. This is my blood poured out for many'. Was it then given? Was it then poured out? It was not. What then? It would be given, it would be poured out.

If he had given his body then, if he had poured out his blood at that moment, would this have done any good? It would never have been for the forgiveness of sins, for which he said this would be done. For this all took place before he became an offering and a sacrifice for sins, before he was crucified. It was necessary therefore that his body and his blood should signify things that were not then present.

But when he became an offering and a sacrifice, did not these things become present to those who eat? In no way, by no means. For after he had offered himself as a sacrifice on the cross, he was buried, he rose again, he ascended into heaven, where he now is, as it is said, 'whom heaven must receive until the time of universal restoration comes' (*Acts* 3.21). So 'how can this man give us his flesh to eat' (*John* 6.52) or his blood to drink?

It is time now to look at what follows from these things.

If Jesus said: 'Take, eat, drink' that which was then present;

If that which was then present was the bread and the wine;

And if that about which he said 'Take' was also what he took;

If that bread and that wine were what he said, namely his body and his blood;

But if neither his body nor his blood was perceptible to the senses, for he did not 'take' these, it being impossible for him to take his own body and blood separately from himself,

whereas what he did take was separate from him; what conclusion now comes from what follows from these things? One,
clearly: all these things are spiritual matters; the bread is to be
taken spiritually as his body, and the wine is similarly to be
taken spiritually as his blood.

He himself in fact spoke beforehand that we must indeed
take it all in this way. He did so very exactly as can be seen
from his discourse about eating his flesh and drinking his
blood in *John* 6.26–63. It is not possible to eat his flesh and to
drink his blood except in this holy sacrament. His words were
these: 'It is the spirit that gives life, the flesh is of no avail; the
words that I have spoken to you' (and his words were 'take,
eat, this is my body given for you, take, drink, this is my blood;
my body is given for you, my blood is poured out for many)
'they are spirit and life'. Spirit, since they are spoken by me;
life, since this comes to those of you who receive these with
faith. And so now, when all have received, the instructions
about the holy sacrament of the eucharist no longer seem to
have been obscure and difficult to understand. If it were not
so, we could never come to the conclusion from this that Holy
Scripture contains all things necessary for salvation.

APPENDIX

Cyril of Jerusalem: 'Come, and with joy eat your bread,
that spiritual bread.' 'Those who did not hear what was said in
a spiritual sense, went away scandalised, imagining that it was
an invitation to cannibalism' (*Catecheses* 4).

Chrysostom: 'Our soul is spiritually blinded, whenever we
do not partake of our food in a spiritual manner' (*Homily* 3 *on
Ephesians*).

Theodoret: 'He honoured the visible symbols with the
designation "body and blood", not by changing their nature,
but by adding grace to nature.' 'You are caught in nets of your

own weaving! For after the consecration the sacramental symbols do not change from their own nature, but remain what they were before in their own being, shape and form. We see and touch what was there before; but we perceive and believe what they have become, and we venerate them as being that which we believe' (*Dialogue* 2).

Ephraim Patriarch of Antioch: 'So also when the body of Christ is received by the faithful, it does not change from being that which is perceived by the senses, but it also remains inseparable from the grace which is perceived therein.'

Makarios of Egypt: 'In the church bread and wine are offered as signs of his flesh and blood; and those who receive that which is outwardly visible as bread, spiritually eat the Lord's flesh' (*Homily* 27).

SECOND LECTURE

O UR FATHER, Which art in Heaven, Hallowed be thy
  name &c.

The Questioner: ROGER BOURCHIER of BRITAIN
The Responder: GEORGIOS MAROULES of SMYRNA

THE QUESTION:

Whether Holy Scripture should be read by all?

The Tutor's Introduction.

After opening your eyes (O educated ones) to see the
wonderful things of the law, that is to say the things contained
in Holy Scripture which are necessary for salvation, what now
hinders you from reading these? St Paul says, 'If anyone is
preaching to you a gospel contrary to that which you received,
let him be accursed' (*Galatians* 1.9). So what should be said to
those who are unwilling to receive us and the gospel which we
have? Not to read it is the same thing as not receiving it. O
the hypocrisy of those pseudo-evangelists! They preach the
importance of accuracy in our faith and piety, yet they also
condemn the one sure rule of faith and piety! 'Their venom is
like that of a serpent', says the royal Psalmist, 'as that of a deaf
asp, that stops her ears' (*Psalm* 58.4). Now the first stratagem
of the ancient serpent (who is the Devil or Satan) is to disarm
those with whom he is at war. But Holy Scripture is indeed
'the whole armour of God' which we 'put on, and so are able
to withstand in the evil day'. From it comes 'the truth, having
girded our loins' with which 'we stand firm'; from it too comes
'the breastplate of righteousness', which we must 'put on';

from it comes 'the equipment of the gospel of peace', with which 'our feet are shod'; from it we can 'take the shield of faith, with which we can quench all the flaming darts of the evil one'; from it we can 'take the helmet of salvation, and the sword of the Spirit, which is the word of God' (*Ephesians* 6.13–17). And having obtained victory (O fellow-soldiers in Christ) and glory, never despair; for thus you will 'resist the Devil and he will flee from you' (*James* 4.7). Three times Jesus triumphed over him with the words 'IT IS WRITTEN' (*Matthew* 4.4, 7, 10), and he gave to his disciples for ever the power to triumph over the devil through this.

The Tutor to GEORGIOS MAROULES who was now to speak:

And now to arms (O fully-armed one) and to victory!

Response of the speaker:

Willingly I hasten towards the arms you command me to take up, for I would despair of victory completely unless you had armed me with the shield that you yourself (O mighty champion) have worn.

The Question is: Whether Holy Scripture should be read by all?

I say, Yes, it should be.

It has already been established in the first lecture that Holy Scripture contains all things necessary for salvation. It follows therefore, and this is the subject of our enquiry, that the same should be read by all. For how absurd it would be to declare that Holy Scripture is of such great benefit to people, whom we then forbade to use it at all! Let them tell me, those who, not only as I might say in an unchristian way but in an inhuman manner dominate and tyrannize over the conscience of their spiritual equals, how they will answer on that day when the books are opened, and they will all be judged by the Gospel, which they wrongly kept to themselves? Christ says, 'till heaven and earth pass away, not an iota, not a dot, will pass from the law until all is accomplished' (*Matthew* 5.18). But they say, 'not one iota or dot, whatsoever it be, will be passed on to anyone, unless we ourselves decide to whom and how much of it'.

'Love is the fulfilling of the law' (*Romans* 10.10), but how can they fulfil it if they refuse to let a brother have this priceless treasure, God's greatest gift to us?

The Apostle Paul asks: 'Then what advantage has the Jew? Or what is the value of circumcision? Much in every way. To begin with, the Jews are entrusted with the oracles of God' (*Romans* 3.1–2). But what advantage would it be to a Christian not to be entrusted with them?

'What is written in the law?' was the Teacher's reply to the lawyer who asked him, 'What shall I do to inherit eternal life?' (*Luke* 10.25). No greater question was ever put to him, nor any greater answer given by him. Moreover, Philip said to the eunuch: 'Do you understand what you are reading?' (*Acts* 8.30). Yet those others say, 'How are you not afraid to read? How arrogantly you also behave, thinking you can read or understand! Salvation is what Holy Scripture teaches; all that it contains is for our Salvation; see that you have nothing to do with it!' In this way they terrify us, thinking that only they are worthy members of the Church, and not granting Salvation of any kind to anyone else outside their own Church.

So I want to ask them one question, and let them answer me: if there is so much danger in understanding the things that bring us Salvation, how great is the danger in knowing nothing at all that brings Salvation to us?

These matters would seem to have been addressed already, as being close to those in the first lecture on 'Whether Holy Scripture contains all things necessary for salvation?'

Now as to the matter of reading it, and how it is possible for all to do this together, I shall try to demonstrate:

> (a) What Holy Scripture is about, and whether it is about the surpassing excellence of the things it contains.
>
> (b) Who is the author of Holy Scripture, and why it was written.
>
> (c) What God commanded us about reading it.
>
> (d) How first the Jews and then the Christians obeyed this command. I shall also add some excellent quotations from the holy Fathers about reading the Sacred Writings.

(a) What Holy Scripture is about, and whether it is about the surpassing excellence of the things it contains.

It is about the works of God himself;

About 'his eternal power and divinity', and about how 'his invisible nature has been clearly perceived in the things that have been made' (*Romans* 1.20);

About his goodness, his righteousness, his truth and his wisdom;

About the divine providence exercised over all things in accordance with these qualities, and in other words also about his grace exercised over man;

About what creation is, what redemption is, and how 'God made man upright, but he has sought out many devices' (*Ecclesiastes* 7.30);

How 'all have sinned and fall short of the glory of God' (*Romans* 3.23);

How those who have sinned may be restored 'being justified by his grace as a gift, through the redemption which is in Christ Jesus' (*Romans* 3.24);

I refrain from saying (as it is beyond us) 'that through the church the manifold wisdom of God has been made known to the principalities and powers in the heavenly places, according to the eternal purpose which he has realised in Christ Jesus' (*Ephesians* 3.10–11);

That he 'chose us before the foundation of the world' (*Ephesians* 1.4);

That he 'destined us to be his sons' (*Ephesians* 1.5). These are all great mysteries, but here they have been revealed.

In addition, where else could we find:

The antiquity and authenticity of history?

The solemnity and magnificence of the stories that are told?

The glory of prophecies both those already fulfilled and those that will be fulfilled?

The perfection of the law?

The beauty and good order of rites and ceremonies?

The truth and accuracy of those earthly forms which correspond so closely to the heavenly realities which are here described?

'O the depth of the riches and wisdom and knowledge of God!' (*Romans* 11.33). Who would refuse to read the Scriptures after hearing all this? Who would not keep vigil outside the doors of Wisdom? For as Jacob said, when he awoke, about the place where he had slept, 'This is none other than the house of God, and this is the gate of heaven' (*Genesis* 28.17). So also we can say of Holy Scripture, 'This is where God dwells'. For every book, every chapter, the whole of the Old Testament and the whole of the New, all disclose his presence. It is indeed the gate of heaven. What great things, what mysteries it reveals! And what diligence and attention it deserves, or even competitive or friendly rivalry in struggling with it!

That is my answer to the first question, what is Holy Scripture about, and whether it is about the surpassing excellence of the things it contains.

(b) Who was the author of Holy Scripture, and why was it written?

Who was its author but God himself alone? This is why it is said to be 'inspired by God' (*II Timothy* 3.16). For 'no prophecy ever came by the impulse of man, but moved by the Holy Spirit, holy men of God spoke' (*II Peter* 1.21).

Divine inspiration is to be established in many different ways.

(a) From the things recorded about it, for it includes the following: 'And the Lord spoke all these words, saying, I am the Lord your God &c' (*Exodus* 20.1). It is clear that it is God who spoke because of all the signs and wonders which he performed at that time, and because of the power by which Moses received from his mouth the words that he had written. 'And there rose up no more a prophet in Israel like Moses, whom the Lord knew face to face, in all the signs and wonders which the Lord sent him to work in the land of Egypt on Pharaoh and his servants' (*Deuteronomy* 34.10–11).

(b) From the internal evidence or impression of divine authorship, which is not to be found elsewhere, such as the grandeur, sublimity, purity or holiness of the word, and its absolute truthfulness and perfection, and, above all, the demonstration and power of the Holy Spirit's work and collaboration. 'For the word of God is living and active, sharper than any two-edged sword, piercing to the division of soul and spirit, of joints and marrow, and discerning the thoughts and intentions of the heart' (*Hebrews* 4.12).

(c) From the mysteries that are investigated therein, such as that of the Holy Trinity, or the incarnation of Christ, the true worship of God, the resurrection of the dead, life eternal, and so on.

(d) That Scripture is from God is shown by its antiquity and by the fact that in the face of every danger, every device of the devil or of men it remains invincible and unconquerable, and as St Peter says, 'the word of the Lord abides for ever' (*I Peter* 1.25).

(e) This is also shown by the fact that it 'tells beforehand the latter events before they come to pass' (*Isaiah* 46.10). For the ability to foretell and also to fulfil that which was foretold belongs only to God.

(f) So does the evident unanimity between the Old and New Testaments, and of all the parts of each with one another, and the fact that all writers of all nations, times and places, wherever the fame of Scripture has spread, have the same opinion of its truth and authority.

That is my answer, for the first part of this chapter, to the question 'Who is the author of Holy Scripture?'

The second part answers the question
'Why was it written?'
The answer is clear from what has been written, which we touched on above in examining 'What Scripture is about':

For we spoke about:

>The goodness, righteousness, truth and wisdom of God,
>Divine providence,
>God's grace,
>Man's creation and redemption,
>The restoration of sinners,
>The manifold wisdom of God,
>His choosing us before the foundation of the world,
>Our being destined to be his sons.

Now in saying all this about Holy Scripture as being inspired by God, we also answered the question, why God wrote the Scriptures, namely for the salvation of mankind, which is the aim and purpose of all these things.

Now let us hear how Scripture itself makes this clear. And first, St Peter says of the Old Testament: 'As the outcome of your faith you obtain the salvation of your souls. The prophets who prophesied of the grace that was to be yours searched and inquired about this salvation' (*I Peter* 1.9–10). Whilst St Paul speaks as follows about the New: 'For I am not ashamed of the gospel: it is the power of God for salvation to every one who has faith, to the Jew first and also to the Greek' (*Romans* 1.16). And again, 'In him you also, who have heard the word of truth, the gospel of your salvation and have believed in him, were sealed with the promised Holy Spirit' (*Ephesians* 1.13). And again, 'For the grace of God has appeared for the salvation of all men, training us to renounce irreligion and worldly passions, and to live sober, upright and godly lives in this world, awaiting our blessed hope, the appearing of the glory of our great God and our Saviour Jesus Christ, who gave himself for us to redeem us from all iniquity and to purify for himself a people of his own who are zealous for good deeds' (*Titus* 2.11–14).

And St Paul speaks of the Old and New Testaments, that is the whole of Scripture together, 'All scripture is inspired by God and profitable for teaching, for reproof, for correction, and for training in righteousness' (*II Timothy* 3.16). And in the preceding verse, 'You have been acquainted with the sacred writings which are able to instruct you for salvation' (*II Timothy* 3.15). And again, 'For whatever was written in former days was written for our instruction, that by steadfastness and by the encouragement of the scriptures we might have hope' (*Romans* 15.4). And again in the Gospels, 'These are written that you may believe that Jesus is the Christ, the Son of God, and that believing you may have life in his name' (*John* 20.31). Let that much be said for our second chapter; now it is time to look at the third, namely:

(c) What God commanded us about reading Holy Scripture.

God gave us instructions in both Testaments. In the Old, he said to all the people: 'And these words, all that I command you this day, shall be in your heart and in your soul. And you shall teach them to your children, and you shall speak of them sitting in the house, and walking by the way, and lying down, and rising up. And you shall fasten them for a sign upon your hand, and it shall be immovable before your eyes' (*Deuteronomy* 6.6–8). And these words are specifically directed to the king: 'And when he is established on his throne of government, he shall read this book of the law all the days of his life, that he may learn to fear the Lord your God, and to keep all these commandments' (*Deuteronomy* 17.18–19).

What God commanded, Christ also commanded. 'You search the scriptures, because you think that in them you have eternal life; and it is they that bear witness to me' (*John* 5.39). St Paul also exhorts this: 'Let the word of Christ dwell in you richly, in all wisdom, as you teach and admonish one another, and as you sing psalms and hymns and spiritual songs with thankfulness in your hearts to the Lord' (*Colossians* 3.16). And St Peter praised the word of the Lord, adding: 'You will do well to pay attention to this' (*II Peter* 1.19).

That is my reply to the question about God's commands.

(d) How first the Jews and then the Christians obeyed this command.

It is clear from what has just been said how the king and all the people had each to read every day the command (called 'Sema' from its first word) 'Hear O Israel, the Lord our God is one Lord' &c (*Deuteronomy* 6.4).

The Hebrews therefore went through the law, dividing it into suitable sections (called 'Parseioth'), one for each Sabbath throughout the year.

During the tyranny of Antiochus the ungodly, who deprived them of the temple and all worship there, and took from them both the Sabbaths and circumcision, as well as burning the books of the law, and completely forbidding the reading of it, they substituted readings of the prophets in sections as they had previously done with the law. And these sections which were substituted in this way for those of the law were called 'Aftaroth'.

This practice is confirmed by the account of the Synod in Jerusalem: 'For from early generations Moses has had in every city those who preach him, for he is read every Sabbath in the synagogues' (*Acts* 15.21).

It is confirmed too by what Jesus did when 'he came to Nazareth, where he had been brought up; and he went to the synagogue, as his custom was, on the Sabbath day. And he stood up to read; and there was given to him the book of the prophet Isaiah. He opened the book and found the place where it was written, "The Spirit of the Lord" &c' (*Luke* 4.16–18).

What Jesus did, his disciples and the Jews did also, as can be seen from this passage: 'And on the Sabbath day they went into the synagogue and sat down. After the reading of the law and the prophets, the rulers of the synagogue sent to them &c' (*Acts* 13.14–15).

We do the same, as all Christians have always done, except when, as now, where he rules, Antichrist forbids the reading of Holy Scripture.

Now it is time to add the testimony of the Fathers. This is so vast, that we must be content with the following.

CHRYSOSTOM: 'Listen, whoever is in the world, and tell your wife and children that you are allowed to read the Scriptures, and not simply randomly, but with great care' (*Homily 9 on Colossians*).

'Listen, all lay people, I beg you to buy books that will provide medicine for your souls. If this is what you wish, at least acquire the New Testament, and the Acts of the Apostles and the Gospels will be your constant teachers' (*Homily 9 on Colossians*).

'But what defence is given against my complaints? "I am not a monk", a man says. "I have a wife and children, and houses to take care of." Yet this is what spoils everything, your idea that reading the Holy Scriptures is only for monks. Yet your need is far greater than theirs; for it is those who go round in public, and are wounded every day, who most need healing of this kind' (*Homily 2 on the Gospel of Matthew*).

'This is the respect in which we are better than animals, even if for other reasons we are very much less than them. It is the nourishment of our souls, it is our world, it is our security. Just as not to listen to Scripture means hunger and decay. For I shall not give them, he says, a hunger for bread and a thirst for water, but a hunger for hearing the word of God. So what could be more wretched than automatically bringing on your own head the evil which God threatens by way of punishment' (*Homily 2 on the Gospel of Matthew*).

'For it is not necessary on your return from worship to throw yourself into matters that have nothing to do with worship, but as soon as you reach home you should get hold of your Bible and call your wife and children and share with them a summary of what has been said in church' (*Homily 5 on the Gospel of Matthew*).

'We should therefore blush and be ashamed of ourselves. For a woman who has had five husbands, and is a Samaritan, has shown such serious concern for doctrines, that she has not been concerned with the time of day or anything else, but has made sure that nothing has kept her away from enquiring into these things. Whereas we not only do not enquire into matters of doctrine, but we simply pay attention quite randomly to everything. For this reason, we are careless about everything. For which of us, tell me, when at home, has taken a Christian book in his hands and looked at its contents, and has then searched the Scriptures? None of us would say we have, but instead we shall find that most possess dice and draughts, but nowhere are there books, except among a few. And those who possess them have the same attitude as those who do not, for they have them bound and always keep them in boxes, and are keen to admire the quality of the parchment or the beauty of the lettering, not actually to read them' (*Homily* 32 *on the Gospel of John*).

'For the Scriptures were not given only so that we should have them in books, but in order that we should inscribe them on our hearts' (*Homily* 32 *on the Gospel of John*).

'And this I say, far from forbidding it, I urge you to acquire books, and very much pray that you will do so. For I wish that both their words and meanings should be carried round in our thoughts and minds' (*Homily* 32 *on the Gospel of John*).

'Ignorance of the Scriptures is the source from which a thousand evils have grown. From this sprang the great outrage of the heresies, wasted lives and fruitless labours. For just as those deprived of the light cannot walk straight, so those who do not look towards the rays which shine from the sacred Scriptures, are bound to sin often and continually, for they are walking in the most terrible darkness' (*Introduction to Romans*).

CLEMENT OF ROME: 'Call to mind the words of Christ and study them continuously, for Scripture says to you, "Meditate on the law day and night, walking in the country, sitting in the house, lying down and rising up, that you may be wise in all things" ' (*Apostolic Constitutions* 1.4, quoting *Joshua* 1.7-8; *Deuteronomy* 6.7).

'Then either approach the faithful and Orthodox, and speak with them and share with them the life-giving words, or sit at home and read the law, the books of the Kings, the Prophets, sing the psalms of David, and go carefully through the Gospel, the fulfilment of all these' (*Apostolic Constitutions* 1.5).

IGNATIUS: 'Fathers, bring up your children through the Lord's teaching and admonition, and teach them the Sacred writings.'

EUSEBIUS: 'With us, a simple reading of the Holy Scriptures is given to those who are recent converts, who are still developing their understanding, and are "babes" in their souls as it were; at the same time tell them to believe in both Old and New Testaments as the words of God. But those who are intellectually well advanced, who are "greybeards" mentally, are allowed to deepen and test their understanding of what is said' (*Preparation for the Gospel* 12).

BASIL: 'All Scripture is inspired and useful, and was therefore written by the Holy Spirit as a sort of "surgery for souls", so that we might each choose the medicine we need for the disease we each suffer from' (*Homily* 1 *on the Psalms*).

CYRIL OF JERUSALEM: 'If you have a zeal for knowledge, then find out from the church which are the Books of the Old Testament, and which are those of the New. Do not for my sake read any of the Apocryphal books, for if you do not as yet know those which are accepted by all, why labour in vain on the disputed ones? Read the Holy Scriptures, the twenty books of the Old Testament.

'Read these twenty-two books. Have nothing to do with the Apocrypha. Read these only, and read them diligently' (*Catecheses* 4).

THEODORET: 'He did not wish that only five or ten people, or fifteen or a hundred or twice that number should drink the water of salvation from the streams of the Gospel, but all people, Greeks and barbarians, the literate and the illiterate, shoemakers and weavers, coppersmiths and other skilled workers; and, as well as those, slaves and beggars, farmers and foresters, and women too, both those surrounded by wealth and those tied to hard work, as well as those compelled to live on alms.' And he writes also: "Shall I neglect the Scriptures? But where then does knowledge come from? Shall I abandon knowledge? Where then does faith come from?" Paul cries out, "How are they to believe without hearing?" and again, "So faith comes from what is heard, and what is heard comes by the word of God" (*Romans* 10.14, 17). If preaching the word is forbidden, then hearing is blocked and believing is excluded. It may not be dangerous for anyone to be ignorant of the laws of the Romans; but what treachery do they not work by forbidding the study and learning of the great decrees of the King of the heavens! Scripture is the soul's nourishment; so, my dear fellow, will you not stop starving the inner man to death, and instead work up a fierce hunger, not for bread and water, but for hearing the word of the Lord? If someone else wounds you, are you going to forbid the application of medicines, or an end to your declaration that the manifold wisdom of medical books is useless? You should respect that eunuch who was in charge of all the Queen's treasure, but was so fond of study that he never stopped reading throughout his journey' (*Graecarum Affectionum Curatio* 8).

Georgios Maroules

Questions & Answers

Question 1: The laity are not fit to be hearers or readers of Holy Scripture, since they are uneducated and ignorant about what is said therein.

Answer: The things that are necessary for salvation are not so difficult to understand that, among those who are otherwise somewhat uneducated and ignorant, any who are fit for salvation cannot accept them.

The Questioner: Your argument is undermined by the following: 'There are some things in them hard to understand, which the ignorant twist to their own destruction, as they do the other scriptures' (*II Peter* 3.16), which means that they are not fit to be hearers or readers of the Holy Scriptures, since 'the ignorant twist the Holy Scriptures like that.' End of argument.

The Speaker: The Apostle says 'ignorant and *unstable*'. Your argument follows from those who are unstable rather than those who are ignorant. When they are both, this is the result of their laziness and bad attitudes; people do not twist things if they just read them, nor if they are merely ignorant.

The Questioner: I can prove the opposite. For from whence have grown a thousand evils? From whence has sprung the great outrage of the heresies, wasted lives and fruitless labours? From the same place as that twisting of Scripture. For 'from ignorant people reading the Scriptures the great outrage of the heresies has sprung, together with wasted lives'. End of argument.

The Speaker: I refuse to accept defeat. I can even recall that Bellarmine used the same argument in a similar way. But Chrysostom's exact words, I remember, were as follows: 'I am amazed that he somehow twisted these things too; for *ignorance of the Scriptures* is the source from which a thousand evils have grown. From this sprang the great outrage of the heresies, wasted lives and fruitless labours' (*Introduction to Romans*).

The Tutor: The boy has answered well, and not ignorantly! And I would like to add something else myself; for on the subject of heresies church history shows that almost all the great heretics were not from the laity nor from the uneducated but rather from those who were educated; they were philosophers or even clergy. These included Marcion, Aetius, Arius, and Anastasius who were all presbyters; and Hyales, Acacius, Achillas, Macedonius, Nestorius, Sergius and Dioscorus, who were all bishops.

Question 2: The Church forbade the reading of Holy Scripture, 'and if someone refuses to listen to the church, let him be to you as a Gentile and a tax collector' (*Matthew* 18.17).

The Speaker: It is rather the one who does not read Scripture who is to be treated as a Gentile! But on what you have said, about the Church forbidding the reading of Scripture, I want to distinguish between:

The Church as a whole or the Church in part;

The Church as pure and uncorrupt or the Church as impure and corrupt.

My reply is, first, that the whole Church does not forbid this now, nor will it ever do so.

My second reply is that any pure and uncorrupt Church does not forbid this. We do not care what an impure and corrupt church determines; in fact we can know that it is impure and corrupt from the fact that it forbids the reading of Holy Scripture. 'If anyone takes away from the words of the book of this prophecy, God will take away his share in the tree of life and in the holy city [which means the church] which are described in this book' (*Revelation* 22.19). So what could be even more terrible or unbearable than to take away the whole book, which is what those who forbid the reading of it are doing?

The Tutor: Well said, my boy; and add to your reply the description of the church as 'the pillar and bulwark of the truth' (*I Timothy* 3.15), for how could it be either if 'in its wickedness it suppressed the truth' (*Romans* 1.18)? And what is a worse example of 'suppressing the truth in wickedness' than to forbid the showing of Scripture to those to whom it was given for their salvation? A 'pillar of the truth' declares to all publicly what is lawful and customary, a 'bulwark of the truth' confirms this.

The Questioner: But Christ himself forbade this, saying, 'Do not give dogs what is holy; do not throw pearls before swine' (*Matthew* 7.6). Is it not therefore not permitted for the laity to read Holy Scripture?

The Speaker: (a) It does not seem that Christ is saying this about Holy Scripture.

(b) Nor does it seem that the laity are to be described as dogs. Let no-one say that, let no-one ever bark that out in contradiction; for, look, if the laity are called dogs, how could the Church ever make them partakers of Holy Baptism or of the Holy Eucharist? Would that not be 'to take the children's bread and throw it to the dogs' (*Matthew* 15.26)?

The Questioner: But God himself forbade this: 'But to the sinner God has said, "Why do you declare my ordinances, and take up my covenant in your mouth?"' (*Psalm* 50.16).

The Speaker: God does not here forbid the reading of Holy Scripture, but only reproves those who read it irreverently, without understanding, or unworthily.

The Questioner: But elsewhere Christ says distinctly to his disciples, 'To you it has been given to know the secrets of the kingdom of heaven, but to them it has not been given' (*Matthew* 13.11). Surely therefore it is not permitted for the laity to read Holy Scripture.

The Speaker: Even if it has not been given to them to know, it has been given to them to hear (for Christ would not have declared that they should not hear), which, as regards the manifestation of the truth, is the same as reading. And what he now gave to his disciples, he intended to give to all through his disciples; for he added this command also: 'Go therefore and make disciples of all nations, teaching them to observe all that I have commanded you' (*Matthew* 28.19–20).

The Questioner: These words of Gregory of Nazianzus are well-known: 'Philosophising about God is not for all, not for everyone. Does that not cheapen it and bring it down to the level of the earthly-minded?' And I would add, it is not for every occasion, nor for everybody, nor for ever.

Response: His own reply to this is also well-known: 'There are occasions when it is appropriate, and people for whom it is so, and for how much time can also be reckoned'; and, as the Apostle says, it is appropriate 'for those who have their faculties trained by practice to distinguish good from bad' (*Hebrews* 5.14).

The Tutor: It is a fine contest, my good people, in which you have engaged today, and my hope is that no-one will ever take away from you that over which you have wrestled, namely the Holy Scriptures. And as Chrysostom says, and I do too, 'If you are eager and willing to pay attention to the reading of Scripture, you will never need anything else' (*Introduction to Romans*).

The grace of our Lord Jesus Christ, and the love of God, and the fellowship of the Holy Spirit be with you all. Amen.

END

To Her Most Excellent Majesty,

The most humble Address

Of the *Greek* Youths Residing in *Oxford*.

Rendred in English.

*S*HEBA's great Queen wise *Solomon* to hear,
     To see what works could with his Wisdom bear
     An Equal Vye, to see the Court, and Train
Fit such a Majesty to entertain,
Comes from remotest parts, but when She came,
How short was all, that could be said by Fame?

     Fame guiding too, far from our Country We
Came in a Queen a *Solomon* to see!
Such is her Meen, so vaste her Mind, so great
Her mighty Works, such, who her Royal Seat
Attend, the Wise, the Great, the Good, Her Court
Where Men, and Vertues equally resort:
Such are Her well built Cities, Rich with Trade
And busy Commerce, but still Richer made
By what so much all other Wealth Excels,
The Piety that there with Vertue dwells.

     Such too Her Universities, the Source
Where Learning, and Religion, have their Force;
From whence as Streams are constantly sent forth
Whom, as the Ornaments of Both, great Worth
Commends to Church, and State; But 'tis to Thee
(Great Queen,) whatever University,
Or Church can breed, is due, 'tis thy blest Breast
(Great Nursing Mother) gives all Growth, and Rest.

Tis not as Queen of th' South, but of the North,
Of East, of West We Thee Revere, the Worth
In thy great Vertues, thy great Graces seen,
Of Men, and Hearts, ev'ry where makes Thee Queen.
Admire it not, that We our Hearts Resign
A few poor Children, for who can Decline
The Conquest, who shall thy great Triumphs hear,
Or what thy Arms by Sea, and Land prepare?
Base Fear be gone! That Hospitable Soul
Which all invites, doth likewise all Controul;
By this, that Ancient Wisdom so long lost,
Is now Restored to the Grecian Coast;
By this, Barbarians are taught to Love
Inspired Truths, Truths that come from Above,
And with Them bring a Power of what's Divine,
To which all Hearts, to which all Souls Resign:
For 'tis to *India* too Thy Fleets Convoy
The Christian Faith, that's Thy true Royal Joy
To give in Heaven It self to every Fraight,
That Pearl of price to make each Cargo weight:
And what but Conquest can attend such Charms!
What less than that attend Your other Arms?

And now, Great Equally in War, or Peace,
Whether He Sail the Terror of the Seas,
Or on the Shoare in glorious Arms appear,
Ormond the Muses Patron, Hopes, and Fear,
[In safety Muses see you back Him bring,
And brought back, his, and his Queen's Triumphs sing!]
And what great *Marlborough*, or *Athlone* shall
Or other *Generals* Atchieve, *Heroes All*,
    May it be prosperous, as thy Vertues are,
'Tis these (great Queen) bless both thy Peace, and War!
'Tis *Solomons* Magnificence, and Zeal

To which Thy glorious Actions still appeal,
'Tis He's thy pattern both in Church and State,
Doubt not but his too is thy happy Fate,
The Temple Thou with Him esteem'st so Dear,
Void of its blessing cannot leave thy Care.

      With Mighty Gifts, with Gold, and Stones of price,
And, what no Age had shown, with richest Spice
Happy *Arabia*'s growth, to see the Store
Of *Solomon*, and add unto it more,
Comes *Sheba*'s Wealthy Queen; but what can We
Poor *Grecian* Youths bring as our Gift to Thee?
Our Poverty, Great Queen, is *All*'s our Own,
And this the greatest Present to the Throne;
Give more who can! With this we Heaven bring,
And with't our payment leave to that Great King
Whose the Debt is, what's to his Subjects done,
What to a Distrest Church, ne'er goes alone:
Let others give what mighty Store affords,
We give what best with our Low State accords,
Accept it Madam, who thus make You Shine
In Charity, make all You do Divine.

Simon Homer.	*George Homer.*
George Aptal.	*Michael Damiral.*
George Marules.	*John Aptal.*
Steph. Constantine.	

THE

HERETICAL

TEACHER

CROSS–EXAMINED

by his

ORTHODOX

PUPIL

A Book very useful to the Orthodox,
confirming their traditions,
And showing the fallacies of Benjamin Woodroffe,
Master of the Greek College in Britain.

Dedicated to
Our Lord and Master, His All-Holiness
The most learned and wise Archbishop GABRIEL of
Constantinople, New Rome,
And Ecumenical Patriarch.

Drawn up and published
Through the efforts and diligence, and at the expense of
The humble Hierodeacon Frangiskos Prossalentis of Kerkyra,
Who spent a considerable time during his twenty-fifth year
Listening to Benjamin Woodroffe in Britain.

AMSTERDAM

Printed by Theodore and Henricius Brousis
In the year of our Lord 1706.

TO OUR LORD THE ALL–HOLY, THE MOST LEARNED AND THE MOST WISE

GABRIEL

ARCHBISHOP OF CONSTANTINOPLE, NEW ROME, AND ECUMENICAL PATRIARCH, WE WISH MANY YEARS OF LIFE.

YOUR ALL–HOLINESS, all those who, because of their own wickedness and ill-will want to destroy a fruit-bearing tree belonging to their neighbour, are not content with chopping off the branches or the fruit, but set out to remove it roots and all. So also the heretics of our age, who want to drag the Catholic Church of Christ into their own hateful blasphemies, do not teach their Greek students that just one unwritten command is false, among those many that we have received from our Saviour and his Apostles and that have been preserved by the Church (such as remembering the faithful departed in the sacred liturgy, or calling upon the Saints, venerating their ikons or some such thing). Instead, being well-instructed by their father the devil, and as fore-runners of the Anti-Christ, they announce shamelessly that every unwritten word of the Lord is untrue. And they imagine that, if the Orthodox will admit just this, there will be no difference any more between us and them.

Given all this, I thought that it was right to show from different quotations from the Old and New Testaments, and from the Holy Fathers and the Ecumenical Synods, that the unwritten word of God, that is to say, the Apostolic traditions, is true and sure.

Knowing those who will slander my book, thanks to those heretics, I endeavoured to adorn it with the gracious name of your All-Holiness, and to hallow it under the mighty protection of the Rod entrusted by God to you which crushes the heads of your enemies.[....]

As Daniel closed the mouths of the lions, so you close the mouths of all those wolves in sheep's clothing who devour the sheep. From this you know how great a desire has possessed my soul to confute the impious teaching of the heretics. For not only have I decided, seeing that I am now out of danger from them myself, to make clear to all their treachery and cunning. But I had to wait patiently, while I stayed in Britain, before I could show to you, my Lord and Master, your All-Holiness the Patriarch Gabriel, the reason why they invite the sons of Greeks to go there. For there is nothing more precious than our true faith in God, whom I ever beseech graciously to grant that I may, both in word and deed, kneel with fitting reverence before you, and kiss the venerable feet of your All-Holiness.

Amsterdam,
15 April 1706.

> Your most humble and unworthy servant, your All-Holiness's footstool,
>
> Frangiskos Prossalentis,
> Hierodeacon of Kerkyra.

[Then follow six dedicatory poems in Greek hexameters: to Patriarch Gabriel; two to Alexander Mavrocordato, Logothete of the Great Church; to the Church of Christ; to the College in Ioannina; and to its teacher Georgios Sougdoures.]

To all Orthodox Readers, Greetings.

The common enemy of Christians, who hates all that is good, has invented many and various heresies, my dear reader, in order to remove Orthodoxy, through his instruments of destruction and through those who follow their own desires. I am therefore right to say that he has gained great power for this purpose through those who disregard our sacred traditions and refuse to accept the unwritten word of God. For if we reject these things which belong to the Church, we are deprived not only of the Holy Fathers and their venerable Synods, but also of the Canons together with the Apostolic Instructions. So, having devoted myself totally to the Church, and sparing nothing, but happy to do whatever I can by every means on behalf of our once fortunate but now unfortunate Greek race, I have not shrunk from the task of demonstrating briefly the strength and authority of the Church's unwritten traditions.

Besides this, I have been given another reason for my work by the Master of the Greek pseudo-college in Britain, Benjamin Woodroffe. For in order to deceive his pupils he has not been ashamed to attack in writing the unwritten tradition of the Apostles (in the book published in Oxford in the year 1704). Having listened to him for some considerable time in Britain and having stayed even longer with other heretics, I decided to make plain their whole stance against the Church of Christ, by cross-examining the fallacies of the aforementioned Woodroffe. For the sole reason behind inviting the sons of Greeks to their country is in order to teach them their impious doctrines. So they refuse to allow them to hold onto their traditional prayers or to observe any of our Eastern Church's other customs, saying that all such things are inventions of the Latin Church.

They do not do this arbitrarily or without cunning, but they know how young people always desire fame and glory and for this reason are only too ready to abandon their Orthodoxy (for the heretics simply cannot stand the name of the Latins). And since I remember these things, it is not beyond my purpose to describe a promise which their Teacher made to his pupils.

He called them all together and began to address them as follows: 'My dear children, my heart aches when I hear that you want to return home. But hold onto the faith you have been taught here, do not discard the truth which you have recently discovered. For God lives, and our Queen lives, and through both you will all attain the highest honours in the Eastern Church. You, my fellow, will have the throne of Constantinople' (God forbid!), 'and you', naming others, 'that of Alexandria, Jerusalem, Antioch, and the rest of you will have the more splendid bishoprics.' The students would not believe him, so the impious teacher protested, saying, 'What is stopping you? Cannot our Queen, and her ambassador achieve what they wish with the help of money?' [....]

Then when some of the students agreed with this, almost all began to insult the life-giving cross, to throw away the immaculate body of our saviour Jesus Christ [...] and, in a word, to loathe everything to do with orthodoxy.

I would not have believed the person who told me that this had happened, had I not also myself heard much from Benjamin Woodroffe to the detriment of Orthodoxy. For when he wanted to publish his fallacies against the traditions, he tried by every means to persuade me to confirm what was written, just by signing it. When I refused, he said: 'There is no difference between our Church and yours, but you are young. You do not know the teachings of the Eastern Church very well, and you adopt those of the Latins instead.' When I asked him what those things were, which belong to the Latin Church but which we think belong to ours, he replied: 'Making the sign of the Cross on your forehead, invoking the Saints, and greeting their ikons; saying that the Mother of God is ever a virgin; observing fasts and other superstitions. Last, but not least, believing that in the sacred mysteries the bread and wine are changed into the body and blood of Christ.' When I heard this, I said: 'Your words would be fine, had not the Fathers, and the whole of our Church today not believed and taught as I have said.' He replied: 'You do not know what you are saying. Neither the Fathers nor the present-day Church teach that.' I said: 'Where do you get that from?' He said: 'From the several letters that I have received from the Patriarchs of the Eastern Church.' After saying this, he straight away opened a letter signed by one of the Patriarchs. I do not know if he did this truthfully or as a trick. But he would not let me read it. But he said this and did this to show that the Church neither teaches nor believes as I had said. 'Through the Fathers', he said, 'we do not know how to interpret or to understand the mind of the Father.' Realising then his craftiness and his purpose, I went out, praying that God would one day deliver me from that impious teaching and give me strength to make everything clear in a simple way for the Orthodox.

The heretics pride themselves on their 'wisdom' which contrives in this way to destroy our Orthodoxy. May I have enough time speedily to tell all accurately. For I shall not shrink from saying a few of these things. So that, my beloved reader, you may learn as clearly as possible the whole of their villainy, and know therefore that as you read the Holy Fathers and their venerable Synods, it is impossible to say that they are such fables as the heretics pretend them to be, to the extent that they prevent their students from reading them!

Besides this, they cannot bear to teach them in a methodical or orderly way. But now for a few days they teach grammar, then after that physics for five or six days, then again logic for a similar time, after that grammar again, and after that mathematics. In short, in the space of three or four months they read all these subjects to them, but explain none! Yet by saying that this does not matter, for this needs no explanation, and the rest are not necessary for Christians, they keep their own students in great ignorance. But not everyone suffers like this, only the Greeks. And the reason for it is the one I gave earlier, namely to stop them being able, by understanding the Fathers and the Synods, to refute their impious doctrines.

Therefore, dear reader, having seen and heard these and similar things, I could not but take time and trouble to explain and make clear to everyone the fallacies which they have published. So do not be amazed when you read *The Heretical Teacher Cross-examined by his Orthodox Pupil*. For it was not as his pupil that I decided to write against the teacher, nor did I try to copy Icarus, and show myself as superior to him. But being Orthodox, you see, I thought it right to examine the heretical fallacies he craftily imparts.

So much for the title. But I have this to say about the inelegance of the language and the looseness of the composition. I do not aim to be called a devotee of the Muses or of Hermes, but of our Saviour Jesus Christ and of his Apostles and disciples, who spoke and wrote in simple fashion. And I pray that to you, young lovers of education, our Lord and God will grant such power and wisdom that in a better expressed composition you will make clear to your shepherds these wolves in sheep's clothing. *Farewell.*

THE HERETICAL
TEACHER
CROSS–EXAMINED
by his
ORTHODOX
PUPIL

CHAPTER I

In which are examined the fallacies of the Heretic,
when he tried to show that Holy Scripture
contains all things necessary for salvation
by answering the question

'Who is the author of Holy Scripture?'

THE HERETIC:

[Here he quotes Aptal's reply to question (a) section by
section.]

THE ORTHODOX:

This sophist quite unnecessarily sets out to show that the
traditional commands of the apostles should not be taken into
account, and then is forced to prove that the Holy Scripture is
true [...]. But none of us children of the Greek Church ever
rejected Scripture as false [...].

And do the traditions of the Apostles really change Holy
Scripture? Does making the sign of the cross in Baptism do
that? Or honouring the martyrs? [...] No, these give greater
glory to God. [...]

The quotations from Scripture about not adding or subtracting to it do not lead to the taking away of our holy traditions. [...] The apostle was only seeking to prevent the destruction of the Book of Revelation [...]. And what about adding the New Testament to the Old?

Who is unaware of the traditions which the Catholic Church proclaims have been ordained by our Saviour Jesus Christ, and by the Holy Spirit through the Apostles, and by the Fathers? [...] Who is so stupid as not to confess that it is given to us from above that Our Lady Mary the Mother of God was a virgin after giving birth; that we should fast, and pray for the faithful departed, and celebrate the sacraments? [...] See the first Canon of the Seventh Ecumenical Council of Nicaea. [...]

CHAPTER 2

In which it is demonstrated
that the Traditions are true
by answering the question

'Who is the author of the Traditions?'

PART 1

In which it is demonstrated
that both before and after the law
the faithful received many things from Tradition.

PART 2

In which it is demonstrated
that Christ gave nothing to the Apostles in writing,
nor did he command them to write down anything.

PART 3

In which it is demonstrated
that the Apostles handed down many things
both written and unwritten.

CHAPTER 3

In which are examined
the fallacies of the Heretic,
when he tried to show that Holy Scripture
contains all things necessary for salvation
by answering the question

'Why was it written by God?'

CHAPTER 4

In which there is an examination of
the Heretic's misinterpretation of the Scriptures,
and a refutation of the quotations which he took
from Holy Scripture to argue for the rejection
of Tradition. In addition, the authority of Tradition
is demonstrated from the Old Testament.

CHAPTER 5

In which it is demonstrated
from the New Testament that there is
an unwritten word of God handed down to us.

CHAPTER 6

In which there is a refutation
of those quotations from the Holy Fathers
misinterpreted by the Heretic,
and Traditions are shown to be true
through many other quotations from the same
Fathers and others both earlier and later than them.

CHAPTER 7

In which the authority of Traditions
is demonstrated from the Holy Ecumenical Synods.

E. The Visit of Neophytos, Archbishop of Philippopolis, to England in 1701

RICHARD SHARP

Introduction

Neophytos was a native of the island of Milos. In 1687 he signed a Patriarchal letter as Metropolitan of Didymotychon and in 1689 was elected Metropolitan of Philippopolis (modern-day Plovdiv in Bulgaria), Exarch of All Thrace and Dragovia. The immediate initiative for his mission to England was taken by William, 6th Lord Paget, Ambassador to Constantinople from 1693 to 1702, whose success in negotiating peace between the Ottoman Empire and the Habsburgs at Carlowitz in 1699 had earned the deep gratitude of the Turkish authorities. Accordingly, when Neophytos arrived in England in late August 1701, he brought an official retinue of twelve persons with him, including his personal physician and other senior clergy. Archbishop Tenison's letters to Covel make clear that the authorities in London ensured that everywhere the archbishop went he was treated as a visitor of great importance. Although Neophytos had been received by Louis XIV in Paris, he had the good sense to avoid contact with any papal representative. Within days of landing, the delegation was welcomed in London at dinners held in their honour by the Archbishop of Canterbury, Dr Tenison, and by the Chancellor of Oxford University, the Duke of Ormond. They then travelled to Oxford where, although official hospitality was provided by the vice-chancellor, Dr Mander of Balliol, the Greek College must also have been on the itinerary. At a crowded ceremony held in the convocation house on 1 September, Archbishop Neophytos was created Doctor of Divinity, his physician Doctor of Medicine, and three of the other Greek clergy were made Masters of Arts. A contemporary observer, Edward Thwaites, Fellow of the Queen's College, reported that it was 'a mighty show and the solemnity was very decent'. Afterwards, the Archbishop made

> a very excellent speech, all in plain proper hellenistick greek; and continued speaking near half an hour, all with great respect to the house, great gravity, great boldness and a very manly voice. [...] hee's a man of admirable aire and makes a gracefull appearance. [...] Dr Woodroof has exerted himself and shown us that he does understand Greek.

The party then travelled to Cambridge, where, on 13 September, they received identical honours and Archbishop Neophytos made another speech, the text of which probably indicates the character of his Oxford address, which has not survived. They then returned to London, where, on 30 November, Neophytos was taken to Court by the Archbishop of Canterbury and the Bishop of London and introduced to William III. The date of their return is not known, but in February 1702 a handsome engraving of the Archbishop was published, taken from the life by Robert White (illustration 5).

Neophytos remained archbishop until 8 April 1711, when he resigned for reasons of ill health. He died on 2 July 1711.[1]

---

1   Further documents and information regarding Neophytos may be found in Andreas Tillyrides, 'Neophytos of Philippoupolis' Visit in England', Ἐκκλησιαστικὸς Φάρος 60 (1978) 679–691.

The Documents

From Michel le Quien, *Oriens Christianus, in Quatuor Patriarchatus Digestus, quo exhibentur Ecclesiæ, Patriarchæ, Caeterique Præsules Totius Orientis.* (Parisiis: Ex Typographia Regia) 1740, t. I, col. 1162.

Alexander Helladius juvenis græcus, libro quem Lipsiæ anno 1714. Latine edidit *De præsenti statu ecclesiæ græcæ,* bis meminit *Neophyti* nostra ætate Philippopolis metropolitae, cujus nonnullas epistolas apud se servari ait p. 327. huncque in Angliam profectum, orationem Oxonii in Theatro Sheldoniano habuisse. Is nimirum ille ipse est Philippopolis Metropolita, qui anno 1701. Lutetiam quoque venit Christianissimi Regis Ludovici XIV. Videndi salutandique causa, à quo humanissime acceptus auditusque fuit, quum Italica ad eum usus dialecto esset, quam Rex apprime callebat.

From the *Post Boy*
979   (23–26 August 1701)
A Greek Patriarch is arrived here with a Retinue of 12 Persons, having Letters of Recommendations from his Excellency the Lord Paget, and Monsieur Collier, the Dutch Ambassador at Constantinople, since his arrival he dined with his Grace the ArchBishop of Canterbury, as also with his Grace the Duke of Ormond.

985   (6–9 September 1701)
Last Week the Greek Arch-Bishop of Phillipopoli went to Oxford, where, upon the Recommendation of his Grace the Duke of Ormond, Chancellor of that famous University, he was Complimented with the Degree of Doctor of Divinity,

and some of his Deacons were admitted Masters of Arts. There were present on this occasion a great concourse of Learned Men; and 'tis observable, that he made an excellent Speech, in the Lower House of the Convocation, in Old Greek, which is much applauded; after which he was Nobly Treated, &c, and was extremely pleased with his courteous Entertainment.

1023   (4–6 December 1701)
The Grecian Arch-Bishop of Philopouli was introduc'd to his Majesty at Kensington last Sunday, by his Grace the Arch-bishop of Canterbury and the Bishop of London, whose Effigies is near finish'd by Mr White, and will be publish'd very speedily.

1050   (5–7 February 1701)
Lately publish'd, The Effigies of the Grecian Archbishop (who was introduced to his Majesty at Hampton Court, by his Grace the Archbishop of Canterbury and the Bishop of London, the 30th of November last) is now publish'd by R. White, and Sold at his House in Bloomsbury Market.

From MS Ballard 13, f. 37, f. 38 (Bodleian Library)

Septr. 2. 1701

Revd Sir,

Yesterday at three a clock the Archbishop of Philip-popoli was created doctor of divinity in the convocation house. His Physician made D.Med. & his presbyters & deacons,[+] masters of Arts; 'twas a mighty show & the solem-nity was very decent.

After their admission, his grace made us a very excellent speech, all in plain proper hellenistick greek; and contrived speaking near half an hour, all with great respect to the house, great gravity, great boldness, and a very manly voice. If you have not seen him, I hope you will in London; hee's a man of admirable aire, and makes a gracefull appearance.

He commended the English nation for hospitality, the church of England, the University, the chancellors[1] civility to him, the Vice chancellor's[2] kindness, &.[c] in very round periods.

After that, we went to the theatre, had a latin song or two, which made about half an hour's musick, and the company dispersed. The concourse was so great, I have not seen it greater, except the Act.

the forms of presentation had nothing singular in them, except the last by the orator[3]: we had one of his rants. Praesento vobis hunc egregiû virum Athanasium-diaconum, nomine suo apud omnes orthodoxos venerandum, ut gradu magistri in artibus insignitus, tandem fidem acrius, quam ipsi Episcopi, tueatur. they were the words, as I remember.

I am very sorry you were not here at the reception & entertainment of this great man, for reasons I can not tell you in writing.

Indeed D[r] Woodroof has exerted himself & shown us that he does understand Greek.

I could not omitt giving you this small account. be pleased to excuse the freedom

Reverend Sir

Your most humble servant

E. Thwaites

+ Athanasius, archdeacon -Neophytus Archimandrite
-Gregorius Protosyncellus
1 D. Ormond   2 D[r] Mander, Balliol   3 Wm Wyatt, ChCh.

Two letters from Archbishop Tenison to Dr John Covel regarding the visit to Cambridge, from George Williams, *The Orthodox Church of the East in the Eighteenth Century* (London, 1868) lix.

                                                        Lambeth
                                              September 6, 1701
Sir,
The Archbishop of Philippopoli in Romania is coming to Cambridge next week. I think he sets out from hence on Wednesday next. He comes recommended by my Lord Paget, Mr Collier Ambassadour for the Dutch at the Port, and divers others; and to me by my Lord Manchester, who much approved of his wise behaviour at Paris in avoiding the Pope's Nuntio and forbearing everything that might carry with it an appearance of being latinized. He has been very well received at Oxford, and he comes recommended to Cambridge University by the Chancellor, the Duke of Somerset. He has a great desire in particular of seeing yourself, who best under-stand his language and the present state of the Greek Church. Not doubting of your doing him all good offices,
                    I remain with true respect,
                         Your loving Brother,
                         THO. CANTUAR.

                                              September 18, 1701.
Sir,
      I was mighty glad that it so happened that you were in town when the Archbishop of Philippopoli came to the Universitie; you being the person in England who could most agreablie covers with him, and in his own way. And I am sensible that we owe much to you in the conduct of this affair, tho I cannot but say that all have done their parts; and the management is much applauded. I know not whether you are

informed that a book of Nectarius (or perhaps of Dositheus under his name) against the Pope's power &c. is here, in good part, translated already.[2] I suppose it will be publish'd this winter. I will get it printed at Cambridge, if a good Bookseller will undertake it, and the Publishers be willing. The latter (I think) will not be difficult.

I am, with true respect,
Sir,
Your assured Friend,
THOMAS CANTERBURY

A Summary of Neophytos' speech at Cambridge, 13 September 1701, from C. Wordsworth, *Social Life at the English Universities in the Eighteenth Century* (Cambridge, 1874).[3]

The speech begins with an elegant and complimentary comparison of the University to bees, which not only gather honey, but impart their sweets to others. We are fishers of men using the tackle of Wisdom and Learning, and in our turn we are enclosed in the net of God. Again, Man is light, as by wisdom he traverses all things, but he is in turn brought to

---

2   Doubtless Dr Allix's Latin translation of the Ἀντίρρησις of Nectarius, published in 1702. Covel had already prepared a Latin translation for the Press in 1685, now Add. MS. in the British Museum, No. 22,902. [Williams' note.]

3   The address was originally published as Λογος του ἱερωτάτου καί σεβασμιωτάτου Νεοφυτου Μητροπολίτου της Φιλιππουπολεως πρός Ἀκαδημίαν της Κανταβριγιας [...] (Cantabrigiæ: Typis Academicis) 1701. The Greek and Latin texts are reprinted (with other related documents) in Charis Mettis, ' Ὁ Μητροπολιτης Φιλιππουπολεως Νεοφυτος (1689–1711) και 'η ἐλευση του στην Αγγλια (1701)', Ὀρθοδοξος Κηρυξ nos. 144–145 (2000) 13–20, 19–20.

the one Source of Motion, the very Wisdom, and the Light which lighteneth every man that cometh into the world.

A threefold wisdom is known to our Greek theologians; first Natural Wisdom, and next Supernatural Wisdom of two kinds, viz. *Create* (which is Faith) and *increate* which is the Subsisting Wisdom of God, the Son and Word of God the Father, our Lord Jesus Christ.

The first Wisdom leads to the second and the second to the divine Person of Wisdom: and without the first (natural Wisdom) we cannot find the way which leads to Jerusalem which is above through the searching of the Scriptures.

Then follows a comparison of the Chancellor (the duke of Somerset) and the Vice-Chancellor (Bentley) to the Silver Trumpets mentioned in the Book of Numbers (x. 2, 8) ... But I have not words to enumerate the excellences of the Chancellor, the V. C., D. D's, and all the rest. And who can sufficiently praise the harmony, proportions, and elegance of the Colleges, especially the most noble and beautiful College of Trinity?

He concludes with a solemn prayer ... for King William, the archbishop of Canterbury and all the other archbishops and bishops of the English Church, as well as all the members of the University.

F. Greek College and other Ecumenical Documents

Edward Stephens

Introduction

These documents are the work of a man who deeply desired Anglican reunion not only with the Orthodox but also with the whole divided Christian family.

> He remonstrated with the Quakers, while he praised their zeal; he criticised the shortcomings of the Non-jurors, while he sympathised with their political honesty; he inveighed against the corruptions of the Church of Rome as loudly as Calvin or Luther, but in the same breath he testified to her undoubted rights as the first See in Christendom. He was a member, and even a regularly ordained clergyman of the Church of England, but he never ceased to denounce her isolation from the rest of Christendom, and what he calls her Cranmerian Liturgy.[1]

Edward Stephens (1633–1706) was called to the Bar as a member of the Middle Temple, but from about 1660 devoted himself increasingly to the life of the church.[2] In a letter he

---

1 'Mr Edward Stephens and the Churches', *The Union Review* I (1863) 553–570.
2 See 'Stephens, Edward' in *Oxford Dictionary of National Biography* 52:461–462, and W. Jardine Grisbrooke, *Anglican Liturgies of the Seventeenth and Eighteenth Centuries* (London: S. P. C. K.) 1958, 37–55.

wrote to Archbishop Tenison in 1695, he explained how he had first promoted a monthly celebration of the Eucharist with family members in the country; in his own parish in London he brought the community to a weekly celebration, all the time desiring to see the 'daily Sacrifice restor'd'. Still as a layman, he brought together a little company of weekly communicants, among them a priest he had brought over from the Dissenters, and they agreed upon three things: '1. To meet daily at 5. in the morning at a daily communion: 2. To indeavour, as near as we could, in all things to follow the Example of the ancient Christians: and 3. To avoid giving Offense to any, but especially to the Church of England.'[3]

When their priest had to leave them, Stephens himself took orders so that they might continue the daily Sacrifice. When they worshipped in public, they used the Prayer Book form, albeit with the addition of 'part of the General Thanksgiving & four Doxologies of the Revelations', and of the prayer of oblation immediately after the words of institution. In private, Stephens used 'such Enlargements of the Service, as I thought agreeable to the ancient Form'.[4] He believed that the 1549 Eucharist was 'Godly and agreeable to the primitive church', but that the service in the second Prayer Book was 'disordered' and 'dismembered', the work of 'Forrainers' and of the Antichrist.[5] Stephens hoped that the communicants might live together in community; it's not clear whether this ever came into being.[6] Certainly the 'extended' community had some distinguished members, including the leading patristic

---

3   Lambeth Palace Library (LPL) MS 930/35. Edward Stephens to Abp Tenison, 21 February 1694/5.
4   Ibid. Two of Stephens' own liturgies may be found in Grisbrooke, *Anglican Liturgies*, 201–30.
5   LPL MS 933/58.
6   A. M. Allchin, *The Silent Rebellion. Anglican Religious Communities 1845–1900* (London: S.C.M. Press, 1958), 27.

scholar Johann Ernst Grabe, who came to London from Oxford in order to receive communion from Stephens.[7] (Grabe could not accept the Prayer Book rite because of its lack of an epiklesis.) Stephens claimed that he was admitted to Orthodox communion by Archbishop Neophytos of Philippopolis when he visited London in 1701.[8]

Stephens also had a special care for members of the Greek College. When George and John Aptal of Smyrna sought to escape from their Roman adventure, they convinced the English consul at Genoa to send them back to England (see Stephens' account below). Arriving in London in October 1703, they stayed with Stephens. He used this opportunity to publish his own proposal (see below) for continuing the work of the Greek College and to enter into correspondence with Patriarch of Constantinople, sharing both his liturgy and his hopes for a restitution of catholic communion between Anglicans and Orthodox.[9] The Patriarch's reply (also below) provides the only evidence for why the Orthodox ceased sending students to Oxford.

Stephens was regarded as an eccentric by many contemporaries. Thomas Hearne 'recalled that his piety led some to call him Father Stephens or Abbot Stephens, although Stephens complained that he was also branded Madman Convert'.[10] He was unabashedly outspoken in his opinions; indeed his convictions can have an uncannily contemporary resonance. He wrote in a letter to the 'English bishops of the Roman Communion', 'The *Case* is this: I take it to be

---

7   Günther Thomann, 'John Ernest Grabe (1666–1711): Lutheran Syncretist and Anglican Patristic Scholar' *Journal of Ecclesiastical History* 43 (1992), 414–427, here 421.
8   See the reference in LPL MS 929/131. Edward Stephens to the Archbishops and Bishops, 12 December 1705.
9   LPL MS 929/131.
10 *ODNB* 52:462.

undeniable, that whoever is duly baptized in the Name of the
Father, and of the Son, and of the Holy Ghost, does thereby
acquire a *Right of Communion* in all the Rights and Privileges of
the Catholick Church in all parts of it."[11] He believed that the
Greek communion was 'the only true *Catholick Communion* in
the World'. Convinced that the Orthodox Liturgy was both
older and more truly catholic than the Western rites, he was
determined to reshape the Anglican liturgy accordingly. His
faith in the necessity of Orthodox–Anglican unity enabled
him with confidence to look beyond every failure and obstacle
to that goal. Like Derwas Chitty in the twentieth century, he
was committed to a loyal nonconformity for the sake of a
prophetic witness to the unity of the Church.

1. From *A Vindication of Christianity, from and against the Scandals of Popery* [...] (1704)[12]

[The *Calendar of Treasury Papers, 1702–1707* (London, 1874)
207–209, contains another account of the 'Roman captivity'
of the Greek students which agrees with Stephens' but
includes some further details. Because Stephens was so closely
associated with the Aptals and because the additional account
mirrors so closely Stephens' own preoccupations, it seems
likely this other document was also Stephens' work. Part of it
is included here at the end of this selection, enclosed in square
brackets.]

---

11   *The Case of the Roman Catholick Missionars Truly Represented. In a Letter
      to the Right Reverend Bishop G— and the rest of the English Bishops of the
      Roman Communion.* (1704).
12   Pages 22–24.

In *Octob.* 1698. were *Five young Grecians* brought from *Smyrna*, and placed in *Gloucester-Hall, Oxford*, as Students there; and it is not to be doubted, but Notice thereof was soon sent thence to *Rome*. But however they had not been long there before *Attempts* were made *by some Roman Catholick Agents* to withdraw them from thence, and if possible to the Church of *Rome*, and at least two of them who came first, and one who came afterward, were prevailed with to *leave the College*; two of them, who were Brothers, in hopes to return to their own Country, but the other who seduced them, upon Promise of better Accommodations at *Paris*, where the King had lately erected a *College for Grecians*. He carried them with him to *Holland*, and thence, instead of *Middleburg*, (whence they thought they should have gone to their own Country) to *Antwerp*, and so to *Bruxels*, where they were brought to the *Internuncio*, and there they found they were in a Trap, and that they had been brought thither by Procurement of the *Internuncio* and the order of the *Pope*; and from thence they were sent to *Louvan*, where they were kept Five Months till farther Orders came from *Rome*; and then they were sent to *Paris*, and from thence to *Leghorn*, where the two got on Board an *English* Ship, and so returned to *England*. This Business was managed here before they went, by a Person belonging to the *Portugal Ambassador's* Chappel; but after their return a Letter was brought to one of them by one belonging to the *Envoy of Florence*, written by one of his Acquaintance in the *Grecian College* at *Rome*, and acquainting him how much the *Pope* was displeased at their Return to *England*, and blaming him for it, and perswading him still to go; which was also much pressed by him who brought it to him, and desired him to consider better of it: whereupon the next Day he sent him a Letter as here follows.

SIR,

I Have considered your Proposals, and am of Opinion, That no Man ought to forsake the Communion of the Church in which he was baptized, or resides, without special and good Cause: and that no Grecian *may be admitted to Communion with the Church of* Rome, *without Renouncing the Communion of the* Grecians *as Schismaticks, and Swearing to the Profession of* Pius IV. *So that in this Case* two *things are to be considered.* 1. *Whether the* Grecians *are in any Schism, for which their Communion may, and ought to be forsaken?* 2. *Whether the Profession of* Pius IV. *may be sworn with a safe Conscience?*

As to the former, it seems, that either there is no Schism between the Greeks and the Latins; *and then there is no such cause to forsake their Communion; or if there be any, the Guilt is on the side of the* Latins. *For the Original of the Schism was from the Addition of an Article to the Common Faith by the Latins, contrary to the Decrees of several General Councils.*

As to the other, that Profession seems to oblige all, who swear to it, to swear a Lie: For of any one of those Articles be either not True, or not Catholick, or not necessary to Salvation, they swear to a Lie. And that they are so necessary, cannot be determined, but by the Holy Scriptures, or by true Catholick Tradition; which are both wanting for divers of them.

Since you have taken so much pains for my sake, I must make bold to desire this further Favour, that you will be pleased to satisfy me as these Difficulties.

Your Humble Servant.

Jan. 4. 1704.

But to this Letter he could never get any Answer, but that he was gotten in among Hereticks; for it was soon known that they were with me; and at last that Person declined so much as to speak with him, tho' he met him several times. But some time after another, who was an *Italian Gentleman* of the

Envoy's Retinue, desired to speak with him; and when they met was very earnest with him to go to *Rome*, but upon no other Motives than of what Temporal Advantage they should have there.

[At Antwerp, going out of ye boat [George and John Aptaloghi] askt Stephen Constantine (who was ye third who had made his escape from Oxford, & as it afterwards appear'd had long entertained a correspondence with Romish emissaries, having for above 3 years before sold himself & his brethren to them) [...].

At their landing at Antwerp, they were welcomed by 3 priests, who were to take care of them, who attended them to Mechlin & thence to Louvain, where they were presented to ye internuncio of ye Pope, who at ye first view of them said, *Homer is not here! That is not Homer!* pointing at the eldest of them. It seems their greatest aime was at him, & they were troubled he was not with them. This Homer is he who was ye eldest of them all, & is now in London, in order to return into his own countrey, he being already appointed to be druggerman in ye place of one lately deceas'd at Smyrna. [...]

And now they began to deale plainly with them, greately exclaiming against the English as ye worst of hereticks, & telling them that they were to renounce all their errors, & to be instructed that they might be receiv'd into the true Catholick Church. In order whereunto they were put into the Irish College, & often disputed with, to be convinced of their errors; but that not prevailing, they were told that his Holinesse had a desire to see them, & to Rome they must goe, where they should find what it was to offend an Apostolick Minsiter. And so they were sent to Paris, where ye Pope's Nuncio entertain'd them, beyond w^t they had ever seen; & to soften what had been said to them at Louvain, he told them of ye great love his Holiness had for them, & a letter of grace came to them from his Holiness, written in Greek, to confirm them therein. [...]]

2. *A Good and Necessary Proposal for the Restitution of Catholick Communion between the Greek Churches and the Church of England* (1705)

That such a Restitution is *practicable,* will appear in due time by matter of Fact; but for the present, the Vindication of the *Greek* Church by the Learned * Dr. *Stillingfleet* late Bishop of *Worcester*, may satisfy all that they are more truly Catholick than the Papal Faction do pretend and the Protestants, tho their Impostures, have believ'd, in the principal Difference of all, wherein they were thought to have been erroneous. But a

---

*   Rational Account, *p.* 1. *c.*1. §.5. *Where he tells his Adversary;* And truly it was much your Concernment to load her as much as you can; For tho she wants one of the great *Marks* of your Church (which yet you know not how long your Church may enjoy) *viz.* Outward Splendor and Bravery; yet you cannot deny, but *that Church* was planted by the *Apostles,* enjoy'd a continual *Succession* from them, flourish'd with a number of the Fathers *exceeding* that of yours, had more of the *Councils* of greatest Credit in it, and which is a Commendation still to it, it retains more *Purity* under its Persecutions than your Church with all its external Splendor. So Dr. Smith, *who hath not only read much of their Books, but conversed with them in their own Country, saith,* They are most unjustly accus'd by some of the *Roman* Church, as Deserters of the Catholick Faith, *&c. And that,* The Christians of the *East* do still retain with all imaginable Constancy and Firmness of Assent, the intire Profession of the Mysteries of the Faith, as they were believ'd and acknowledg'd in the first Ages; and this in the said Pressures, which daily afflict them, and the continual Scoffs and Blasphemies of the *Turks.*

more just an full Account, than any we have yet had of them, is preparing by one well qualify'd for it by Acquaintance and Conversation amongst them, as well as by their Books, of which he hath brought a considerable Collection with him.

And that it is a matter of great *Duty* and *Obligation* to be heartily endeavour'd on both sides, and will be, when accomplish'd, of like *Benefit* to both, and of mutual *Advantage* against our common Adversaries, the Papal Faction; will be more fully declared, and sufficiently proved in due time. But it is not to be expected but so good a Work will be encounter'd with all the *Opposition* that the Papal Faction and the Devil himself can raise against it. And of this we have a notable *Instance* in this Nation within this seven years last past.

In *Octob.* 1698. divers young Men from *Smyrna,* and others afterward from *Constantinople* and other places, were invited over by our Agents and Merchants by Orders from hence, and more especially by Dr. Woodroffe, by Letters to the Patriarchs, to come and study at *Oxford*, with such *Promises* of all necessary Accommodations, Assistance in Studies, and to be sent home when their Studies should be finish'd, without any Trouble or Charge to their Parents or Friends, as easily prevail'd with them to leave their Parents, Friends and Country too, for the Improvement of their Studies here; and rais'd such Jealousy in the Papal Faction, that the *Pope* was at no little charge to get some of them from *Oxford*, and the *French King* was prevail'd with to order a provision for such as would come thither at Paris; and the Example was soon follow'd by those Pious and Worthy Persons at *Hall* in Saxony, where good Provision is made for the *Greeks*; so that they live very comfortably with very good Success in their Studies there.

But at *Oxford*, tho they who came first were well enough order'd for some time, yet afterwards they, and those who came after them, were so ill accommodated, both for their

Studies and other Necessaries, that some of the staid not many Months, and others would have been gone, if they had known how; and there is now but one left there, two being come lately thence to *London*: so that this good Work, which had rais'd great Expectations among the *Greeks*, no little Jealousy among our Adversaries aforesaid, and perhaps a pious Emulation in our Friends at *Hall*, is now like to prove an occasion of the Indignation of the *Greeks*, the Grief of our Friends, the Derision of our Adversaries, and the Shame of the Church and Nation, unless there appear amongst us some sincere devout Christians and true Lovers of their Country, who will take the matter into good Consideration, and heartily give their Assistance to prevent farther Mischief, and retrieve the good Work begun, to be promoted to a much better purpose.

There is no need of a College at Oxford, nor of a building of a Church here, but a good House well situated, with convenient Lodgings for some *Greek* Clergymen and young Scholars, and a decent Oratory here in *London*, may be so order'd, as to serve all that is necessary, and more to the Satisfaction of the *Greeks*, if pious and devout people be but sensible of the great Value in the sight of *Christ* of Charity to such as suffer for his Name. This alone will do all: so that tho it be a great Work, it may, notwithstanding all Opposition, be easily accomplish'd, if in our Devotions and Charities there be the Spirit and Life of the genuine primitive Christianity, sincere, and pure from all Corruption of Hypocrisy, Formality or Faction. And this alone will clear both Church and Nation from the Scandal which the Miscarriages of two of three unworthy Persons have brought upon it, if the three *Greeks* who are yet here, and understand and speak *English* tolerably well, be kept here at *London* to perfect their Skill in it, and to assist their Countrymen who understand it not; or if any of them desire it, be decently sent home; and some small necessary Provision be made for some Persons to be sent over by the Authority of the Patriarch.

But so much of this is so necessary for this purpose, that otherwise what is only the personal Faults of two or three such Persons as mention'd before, may really become, and reasonably be reputed National; and be resented and censur'd as such: and the rather because this is almost the only considerable Nation, where the *Greeks* have no Church at all. But if we farther consider *the Importance of Catholick Communion, and our Duty, Obligation and Interest* to endeavour for it, in order to that it is very necessary that all *Occasions of Offence* be avoided and removed, and that the most *obliging Offices* readily perform'd upon all occasions: And certainly upon the Consideration also less than what is here said cannot be done upon this Occasion.

There is *one Consideration more*, which in respect to the present *Juncture of Affairs* in the World, ought not to be omitted; and that is, that it is more than possible, that the Restitution of such a Communion between the *Greek* Churches (a Communion of themselves of larger Extent than that of the Roman) and the Church of *England*, may by the good Providence of God, prove an Occasion to bring off *our Confederates* from the *Roman* to this, being truly Catholick; which cannot otherwise be expected; and so break the Papal Faction (and without hands) and bring in such a *Universal Reformation* as has been long since foretold by some, and is much expected by many about this time, and much to be desir'd by all sincere Christians.

[And there is *another Occasion of Offense* which ought to be removed, the Pressing of Grecian Seamen, contrary to the Laws of Nations, call'd Jus Gentium, and the Laws of this Nation in particular: For which such Reasons have been returned by some Great Men, as the Clerks say, that it is not for the Hon^r of the Governmt that Men of so little Sense, Conscience, or Civil Prudence should be imploy'd in such Places. And it is very observable, that at the very Time, when a Positive Denial of their Discharge was return'd to one, who sollicited for it, it pleased God to send such *a Storm*, as besides the Damage in our Shipping, cast away many hundreds of our Men. And for this no man is so proper to intercede as the *Archbp of Canterbury*, both as Archbp, and as a Privy Counsell[r], upon the Consideration both of Religion, and of Civil Prudence; no small Obligations upon him, of which he must give acct ere Long.][13]

Such as are willing to contribute to his Noble and most Christian Proposal, as it is call'd by a Right Reverend Bishop of this Church, who earnestly recommends it to all sincere and publick-spirited Christians, may leave either Mony or Subscriptions with Mr. *Edward Fowler* Linendraper, Mr. *Henry Colchester* Druggist, both near *Bow*-Church *Cheapside*, Mr. *Christopher Todd* Apothecary in *Newgate-Market* or Mr. *William Gardiner* Distiller at *Holborn-Bridg*.

Where they may have farther Satisfaction concerning it.

3. A Letter of Jeremias Xantheus, secretary or registrar of the Greek Orthodox Church, by order of the Patriarch of Constantinople, to Edward Stephens.

[Lambeth Palace Library MS 933/49–50 (f. 49 is the Greek original, f. 50 a Latin translation. This English translation comes from 'Establishment of a Greek College at Oxford in the 17th Century', *The Union Review* i (1863) 490–500, 499–500.]

---

13   This section in square brackets, omitted from the printed version, is the only significant variation in Lambeth Palace Library MS 935/30.

Most worthy and reverend brother in Christ.

It was a matter of wonder to us to hear what had been done through your earnestness and piety with Divine zeal for the common good of the Church; not, however, but that we know that in all ages the Lord has magnified His mercy. When His Blessedness had received your excellent letter, which you sent by the hand of the noble Lord George, his relative, he was not a little surprised – first, on understanding the British nation to be more ready to admit a change for the better and positive amendment, than the stiff-necked Papists, who, from the first, have opposed the orthodox faith, and daily continue doing the same against the Eastern Church of Christ, but all in vain, for their madness is patent to all; next, on hearing from the above-named George, and, indeed, from your own letter, to love and desire which you have to succour and assist the scattered sheep of the Eastern Church. Wherefore, his Blessedness, giving thanks to God, blessed you and all who are with you. Thirdly, when your liturgy had been read to him – in which are contained many good and excellent things, even if not quite perfect in our judgement. Whatever is wanting, time and charity will amend. If you want help in the work, and desire to render it acceptable to the Easterns, we will undertake it, if God see fit. Forasmuch as we have it in our intentions to pay you a visit, in company with a deacon and reader, bringing with us commendatory letters from the Church, for the purpose of confirming and promoting the good work for which God has accepted you as an instrument. But I am detained by certain causes, especially such as are inimical to the truth. Nevertheless, I have written to Smyrna to Lord George, as to what you and we ought to do to set matters straight between your and our reverences, desiring to collect, within their own native folds, the dispersed sheep of the Eastern Church, that they may not stray into Calvino-Lutheranism, or, still more, into Popery, making themselves swords against the Church. I will say no more, for you well know it; and, therefore, we have requested, and farther, written, by command of his Blessedness, to Lord George, that he should study both the usefulness and improvement of the work. Who, having on hand another business in Britain (as he has written to us) willingly arranged to do all in his power, as becomes a faithful and beloved son; so we send you by him, together with our letter, two books, with the blessing, and by the command, of his Blessedness, against the Roman Church, that have just been printed, begging you to receive this small gift from the brethren as a great sign of their love. He will, if God will, when safe arrived in England, declare our counsel and dispositions; and, through him, again, if God be willing, we shall know what the will of God is. The irregular life of certain priests and laymen of the Eastern Church, living in London, is a matter of great concern to the Church. Wherefore, the Church forbids any to go and study at Oxford, be they ever so willing. In conclusion, I write to you by command of the Patriarch that, having made yourself known by your truthfulness and charity throughout the Eastern Church, this Church itself, with one consent, send you, and those with you, blessing and salutation in Christ, and will make mention of you in its prayers, that God would speed the good work at which you are labouring on behalf of his Church; and that we may all, with one consent, hear His blessed voice saying, 'Come unto me all ye that are heavy laden and I will refresh you' – a blessing which may it be the lot of us all to obtain.

Farewell in the Lord,

Your brother in the Lord,

JEREMIAH XANTHEUS,

Registrar of the Greek Church.

March 2, 1705.

To the most reverend and pious brother in the Lord, Lord Stephen, worthily given to London in Britain.

G. An Office for the Sacrifice of the Holy Eucharist, being the Ancient Liturgy of the Church of Jerusalem

Thomas Rattray

Introduction

Thomas Rattray was the leading Scottish Episcopal bishop of his time and also a pre-eminent patristic scholar. He was so committed to the repristination of the government and liturgy of the Scottish church in the image of primitive antiquity that he was even prepared to oppose the continuation of the royal prerogative of the exiled Stuart claimants to the British throne. This was a highly divisive position among Scottish Non-Jurors. Following the abolition of legally established episcopacy in 1688–9, in 1705 the bishops agreed to continue the episcopal succession without diocesan title or jurisdiction but only as members of an episcopal college. This would not then infringe on the rights of their acknowledged (Stuart) sovereign to nominate to dioceses.

Rattray lived for a time in London in contact with the Non-Jurors there and was deeply influenced by their liturgical scholarship and their high theology of the spiritual independence of the church from the state.[1] This independence was embodied in the apostolic succession of the episcopate and expressed in the sort of Catholic liturgy to be found in the 1637

1   Henry Broxap, *The Later Non-Jurors* (Cambridge: Cambridge University Press, 1924), 61.

Scottish Prayer Book. When he returned to Scotland, Rattray advocated the restoration of diocesan episcopacy and the spiritual independence of the church in *An Essay on the Nature of the Church* (1728). Drawing on the Church Fathers, he argued that the episcopate was independent and authoritative and that the unity between the bishop and his diocese constituted the unity of the Church. The royal supremacy had no necessary role to play in the life of the Scottish Episcopal or any other church.[2]

As a liturgist, Rattray was not content simply with encouraging the use of the 1637 rite. He always sought earlier sources in the hope of coming at the end to the primitive foundation. The ultimate fruit of his researches was his posthumously published edition of the Liturgy of St James, a liturgy unlikely to have been used beyond the confines of the bishop's private chapel. It has, however, been revived in modern times and is (in this editor's experience) a powerfully effective and accessible rite, at once identifiably Anglican yet also Orthodox in structure and spirit. Donald Allchin pays tribute to Rattray as a liturgist elsewhere in this volume (chapter 12).[3] As he points out, the patristic spirituality of eighteenth-century Anglicanism is profoundly present in this liturgy, a spirit of adoration of the triune God, of thanksgiving for the gifts of the whole created order, and of the joining together of heaven and earth, of time and eternity.[4]

---

2   See Rowan Strong, *Alexander Forbes of Brechin: The First Tractarian Bishop* (Oxford: Clarendon Press, 1995), 7–9.

3   See also A. M. Allchin, 'Thomas Rattray: The Eucharist and Unity', *Revista Teologica* (Sibiu, Romania) nos 3-4, July/December 1996, 144–161; W. Jardine Grisbrooke, *Anglican Liturgies of the Seventeenth and Eighteenth Centuries* (London: S.P.C.K., 1958), 136–149.

4   The format of the liturgy here follows that of the original edition, in *The Ancient Liturgy of the Church of Jerusalem, being the Liturgy of St James* (London, 1744) 111–122.

AN

OFFICE

FOR THE

Sacrifice of the HOLY EUCHARIST

BEING THE

ANCIENT LITURGY

OF THE

Church of *Jerusalem*

TO WHICH

PROPER RUBRICKS are added for Direction,

AND

Some few NOTES at the Foot of the Page, &c.

The ORDER for celebrating the Sacrifice of the
H O L Y   E U C H A R I S T.

NONE but the * Faithful are to present at this Office. And if any of these shall fall into any Crime for which he ought to do Penance, the Priest, having Knowledge thereof, shall prohibit him from approaching the holy Altar, until he have performed the same.

Likewise, if the Priest shall perceive any Enmity or Hatred betwixt any of them, he shall not suffer them to be Partakers of the holy Eucharist, until he know them to be reconciled. And if one of the Parties so at Variance be content to forgive, from the Bottom of his Heart, all that the other hath trespassed against him, and to make amends for all that he himself hath offended; and the other will not be persuaded to a Reconciliation; the Priest in that Case ought to admit the Person thus willing to be reconciled, and not him that is obstinate. Provided that the Priest so repelling any, as is specified in this or the next precedent Paragraph, shall be obliged to give an Account of the same to the Bishop, within fourteen Days after at the farthest.

The Altar shall stand at the East end of the Church or Chapel: And at the time of celebrating the holy Eucharist shall have a fair white linen Cloth upon it.

Before the Service begin the † Deacon shall prepare so much Bread, Wine, and Water as he judgeth convenient; laying the Bread in the Paten, or in some decent Thing provided for that purpose; and putting the Wine into the Chalice, or into Flagons provided also for that Use; and the Water into some other proper Vessel: And shall place them upon the Prothesis, and cover them with a fair white linen Cloth.

---

*   Note, The Word Faithful is taken here in the primitive Sense, in opposition not only to Hearers and Unbelievers, but also to Catechumens and Penitents, and to all Hereticks and Schismaticks.

†   Note, If there be no Deacon, what is in this Office ordered to be performed by him must be done by the Priest himself.

¶ At the Beginning of the Eucharistick Service, the Priest standing at the Altar, and the People with their Faces towards it: [The Deacon shall bring * Water to the Priest, who shall wash his Hands therein, saying,

I will wash my Hands in Innocency, and so will I compass thine Altar, O Lord.

Then] The Deacon, being turned to the People, shall say with a loud Voice,

Let none of those who ought not to join in this Service stay.

Let none have ought against any one.

Let none come in Hypocrisy.

† [Salute one another with the holy Kiss.

And let the Clergy salute the Bishop, or officiating Priest; and the Laity one another, the Men the Men, and the Women the Women.

Then the Priest being turned to the People shall say,

The Peace of God be with you all.

Answ. And with thy Spirit.

Then the Deacon shall say,

Let us present our Offerings to the Lord with Reverence and godly Fear.

Then ‡ [shall all the People kneel, and] § "The Priest shall begin the "Offertory, turning himself to the People, and saying one or more of these "Sentences following, as he thinketh most convenient in his Discretion *.

---

*   This as it is an ancient, so is a very innocent and significant Ceremony: But where it cannot conveniently and decently be done, it may be omitted.

†   Note, This is not to be used but in such Churches or Chapels as are so ordered as that the Men and Women sit separate, as they ought to do. As to the Antiquity of it, there can be no question, since we find it so frequently mentioned in the Scriptures themselves.

‡   Note, That on all Lord's Days, and during all the Time between Easter and Pentecost, the Faithful are not to kneel, but to stand at Prayer, in memory of our Lord's Resurrection. : See *Tertul. De Coron.* c. 3. *Con. Nic.* 1. can. 20. and *Beverige*'s Notes upon it.

§   Note, These Sentences of the Offertory, which are not in *Lit. Ja.* or any other of the ancient Liturgies (and are therefore included within these " " Marks) but are taken chiefly from the Liturgy composed for

"In Process of Time it came to pass, that *Cain* brought "of the Fruit of the Ground an Offering unto the Lord; and "*Abel* he also brought of the Firstlings of his Flock, and of the "Fat thereof: And the Lord had respect unto *Abel* and to his "Offering, but unto *Cain* and to his Offering he had not "respect. *Gen.* iv. 3, 4, 5.

"Speak unto the Children of *Israel*, that they bring me an "Offering: of every Man that giveth it willingly with his Heart, "ye shall take my Offering. *Ex.* xxv. 2.

"They shall not appear before the Lord empty: Every "Man shall give as he is able, according to the Blessing of the "Lord your God, which he hath given you. *Deut.* xvi. 16.

"Give unto the Lord the Glory due unto his Name: Bring "an Offering, and come into his Courts. *Psal.* xcvi. 8.

"If thou bring thy Gift to the Altar, and there "remembrest that thy Brother hath ought against thee: Leave "there thy Gift before the Altar, and go thy way, first be "reconciled to thy Brother, and then come and offer thy Gift. "*Matt.* v. 23, 24.

" ¶ Lay not up for yourselves Treasures upon Earth, "where Moth and Rust doth corrupt, and where Thieves do "break through and steal: But lay up for yourselves Treasures "in Heaven, where neither Moth nor Rust doth corrupt, and "where Thieves do not break through nor steal. *Matt.* vi. 19, "20.

"He who soweth sparingly, shall reap sparingly: And he "who soweth bountifully, shall reap bountifully. Every Man as "he purposes in his Heart, so let him give, not grudgingly, or "of necessity: for God loveth a chearful giver. 2 *Cor.* ix. 6, 7.

---

the Use of the Church of *Scotland*, and printed at *Edinb.* An. 1637. are inserted here as being very proper to stir up the People to offer willingly with a devout Heart.

* Note, In Lit. 1. *Edw.* VI. the Sentences for the Offertory are directed to be sung by the Clerks.

"Jesus sat over against the Treasury, and beheld how the
"People cast Money into the Treasury; and many that were
"rich cast in much: And there came a certain poor Widow,
"and she threw in two Mites, which make a Farthing. And he
"called unto him his Disciples, and saith unto them, Verily I
"say unto you, that this poor Widow hath cast more in than all
"they who have cast into the Treasury. *Mark* xii. 41, 42, 43.

" ¶ Who goeth a Warfare at any time at his own Charges?
"Who planteth a Vineyard, and eateth not of the Fruit
"thereof? Or who feedeth a Flock and eateth not of the Milk
"of the Flock? 1 *Cor.* ix. 7.

"If we have sown unto you spiritual Things, is it a great
"matter if we shall reap your carnal Things? 1 *Cor.* ix. 11.

"Do ye not know, that they who minister about holy
"Things, live of the Things of the Temple? And they who wait
"at the Altar, are Partakers with the Altar? Even so hath the
"Lord ordained, that they who preach the Gospel, should live
"of the Gospel. 1 *Cor.* ix. 13, 14.

"Let him that is taught in the Word, communicate unto
"him that teacheth in all good Things. Be not deceived, God is
"not mocked; for whatsoever a Man soweth, that shall he also
"reap. *Gal.* vi. 6, 7.

" ¶ Charge them that are rich in this World that they be
"not high-minded, nor trust in uncertain Riches, but in the
"living God, who giveth us richly all Things to enjoy: That
"they do good, that they be rich in good Works, ready to
"distribute, willing to communicate, laying up in store for
"themselves a good foundation against the time to come, that
"they may lay hold on eternal Life. 1 *Tim.* vi. 17, 18, 19.

"God is not unrighteous, to forget your Work and
"Labour of Love, which ye have shewed toward his Name, in
"that ye have ministred to the Saints, and do minister. *Heb.*
"vi. 10.

"Whilst these Sentences are reading" the Deacon, or (if there be no Deacon) any other fit Person appointed for that Purpose, shall receive the free-will Offerings of the People, in a decent Basin provided for that Purpose. And that no one may neglect to come to the holy Eucharist, by reason of having but little to give, the Person who collects the Offerings shall cover the Basin with a fair white linen Cloth, so that neither he himself, nor any other may see or know what any particular Person offers. And when all have offered, he shall reverently bring the said Basin with the Oblations therein, and deliver it to the Priest, who shall humbly present and place it upon the Altar, "saying, Blessed be thou, O Lord God, "for ever and ever. Thine, O Lord, is the Greatness, and the "Power, and the Glory, and the Majesty; for all that is in the "Heaven and in the Earth is thine: All things come of Thee; "and of thine own do we give unto Thee."

Then shall the Deacon go to the Prothesis, and having mixed the Wine and Water, he shall bring the Bread and mixed Wine to the Priest, who shall reverently place them upon the Altar.

Then the priest having first prayed secretly for a short Space, shall turn to the People, and signing himself with the Sign * of the Cross upon the forehead, shall say,

* The Grace of our Lord Jesus Christ, and the Love of God, and the Communion of the Holy Ghost be with you all.

---

* They must be great Strangers to Antiquity who do not know that the Sign of the Cross was used by the primitive Christians from the apostolical Age downward, not only in the sacred Mysteries of Religion, but even in the ordinary Occurrences of Life. See *Tertul. de Coron.* c. 3, *ad Uxor.* l. 2. c. 5. *de Resur. Carn.* c. 8. S. *Cyprian. Ep.* 73. S. *Cyril. Catech.* 13. §. 18. S. *Basil. de Sp. Sanct.* c. 27. *Chrysost. Hom.* 55. in *Matth. Lactan. de Mort. Persec.* c. 10. &c. And no serious and judicious Christian, who founds his Belief on rational Evidence, can disregard, far less oppose the venerable Usages universally received in the first and purest Ages immediately succeeding the Apostles, and which the Catholick Church could not then have been so agreed in, had they not been undoubtedly derived from apostolical Tradition.

People
And with thy Spirit.
Priest
Lift up your Hearts.
Peop. We lift them up unto the Lord.
Pr. Let us give Thanks unto the Lord.
Peop. It is meet and right so to do.

Then the Priest shall turn to the Altar, and say,

It is very meet, right, and our bounden Duty to praise Thee, to bless Thee, to worship Thee, to glorify Thee, to give Thanks unto Thee, the Maker of all Creatures visible and invisible, the Treasure of † all" good Things; the Fountain of Life and Immortality; the God and Governor of the Universe: To whom the Heaven and the Heaven of Heavens sing Praise, with all their Hosts: the Sun and Moon, and the whole Choir of Stars: The Earth and Sea, and all Things that are in them: The Angels, Archangels, Thrones, Dominions, Principalities, Authorities, and tremendous Powers: The many-eyed Cherubim, and the Seraphim with six Wings, who with twain cover their Faces, and with twain their feet, and with twain they fly, crying one to another with never-ceasing Voices, and uninterrupted Shouts of Praise, and saying,

Here the People shall join with the Priest, and say,

Holy, Holy, Holy, Lord of ‡ Sabaoth, Heaven and Earth are full of thy Glory.

Hosanna in the Highest: Blessed be he that cometh in the Name of the Lord; Hosanna in the Highest.

Then the Priest shall say,

Holy art thou, O eternal King, and the Giver of all Holiness: Holy is thine only-begotten Son, our Lord Jesus Christ,

---

*   In *Lit. Ja.* it is The Love of the Father, the Grace of the Son, and the Communion of the Holy Ghost be with you all.

†   In *Lit. Ja.* eternal.

‡   *i. e.,* Hosts, or Armies.

by whom thou madest the Worlds: Holy also is thy holy
Spirit, who searcheth all Things, even the Depths of Thee, O
God. Holy art Thou, who rulest over all, almighty and good
God, terrible, yet full of Compassion: But especially indulgent
to the Workmanship of thy own Hands; for thou didst make
Man, formed out of the Earth, after thy own Image, and
graciously gavest him the Enjoyment of Paradise: And when
he had lost his Happiness by transgressing thy Commandment, thou of thy Goodness didst not despise nor abandon
him; but didst discipline him as a merciful Father, and train
him up by the Pedagogy of the Law and the prophets: And
last of all thou didst send thine own only-begotten Son, our
Lord Jesus Christ, into the World, that by his Coming he
might renew thy Image in us: Who descended from Heaven,
and was incarnate by the Holy Ghost of the Virgin *Mary*,
conversed with Mankind, and directed his whole Dispen-
sation to our Salvation. And when the Hour was come, that he
who had no Sin, was to suffer a voluntary and life-giving Death
upon the Cross for us Sinners, in the same Night that he was
betrayed, or rather offered up himself for   a Here the Priest is to
the Life and Salvation of the World,   take the Paten into his
                                               Hands.
taking ᵃ Bread into his holy and immacu-
late Hands, looking up to Heaven and presenting it to Thee
his God and Father, he gave Thanks,   b And here to break
sanctified, and ᵇ brake it, and gave it to   the Bread.
                                               c And here to lay his
his Disciples, saying, Take, eat, ᶜ THIS IS   Hands upon all the
MY BO✠DY which is broken and given   Bread.
for you: For the Remission of Sins.

In like manner after Supper he took   d Here he is to take
the ᵈ Cup, and having * mixed it of Wine   the Chalice into his
                                               Hands.

---

*   The Testimonies of the Mixture of Water and Wine in the Eucharist
       are so many, and so early, as plainly prove it to be an apostolical
       Practice and Tradition, and consequently derived from Christ

and Water he gave Thanks, sanctified, and blessed it, and gave it to his Disciples, saying, Drink ye all of this, THIS ᵉ IS MY BLO✠OD of the New Testament, which is shed and given for you and for many, for the Remission of Sins. Do this in Remembrance of me.

e And here to lay his Hands upon every Vessel in which there is any Wine to be consecrated.

Wherefore in Commemoration of his life-giving Passion, salutary Cross, Death, Burial, and Resurrection from the Dead on the third Day, his Ascension into Heaven, and Sitting at the right Hand of Thee his God and Father, and * looking for" his second glorious and terrible Advent, when he shall come again with Glory to judge the Quick and the Dead, and shall render to every one according to his Works, we Sinners offer to Thee, O Lord, this tremendous and unbloody Sacrifice: Beseeching Thee, that thou wouldst not deal with us after our Sins, nor reward us after our Iniquities; but according to thy Clemency and ineffable Love to Mankind overlooking and blotting out the Hand-writing that is against us thy Servants, wouldst grant us thy heavenly and eternal good Things; for thy People and thine Inheritance make their Supplications unto Thee: Have Mercy upon us, O Lord God, Almighty Father, have Mercy upon us according to thy great Mercy, and send down thy holy Spirit upon us, and upon these Gifts which are here set before Thee, that by his Descent upon them, he may make this ᵃ Bread the holy BO✠DY of thy Christ,

a Here the Priest shall lay his Hands upon all the Bread.

b And here upon the Chalice, and every Vessel in which there is any Wine.

and this ᵇ Cup the precious BLO✠OD of thy Christ; that they may be to all who partake of them, for the Sanctification of

---

himself. See *Just. M. Apol.* 1. p. 125, 128, 131. *Iren.* l: iv. c. 57. l. v. c. 2. *Clem. Alex. Pæd.* l. ii. c. 2. *Cyprian.* Ep. 63. *Con. Carth.* 3. can. 24. *Con. Aurel.* 4. can. 4. *Lit. Clem. Mar. Bas.* &c.

* This is added from *Lit. Mar.*

Soul and Body, for bringing forth the Fruit of good Works, for Remission of Sins, and for Life everlasting.

We offer to Thee, O Lord, for thy holy Catholick and Apostolick Church throughout the whole World; do thou now also plentifully furnish her with the rich Gifts of thy holy Spirit.

Remember, O Lord, the holy Bishops in the same, [especially thy Servant *N.* our Bishop] * endow them with Wisdom, and fill them with the holy Ghost" † that they may" rightly divide the Word of thy Truth.

‡ Remember, O Lord, according to the Multitude of thy Mercies and Compassions, me thy unworthy and unprofitable Servant, and all the Presbyters and Deacons who compass thy holy Altar, grant to those an unblameable Presbyterate, and preserve these unspotted in their Ministry, and purchase for them good Degrees.

§ Remember, O Lord, all Kings and Princes whom thou hast appointed to reign upon Earth, and especially thy Servant our King, and all in Authority; establish their Kingdoms in Peace, and incline their Hearts to be favourable to thy Church, that in their Tranquillity we may lead a quiet and peaceable Life in all Godliness and Honesty.

Remember, O Lord, this City [or, this Diocese], and every City and Country, with all the Faithful that dwell in them; preserve them in Peace and Safety.

Remember, O Lord, our Christian Brethren that travel by Sea or Land, or are in foreign Countries; that are in Chains

---

*   This is added from *Lit. Clem.*
†   In *Lit. Ja.* who.
‡   This Petition which in *Lit. Ja.* comes in afterwards, is inserted in this Place, that the Prayers for the Clergy may all come together as in *Lit. Clem.*
§   The Petition, which is wanting in *Lit. Ja.* is here supplied from the other Liturgies.

or Imprisonment; that are in Captivity or Banishment * or in hard Slavery.

Remember, O Lord, those that are sick or diseased, [especially —] and such as are infested with unclean Spirits; and make haste to heal and deliver them.

Remember, O Lord, every Christian Soul under Affliction, or Calamity, and who stand in need of thy divine Mercy and Help.

Remember also the Conversion of those that are in Error.

† [Remember, O Lord, the Catechumens, and perfect them in the Faith.]

† [Remember, O Lord, our Brethren who are in a State of Penance, accept their Repentance, and forgive both them and us whatever Offences we have committed against Thee.]

Remember, O Lord, those who ‡ minister to us for thy holy Name's Sake.

Remember all, O Lord, for good: Have Mercy upon all, O Lord; be reconciled to us all: Settle the Flocks of thy People in Peace: Remove all Scandals: Make Wars to cease: Put a stop to the Violence of Heresies: § Heal the Schisms of the Churches:" And grant us thy Peace and Love, O God, our Saviour, and the Hope of all the Ends of the Earth.

Remember, O Lord, *to grant us* temperate Weather, moderate Showers, pleasant Dews, and Plenty of the Fruits of the Earth; and *to bless* the whole Circle of the Year with thy Goodness: For the Eyes of all hope in Thee, and thou givest them Food in due Season; thou openest thy Hand and fillest every living Creature with thy gracious Bounty.

---

*   In *Lit. Ja.* is added here, in the Mines, under Torture.
†   These two Petitions are added from *Lit. Clem.* and are only to be said when there are any Catechumens, or Penitents.
‡   In *Lit. Ja.* is added here, Labour and.
§   This is added from *Lit. Bas.*

Remember, O Lord, all who bring forth Fruit and do good Works in thy holy Churches, and who are mindful of the Poor: The Widows, Orphans, Strangers, and indigent Persons; and all who desire to be remembred in our Prayers.

Vouchsafe also, O Lord, to remember those who have this Day offered these Oblations at thy holy Altar, and for whom, * or for what Ends" every one has offered, or has in his Thoughts, [and those whose Names we have lately read before Thee.]

† *And grant* that we may *all* find Mercy and Favour, with all thy Saints, who from the Beginning of the World have pleased Thee in their several Generations, Patriarchs, Prophets, Apostles, Martyrs, and every just Spirit made perfect in the Faith of thy Christ, [particularly *N.* whom we this Day commemorate.]

‡ Here the Priest shall pause a while, he and the People secretly recommending those departed whom each thinks proper.

And then the Priest shall go on as follows,

Remember, O Lord, the God of Spirits and of all Flesh, those whom we have remembred, and those also whom we have not remembred from righteous *Abel* even unto this Day: Do thou give them § Rest in the Region of the Living, in the

---

*   This is added from *Lit. Bas.*

†   Here the Petition which is inserted above p. 535 with this † Mark comes in, in *Lit. Ja.*

‡   Of old the Deacon read the Names contained in the Diptychs; instead of which this Rubrick is inserted.

§   Prayers for the Dead, especially at the holy Altar, is so very early a Practice of the primitive Church, that undoubtedly it must have been derived from apostolical Tradition. See *Tertul. de Coron.* c. 3. *de Monog.* c. 10. *de Exhort. Cast.* c. 11. *Cypr. Ep.* 1, 12, 39. *Orig.* l. 9. in *Rom.* xii. *Arnob.* l. 4. p. 152. *Cyril. Myst. Catech.* 5. §. 6. &c. and all the ancient Liturgies. It is founded on that plain Scripture-Doctrine of an intermediate State betwixt Death and the Resurrection; and that the Righteous are not to receive their Crown of Reward (2 *Tim.* iv. 8.)

Bosoms of our holy Fathers *Abraham, Isaac,* and *Jacob,* whence Sorrow, Grief, and Lamentation are banished away, where the Light of thy Countenance visits, and shines continually; * And vouchsafe to bring them to thy heavenly Kingdom." And dispose the End of our Lives, O Lord, in Peace, that they may be Christian, well pleasing to Thee, and free from Sin; gathering us with thine Elect: Through thy only begotten Son, our Lord, and God, and Saviour Jesus Christ, for he alone appeared without Sin upon the Earth; through whom, and with whom, Thou are blessed and glorified, together with thy Holy Spirit, now and ever, World without end.

And all the People shall say with a loud Voice,

Amen.

Then shall the Priest turn to the People, and say,

Peace be with you all.

Answ. And with thy Spirit.

Then shall the Deacon say,

Let us again and again pray to the Lord.

Let us pray for the Gifts which are offered to the Lord God; that the Lord our God, receiving them upon his heavenly Altar for a sweet-smelling Savour, would send down upon us the divine Grace, and the Gift of his holy Spirit.

---

nor to enter into the Joy of their Lord in the Kingdom of Heaven, till the Resurrection and Judgment (*Matth.* xxv. 19, 20–31–34.) And that though they are to be judged according to their Works, yet there is Mercy to be found of the Lord in that Day, (2 *Tim.* i. 18) else if God should enter into strict Judgment with his Servants, no Man could be justified in his Sight. This Prayer here is not to be so understood as if none of those here commemorated were as yet in Rest in the Region of the Living; but as an Acknowledgment that their present Happiness is the free Gift of God, not due to their Nature or their Merit; to congratulate the same; and to wish the Increase of it; and the final Consummation of their Bliss at the last Day.

* These Words, which it is probable have been casually omitted in *Lit. Ja.* are here added from *Lit. Mar.*

Answ. Lord have Mercy *.

Deac. Let us pray for the Tranquillity of the whole World: And for the Peace of the holy Churches of God.

Answ. Lord have Mercy.

† Deac. Let us pray for the whole Episcopate, for all the Presbyters and Deacons in Christ, and for the whole Body of the Church; that the Lord would keep and preserve them all.

Answ. Lord have Mercy.

† Deac. Let us pray for Kings and all in Authority; that our Affairs may be in Peace.

Answ. Lord have Mercy.

Deac. Let us pray for those who have this Day offered these Gifts, and for whom, ‡ or for what Ends" every one has offered, or has in his Thoughts, and for all the People that stand about the Altar; for the Remission of our Sins, and the Propitiation of our Souls.

Answ. Lord have Mercy.

Deac. Let us pray for every Soul that is in Affliction or Calamity, and stands in need of the Mercy and Help of God: For the Conversion of those that are in Error: For Health to the Sick: For Deliverance to the Captives: And for § Rest to our Fathers and Brethren who have gone before us.

Answ. Lord have Mercy.

Deac. Let us all earnestly say, Lord have Mercy.

Answ. Lord have Mercy.

Then shall the Priest say,

---

*   Note, The Deacon is to pause a little after every Response, to allow the People time for short Ejaculations.

†   These two petitions are added from *Lit. Clem.*

‡   This is added from *Lit. Bas.* as above, p. 536.

§   *Rev.* vi. 9, 10, 11. *Isa.* xxvi. 20. *Clem. Rom. Ep.* 1. c. 50. 4 *Esdr.* iv. 35, 36. *Heb.* iv. *Barnab. Ep.* c. 15. *Iren.* l. v. c. 30. p. 450. col. 2. and c. 33. p. 454. col. 1. 2 *Thess.* 1. 7.

Vouchsafe us, O Lord, thou Lover of Men, with Freedom, without Condemnation, and with a pure Conscience, to call upon Thee, the holy God who art in the Heavens, as our Father, and say,

Here the People shall join with the Priest.

Our Father, who art in Heaven, hallowed be thy Name. Thy Kingdom come. Thy Will be done on Earth, as it is in Heaven. Give us this Day our daily Bread. And forgive us our Trespasses, as we forgive them that trespass against us. And lead us not into Temptation: But deliver us from evil. Amen.

Then shall the Priest turn to the People, and say,

Peace be with you all.

Answ. And with thy Spirit.

Deacon.

Let us bow down our Heads unto the Lord.

Answ. To Thee, O Lord.

Then the Priest turning to the Altar, shall say,

We thy Servants, O Lord, bow down our Necks to Thee, before thy holy Altar, in Expectation of thy rich Mercies: Send down upon us, O Lord, thine abundant Grace and Benediction; and sanctify our Souls and Bodies, that we may be made worthy to be Communicants and Partakers of thy holy Mysteries, for the Remission of our Sins, and for Life everlasting: For to Thee, our God, belongs Adoration and Glory, and to thy only begotten Son, and Holy Spirit, now and for ever. Amen.

Then the Priest turning to the People, shall say,

Grace be with you all.

Answ. And with thy Spirit.

Deacon.

Let us attend in the Fear of God.

Priest.

Holy Things for holy Persons.

People.

There is one holy, one Lord Jesus Christ, to the Glory of God the Father, to whom be Glory for ever.

Then shall the Priest receive the Eucharist in both Kinds himself: And then proceed to deliver the same in like manner to other Priests and Deacons, if any be present, in order, into their Hands.

And when he receiveth, or delivereth the Sacrament of the Body, he shall say,

* The Body of Christ.

And the person receiving shall say,

Amen.

And when he receiveth, or delivereth the Cup, he shall say,

The Blood of Christ.

And the person receiving shall say,

Amen.

After all the Clergy have communicated, the officiating Priest, or according to his Direction, any, or all of the Priests, or Deacons there present, shall administer the Eucharist in both Kinds to the People, in order, into their Hands, according to the Form above prescribed.

Whilst the Faithful are communicating, *Psalm* xxxiv. and cxlv. may be sung.

When all have communicated, what remaineth of the consecrated Elements shall be reverently placed upon the Altar, and covered with a fair linen Cloth.

Then the Deacon, being turned to the People, shall say,

Let us give Thanks to God that he hath vouchsafed to make us Partakers of the Body and Blood of Christ, for Remission of Sins, and for Life everlasting. And let us pray to him that he would keep us unblameable, as he is good and a Lover of Men.

Then the Priest, standing before the Altar, shall say,

O God, who of thy great and inexpressable Love to Man, dost condescend to the Weakness of thy Servants; We give Thanks to Thee, that thou hast vouchsafed to make us Partakers of this heavenly Table: Let not the receiving of thy

---

*   See *Cyril. Myst. Catech.* v. §. 18, 19. comp. with *Lit. Clem.*

unspotted Mysteries be to the Condemnation of us Sinners; but keep us, good God, in the Sanctification of thy holy Spirit; that being made holy, we may obtain a Part and Inheritance with all thy Saints, who have pleased Thee from the Beginning of the World; through the Mercies of thy only begotten Son, our Lord, and God, and Saviour Jesus Christ, with whom, and thy holy Spirit, Thou art blessed, now and for ever, World without end. Amen.

Then the Deacon, being turned to the People, shall say,

Let us bow down our Heads to the Lord.

Then the Priest shall say the following Benediction, the People bowing their Heads.

O God, great and wonderful, look upon thy Servants, who bow down their Necks unto Thee: Stretch forth thy powerful Hand, full of Blessings, and bless thy People. Preserve thine Inheritance, that we may continually glorify Thee, for ever, the only living and true God: For to Thee, O Father, belongs Glory, Honour, Adoration, and Thanksgiving; and to thy Son; and holy Spirit, now and ever.

And all the People shall answer,

Amen.

Then, after a Pause, the Deacon shall say to the People,

Depart in Peace.

The holy Eucharist shall be celebrated on every Sunday, and on every other Festival at least for which a proper Epistle and Gospel are appointed: And every Priest shall then either administer or receive the same, except he be hindred by some urgent and reasonable Cause; or cannot get two Persons to communicate with him: For there shall be no Celebration of the Eucharist, except two Persons at least communicate with the Priest.

And to the end, that all the Faithful may constantly frequent it, every Priest shall diligently inform the People of the Nature and Importance of this holy Mystery; and inculcate upon them the great Advantage and Necessity of frequent Communion. He shall also exhort them not to neglect coming often to God's Altar, because they have but little to give at the Offertory; for he shall instruct them, that provided they frequent the Christian Sacrifice, their Offering will be accepted by God, though it be never so little, if it be given according to their Abilities, with a chearful and devout Heart.

The Priest shall always consecrate more than is necessary for the Communicants; and he shall carefully reserve so much of the consecrated Elements as shall serve for the Use of the Sick, or other Persons who for any urgent Cause cannot come to the publick Service.

And if, after that, any of the consecrated Elements remain, the officiating Priest, with other Priests and Deacons, if any be present, and with such other of the Communicants as he shall call unto him, shall reverently receive them. Always observing that some of the consecrated Elements be constantly reserved in the Vestry, or some other convenient Place in the Church, under a safe Lock, in case of any sudden Emergency, wherein they may be wanted. But he shall take Care that they never be too long kept, but renewed from Time to Time.

The Money given at the Offertory, being the freewill Offerings of the People to God, and solemnly devoted to him; the Priest shall take so much out of it as will defray the Charge of the Bread and Wine: And the remainder he shall keep, or part of it, or dispose of it, or part of it, to pious or charitable Uses, according to the Direction of the Bishop.

F I N I S.

Contributors

The Revd Canon A. M. ALLCHIN is Honorary Professor in the Department of Theology and Religious Studies in the University of Wales, Bangor. The author of many works of ecumenical theology, his recent research into patristic influences in Welsh early mediaeval theology has appeared in John Behr, ed., *Abba: The Tradition of Orthodoxy in the West: Festschrift for Bishop Kallistos (Ware) of Diokleia* (2003).

JOHN P. BARRON was Master of St Peter's College, Oxford, 1991–2003, and previously Dean of the University of London Institutes for Advanced Study and Director of the Institute of Classical Studies. Having written his doctoral dissertation on the ancient history of Samos and published a book on *The Silver Coins of Samos* (1996), he is currently engaged on a biography of the island's Archbishop Joseph Georgirenes, the subject of his paper in the present volume.

The Rt Revd and Rt Hon RICHARD CHARTRES is the 132nd Bishop of London. Deeply engaged in the cause of Anglican–Orthodox unity, he has also published in the field of Religion, Science and the Environment.

The Revd Canon CHAD COUSSMAKER, a graduate of Worcester College, has spent much of his Anglican ministry in close contact with Orthodox churches. As chaplain in Istanbul and later in Moscow, he served as the Archbishop of Canterbury's apokrisarios to the Ecumenical Patriarch and to the Patriarch of Moscow.

The Revd Dr COLIN DAVEY was a research student in Athens in the 1950s and then held a number of college, parish and ecumenical staff posts, serving as Secretary of both the Anglican/Roman Catholic International Commission and the Anglican/Orthodox Joint Doctrinal Discussions. He is the author of *Pioneer for Unity: Metrophanes Kritopoulos (1589–1639)* and *Relations between the Orthodox, Roman Catholic and Reformed Churches* (1987).

The Revd Dr PETER M. DOLL, formerly chaplain of Worcester College, now serves as a parish priest in Abingdon. He is author of *Revolution, Religion and National Identity: Imperial Anglicanism in British North America, 1745–1795* (2000) and *'After the Primitive Christians': The Eighteenth-Century Anglican Eucharist in its Architectural Setting* (1997).

The Revd Canon EDWARD EVERY was from 1952 to 1979 residentiary canon of St George's Cathedral, Jerusalem, where he worked to foster ecumenical links. As a member of the Anglican–Orthodox International Theological Dialogue, he contributed several papers on the *filioque*.

The Revd Canon WILLIAM B. GREEN is Clinton S. Quin Professor Emeritus of Systematic Theology in the Episcopal Theological Seminary of the Southwest, Austin, Texas. At the 2004 meeting of the International Commission of the Anglican–Orthodox Theological Dialogue, he presented a paper on 'Heresy and Schism'.

Archimandrite EPHREM (LASH), formerly lecturer in the Department of Theology, University of Newcastle, is presently engaged in the translation of patristic and liturgical material.

VASILIOS N. MAKRIDES is Professor of Religious Studies (with a specialization in Orthodox Christianity) at the Faculty of Philosophy in the University of Erfurt, Germany. He is the editor of *Alexander Helladius the Larissaean* (2003).

The Revd Dr CHARLES MILLER, until recently Rector of the Church of the Transfiguration, New York City, is a specialist in seventeenth-century English theology. His books include *Toward a Fuller Vision. Anglicanism and the Orthodox Experience* (1984) and *The Gift of the World. An Introduction to the Theology of Dumitru Staniloae* (2000).

W. B. PATTERSON is Francis S. Houghteling Professor of History Emeritus at the University of the South, Sewanee, Tennessee. He is the author of *King James VI and I and the Reunion of Christendom* (1997) and of several articles dealing with the British king's efforts to bring about closer relations between the Church of England and the Greek Orthodox Church, as well as the major western churches. His current research deals with theology at Cambridge University in the late sixteenth and early seventeenth centuries.

RICHARD SHARP was Senior Research Fellow of Worcester College from 1995–2002. As an ecclesiastical historian he has worked on the nonjuring movement with particular reference to its wider links to the High Church tradition in England during the 'long' eighteenth century, and he is also interested in the study of engraved clerical portraiture.

The Revd Dr ANN SHUKMAN first became interested in the Nonjurors when preparing a course of lectures for the Alexander Men University in Moscow on the Anglican Church. She has recently completed a translation of the main source for our knowledge of St Seraphim of Sarov, *The Chronicles of the Seraphim-Diveyevo Monastery*.

E. D. TAPPE (1910–1992) was from 1974 Professor of Romanian Studies at the School of Slavonic and East European Studies in the University of London. He was the first holder of such a post in the English-speaking world.

Bishop KALLISTOS (WARE) of Diokleia is an Assistant Bishop in the Greek Orthodox Archdiocese of Thyateira and Great Britain, and for thirty-five years he taught Eastern Orthodox Studies in the University of Oxford. His publications include *The Orthodox Church* (Penguin Books), *The Orthodox Way*, and (under his secular name Timothy Ware) *Eustratios Argenti: A Study of the Greek Church under Turkish Rule*.

Priestmonk GREGORY (WOOLFENDEN) was lecturer in Liturgy at Ripon College, Cuddesdon, and a member of the Oxford University Faculty of Theology for some fifteen years. Since 2004 he has been pastor of a Ukrainian Orthodox parish in Monessen, Pennsylvania, and doing part-time teaching. He is the author of *Daily Liturgical Prayer: Origins & Theology* (2004). Readers of this volume may be interested in his article on Western-rite Orthodox experiments in *St Vladimir's Theological Quarterly* 45.2 (2001) 163–192.

Index

Items in italic are reproduced documents.

Aaron, St, 334
Abbot, George, Abp: and Balliol, 62 & n. 13; career of, 43–4; correspondence with Lucaris, 39–40, 58, 60, 63–4; and King James, 44, 50–1; and Orthodox scholars, 22, 39, 61–2, 63, 72, 73, 153, 433
Abbot, Maurice, 44
Abbot, Robert, 62
Adams, William, 163
Addison, Lancelot: *Introduction to the Sacrament*, 216
Alban, St, 334
Alexei II, Patriarch of Moscow, 370, 371, 372
Alphery, Michael, 401
Andrewes, Lancelot, Bp, 202, 335, 345; and prayer of oblation, 208
Angelomati-Tsougaraki, Dr Eleni: doubts North's Orthodox baptism, 318
Angelos, Christophoros, 54–5; on England, 22; at Oxford, 48, 62
Anglican–Orthodox International Commission, *see* International Commission of the Anglican–Orthodox Dialogue
Anglican–Orthodox Joint Doctrinal Discussion (A/OJDD), 382, 384–7, *see also* International Commission of the Anglican–Orthodox Dialogue
Anglican–Orthodox relations, 54, 55, 114, 153, 193–4, 293–5; character of, 329; and Christian unity, 36, 331–2, 353–4, 382, 405; and dialogue, 29, 35, 337, 379–93; and joint agenda, 410–11; and Kritopoulos, 75; misunderstandings, scope for in, 407–8; obstacles to, 336; official, 22, 40, 331, 335–6, 395, 404–8, 505–6; and personal friendships, 412; *see also* Church of England
Anglo-Catholicism, 236–37
Anne, Queen: address to by Greek students, 164, 173, 260–1, *490–2*; *Sufficiency of the Holy Scriptures* dedicated to, 439, 442–3
Anson, Peter: *Fashions in Church Furnishings*, 247
Anthony, Metropolitan of Sourozh, 330
Anthrakitis, Methodios: and Aristotelianism, 282
apokrisarioi, 412; canine diplomacy by, 374–5; function of, 28–9, 365–78; personal contacts important to, 369, 371
Apostolis, Michael, 264

Plate Section

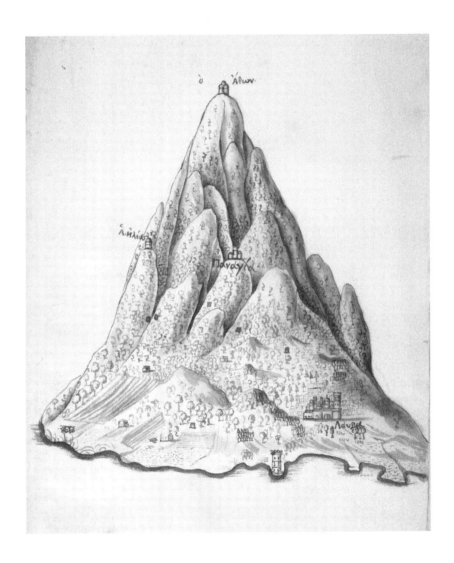

Plate 3

B. *Woodroffe* S.T.P. *Canonic. Ædis Christi. Oxon.*
Ἕλλησί τε ᾗ βαρβάροις ὀφθλέτης εἰμί. *Rom. 1. 14.*
In magnis voluisse sat est. —

Plate 4

The original Greek Church (now St. Mary's), Soho

Plate 1

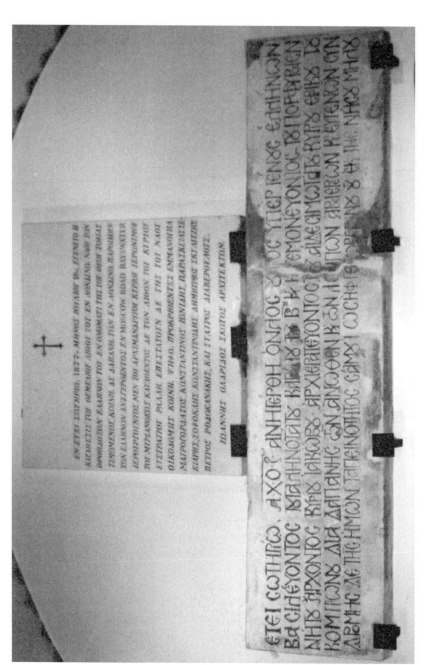

Plate 2

Reverendiſsimus in Christo Pater,
NEOPHYTUS PHILIPPOPOLEOS ARCHIEPISCOPUS,
totius Thraciæ et Tergovitiæ Exarchus.

Plate 5

Plate 6a

Plate 6b

Matth. XVIII. 19. 20. I. Cor. XI. 23. 24. 25. 26.
Printed for A. Bettesworth, C. Clements & C. Rivington.

Plate 7

Agite, veneremur supplices, flexis ante Dominum
Creatorem nostrum genibus. PSAL. XCV. 6.

Plate 8

Plate 9

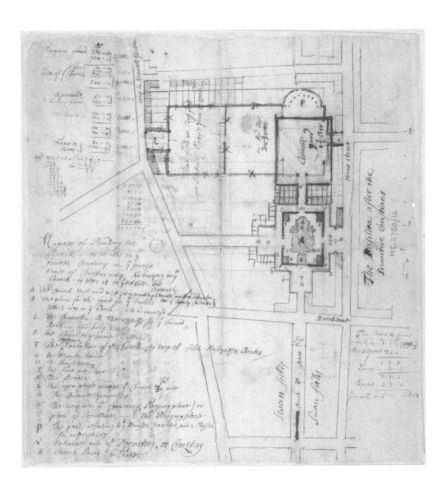

Plate 10

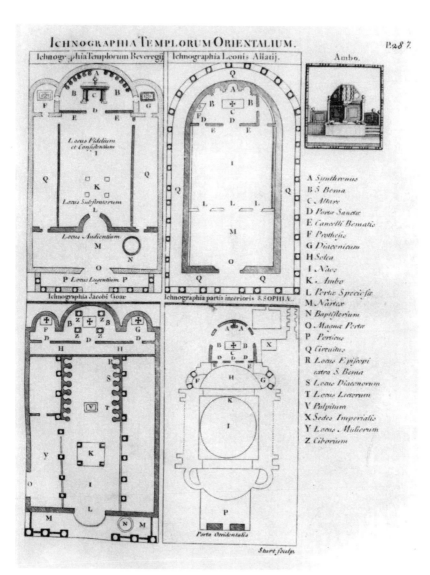

ICHNOGRAPHIA TEMPLORUM ORIENTALIUM.   P.28 7.

Ichnographia Templorum Beveregij | Ichnographia Leonis Allatij. | Ambo.

Locus Fidelium et Consistentium

Locus Substratorum

Locus Audientium

P Locus Lugentium P

Ichnographia Jacobi Goar | Ichnographia partis interioris S.SOPHIÆ.

A Synthronus
B S. Bema
C Altare
D Portæ Sanctæ
E Cancelli Bematis
F Protheſis
G Diaconicum
H Solea
I Naos
K Ambo
L Portæ Speciofæ
M Nartex
N Baptifterium
O Magna Porta
P Porticus
Q Circuitus
R Locus Epifcopi extra S. Bema
S Locus Diaconorum
T Locus Lectorum
V Pulpitum
X Sedes Imperialis
Y Locus Mulierum
Z Ciborium

Porta Occidentalis

Stuart sculp.

Plate 11

FREDERIC (NORTH) EARL OF GUILDFORD.
Nat 7 Feb. 1766.

Plate 12

225, 229; (1928), 238–9;, *Alternative Service Book* 241; *Book of Alternative Services ... Canada*, 242–3; *Common Worship*, 241, 242; Scottish (1637), 230, 528; *see also* Cranmer, Thomas
prayers: for the dead, 23, 81, 93, 344; in Orthodox tradition, 408; by saints, 344; to saints, 118
Prideaux, Humphrey: on Woodroffe, 171, 172
Propaganda (Rome), 65 n.28, 420
Prosalendis, George, 297 & n. 20, 299–300, 301–9, 312, 325; veracity of, 318
Prossalentis, Frangiskos (Francis Prossalenos/Prossalento), 21, 31, 150–1, 167–8, 170, 173, 174, 268, 439; *The Heretical Teacher...*, 31, 151–2, 170, 268–70, 435–6, 493–503
Pylarinos, Iakovos, 261–2

Queen's College (Oxford), 100
Quien, Michel le: *Oriens Christianus ..., 507*

Ralli, Pandely Thomas, 313 n. 59
Ramon, Brother, S. S. F., 339
Ramsey, Michael, Abp, 330, 351–2, 406; and Anglican–Orthodox dialogue, 379–80; quoted, 35–6, 331, 337
Ratcliff, E. C., 228
Rattray, Thomas, Bp, 181 n. 12, 207, 234, 333, 340–6, 527; *Essay on the Nature of the Church,* 528; on eucharistic prayer, 342–3; as liturgist, 342, 528; 'Of the Necessity of a Positive Revelation

...', 341–2; and Non-Jurors, 527–8; *An Office for the Sacrifice of the Holy Eucharist ...* (Liturgy of St James), 32, 341, 529–46; patristic influences on, 28, 233
Reformation: and Anglicanism, 333; and ecumenism, 19; and Greek Church, 54; and patristic heritage, 399, 400
Renaudot, Eusèbe, 134, 151–2
Rhodocanaces, Constantine, 80 n. 4
Rhoedus, Thomas: praises Kritopoulos, 67
Ricaut, Paul, *see* Rycaut, Paul
Roe, Sir Thomas, 59 & n. 4, 72
Roman Catholicism: attacked by Anglicans, 31; and ancient tradition, 20; and reunion with Orthodox, 292; and training of Orthodox clergy, 21, 58–9
Rome: supremacy of, 20
Rous, John, 69
Routh, Dr Martin: on Palmer's Russian journey, 293
Runcie, Robert, Abp, 381, 407, 409
Runciman, Steven: Chartres on, 396–7; on Greek College, 32–3, 150
Russian Embassy Chapel (*or* church; London), 296 & n. 17, 313; and Peter the Great, 190–1 & n. 37
Rutt, Richard, Bp, 384
Rycaut, Paul, 271; *Present State of the Greek and Armenian Churches,* 101, 154

St Andrew Service Book, 234
St Andrew's Trust, 401